3rd Workshop on Human Evaluation of NLP Systems (HumEval 2023)

Varna, Bulgaria
7 September 2023

ISBN: 978-1-7138-9052-2

Printed from e-media with permission by:

Curran Associates, Inc.
57 Morehouse Lane
Red Hook, NY 12571

Some format issues inherent in the e-media version may also appear in this print version.

Association for Computational Linguistics
209 N. Eighth Street
Stroudsburg, Pennsylvania 18360

Phone: 1-570-476-8006
Fax: 1-570-476-0860

acl@aclweb.org

Additional copies of this publication are available from:

Curran Associates, Inc.
57 Morehouse Lane
Red Hook, NY 12571 USA
Phone: 845-758-0400
Fax: 845-758-2633
Email: curran@proceedings.com
Web: www.proceedings.com

HumEval 2023

Proceedings of the 3rd Workshop on Human Evaluation of NLP Systems

associated with

The 14th International Conference on Recent Advances in Natural Language Processing'2023

7 September 2023
Varna, Bulgaria

3RD WORKSHOP ON HUMAN EVALUATION OF NLP SYSTEMS
ASSOCIATED WITH THE 14TH INTERNATIONAL CONFERENCE
RECENT ADVANCES IN
NATURAL LANGUAGE PROCESSING'2023

PROCEEDINGS

7 September 2023
Varna, Bulgaria

Designed by INCOMA Ltd.
Shoumen, BULGARIA

Preface

Welcome to HumEval 2023!

We are pleased to present the third workshop on Human Evaluation of NLP Systems (HumEval) which is taking place as part of the Conference on Recent Advances in Natural Language Processing (RANLP 2023).

Human evaluation is vital in NLP, and it is often considered as the most reliable form of evaluation. It ranges from the large-scale crowd-sourced evaluations to the much smaller experiments routinely encountered in conference papers. With this workshop we wish to create a forum for current human evaluation research, a space for researchers working with human evaluations to exchange ideas and begin to address the issues that human evaluation in NLP currently faces, including aspects of experimental design, reporting standards, meta-evaluation and reproducibility.

We are truly grateful to the authors of the submitted papers that showed interest in human evaluation research. The HumEval workshop accepted 15 submissions. The accepted papers cover a broad range of NLP areas where human evaluation is used: machine translation, natural language generation, summarisation, text-to-speech. Several papers are addressing reproducibility of human evaluations.

This workshop would not have been possible without the hard work of the programme committee. We would like to express our gratitude to them for writing detailed and thoughtful reviews in a very constrained span of time. We also thank our invited speaker, Elizabeth Clark, for her contribution to our program. We are grateful for the help from the RANLP organisers, especially Galia Angelova and Ivelina Nikolova, and we are grateful to all the people involved in setting up the infrastructure.

You can find more details about the worskhop on its website: `https://humeval.github.io/`.

Anya, Ehud, Craig, Maja, Joao, Simone, Rudali

Organizers:

Anya Belz (ADAPT Centre, Dublin City University, Ireland)
Ehud Reiter (University of Aberdeen, UK)
Maja Popović (ADAPT Centre, Dublin City University, Ireland)
João Sedoc (New-York University, US)
Craig Thomson (University of Aberdeen, UK)
Simone Balloccu (University of Aberdeen, UK)
Rudali Huidrom (ADAPT Centre, Dublin City University, Ireland)

Programme Committee:

Gavin Abercrombie (Heriot Watt University, UK)
Jose Alonso (University of Santiago de Compostela, Spain)
Mohammad Arvan (University of Illinois, Chicago, USA)
Mohit Bansal (UNC Charlotte, USA)
Alberto BugarÃín-Diz (University of Santiago de Compostela, Spain)
Aoife Cahill (Dataminr, USA)
Eduardo Caló (Utrecht University, Netherlands)
Tanvi Dinkar (Heriot Watt University, UK)
Steffen Eger (Bielefeld University, Germany)
Mingqi Gao (Peking University, China)
Dimitra Gkatzia (Edinburgh Napier University, UK)
Javier González Corbelle (University of Santiago de Compostela, Spain)
Rudali Huidrom (ADAPT Centre, Dublin City University, Ireland)
Manuela Hürlimann (Zurich University of Applied Sciences, Switzerland)
Takumi Ito (Utrecht University, Netherlands)
Huiyuan Lai (Groningen University, Netherlands)
Yiru Li (Groningen University, Netherlands)
Saad Mahamood (Trivago N.V., Germany)
Margot Mieskes (University of Applied Sciences, Darmstadt, Germany)
Pablo Mosteiro (Utrecht University, Netherlands)
Natalie Parde (University of Illinois, Chicago, USA)
Joel Tetreault (Dataminr, USA)
Xiaojun Wan (Peking University, China)

Invited Speaker:

Elizabeth Clark (Google Research, USA)

Table of Contents

Conference Programme

No Day Set (continued)

With a Little Help from the Authors: Reproducing Human Evaluation of an MT Error Detector
Ondrej Platek, Mateusz Lango and Ondrej Dusek

HumEval'23 Reproduction Report for Paper 0040: Human Evaluation of Automatically Detected Over- and Undertranslations
Filip Klubička and John D. Kelleher

Same Trends, Different Answers: Insights from a Replication Study of Human Plausibility Judgments on Narrative Continuations
Yiru Li, Huiyuan Lai, Antonio Toral and Malvina Nissim

Reproduction of Human Evaluations in: "It's not Rocket Science: Interpreting Figurative Language in Narratives"
Saad Mahamood

A Manual Evaluation Method of Neural MT for Indigenous Languages

Linda Wiechetek
UiT Norgga árktalaš universitehta
linda.wiechetek@uit.no

Flammie A. Pirinen
UiT Norgga árktalaš universitehta
flammie.pirinen@uit.no

Per E Kummervold
National Library of Norway
per.kummervold@nb.no

Abstract

Indigenous language expertise is not encoded in written text in the same way as it is for languages that have a long literal tradition. In many cases it is, on the contrary, mostly conserved orally. Therefore the evaluation of neural MT systems solely based on an algorithm learning from written texts is not adequate to measure the quality of a system that is used by the language community. If extensively using tools based on a big amount of non-native language this can even contribute to language change in a way that is not desired by the language community. It can also pollute the internet with automatically created texts that outweigh native texts. We propose a manual evaluation method focusing on flow and content separately, and additionally we use existing rule-based NLP to evaluate other factors such as spelling, grammar and grammatical richness. Our main conclusion is that language expertise of a native speaker is necessary to properly evaluate a given system. We test the method by manually evaluating two neural MT tools for an indigenous low resource language. We present an experiment on two different neural translations to and from North Sámi, an indigenous language of North Europe.

1 Introduction

Indigenous languages with few speakers are often left out in the development of high-level NLP tools that require a lot of data and have therefore not been subject to evaluation either. However, recently neural machine translation has become more effective and more available for even lesser resourced languages than before. While the technology has made the use of neural machine translators plausible, it is not clear whether the quality of the translation really is good enough for the common use cases within language communities. High-resource languages typically apply data-hungry evaluation methods. The demand for big data is known to be problematic for smaller languages. An additional factor is, that while big languages with a long literary tradition have their language expertise encoded in large amounts of written texts, typically this is not the case for indigenous languages with a much shorter literary tradition. Here language expertise is often transmitted orally and may not be reflected in written text at all, partly due to lack of literacy and tradition. It is problematic if we base our knowledge of a language on existing written text for a language community that does not have a long tradition in writing. Written texts need to be treated much more critically with regard to who wrote it (was it even a native speaker?), if it was a translation, and which genre it belongs to. Written texts can have systematic spelling and grammar errors. Their authors can be second language learners instead of language experts, or they can be synthetically created by machine translation programs. Taking into account the distribution of human resource and language expertise is an important factor in the thought process. Language communities that put a great deal of work into preserving and strengthening their language typically use a lot of resources in teaching the younger generation. That also means that expertise may be found to a great deal in oral contexts rather than being reflected in text corpora. Basing evaluation on algorithms that learn from written corpora is therefore a thinking error in these contexts.

Consequently, we find a manual evaluation of neural MT tools by language experts in this context unavoidable. By *language experts* we mean native speakers with a profound understanding of their own language, which allows them to make judgements about the grammaticality and idiomaticity of a sentence. Especially since indigenous written grammars are far from exhaustive, good language intuition is a key qualification.

Proceedings of the Third Workshop on Human Evaluation of NLP Systems, pages 1–10, Varna, Bulgaria, Sep 7, 2023.
https://doi.org/10.26615/978-954-452-088-5_001

In this article we suggest a grading system for a language expert evaluator that is an expert of both source and target language. The scale distinguishes between flow and content, where flow (which has a main focus on the target sentence) is evaluated before content (which again requires an analysis of the source sentence). Our main hypothesis is, we need native language/linguistic expertise to even know how good the translation is.

We do a small-scale but detailed manual evaluation of two neural MT tools for an indigenous low resource language (North Sámi). Our aim is to develop a workflow for future evaluations of similar languages and systems and those with even less resources, than the ones we work on, should they become available in the popular NMT toolkits.

2 Background

Methods of evaluating machine translation are often based on two approaches: automatic that requires high quality parallel texts and human-based, which requires a large amount of humans doing annotation or rating of large number of sentences for example. In a low-resource minority language situation, neither of these resources is easily available; there are no parallel texts and very few humans to do annotation or rating. That is to say, the amount of sentence-aligned parallel texts that is needed to automatically verify quality is larger than amount of any translated texts in the language in the foreseeable future and the amount of people required to do a meaningful comparison is well larger than available people as well, it is physically impossible to do perform such tests. The typical automatic evaluation metrics like word error rate require either post-editing or parallel corpora which typically are not available in large quantities in indigenous low-resource contexts.

Thus we will be able to identify the criteria that matter for a good translation of or into the language in question. Based on their feedback, automatic processes to perform an adequate evaluation can be developed.

Also with regard to human resources the indigenous context is a challenging one. Those that are language experts with a linguistic background and a high degree of literacy are typically recruited by schools, media, as translators or any other context where language knowledge is highly sought-after.

Generally, the machine translation use cases can be divided in two main categories: translations that can be read to understand the source texts (assimilation, gisting) and translations that can be edited for further use (dissemination). If the tools are useful as a basis for post-editing has to be decided by members of the the language communities, which is why we also think that feedback from the community is needed to evaluate the quality. Because of the systems' fluency, new machine translation tools tend to get adopted quickly by businesses (e.g. Facebook, Google reviews) and even official bodies. An early and critical evaluation by language community is therefore essential. Machine-learning MT is now almost a standard and being used in every day life without much thought. How does it look like in an extremely low resource language context? (Moorkens et al., 2018)

2.1 Languages

North Sámi is a Finno-Ugric language belonging to the Uralic language family, it is spoken in Norway, Sweden, and Finland by approximately 25,700 speakers (Eberhard et al., 2018). It is a synthetic language, where the open *parts-of-speech* (PoS) — e.g. nouns, adjectives — inflect for case, person, number, and more. The grammatical categories are expressed by a combination of suffixes and stem-internal processes affecting root vowels and consonants alike, making it perhaps the most fusional of all Uralic languages. In addition to compounding, inflection and derivation are common morphological processes in North Sámi. The Sámi languages are typically described as verb heavy languages, with at least few hundred distinct inflectional verb forms (both finite and non-finite, varies a bit based on paradigms and depending on what you include as inflectional). Sammallahti (1998) notes that in a list of the most common North Sámi words, verbs are in first place (33%), followed by 28% nouns. English and Norwegian, on the other hand, are Indo-European languages, with relatively low morphological complexity: less than 10 word-forms per word in productive inflection. The word order in English and Norwegian is stricter than in North Sámi and our hypothesis is that the distribution of parts-of-speech and derivations is different as well. We expect this to have an effect on the translated language and non-translated, as well as different profiles between machine and human translated texts.

The syntactic differences between Sámi and the two Germanic languages are notable. While the neutral word order for all of them is Subject-Verb-

Object (SVO), there are a number of mismatching features in the syntax. Unlike Norwegian and English, Sámi has pro-drop (pronoun dropping) for 1. and 2. person. Sámi uses mostly postpositions as opposed to prepositions. Other differences are adverbial positioning, word order in sub-clauses, question clauses or after adverbial extensions, etc.

2.2 Previous research

There has been a lot of research in the evaluating of machine translation. There are many ways to evaluate the machine translation quality, some are standardised like MQM (Multidimensional Quality Metrics) and others are purpose-built for one specific experiment or study. Lommel (2018) use a very fine-grained system for categorising translation errors. Popović (2018) use a less fine-grained system. OpenAI has used following criteria (Stiennon et al., 2020) for their human evaluation work of a summarisation system, we have taken some inspiration from that, for example in our 7-grade scale for judgments. The machine translation systems we evaluate are based on neural machine translation. The translation system between English and North Sámi is described in Yankovskaya et al. (2023). Mager et al. (2023) have studied machine translation in similar contexts than as we work in.

Human evaluation of machine translated texts often is based on crowd-sourced quick evaluations based on superficial reading of the sentences without context (c.f. WMT shared tasks (Weller-di Marco and Fraser, 2022), AppRaise (Federmann, 2018)). While this kind of quick eyeballing by average language users can give some impression of fluency of the translations it may be insufficient to determine if the text is translated accurately and language is truly idiomatic. A lot of evaluation approaches use scales of fluency and adequacy, in a way to measure separately the overall readability of the text from the accuracy of the translated content.

2.3 Data

The corpora available for a low resource language like North Sámi is very limited. In Table 1 we list the corpora that we have used in the experiments: the largest electronically available Sámi corpus SIKOR (2018) has been used both for training the North Sámi—Norwegian and English—North Sámi machine translation. We did not train the English—North Sámi model ourselves but used TARTUNLP that is partly trained on *SIKOR*, cf. Section 3.2.

We also use part of *SIKOR* to calculate the linguistic features of non-machine translated, open domain texts. *Alice in Wonderland*[1] (henceforth referred to as 'Alice'; we evaluated here the first three chapters), CTV.ca news item: *What's behind the increase in orca-human interactions, boat attacks?* (CTV), BBC.co.uk news item: *Multi-cancer blood test shows real promise in NHS study* (BBC) and *ILO-169 declaration of indigenous peoples' rights*[2] (ILO-169) are texts we have manually harvested from the internet and represent different genres: fiction, news texts in two variants of English and a legal / political text respectively. These texts were used as sources for machine translation from English.

Corpus	Size
SIKOR	23,923,558
Alice in Wonderland	3,509
CTV	722
BBC	413
ILO-169	2,978

Table 1: Sizes of corpora in simple, space-separated tokens (`wc -w`).

The data used for training the Sámi—Norwegian machine training system is described in 3.1.

3 Methods

Despite limited amount of corpora North Sámi has in recent years gained some experimental neural machine translators. By evaluating their current state-of-the-art we present a manual evaluation method and relevant criteria. As a test case we looked at one system to and another one from North Sámi.

Previously North Sámi has been unreachable for neural approaches to language technology due to low resourcedness. The majority of resources are therefore rule-based tools. For machine translation, language pairs included other closely related Sámi languages, as well as Finnish, which is in same language family, but not closely related. There also exists translators for Norwegian, which is another majority language in North

[1] `https://www.gutenberg.org/ebooks/11`

[2] `https://www.ilo.org/dyn/normlex/en/f?p=NORMLEXPUB:55:0::NO::P55_TYPE,P55_LANG,P55_DOCUMENT,P55_NODE:REV,en,C169,/Document`

Sámi territory. Many of the existing majority-to-minority language translators are primarily developed in one direction first (Trosterud and Unhammer, 2012). The rule-based machine translators are based on other language technology resources, such as dictionaries, morphological analysers, syntactic analysers and so forth. We use these morphological analysers, as well as spell-checkers and grammar checkers as tools to find out if there are differences between the human and machine translated texts for potential spelling errors, grammatical errors as well as differences in distributions of the grammatical features. The systems for linguistic analysis and grammar and spell-checking have been acquired from the GiellaLT infrastructure[3], that contains freely available open source language technology tools for minority languages (Pirinen et al., 2023).

We used the existing neural machine translation systems as a black box, we fed in the source texts and evaluated the target translations without post-editing in between; only the cases where formatting went destructively wrong (line breaks and spaces added or disappeared in unusual places, like intra-word spaces) were corrected.

3.1 North Sámi to Norwegian NMT

In the development of the North Sámi—Norwegian machine translator, we utilized a standard sequence-to-sequence model based on mT5 (Xue et al., 2020). Our starting point was the pretrained NorthT5 checkpoint[4], a checkpoint that is additionally pretrainedfrom the mT5 checkpoint using additional Scandinavian and English data. Notably, while both these are multilingual models, North Sámi is not included in the listed training corpus.

We retrieved a set of bilingual translations from *SIKOR*. This was divided into a train and test set, and we proceeded to fine-tune a translation model on the train set with 3,800 parallel North Sámi—Norwegian sentences for 10,000 steps. After training, the model was applied to translate sentences in the test set, and a professional translator evaluated the output. As mentioned earlier, human resources are limited, which is why finding even a single adequate evaluator can be difficult.

[3] https://github.com/giellalt/

[4] https://huggingface.co/north/t5_large_NCC

3.2 English to North Sámi NMT

The English-North Sámi machine translation was built by university of Tartu NLP group as a part of their low resource Uralic neural machine translators[5] and it is based on North Sámi corpus SIKOR (2018) and its parallel parts have been used to train the machine translation (Yankovskaya et al., 2023). The output was analyzed by our rule-based tools. Hand-picked examples show shortcomings of the system. As we were short on human resources for this task, i.e. language experts, we were not able to apply the same method as for North Sámi to Norwegian.

4 Evaluation method

We evaluate separately for the from and to North Sámi scenarios.

4.1 North Sámi as a source language

We study the evaluation of the translations by a language expert. We want to gain an insight on how useful the translated texts are for their use cases within the speaker community: for the speakers who are proficient in the source and target languages with different levels and aims, and relevant to the user experience. We expect that the results of the neural machine translation may partially reflect the style and features of the available corpora in the language, which is not necessarily representative of the norms and standards in the same proportion as with largely resourced majority languages. We also study to what extent the translated texts look translationese versus texts written by native speakers. The commonly translated languages in a neural MT setting at the moment are Indo-European majority languages: English, Norwegian etc., that are in a whole different language family, it is possible that this reflects in the (machine) translated texts more heavily. As it is well-known that neural machine translations get more fluent-looking before they get content-accurate, we also attempt to study how expensive it is to evaluate the translations on this. A professional translator with North Sámi and Norwegian as her native languages evaluated the machine translation from North Sámi to Norwegian described in Section 3.1.

For evaluation we developed a 7-level scale for two main criteria inspired by the scale automatic summaries described in Stiennon et al. (2020, p.23)

[5] https://translate.ut.ee

and based on initial comments on translation quality of our professional North Sámi translator. In developing categories for MT evaluation and looking at actual translations we found to main categories: flow and content. First reactions to the quality of a translation typically focus on the output and if there is a good flow in the target language, rather than meticulously comparing the input to the output. However, when knowing the source language in addition to the target language, one will have a second look at the source sentence, and be more critical to the well-sounding translation when parts of the source sentence are missing or incorrectly translated.

A professional translator who is trained in exactness, idiomaticity, and polysemy will quickly be able to identify not only critical errors that change the whole meaning of the sentence, but also other errors that reduce the quality of the translation.

We will therefore distinguish between the first impression of the output with regard to idiomaticity, grammatical and semantic coherence of the text on the one hand, and the exactness of which grammatical structures and content are transferred from the source language into the target language on the other hand. In order to get an unbiased result, the method is the following:

1. read the target translation and evaluate the flow
2. read the Sámi translation and decide on the quality of the translation of the content

The score of 1 stands for the worst possible result, while a score of 7 stands for the best possible result.

The scale for flow is the shown in Table 2. Candidates for flow errors are agreement, valency and word order errors, errors in definiteness, missing articles, morphology and spelling errors, punctuation errors, missing conjunctions and non-idiomaticity.

Grade	Description
7	Perfect flow
6	Good flow (nothing stopping it)
5	Spelling error, smaller idiomatic error
4	Grammatical error, bigger idiomatic error
3	Several grammatical/idiomatic errors
2	A lot of grammatical/idiomatic errors
1	Sentence is unintelligible, cannot be understood or unrelated to the original

Table 2: Flow grades and descriptions.

The scale for content is shown in Table 3. Error candidates are (central) verb meanings in either sub-clause or main clause, where a the meaning difference is not a slight connotation deviation as it would be with synonyms, but a bigger lexical error. Secondly participants, which change the content of a sentence. If a sentence about reindeer would suddenly refer to dogs instead, the meaning of the sentence would be critically changed. Other critical errors can involve time and place errors or errors in quantities and temporal descriptions. Lastly, relevant extra content or missing content.

Grade	Description
7	Perfect, translation contains every single detail and translates it accurately
6	Good content (good enough synonyms)
5	Smaller content errors of the type above/missing information, extra content
4	Big content error/missing information
3	Several big content errors/missing information
2	A lot of big content errors/missing information (more than 50% of the sentence)
1	Nothing is as it should be, translation is (almost) unrelated to original (more than 90% is incorrect)

Table 3: Content grades and descriptions.

The human translation of ex. (1) is exx. (2-a) and the (2-b).[6] In a blind evaluation, the evaluator gave good flow scores to both (6) and slightly better content scores to the neural translation (5) than the human translation (4). *verddevuođa sullasaš ortnegat* is translated into 'the same system with ear clips' which includes extra information compared to the more literal neural translation saying 'verde-like relations'. This yields several issues:

1. If we only evaluate one sentence at a time, we may not get contextual information, where simply the distribution of content onto different sentences is different in manual translation.
2. Automatic translation evaluation based on parallel corpora will have to take into account that the output sentence may be of better quality than the target sentence.

(1) Departemeanta deattuha
department.N.SG.NOM accentuate.V.PRES.3.SG
ahte vejolašvuohta addit
that.C possibility.N.SG.NOM give.V.INF
sierralobi ii
special.dispensation.N.SG.ACC not..V.NEG.3.SG
galgga mielddisbuktit ahte
shallV.CONNEG entail.V.INF that.C

[6]Linguistic examples follow Leipzig glossing standards: `https://www.eva.mpg.de/lingua/resources/glossing-rules.php`

verddevuođa sullasaš
verddevuohta.N.SG.GEN like.A
ortnegat galget
arrangement.N.PL.NOM shall.V.PAST.3.PL
fas ásahuvvot.
again.ADV build.V.PASS.INF.

(2) a. The department would like to emphasise that the possibility to give special dispensations should not lead to that the same system using ear clips should be reestablished.

b. The departments accentuates that the possibility to give special dispensations should not lead to a reestablishment of *verde*-like relations.

Ex. (3) is a good example where the flow in the neural translation is good (6), and content scores low (2) in the neural translation in ex. (4-b). The reason for that is missing of substantial content, i.e. a translation of *Almmolašvuođagažaldat ja oktavuohta dábálaš láhkaprosedyraide*.

(3) Almmolašvuođagažaldat ja
publicity.question.SG.NOM and
oktavuohta dábálaš
relation.N.SG.NOM normal
láhkaprosedyraide leat
legal.procedure.PL.ILL be.V.PRES.3.PL
guovddážis dán dáfus.
central.SG.PX3SG this.SG.GEN context
'Publicity questions and relations to normal legal procedures are in the center in this context.'

(4) a. The issue of publicity and the relationship with ordinary legal procedures is central in this context.

b. This is a core point in this context.

Table 4 is based on 34 sentences and sentence fragments. It shows only slight differences between human and neural translations. It is however revealing that even human translations do not get perfect scores. This means that automatic evaluations that contrast machine vs. manual translations will not necessarily be able to make judgements about the machine translation quality, but only its similarity to the (possibly bad) human translation. One important factor that was revealed while discussing the evaluation was that in many cases sentences cannot be adequately evaluated without their context as certain terms only get their meaning from the context in which they are used. Therefore, an evaluation of out-of-context sentences' MT test sets can never be entirely satisfactory.

	Neural MT	Human
Flow	5.8	6
Content	5.5	5.6
Average	5.6	5.8

Table 4: Score for neural vs. human ML evaluation

4.2 North Sámi as a target language

For North Sámi as target language, we use the Tartu neural machine translation system for Uralic low resource languages by Yankovskaya et al. (2023). We picked samples from different genres, fiction, news, legal texts, and evaluated these both manually and with our rule-based tools. The only text in our corpora that has pre-existing translations for both North Sámi and English is the ILO declaration.

Ex. (5) from a news text is translated into ex. (6). Flow scores 3 and content scores 4. Flow is negatively affected by both, a case error and word order error *boazodolliid (Gen Pl) orohagaide (Ill Pl) > orohaga (Gen Sg) boazodolliid (Pl Acc)*. In addition, the output sentence contains a non-idiomatic term / lexical error *bohccofuođđut* (Nom) which should be *bieggaturbiinnaid* (Acc). It also involves a case error.

(5) "I have apologised (today) on behalf of the government to the reindeer herding districts for the fact that the permits (to build wind farms) constituted a violation of human rights," Aasland told a at a news conference.

(6) Mun lean áššáskuhttán (dál)
I.NOM have.PRES.SG1 accuse.PTCP (now)
ráđđehusa bealis
government.SG.GEN side.SG.LOC
boazodolliid orohagaide
reindeer.herder.PL.ACC dwelling.PL.ILL
dan go lobit
it.SG.GEN QST permit.PL.NOM
(bohccefuođđuid hukset)
(wild.reindeer.PL.GEN build.INF)
ledje olmmošvuoigatvuođaid
have.PAST.3.PL human.right.PL.ACC
rihkkun," Aasland
violation.SG.GEN," Aasland.SG.NOM,
muitalii odaskonferánssas.
tell.PAST.3.SG news.conference.SG.LOC.

'I have accused (now) on the side of the government the reindeer herders dwellings as the permits (to build wild reindeer) were a violation of the human rights," Aasland told on the news conference.'

We evaluate the translations on linguistic level using several approaches. We use spelling checking and correction to find out where machine translation has created non-words and whether those are near to right words by automatic spelling corrections, we also use grammatical error correction to find out some of the grammatical errors and suspicious constructions the MT system has constructed, we evaluate the errors found this way using linguistic and language understanding. We also calculate some linguistic metrics such as morpho-syntactic form distributions from the translated texts and compare those to texts that are not machine translated; to see if machine translation uses same kind of word-forms and grammatical structures as non-translated or professionally translated texts.

As is expected, the output text of *Alice* involves a number of non-word and probably also real word spelling errors, the latter of which are not handled entirely by the grammar checker yet. There are several spelling errors such as **teleskopa* for *teleskohpa* and **beallahemiin* for *bealjahemiin*.

Grammatical errors include incorrect attributive forms such as **golmmageardánis* for *golmmageardán* in ex. (7), although here the main error is a lexical error. Three-legged in the original sentence ex. (8) is translated with *golmmageardánis* 'three-times'.

(7) Fáhkka son bođii unna
suddenly s/he.NOM come.PAST.3.SG small
golmmageardánis beavdái, buot
three-times.SG.LOC table.SG.ILL, all
duddjojuvvon čavga *glássas
craft.PASS.PTCP tight glass.
'Suddenly she came to a three-time table, all crafted in tight glass.'

(8) 'Suddenly she came upon a little three-legged table, all made of solid glass'

In ex. (9), both flow and content are affected. The sentence sounds weird as such even from a logical point of view as to using future tense and the adverb *ikte* in the same sentence. The comparison with the source sentence (10) shows that the adverb is a wrong translation of *never* and *fall* is wrongly translated as *čakča* 'autumn' instead of a form of *gáhččat* 'to fall'. I.e. when translating a word with polysemy to a target language without the same polysemy, the MT system fails. The verb *loahpahuvvat* has a spelling error, it should be loahpahuvvot and is therefore erroneously analyzed as a compound noun with possessive suffix ending instead of as a passive verb.

(9) Boahtá go čakča
come.PRES.3.SG QST autumn.SG.NOM
ikte loahpahuvvat?
yesterday be.finished.SG.NOM.PX2SG?
'Will autumn be finished yesterday?'

(10) Would the fall never come to an end?

Table 5 shows translation errors by type.

4.3 Some automatic measures

The emphasis in our study is in the linguistic evaluation of the translations, but we were also interested if we can quantify if the translations are similar to texts written by native speakers in terms of grammatical features, and also how many errors there are.

Table 6 shows how many spelling and grammar errors are detected in the target text. Grammatical errors include subject-verb agreement errors, compound errors.

The amount of non-words that the system has generated is quite notable, although several of these are reflected in non-translated corpus as well, for example confusion between á and a. It is more surprising that the neural MT has not generated many grammatical errors, at least ones that can be automatically detected.

Table 7 contains distributions of grammatical features in machine translated texts and large corpus.

There does not appear to be large difference between the machine translated and reference corpus, with the exception of lack of dual forms. This is not totally unsurprising, the forms are rare in use in general and do not have any comparable equivalent in source language: virtually all word-forms that concern two individuals fall under generic plurals in English, very few lexical selections can be used to refer two people specifically.

Type	**error**	**correct**
Nonsense words based on orthographic similarity	*Rabihtta-Hole*	*njoammilbiedju* 'rabbit hole'
	"Vel!" for "Well!"	*de*
Postpostition vs. preposition	*haga govaid*	*govaid haga* 'without pictures'
Wrong PoS	*hui oađđin* 'very sleep' (noun)	*hui váiban* 'very tired' (adjective)
Lexical error	*álggii čuožžut su bálgáide* 'started to stand his paths'	*álggii čuovvut su bálgáide* 'started to follow his paths'
	su ***čivga*** *lei lohkame* 'baby animal'	*su* ***oabbá*** *lei lohkame* 'sister'
Literal/Non-idiomatic	*Aliceas ii lean boddu smiehttat* 'Alice did not have a break to think'	*Alice ii ribahan smiehttat*
Polysemy error	*girjái* ***ahte*** *(subjunction 'that') su čivga lei lohkame*	*girjái maid (relative pronoun 'that') su čivga lei lohkame*
	mii lea girjji geavaheapmi 'how can the book be used'	*mii lea girjji* ***ávki*** 'what is the use of the book'
Periphrastic > synthetic construction	*ALICE lei šaddagoahtán váiban čohkkedit*	*ALICE lei váibagoahtán čohkkedeamis* 'Alice started to be tired of sitting'
Valency error	*váiban čohkkedit* (infinitive)	*váiban čohkkedeamis* (locative) 'tired of sitting'
Agreement error	*das eai lean govat* ***iige*** *ságastallamat* 'there weren't pictures and there wasn't conversations either'	*das eai lean govat* ***eaige*** *ságastallamat* 'there were neither pictures and there weren't conversations either'

Table 5: Error types found in English-North Sámi neural MT

Text	Spelling (%)	Grammar (%)
Alice	232 (5%)	9 (0.1%)
BBC	23 (5%)	0
CTV	33 (4%)	1 (0.1%)
ILO-169	0	3 (0.1%)
SIKOR	399,282 (1.8%)	59,611 (0.3%)

Table 6: Automatically detected spelling (non-word) and grammar errors (real-word) in machine translated texts

5 Conclusion

We manually evaluated two neural machine translation systems in an indigenous low-resource context, one of which has North Sámi as a source language and the other of which has North Sámi as a target language. Translation is done either into or from a higher resource language, i.e. Norwegian and English, which are both morphologically simple compared to North Sámi. The Sámi to Norwegian evaluation is done by a native North Sámi speaker who has worked as a professional translator. We developed a scale according to which first the flow of the target language is evaluated and then the representation and exactness of the source language content in the target language. Both scales have 7 grades. Flow and content evaluation can differ very much from each other as flow mostly focuses on the target sentence, while content takes into account the source sentence to a much higher degree. The evaluation shows that flow typically scores higher than content, which means that a clear understanding of both source and target sentence is necessary to evaluate how well the matching is done. This supports our hypothesis that high-level language expertise is necessary to evaluate the quality of a translation.

For the English to Sámi evaluation we applied a different evaluation method. We applied high-quality rule-based proofing tools for Sámi for spellchecking and basic grammar checking of the target text. As human resources for indigenous languages are typically low, we find that this method - while it cannot replace human evaluation - can be revealing as regards certain shortcomings of the MT system, which affect its quality. We discovered that spelling errors in the neural translation are more than twice as much as in the Sámi text collection SIKOR. Additionally, a low-scale manual evaluation of the fictional text *Alice*, showed that shortcomings of the system included a variety of different morpho-syntactic errors as well of non-idiomatic constructions and nonsense translations.

The second system evaluation regards the newly released multi-lingual neural MT tool by Tartu university, where we had a look at English-North Sámi machine translation. None of the developers has knowledge of North Sámi and is therefore not able to properly evaluate the results in all its relevant details. We regard it as important that these systems are evaluated by those that have knowledge of the language, and give a reliable picture of what can and what cannot be expected of such a system. As a user can have varying knowledge themselves about either source or target language,

Text		Poss		Dual		Actio
	n	%	n	%	n	%
Alice	34	0.8%	0	0	26	0.6%
BBC	1	0.2%	0	0	1	0.2%
CTV	4	0.5%	0	0	2	0.2%
ILO-169	23	0.7%	1	0.0%	3	0.1%
SIKOR	130,257	0.5%	59,623	0.2%	58,850	0.2%

Table 7: Distribution of grammatical features in machine translated documents (first four) and the large corpus (SIKOR).

expectations to the system can be different. We apply our rule-based proofing tools to test both spelling and grammar, provide an overview of prevailing error types of the MT tool, and show if the outcome reflects the morpho-syntactic reality of the monolingual Sámi corpus SIKOR written by native language users.

In the future we would like to manually evaluate neural MT both from and to an indigenous language (starting with North Sámi) on a larger scale in order to get more insights in refining the criteria of our evaluation method to come to adequate conclusions of the systems' quality. As this highly depends on human resources and language expertise, we also plan to focus on recruitment of language experts.

Acknowledgments

Máret Láila Anti contributed with her language expertise in North Sámi and Norwegian, as well as her professional knowledge regarding translation practices and Sámi linguistics.

This research was supported by Cloud TPUs from Google's TPU Research Cloud (TRC).

References

David M. Eberhard, Gary F. Simons, and Charles D. Fennig, editors. 2018. *Ethnologue: Languages of the World*, twenty-fifth edition. SIL International, Dallas, Texas.

Christian Federmann. 2018. Appraise evaluation framework for machine translation. In *Proceedings of the 27th International Conference on Computational Linguistics: System Demonstrations*, pages 86–88, Santa Fe, New Mexico. Association for Computational Linguistics.

Arle Lommel. 2018. *Metrics for Translation Quality Assessment: A Case for Standardising Error Typologies*, pages 109–127. Springer International Publishing, Cham.

Manuel Mager, Elisabeth Mager, Katharina Kann, and Ngoc Thang Vu. 2023. Ethical considerations for machine translation of indigenous languages: Giving a voice to the speakers.

Marion Weller-di Marco and Alexander Fraser. 2022. Findings of the WMT 2022 shared tasks in unsupervised MT and very low resource supervised MT. In *Proceedings of the Seventh Conference on Machine Translation (WMT)*, pages 801–805, Abu Dhabi, United Arab Emirates (Hybrid). Association for Computational Linguistics.

Joss Moorkens, Sheila Castilho, Federico Gaspari, and Stephen Doherty, editors. 2018. *Translation Quality Assessment*, volume 1 of *Machine Translation: Technologies and Applications*. Springer.

Flammie Pirinen, Sjur Moshagen, and Katri Hiovain-Asikainen. 2023. GiellaLT — a stable infrastructure for Nordic minority languages and beyond. In *Proceedings of the 24th Nordic Conference on Computational Linguistics (NoDaLiDa)*, pages 643–649, Tórshavn, Faroe Islands. University of Tartu Library.

Maja Popović. 2018. *Error Classification and Analysis for Machine Translation Quality Assessment*, pages 129–158. Springer International Publishing, Cham.

Pekka Sammallahti. 1998. *The Saami languages – An Introduction*. Davvi Girji, Kárášjohka.

SIKOR. 2018. SIKOR uit norgga árktalaš universitehta ja norgga sámedikki sámi teakstačoakkáldat, veršuvdna 06.11.2018. http://gtweb.uit.no/korp. Accessed: 2023-06-12.

Nisan Stiennon, Long Ouyang, Jeffrey Wu, Daniel Ziegler, Ryan Lowe, Chelsea Voss, Alec Radford, Dario Amodei, and Paul F Christiano. 2020. Learning to summarize with human feedback. *Advances in Neural Information Processing Systems*, 33:3008–3021.

Trond Trosterud and Kevin Brubeck Unhammer. 2012. Evaluating North Sámi to Norwegian assimilation RBMT. In *Proceedings of the Third International Workshop on Free/Open-Source Rule-Based Machine Translation*, pages 13–26, Gothenburg, Sweden.

Linting Xue, Noah Constant, Adam Roberts, Mihir Kale, Rami Al-Rfou, Aditya Siddhant, Aditya Barua, and Colin Raffel. 2020. mt5: A massively multilingual pre-trained text-to-text transformer. *arXiv preprint arXiv:2010.11934*.

Lisa Yankovskaya, Maali Tars, Andre Tättar, and Mark Fishel. 2023. Machine translation for low-resource Finno-Ugric languages. In *Proceedings of the 24th Nordic Conference on Computational Linguistics (NoDaLiDa)*, pages 762–771, Tórshavn, Faroe Islands. University of Tartu Library.

Hierarchical Evaluation Framework: Best Practices for Human Evaluation

Iva Bojic[1] and **Jessica Chen**[2] and **Si Yuan Chang**[1] and **Qi Chwen Ong**[1] and **Shafiq Joty**[1,3] and **Josip Car**[1,2]
[1]Nanyang Technological University Singapore
[2]Imperial College London, United Kingdom
[3]Salesforce Research, USA

Abstract

Human evaluation plays a crucial role in Natural Language Processing (NLP) as it assesses the quality and relevance of developed systems, thereby facilitating their enhancement. However, the absence of widely accepted human evaluation metrics in NLP hampers fair comparisons among different systems and the establishment of universal assessment standards. Through an extensive analysis of existing literature on human evaluation metrics, we identified several gaps in NLP evaluation methodologies. These gaps served as motivation for developing our own hierarchical evaluation framework. The proposed framework offers notable advantages, particularly in providing a more comprehensive representation of the NLP system's performance. We applied this framework to evaluate the developed Machine Reading Comprehension system, which was utilized within a human-AI symbiosis model. The results highlighted the associations between the quality of inputs and outputs, underscoring the necessity to evaluate both components rather than solely focusing on outputs. In future work, we will investigate the potential time-saving benefits of our proposed framework for evaluators assessing NLP systems.

1 Introduction

Human evaluation is crucial for assessing the quality, validity, and performance of Natural Language Processing (NLP) systems especially as automatic metrics are usually not sufficient (Van Der Lee et al., 2019). Human evaluation can deal with complex generated natural language and its nuances such as pragmatics, context and semantics which often requires some expert knowledge (Sudoh et al., 2021). Automatic evaluation may be used to assess individual dimensions (e.g., fluency, accuracy) of natural language, however, may often lose to humans in terms of accuracy and understanding.

Various methodologies are often employed in human evaluation such as ranking, pairwise comparison, or a state-of-the-art machine translation metric that was used in Castilho (2021). They can provide valuable insights into the strengths and limitations of an NLP system; however, it is notably time-consuming and expensive and significant trade-offs may exist in consideration of different goals or requirements (Zhang et al., 2020). The human evaluation also comes with its own set of limitations, such as fatigue effect (van der Lee et al., 2021) and inconsistencies between evaluators. The role of human evaluators should also be considered as some tasks may require domain expert knowledge or provide specific training evaluators.

There is currently a lack of consensus on which metrics to use for the human evaluation of NLP systems (Paroubek et al., 2007). As there tend to be different research goals, requirements and task-dependent metrics, there exists the challenge of standardizing human evaluation metrics and essentially reaching an overall consensus. A unique combination of metrics can be used for a more comprehensive assessment depending on the desired objectives. These combinations can be grouped based on different evaluation aspects (Liang and Li, 2021). Metrics may also vary depending on the task (e.g., machine translation, sentiment analysis) and thus task design can affect the criteria used for evaluation (Iskender et al., 2021).

To identify gaps in the literature pertaining to human evaluation, we conducted a scoping review to systematically examine various aspects of human evaluation experiments in NLP tasks, including the characteristics of evaluators, evaluation samples, scoring methods, design of evaluation and statistical analysis. The findings of our literature review revealed three significant gaps: (i) the absence of evaluation metrics for NLP system inputs, (ii) the lack of consideration for interdependencies among different characteristics of assessed NLP systems, and (iii) a limited utilization of metrics for extrinsic evaluation of NLP systems.

Proceedings of the Third Workshop on Human Evaluation of NLP Systems, pages 11–22, Varna, Bulgaria, Sep 7, 2023.
https://doi.org/10.26615/978-954-452-088-5_002

We hope to bridge the aforementioned gaps by providing a standardized human evaluation framework that can be used across different NLP tasks. Our proposed framework employs a hierarchical structure that divides the human evaluation process into two phases: testing and evaluation. This division enables evaluators to assess the quality of inputs used by testers when evaluating NLP systems. Furthermore, the hierarchical design of the evaluation metric allows for the computation of a composite score that reflects the overall quality of the NLP system.

This paper is organized as follows. Section 2 presents the analysis from a scoping review that included more than 200 papers published within the last three years in the top 5 NLP venues. The results of the aforementioned analysis informed the development of the proposed hierarchical evaluation framework, which is presented in Section 3. Section 4 presents the results of adopting the proposed framework for the human evaluation of the Machine Reading Comprehension (MRC) system developed as a part of the human-AI symbiosis model. Finally, Section 5 concludes the paper.

2 Scoping Review

2.1 Structured Review

To inform our development of a hierarchical framework for human evaluation, we conducted a scoping review to examine existing literature systematically. Our paper selection process followed the Preferred Reporting Items for Systematic Reviews and Meta-Analyses (PRISMA) extension for Scoping Reviews checklist (PRISMA-ScR) (Peters et al., 2015) (see Figure 1). We searched for relevant publication venues on Google Scholar. We selected the category of Engineering and Computer Science, followed by the sub-category of Computational Linguistics. Subsequently, we chose the top five venues with the highest h5-index, namely:

- Meeting of the Association for Computational Linguistics (ACL),
- Conference on Empirical Methods in Natural Language Processing (EMNLP),
- Conference of the North American Chapter of the Association for Computational Linguistics: Human Language Technologies (NAACL),
- Conference of the European Chapter of the Association for Computational Linguistics (EACL),
- International Conference on Computational Linguistics (COLING).

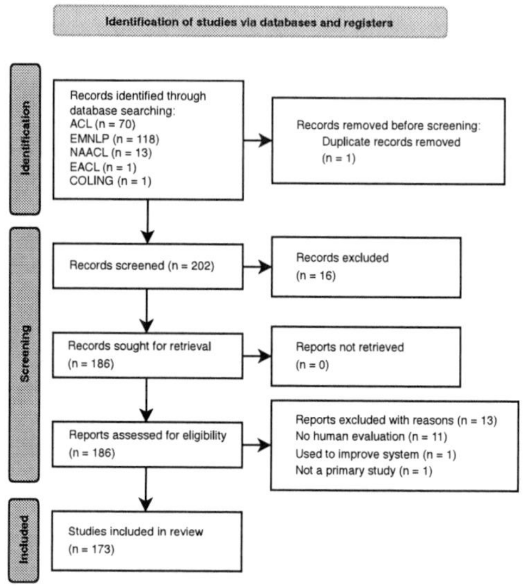

Figure 1: This PRISMA flow diagram depicts the study selection process throughout this scoping review. 203 studies in total were identified through a search on Google Scholar. After one duplicate was removed, the total remaining studies was 202. After title and abstract screening, 16 studies were excluded, leaving 186 studies for full-text screening. A final 173 studies were included in this scoping review for data extraction and analysis.

Due to the rapid development in the NLP field, only studies published between 2019 and 2023 were included. The Google Scholar search strategy is shown in Figure 2.

2.2 Selection of Articles

Eligible articles were identified in two stages: (1) title and abstract screening, (2) full-text screening. To maintain consistency of decision-making in the selection process, both title and abstract screening and full-text screening were conducted by two of the three reviewers (IB, JC, QCO) independently based on pre-defined inclusion and exclusion criteria (see Figure 3). Conflicts were resolved through discussion with a third reviewer to establish consensus. The resolution of inconsistencies or disagreements amongst reviewers was guided by pre-defined eligibility criteria and reference to initial objectives. Reasons for exclusion were recorded during full-text screening.

Hierarchical Human Evaluation Framework Search Strategy
(Literature Search performed: April 24, 2023)

1. "human evaluation" source:"ACL" OR source:"EMNLP" OR source:"NAACL" OR source:"EACL" OR source:"COLING"
2. "human evaluation" source:"ACL"
3. "human evaluation" source:"EMNLP"
4. "human evaluation" source:"NAACL"
5. "human evaluation" source:"EACL"
6. "human evaluation" source:"COLING"
7. Limit 1-6 to yr=2019-current

Figure 2: Search strategy used for the scoping review. After performing 1, we also performed 2-6 to find all papers from individual venues that did not appear after the first combined search.

Inclusion criteria:

1. It is a full-text article that reported empirical research in NLU, NLG or both.
2. It reported human evaluation for the purpose of evaluating the performance of the system.
3. It was published in English.
4. It was published in 2019 or later.
5. It is a peer-reviewed article published in ACL, EMNLP, NAACL, EACL or COLING.

Exclusion Criteria:

1. It reported secondary research such as a literature review, rapid review, systematic review, or scoping review.
2. It is a pre-print article, book chapter, conference abstract, expert opinions, perspectives, or commentary.
3. Human evaluation was conducted for other purposes, such as improving the system.
4. It was published in a language other than English.
5. It was published before 2019.
6. It does not involve an NLP system.
7. It was published in other venues that are not listed above.

Figure 3: This figure lists the inclusion and exclusion criteria that formed the basis of our screening process.

2.3 Data Extraction

A standardized data extraction form (see Appendix 1) was developed through iterative discussions between three reviewers (IB, JC, QCO) based on insights gained during the initial literature review of related work. The data extraction form was first piloted on three randomly selected articles by the three reviewers to ensure consistent and accurate extraction of data. The data extraction process involved all three reviewers and was done independently. Ambiguities or uncertainties were resolved by discussion between reviewers and by referring to the original papers used for the creation of the extraction matrix (Van Der Lee et al., 2019; Amidei et al., 2018a; Liang and Li, 2021; Howcroft et al., 2020). We extracted a range of variables from certain chosen sources and tailored them to the objectives of our review. These variables are categorized as follows in Section 2.4: (1) characteristics of evaluators, (2) evaluation samples, (3) scoring methods, (4) design of evaluation and (5) statistical analysis.

2.4 Synthesis of Results

2.4.1 Characteristics of Evaluators

A large proportion of papers (83%, 144/173) provided information on the number of evaluators that participated in the human evaluation. This shows that there is a general consistency in the reporting of human evaluation methods across all papers reviewed. The number of evaluators employed can be defined as *small* (1-5), *medium* (6-9) and *large* ($\geq$ 10) scale (van der Lee et al., 2021). Papers reported a small number of evaluators in 62% of cases (107/173), a medium number in 6% (11/173), and a large number in 15% (26/173). The median number of evaluators was three per study.

71% of the reviewed papers (122/173) reported the background of the evaluators, differentiating between *experts* and *non-experts*, detailed which platform they were from or set standards for crowd-sourced workers. One example, proposed in Zhu et al. (2020), was to set standards by only using workers with a high enough approval rate to ensure quality. This helps alleviate the problem of quality control when using larger-scale crowd-sourcing platforms such as Amazon Mechanical Turk.

2.4.2 Evaluation Samples

All of the papers reported that human evaluation was done only on *outputs* of NLP systems, with the median number of evaluation instances being 100. Most papers (60%, 103/173) created samples *randomly*, but some (3%, 6/173) specified *their methodology*. For instance, in Zeng and Nie (2021), discussions that were difficult to understand were filtered out. In this case, human evaluation was used to compare the dialogue generation between two different models. In order to create a more relevant dataset for human evaluation, filtering out professional texts that were difficult to understand, ensured that the data was closer to daily dialogue. This allowed for more accurate and reproducible human evaluation results. Using alternative methods to random sampling can have certain benefits such as cost-effectiveness, time efficiency and focused research objectives (Zeng and Nie, 2021).

2.4.3 Scoring Methods

Overall, 68% of papers (118/173) used a *scale* as their evaluation scoring system. A scoring system should also be defined by assigning attributes or certain qualities to a number in the scale that they are using. Further, 23% of papers (39/173) reported using *comparison* between different models or question answering to achieve more qualitative results. Examples include win, tie, loss, A/B testing, and a direct comparison.

The characteristics of evaluation can be referred to as evaluation attributes or text quality dimensions such as *fluency*, *adequacy*, and *grammar* (Gehrmann et al., 2023). These characteristics can be considered for both qualitative and quantitative methods and are often specified to guide the evaluation task. For example, Liang and Li (2021) divided various characteristics into seven groups based on their similarity and overall purpose for the human evaluation of chatbots. These groups further tailor the characteristics of evaluation to the unique task, allowing the reader to understand the reason for their selection.

Dependencies can exist among characteristics of evaluation. In other words, human evaluation can be done in sequential order when the order in which characteristics are evaluated matters. Moreover, evaluation can be prematurely stopped if some characteristics were not deemed of a satisfactory quality. Consequently, dependencies among characteristics of evaluation could also allow for a NLP system to have a composite score that would reflect its overall quality. For instance, an overall performance score can be produced based on pre-defined threshold criteria that need to be fulfilled. This threshold could be a specified performance level reached by a specific combination of characteristics. We have not observed any dependencies reported among different evaluated characteristics in the reviewed literature. Namely, all characteristics were evaluated separately, and the quality of a certain characteristic was never put in relation with the quality of another one.

2.4.4 Design of Evaluation

Extrinsic and *intrinsic* evaluation are two different types of human evaluation. Extrinsic evaluation assesses the ability of the system to perform an over-arching task with a real-world application. On the other hand, intrinsic evaluation assesses specific qualities or attributes and is evaluated independently of the over-arching task. Therefore, a system could perform well intrinsically without performing well extrinsically. Most papers (88%, 153/173) performed intrinsic evaluation, 4% (7/173) performed extrinsic evaluation, and 8% (13/173) involved aspects of both intrinsic and extrinsic evaluation. Intrinsic evaluation remains popular likely due to its simplicity, cost-efficiency, ease in tracking progress and benchmarking (Gehrmann et al., 2023), (Belz and Gatt, 2008). The lack of extrinsic evaluation may also be affected by the difficulty of designing an evaluation that effectively emulates its usage in the real-world setting.

Bias mitigation is important due to the potential compromise of human evaluation caused by order effects (Van Der Lee et al., 2019). Order effects include practice, carryover, and fatigue effects (Van Der Lee et al., 2019), all of which have the potential to affect human evaluation and lead to misleading and biased results. To mitigate this, Van Der Lee et al. (2019) suggested potential solutions including practice trials, increasing the time between tasks, shortening tasks, and proposed specific evaluation designs such as counterbalancing (systematically varying the order of presentation) and randomization. Further solutions include multiple evaluators assessing the same point (Son et al., 2022) to increase the reliability of their human evaluation and randomized counterbalancing, which is a combination of randomization and counterbalancing methods (Kurisinkel and Chen, 2019). However, the method of bias mitigation was only specified in 14% (24/173) of papers. This may be due to the high costs of evaluation designs, specifically counterbalancing. However, according to Van Der Lee et al. (2019), randomization or limiting the evaluation to one judge per system (if order effects are suspected) should be sufficient to mitigate order effects and avoid biased results.

2.4.5 Statistical Analysis

Inter-annotator agreement (IAA) scores should be reported to confirm consistency between evaluators and the reliability of the evaluation. Typically, a higher score indicates increased IAA. 34% of included papers (58/173) reported IAA using Kendall's τ, Fleiss' κ, Cohen's κ, Krippendorf's α and percentage agreement to name a few. However, a detailed analysis of the IAA scores and how they affected the overall evaluation is important. In some cases, IAA scores can prove to not be a useful measurement of agreement - as alluded to further in (Amidei et al., 2018b).

The importance of ensuring the reliability and validity of human evaluation is further highlighted by Liu et al. (2022) through the need for using statistical tests. Other methods of presenting data and analyzing results include displaying 1st and 2nd best performances in a table by highlighting the specific performance values (Gangal et al., 2022); or summary statistics such as standard deviations or mean scores (Qian and Levy, 2022). Only 16% of papers (28/173) used statistical tests as a form of analysis of their human evaluation such as student's t-test and Wilcoxon ranked test (Van Der Lee et al., 2019). This could be due to a lack of statistical power attributed to inadequate sample sizes, which could lead to misleading or different conclusions as they are more subject to the effects of chance (Otani et al., 2023).

3 Hierarchical Evaluation Framework

The review of existing literature identified 3 gaps:

- Majority of human evaluation was *intrinsic*.
- The characteristics of NLP systems were evaluated *independently*.
- Human evaluation focused on assessing the *outputs* of NLP systems, neglecting the evaluation of their *inputs*.

The analysis of existing literature revealed that the majority of papers (88%, 153/173) focused solely on an intrinsic evaluation of NLP systems. To avoid conducting an evaluation merely for the sake of it, we suggest that first a clear purpose for an NLP system is defined, and subsequently, an extrinsic evaluation is designed to gauge the systems' performance in fulfilling that specific purpose.

Additionally, the evaluation of various aspects of NLP systems' outputs (e.g., truthfulness) is usually conducted independently, without providing a composite score for the overall system performance. We suggest adopting a hierarchical approach, where the characteristics of the systems are interdependent, and the evaluation process continues only if the preceding characteristic(s) is deemed satisfactory. Conversely, if a characteristic is unsatisfactory, the evaluation can be discontinued, allowing evaluators to save time by not evaluating all characteristics for the low-quality outputs.

Lastly, to date, the existing literature has focused solely on the human evaluation of NLP systems' outputs, assuming that the inputs provided to these systems were of good quality. However, this assumption may not always hold true. We thus propose a two-phase approach for human evaluation, wherein testers initially assess NLP systems, followed by evaluators who evaluate both the inputs and outputs of the systems. By dividing the evaluation process into two phases, we enable evaluators to also assess the quality of the inputs used by testers during the testing phase of NLP systems. In essence, our hypothesis is that the quality of the outputs may not only be influenced by the system itself but also by the quality of the inputs.

In order to address those gaps, we propose a framework as shown in Figure 4. By defining a system's purpose as the first step, our framework supports extrinsic evaluation. The second step is to define interdependencies between the evaluated characteristics and consequently to design a hierarchical evaluation metric that supports calculating a composite score that encompasses the overall quality of an NLP system. Namely, the evaluation stops if any of the evaluated characteristics is deemed unsatisfactory and, in this case, the composite score is "bad" as the system did not pass the evaluation. Otherwise, if the evaluation goes to the end, then the composite score is "good". We hypothesize that our framework facilitates a shorter evaluation time for evaluators by allowing early termination of evaluation in cases where any evaluated characteristic does not meet satisfactory quality. The third step is to do testing of the system according to the defined purpose. Testers are independent of evaluators who evaluate the system's inputs and outputs using the designed hierarchical evaluation metric in the fourth step. This allows for independent evaluation of the system's inputs as well. Consequently, our framework enables an examination of whether the quality of a system's outputs is influenced by the quality of its inputs.

1) define the purpose of the system

2) design a hierarchical evaluation metric

3) conduct testing of the system

4) do an evaluation of system's inputs and outputs

5) calculate the composite score

Figure 4: Steps explaining how to create a hierarchical evaluation framework for an NLP system.

4 Case study: Hierarchical Evaluation for an MRC System

We evaluated a Machine Reading Comprehension (MRC) system using the framework outlined in the previous section. In an MRC system, answers come in the form of short text spans which are directly extracted from the text corpus (i.e., relevant text database). Questions asked, on the other hand, need to be relevant to the topic that the text corpus covers, factoid, answerable and mistake-free (i.e., no spelling or grammar mistakes).

4.1 The purpose of the MRC System

The purpose of the developed MRC system was to support health coaches during their sessions with clients, coaching them on the importance of good quality sleep. Namely, the developed system is part of the human-AI symbiosis model shown in Figure 5 (Bojic et al., 2023b). The system is a pre-trained BERT model that was fine-tuned on a human-annotated domain-specific dataset.

The entire health coaching process takes place online through text messaging. To address factoid questions raised by clients, the health coach may utilize the MRC system for additional support during coaching sessions (Bojic et al., 2022, 2023a). Health coaches were given the liberty to use, modify, or disregard the answers provided by the MRC system. This integration enhances the human coaching experience by incorporating evidence-based knowledge given by the MRC system. As a result, the health coaches' response time improves, and the information they offer is grounded in reliable evidence.

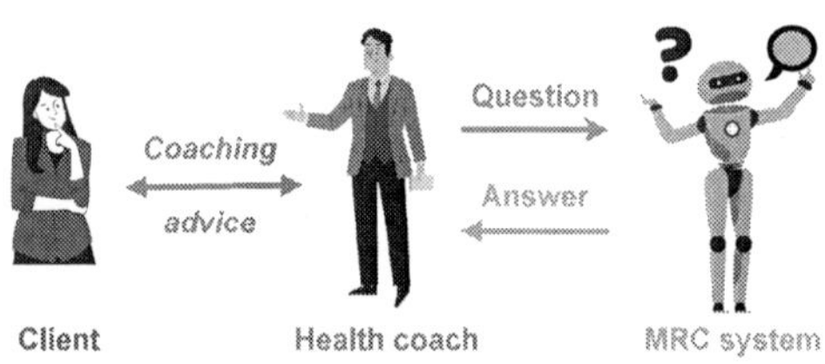

Figure 5: Human-AI health coaching model.

4.2 Hierarchical Evaluation Metrics

We developed two evaluation metrics: one for the inputs (i.e., questions) of the MRC system and the other for the outputs (i.e., answers), in order to be able to detect whether the quality of the MRC system output is affected by the quality of its input.

4.2.1 Evaluation of Inputs

Figure 6 shows a set of evaluation criteria for evaluating the MRC questions. The question is *relevant* if it is on the topic covered in the corresponding text corpus. *Factoid* questions are questions that start with one of the following words: "who", "what", "where", "when", "why" or "how". They ask about facts that can be expressed as short texts (Parsing, 2009). The question is *answerable* if there exists an answer to it. The evaluators are asked if the posed question contains any *spelling* or *grammar* errors. The *difficulty* of the posed question can be chosen from three levels – *easy*, *medium*, or *hard* (please refer to Table 1).

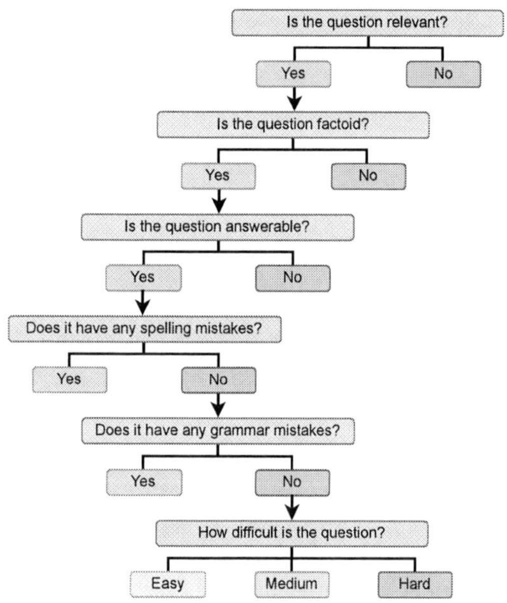

Figure 6: Hierarchical evaluation of the questions.

Table 1: Three different levels of difficulty of the posed questions.

Easy	The correct answer is obvious after reading the passage only one time.
Medium	To find the correct answer, one needs to carefully read and understand both the question and the paragraph.
Hard	To find the correct answer, one needs to read the paragraph many times, sometimes even use logical reasoning to find the correct answer.

4.2.2 Evaluation of Outputs

The evaluators were asked to evaluate the retrieved *short answer* and if necessary its *explanation*. Namely, the output of the whole MRC system is a text span (i.e., short answer). However, an MRC system can be seen as a pipeline of two NLP models - *document retrieval* and *document reader*, where the output of the former model is the *relevant passage(s)* and the output of the latter model (i.e., the whole system) is a *text span*. Our metric first evaluates the characteristics of the output of the whole system (i.e., text span). If the output of the whole system was not satisfying, then we evaluate its explanation (i.e., relevant passage) that was provided by the document retrieval component.

The retrieved short answer is *clear* if its meaning is easy to understand. The retrieved short answer/explanation is *relevant* if it answers the posed question. *Clinical accuracy* of the retrieved short answer/explanation denotes the degree to which it is clinically accurate – (i) clinically accurate, (ii) partially clinically accurate, and (iii) clinically inaccurate (see Table 2). Finally, the health coaches judged the usefulness of the retrieved short answer/explanation (see Figure 7).

Table 2: Three different levels of clinical accuracy.

Clinically accurate	The retrieved short answer/ explanation is clinically accurate and is based on evidence-based information.
Partially clinically accurate	The retrieved short answer/ explanation is partially clinically accurate and somewhat lacks evidence-based information.
Clinically inaccurate	The retrieved short answer/ explanation is not clinically accurate and is not based on evidence-based information.

4.3 Testing of the MRC System

Testing of the developed MRC system was conducted during a pilot Randomized Controlled Trial (RCT). In this RCT, 30 participants in the intervention group (i.e., clients) interacted with 10 health coaches who utilized the MRC system to answer factoid questions. Clients were recruited from a general student population if they (1) were older than 21 years, (2) were available for weekly interaction with a health coach for four weeks, (3) were not currently undergoing any treatment for a sleep disorder or mental disorder and were not under the care of a psychologist or psychiatrist, and (iv) had PHQ-9 score less than 10.

Health coaches were recruited from the cohorts of graduated students from the health coaching course if they (1) were older than 21 years, (2) were available for weekly interaction with three clients for four weeks, and (iii) successfully completed and passed the health coaching course. During the study period of four weeks, clients had weekly 30-minute sessions with their respective health coaches. All questions asked by health coaches and their corresponding answers were saved during the testing phase and were subsequently used in the evaluation phase. By dividing human evaluation into two parts, we were able also to judge whether questions were posed in the way we asked our health coaches to ask them, i.e., if they can be answered by the developed MRC system.

4.4 Evaluation of the MRC System

Following a 4-week pilot RCT, the developed MRC system underwent evaluation by 10 health coaches. A total of 387 unique question-answer pairs were evaluated by the health coaches during this period. The heat map depicted in Figure 8 illustrates the number of inputs and outputs evaluated by each health coach, while Figure 9 showcases the average evaluation time required for each input/output assessed by the health coaches.

Almost all questions (99%, 383/387) were evaluated as *relevant*. One example of a question that was marked as not relevant was: "*Food nutrition tips*". The next 87% of questions (335/383) were judged as factoid. Some examples of not factoid questions are as follows: "*About REM sleep, is it the phase that I'm dreaming?*", "*Can you exercise before sleeping?*", "*I often run around campus for 3-5km at night 1-2h before sleeping. Is it good or bad for sleep?*". 2% of the remaining questions (8/335) were marked as not answerable: "*How long should I be awake during sleep?*", "*How bad would you say is my sleep health like compared to the average?*", while additional 2% (6/327) had spelling errors (e.g., "*How long before bedtime shld i stop screentime?*"). Finally, the last 23% (74/321) had grammar errors: "*How do ensure naps have good quality?*", "*Why wake up during night?*". The results of the complete external human evaluation for questions are shown in Figure 10.

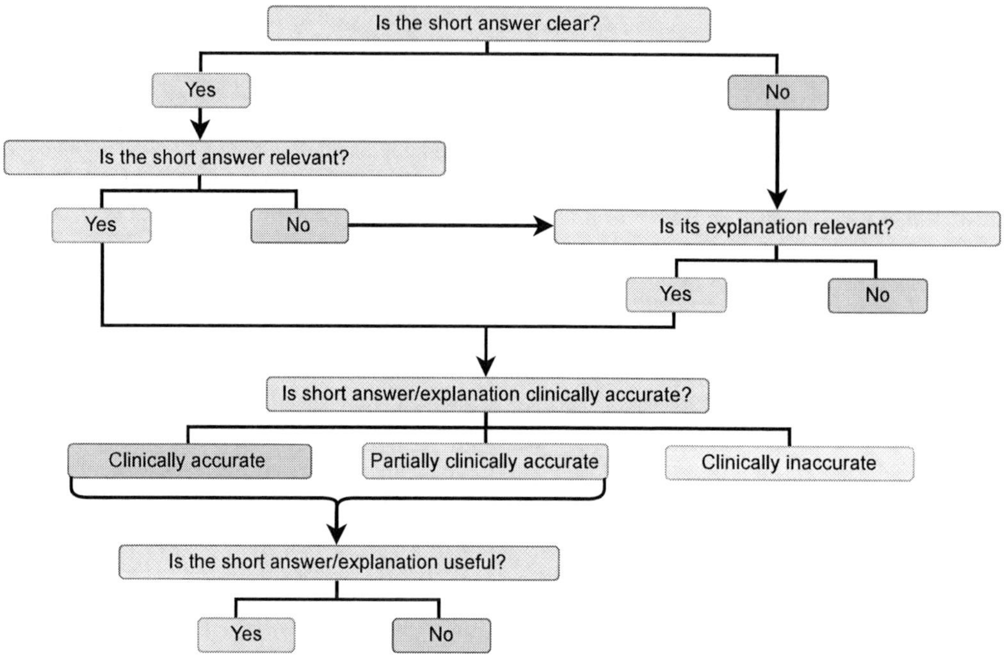

Figure 7: Hierarchical evaluation of the answers.

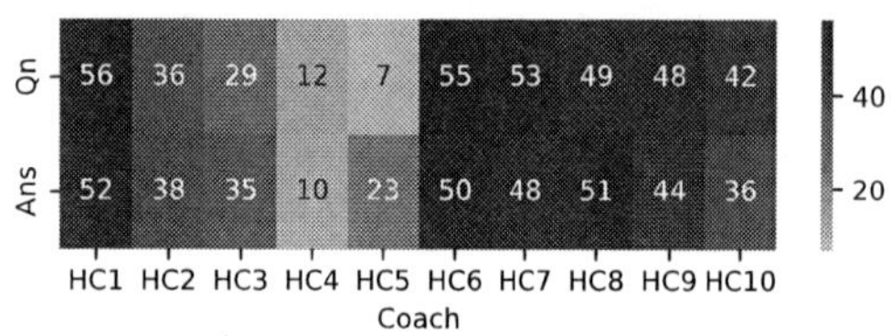

Figure 8: The total number of questions and answers evaluated by each health coach.

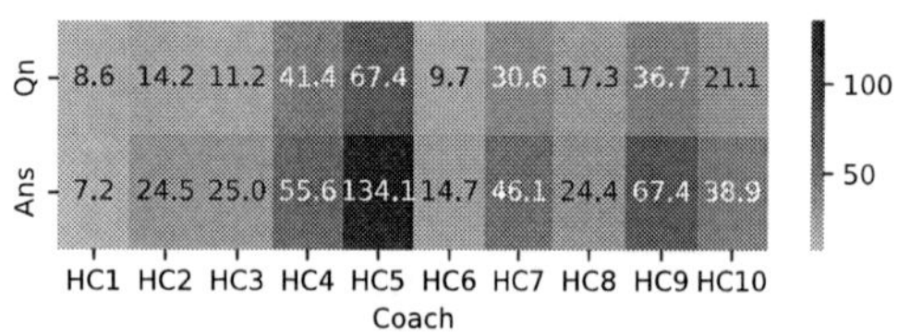

Figure 9: Average time in seconds per health coach needed to evaluate questions and answers.

More than 40% (157/387) of short answers were evaluated as not *clear*, out of which in 57% of cases (89/157), their explanations were marked as relevant. For example, "***Question***: *When does melatonin peak?* ***Answer***: *release of melatonin, the hormone that induces feelings of tiredness and relaxation.* ***Explanation***: *When the sun goes down, your eyes will perceive darkness and signal the scn accordingly. This triggers the release of melatonin, the hormone that induces feelings of tiredness and relaxation. This also causes your core temperature to dip.*". 63% of clear answers (146/230) were also evaluated as relevant of which 99% (144/146) was indicated as being (partly) clinically accurate. Furthermore, 97% (113/116) of the short answers that were not clear, but their explanations were relevant, were (partly) clinically accurate. The results of the complete external human evaluation for answers are shown in Figure 11.

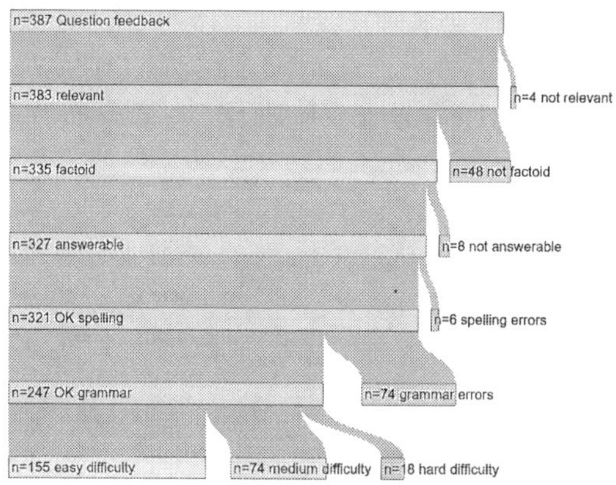

Figure 10: Extrinsic evaluation of questions.

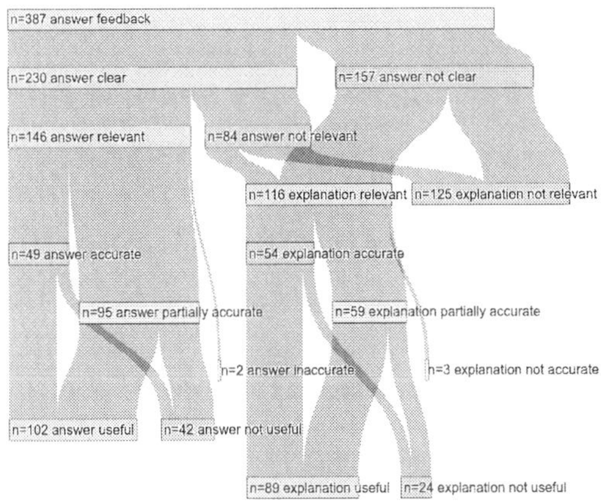

Figure 11: Extrinsic evaluation of answers.

4.5 Composite scores of the MRC System

The results of our evaluation showed that 63.8% (247/387) of unique questions were evaluated as relevant, factoid, answerable, spelling and grammar mistakes-free (i.e., *good* questions). Out of those, 63% (155/247) were judged as easy, 30% (74/247) as medium and 7% (18/247) as hard questions. Furthermore, 49.4% (191/387) of unique answers were evaluated as clear, relevant, clinically accurate and useful (i.e., *good* answers). In order to check if there are any associations between the quality of outputs and inputs, we performed a χ^2 test. The result showed significant associations between the two (χ^2 = 4.56, p=0.03). The distribution of the performance matrix is shown in Table 3.

Table 3: 2x2 matrix for the performed χ^2 test.

		Questions	
		good	bad
Answers	good	132	59
	bad	115	81

5 Discussion and Conclusions

In this study, we conducted a scoping review to identify gaps in the literature regarding human evaluation in NLP. The findings revealed three significant gaps that need to be addressed: the lack of evaluation metrics for NLP system inputs, limited consideration for interdependencies among different characteristics of NLP systems, and a scarcity of metrics for extrinsic evaluation.

To bridge these gaps and enhance human evaluation in NLP, we proposed a hierarchical evaluation framework. Our framework offers a standardized approach that considers both the inputs and outputs of NLP systems, allowing for a more comprehensive assessment. Moreover, our hierarchical approach considers the interdependencies among different characteristics of NLP systems. Rather than evaluating characteristics independently, our framework emphasizes their interconnectedness and the impact they may have on each other. This approach enables a more holistic evaluation that captures the overall performance of NLP systems.

To validate the effectiveness of our proposed framework, we conducted a pilot RCT evaluating an MRC system. The evaluation phase of our study involved 10 health coaches who evaluated a total of 387 question-answer pairs generated during the RCT. The evaluation metrics developed for inputs focused on aspects such as relevance, factoid nature, answerability, spelling, grammar errors, and difficulty levels of the questions. For outputs, the evaluation criteria included clarity, relevance, clinical accuracy, and usefulness of the retrieved short answers and explanations.

The results of the evaluation provided valuable insights into the strengths and weaknesses of the MRC system and demonstrated the practical application of our hierarchical evaluation framework. The findings supported the notion that evaluating both inputs and outputs is crucial for obtaining a comprehensive understanding of the performance and effectiveness of NLP systems. Future research should focus on validating the scalability and time-saving benefits of our proposed framework.

Limitations

We recognize the potential limitations that may arise with a small-scale scoping review that is limited to a few venues. As our sample size is small, our results and proposed solutions may lack generalizability and applicability. To mitigate the potentially negative effects, we carefully chose the most appropriate venues - as further explained in 2.1 - and limited the search to the most recent papers as the field of computer science is rapidly and constantly evolving. Solely reviewing papers in the English language could also potentially limit the scope of our research. We also tried to delve into a broad range of aspects of human evaluation whilst keeping our objectives focused. However, we recognize the inevitability of potential factors that may exist outside of our considerations - which may also affect results and conclusions.

Ethics Statement

We aim to conduct our study with the highest ethical standards and maintain continuous referral to the ACL code of ethics throughout our research. We obtained articles via Google Scholar and have anonymized most of the papers and authors - excluding a few that were cited in our main text. This paper should be used to provide insight into the current practices of human evaluation and a potential solution to streamline the process. It is not used to penalize any research or draw any negative attention to certain papers.

We also recognize that some potential biases and errors may arise amongst human reviewers which may lead to potentially inaccurate data extraction. This may have a potential knock-on effect on derived conclusions. These issues are considered and mitigated through multiple reviewers performing the same task, frequent discussions, and good communication.

Acknowledgements

The authors would like to acknowledge the Accelerating Creativity and Excellence (ACE) Award (NTU-ACE2020-05) and center funding from Nanyang Technological University, Singapore. Josip Car's post at Imperial College London is supported by the NIHR NW London Applied Research Collaboration. Finally, the authors would also like to acknowledge Jintana Liu and Ashwini Lawate who were included in the pilot RCT running and supported the data collection process.

References

Jacopo Amidei, Paul Piwek, and Alistair Willis. 2018a. Evaluation methodologies in automatic question generation 2013-2018. In *Proceedings of the 11th International Conference on Natural Language Generation*.

Jacopo Amidei, Paul Piwek, and Alistair Willis. 2018b. Rethinking the agreement in human evaluation tasks. In *Proceedings of the 27th International Conference on Computational Linguistics*, pages 3318–3329.

Anja Belz and Albert Gatt. 2008. Intrinsic vs. extrinsic evaluation measures for referring expression generation. In *Proceedings of ACL-08: HLT, Short Papers*, pages 197–200.

Iva Bojic, Josef Halim, Verena Suharman, Sreeja Tar, Qi Chwen Ong, Duy Phung, Mathieu Ravaut, Shafiq Joty, and Josip Car. 2023a. A data-centric framework for improving domain-specific machine reading comprehension datasets. In *The Fourth Workshop on Insights from Negative Results in NLP*, pages 19–32, Dubrovnik, Croatia. Association for Computational Linguistics.

Iva Bojic, Qi Chwen Ong, Shafiq Joty, and Josip Car. 2023b. Building extractive question answering system to support human-ai health coaching model for sleep domain. *arXiv preprint arXiv:2305.19707*.

Iva Bojic, Qi Chwen Ong, Megh Thakkar, Esha Kamran, Irving Yu Le Shua, Jaime Rei Ern Pang, Jessica Chen, Vaaruni Nayak, Shafiq Joty, and Josip Car. 2022. Sleepqa: A health coaching dataset on sleep for extractive question answering. In *Machine Learning for Health*, pages 199–217. PMLR.

Sheila Castilho. 2021. Towards document-level human mt evaluation: On the issues of annotator agreement, effort and misevaluation. In *Proceedings of the Workshop on Human Evaluation of NLP Systems (HumEval)*. Association for Computational Linguistics (ACL).

Varun Gangal, Steven Y Feng, Malihe Alikhani, Teruko Mitamura, and Eduard Hovy. 2022. Nareor: The narrative reordering problem. In *Proceedings of the AAAI Conference on Artificial Intelligence*, pages 10645–10653.

Sebastian Gehrmann, Elizabeth Clark, and Thibault Sellam. 2023. Repairing the cracked foundation: A survey of obstacles in evaluation practices for generated text. *Journal of Artificial Intelligence Research*, 77:103–166.

David Howcroft, Anya Belz, Miruna Clinciu, Dimitra Gkatzia, Sadid A Hasan, Saad Mahamood, Simon Mille, Emiel Van Miltenburg, Sashank Santhanam, and Verena Rieser. 2020. Twenty years of confusion in human evaluation: Nlg needs evaluation sheets and standardised definition. In *Proceedings of the 13th International Conference on Natural Language Generation*. Association for Computational Linguistics (ACL).

Neslihan Iskender, Tim Polzehl, and Sebastian Möller. 2021. Reliability of human evaluation for text summarization: Lessons learned and challenges ahead. In *Proceedings of the Workshop on Human Evaluation of NLP Systems (HumEval)*, pages 86–96.

Litton J Kurisinkel and Nancy Chen. 2019. Set to ordered text: Generating discharge instructions from medical billing codes. In *Proceedings of the 2019 Conference on Empirical Methods in Natural Language Processing and the 9th International Joint Conference on Natural Language Processing (EMNLP-IJCNLP)*, pages 6165–6175.

Hongru Liang and Huaqing Li. 2021. Towards standard criteria for human evaluation of chatbots: A survey. *arXiv preprint arXiv:2105.11197*.

Yixin Liu, Alexander R Fabbri, Pengfei Liu, Yilun Zhao, Linyong Nan, Ruilin Han, Simeng Han, Shafiq Joty, Chien-Sheng Wu, Caiming Xiong, et al. 2022. Revisiting the gold standard: Grounding summarization evaluation with robust human evaluation. *arXiv preprint arXiv:2212.07981*.

Mayu Otani, Riku Togashi, Yu Sawai, Ryosuke Ishigami, Yuta Nakashima, Esa Rahtu, Janne Heikkilä, and Shin'ichi Satoh. 2023. Toward verifiable and reproducible human evaluation for text-to-image generation. In *Proceedings of the IEEE/CVF Conference on Computer Vision and Pattern Recognition*, pages 14277–14286.

Patrick Paroubek, Stéphane Chaudiron, and Lynette Hirschman. 2007. Principles of evaluation in natural language processing. In *Traitement Automatique des Langues, Volume 48, Numéro 1 : Principes de l'évaluation en Traitement Automatique des Langues [Principles of Evaluation in Natural Language Processing]*, pages 7–31, France. ATALA (Association pour le Traitement Automatique des Langues).

Constituency Parsing. 2009. Speech and language processing. *Power Point Slides*.

Micah DJ Peters, Christina M Godfrey, Patricia McInerney, Cassia Baldini Soares, Hanan Khalil, and Deborah Parker. 2015. *The Joanna Briggs Institute reviewers' manual 2015: methodology for JBI scoping reviews*, chapter 11. The Joanna Briggs Institute.

Peng Qian and Roger Levy. 2022. Flexible generation from fragmentary linguistic input. In *Proceedings of the 60th Annual Meeting of the Association for Computational Linguistics (Volume 1: Long Papers)*, pages 8176–8196.

Juhee Son, Jiho Jin, Haneul Yoo, JinYeong Bak, Kyunghyun Cho, and Alice Oh. 2022. Translating hanja historical documents to contemporary korean and english. In *Findings of the Association for Computational Linguistics: EMNLP 2022*, pages 1260–1272.

Katsuhito Sudoh, Kosuke Takahashi, and Satoshi Nakamura. 2021. Is this translation error critical?: Classification-based human and automatic machine translation evaluation focusing on critical errors. In *Proceedings of the Workshop on Human Evaluation of NLP Systems (HumEval)*, pages 46–55.

Chris van der Lee, Albert Gatt, Emiel van Miltenburg, and Emiel Krahmer. 2021. Human evaluation of automatically generated text: Current trends and best practice guidelines. *Computer Speech & Language*, 67:101151.

Chris Van Der Lee, Albert Gatt, Emiel Van Miltenburg, Sander Wubben, and Emiel Krahmer. 2019. Best practices for the human evaluation of automatically generated text. In *Proceedings of the 12th International Conference on Natural Language Generation*, pages 355–368.

Yan Zeng and Jian-Yun Nie. 2021. An investigation of suitability of pre-trained language models for dialogue generation–avoiding discrepancies. In *Findings of the Association for Computational Linguistics: ACL-IJCNLP 2021*, pages 4481–4494.

Hugh Zhang, Daniel Duckworth, Daphne Ippolito, and Arvind Neelakantan. 2020. Trading off diversity and quality in natural language generation. *arXiv preprint arXiv:2004.10450*.

Qingfu Zhu, Weinan Zhang, Ting Liu, and William Yang Wang. 2020. Counterfactual off-policy training for neural dialogue generation. In *Proceedings of the 2020 Conference on Empirical Methods in Natural Language Processing (EMNLP)*, pages 3438–3448.

Appendix

Appendix 1: Data Extraction Form

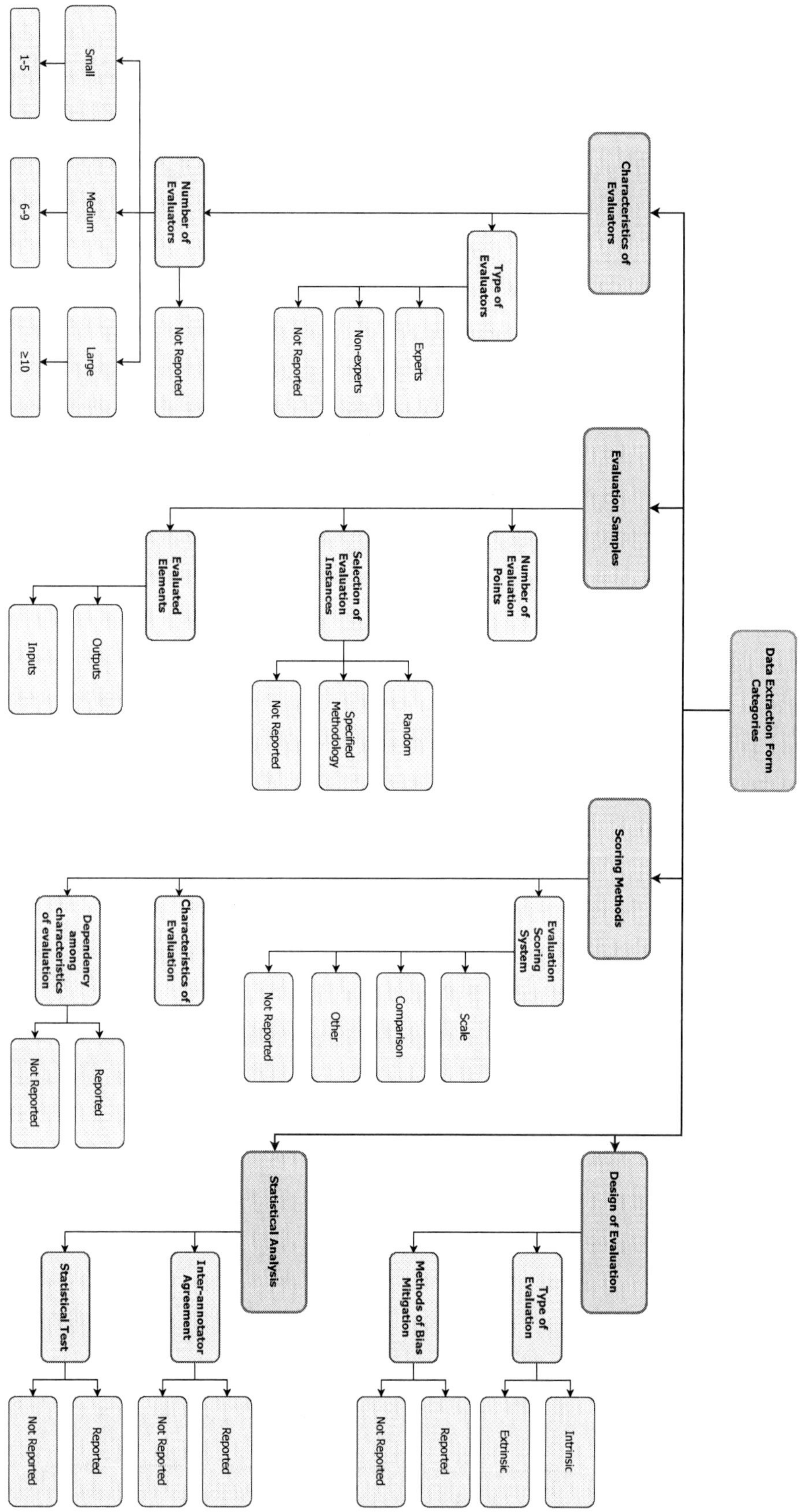

Figure 12: Data extraction form categories.

Designing a Metalanguage of Differences Between Translations: A Case Study for English-to-Japanese Translation

Tomono Honda[†*] **Atsushi Fujita**[‡] **Mayuka Yamamoto**[†] **Kyo Kageura**[†]
[†]The University of Tokyo, Tokyo, Japan
[‡]National Institute of Information and Communications Technology, Kyoto, Japan
[†]{tomono20@g.ecc, yamamoto.mayuka@mail, kyo@p}.u-tokyo.ac.jp
[‡]atsushi.fujita@nict.go.jp

Abstract

In both the translation industry and translation education, analytic and systematic assessment of translations plays a vital role. However, due to lack of a scheme for describing differences between translations, such assessment has been realized only in an ad-hoc manner. There is prior work on a scheme for describing differences between translations, but it has coverage and objectivity issues. To alleviate these issues and realize more fine-grained analyses, we developed an improved scheme by referring to diverse types of translations and adopting hierarchical linguistic units for analysis, taking English-to-Japanese translation as an example.

1 Introduction

In translation, assuring quality is the primary and indispensable issue. In translation industry, translation quality assessment (TQA) is introduced to ensure a certain level of quality for clients and end-users, whereas in research, TQA is conducted to gauge the differences in quality between different translation processes and systems (Castilho et al., 2018). The goals of TQA are diverse depending on situations, but regardless of situations, we need to compare translations as systematically and objectively as possible (Koby et al., 2014).

In translation education, learners should acquire competence to analyze and justify their translations, and explain their decisions with appropriate metalanguages and theoretical approaches (European Master's in Translation, 2022). Lacking systematically organized concepts and precise descriptions, however, instructors can explain several possible translations and their differences only by using their own languages in an ad-hoc manner, and learners are not able to grasp the whole picture of differences. In the translation production workflow in industry, machine translation (MT) systems are often used with manual post-editing (ISO/TC37, 2017). However, no study has analytically assessed how post-edited MT output (MT+PE) and translation produced exclusively by human translators (HT) differ and what cause the differences. These situations suggest the necessity of a comprehensive typology, or metalanguage (Kageura et al., 2022), of differences between translations (target documents, henceforth TDs) for the same source document (SD), as a scaffold to discuss such differences objectively, analytically, and precisely.

There is only one scheme that enables us to describe differences between independently produced TDs (Honda et al., 2022). While their scheme has been tailored for analytic and systematic assessment of differences, it has two vital problems. First, the covered phenomena would be limited; the TDs they analyzed were all from the same content domain and produced by human translators. Another problem is the vagueness and subjectivity of units employed to capture sub-sentential pairs within given TDs.

This paper presents our scheme for describing differences between TDs, which we have developed to alleviate these two problems. To cover a wider variety of phenomena, we used several SDs from various content domains and obtained their translations via substantially different methods, i.e., HT and MT+PE. For tangible and objective analyses, we adopted general linguistic units. Our scheme has two notable features: (i) it serves as scaffolding metalanguage for discussing differences between TDs, and (ii) it can be used as a research tool as well as a learning material.

The remainder of this paper is structured as follows. Section 2 describes related work. Section 3 explains how we have developed the scheme. Section 4 presents our scheme. Section 5 reports on

[*]This work was done during an internship of the first author at National Institute of Information and Communications Technology.

Proceedings of the Third Workshop on Human Evaluation of NLP Systems, pages 23–34, Varna, Bulgaria, Sep 7, 2023.
https://doi.org/10.26615/978-954-452-088-5_003

our intrinsic evaluation, and Section 6 discusses the current status of our scheme and remaining issues. Section 7 concludes this paper.

2 Related Work

Many studies have so far addressed analytic and systematic assessment of translation quality. Existing evaluation schemes, e.g., MQM (Lommel et al., 2014), focus on translation errors (or *issues*) (Castilho et al., 2018). However, none of them can be used to describe differences between pairs of issue-free translations: how they differ and what cause the differences. Recent MT systems, which cause less translation issues (Freitag et al., 2021), will require such schemes sooner or later.

There is a large body of studies comparing issue-free translations independently produced by various translators, such as students and professional translators (Pastor et al., 2008; Lapshinova-Koltunski, 2015; Rubino et al., 2016; Ghent et al., 2018; Bizzoni and Lapshinova-Koltunski, 2021; Lapshinova-Koltunski et al., 2022), and MT+PE and HT (Toral, 2019). They revealed differences in terms of linguistic features, i.e., *translationese* (Baker, 1993; Laviosa-Braithwaite, 1998) and *post-editese* (Toral, 2019). However, they only observed general tendencies of TDs as a whole, and none of them established a means to analytically and systematically explain individual instances that exhibit some kind of differences.

Unlike above, Yamamoto and Yamada (2022) made an analytic comparison of draft and final versions of TDs. They compiled a typology of manipulations applied to TDs during the production process, called *translation strategies* (Chesterman, 2016),[1] extending the work by Chesterman (2016), and ensuring the coverage and systematicity through analyzing actual revision examples extracted from pairs of draft and final versions of TDs. Their typology consists of syntactic, semantic, and pragmatic subparts[2] comprising 13, 9, and 10 types, respectively. The syntactic and semantic strategies have been adopted from linguistic theories (Morris, 1938). The pragmatic strategies are, on the other hand, more specific to translation, e.g., referring to external information and ensuring quality for target readers, performed to produce a TD that is more appropriate for the predetermined purposes. However, the typology of translation strategies would not be applicable to the pairs of independently produced TDs, since it has been developed only on the basis of revision examples performed during the process of producing TDs.

Honda et al. (2022) is the pioneer of constructing a scheme for extracting and explaining differences between independently produced TDs for the same SD. To identify differences between any pair of linguistic expressions observed in given pairs of TDs, they proposed a two-step procedure: decompose given pairs of TDs and classify the differences between each constituent pair. The latter is realized with decision lists, consisting of 13, 8, and 4 types of categories for syntactic, semantic, and pragmatic differences incorporated from translation strategies (Chesterman, 2016; Yamamoto and Yamada, 2022). Their work has two major defects. One is the limited variety of phenomena it covers. They used a set of abstracts of scientific articles and their human translations (HT) produced by different translators. Due to the relatively limited range of textual domain, homogeneous text type, and the same method for translation production, they observed only a limited range of differences. The other problem is the intermediate unit called "chunk." They introduced it in between sentence and word, and proposed criteria to extract pairs of chunks from given pairs of TDs. However, the vague definition of chunk leads to subjective analyses.

3 Construction of the Scheme

We developed an improved scheme for describing differences in TDs. In our scheme, we adopted the two-step workflow proposed in the previous work (Honda et al., 2022): top-down recursive decomposition of pairs of TDs followed by classification of each constituent pair into pre-defined categories. We also followed Honda et al. (2022) to implement a procedure for the first step and decision lists for the second step. In contrast, we addressed the two problems in Honda et al. (2022) as follows.

- To cover a wider variety of differences, we used the TDs that belong to various content domains and produced by different methods (Section 3.1), and reconsidered to incorporate translation strategies that Honda et al. (2022) did not adopt (Section 3.2.2).

[1] Yamamoto and Yamada (2022, p.83) explain that translation strategies are "methods applied to achieve a proper translation that moves beyond the literal."

[2] Chesterman (2016, p.104) defined the three groups of strategies as follows: "if syntactic strategies manipulate form, and semantic strategies manipulate meaning, pragmatic strategies can be said to manipulate the message itself."

Usage	ID	# seg	# sentences			# words (tokens)			Topic
			SD	HT	MT+PE	SD	HT	MT+PE	
Development	Doc1	11	21	25	26	524	774	762	Clean energy
	Doc2	8	15	18	18	415	593	588	Medical equipment
	Doc3	7	13	14	14	273	339	362	CAD software
	Doc4	11	21	21	22	399	555	575	Travel health
	Doc5	18	34	34	34	895	1,184	1,197	Radio frequency devices
Refinement	Doc6	19	32	30	30	384	541	499	Complaint letter
	Doc7	31	39	42	41	463	632	630	Game application
Validation	Doc8	36	47	48	48	446	621	602	Licensing procedure
	Doc9	32	39	40	41	530	729	715	Contract renewal

Table 1: Usage of and statistics for documents and translations: words (token) counts were obtained by NLTK (Bird et al., 2009) for the SDs in English and MeCab and IPAdic (Kudo et al., 2004) for the two types of TDs in Japanese. "seg" indicates "segments" given as original units aligned across SD, MT+PE, and HT.

- To carry out tangible and objective analyses, we adopted hierarchical linguistic units in the target language widely used in linguistics (Section 3.2.1).

We developed and refined our scheme through repeating annotation and discussion in order to ensure its systematicity and coverage as much as possible (Sections 3.2 and 3.3), taking English-to-Japanese translations.

3.1 Collecting Translation Data

When designing and validating an annotation scheme, in general, it is ideal to take as diverse examples as possible into account.

To ensure the diversity of SDs, we used technical documents in various specialized fields, considering their nature and purposes; they are rather literal and logical than figurative and emotional. We also expected that the requirements in translating them should potentially be identified and explained in the form of translation brief, and that the subtle differences seen in their translations would be explainable by ourselves. For our study, we collected nine technical documents written in English.[3]

To ensure the diversity of translations, we decided to compare human translation (HT) and post-edited version of machine translation (MT+PE). HT is eligible as one side of document pairs for comparison, because it should have the highest quality among conceivable ways of obtaining translations. As the counterpart, we chose MT+PE, assuming that it assures certain quality if it follows ISO 18587 (ISO/TC37, 2017), and that it should be substantially different from HT due to the certain level of reliance on MT outputs. Even if MT+PE is close enough to HT, analyzing their differences still contributes to research on MT.

HT and MT+PE for the nine documents were produced by two different Translation Service Providers (TSPs). For HT, we asked an ISO-certified TSP to produce HT following ISO 17100 (ISO/TC37, 2015). For MT+PE, we first obtained English-to-Japanese MT outputs using TexTra[4] and asked another ISO-certified TSP to post-edit the MT outputs following ISO 18587 (ISO/TC37, 2017) but avoiding excessive editing.

Table 1 summarizes the statistics for the collected tuples of SD, HT, and MT+PE. We used five tuples for development, other two for refinement, and the rest two for validation of the scheme.

3.2 Development of the Initial Scheme

The authors, whose native language is Japanese and thus have sufficient linguistic competence in Japanese, first created the scheme for English-to-Japanese translation through repeating annotation and discussion. Annotation, i.e., decomposition of paired TDs and classification of extracted pairs, was carried out by one of the authors of this paper, and another author joined in discussion to revise the scheme. Five tuples of SD, HT, and MT+PE (Doc1 to Doc5 in Table 1) were used.

3.2.1 Decomposing Unit Pairs

Within pairs of relatively large units, such as sentence pairs, several types of differences can coexist. Aiming at analytically describing each difference, Honda et al. (2022) proposed to decompose

[3]We searched for documents on the Web considering their license for our future release of documents with our translations and annotations.

[4]`https://mt-auto-minhon-mlt.ucri.jgn-x.jp/`, GPMT-3.9_200930_nmt

given sentence-aligned TDs into smaller units. To better handle the hierarchical structures in TDs, we adopted linguistic units in Japanese.

First, we extracted pairs of linguistic units from each pair of TDs, making sure that each unit to be well-defined in linguistics, such as clause and noun phrase, referring to literature on Japanese grammar (Masuoka and Takubo, 1992; SIG for Descriptive Grammar in Japanese, 2008, 2009a, 2010). Each unit is also aligned with corresponding unit in SD in order to identify the corresponding units in different TDs. Then, based on the results, we refined the procedure for decomposition as well as the types of units by grouping them based on linguistic features. In this refinement process, we decided to distinguish the "non-linguistic units" that play some role in document from linguistic units.

We present the resulted procedure and the types of units in Section 4.1.

3.2.2 Classifying Differences

Following Honda et al. (2022), we used three exclusive groups of categories (syntactic, semantic, and pragmatic categories) and decision lists for describing differences. To cover a wide variety of differences, we reconsidered to incorporate the categories discussed in the literature of translation strategies (Chesterman, 2016; Yamamoto and Yamada, 2022) that Honda et al. (2022) did not adopt.

Given extracted pairs of units, one of the authors first classified them into one of the categories within a union of those presented in Chesterman (2016), Yamamoto and Yamada (2022), and Honda et al. (2022). Syntactic, semantic, and pragmatic differences were separately analyzed, as in previous work. We then examined the results to refine the categories. When we found problems, such as phenomena that are not covered by existing categories, we refined the decision lists by adding new categories, revising definition statements to extend the scope of existing categories, and/or dividing or merging existing categories, referring to literatures of linguistics (SIG for Descriptive Grammar in Japanese, 2003, 2009b,c, 2010). In the decision lists, we prioritized categories that describe a more specific and/or easily identifiable phenomena.

The resulted three sets of categories are presented in Section 4.2.

3.3 Refinement of the Scheme

After a couple of iterations of the initial phase (Section 3.2), the same two of the authors refined the scheme in a more rigorous setting: independent annotation followed by comparison of the results. First, they only decomposed TDs for Doc6, and refined the procedure for decomposition through comparing the results. Then, they did both decomposition and classification for Doc7. Through comparing the results, they determined the issues of the scheme from the viewpoint of consistency, coverage, and understandability of the instructional materials, and improved them.

4 Our Improved Scheme

Through the process described in Section 3, we developed a scheme for describing differences between pairs of TDs. During the process, we also assembled instructional materials for annotators. These documents are made publicly available;[5] they are mainly written in Japanese, since we have compiled them for analyzing TDs in Japanese.

In this section, we explain their summary, using examples of unit decomposition and classification shown in Table 2.

4.1 Procedure for Decomposing Unit Pairs

We defined a total of nine types of units for analysis. Seven out of them are "linguistic unit" well-defined in linguistics: paragraph, sentence, clause, phrase, compound expression, word, and punctuation. The remaining two are called "non-linguistic unit" since they play specific roles within document: "sentence-equivalent unit," such as headlines and bibliographic information, and "phrase-or-word-equivalent unit," such as terms, named entities, and inline quotations.

The overview of our procedure for decomposing and extracting units for analysis is as follows.

Step 1. Check if the stopping conditions apply: assess whether the given pair of units for analysis must be decomposed or not.

Step 2. Decompose each TD unit: decompose each unit into smaller units "without nesting;" the extracted units must be as large as possible and must not overlap with each other.

Step 3. Align with SD: align each extracted unit of TD with its corresponding unit of SD.

Step 4. Align between TD units: identify pairs of constituent units extracted from different TDs that correspond to the identical unit of

[5] https://github.com/tntc-project/translation-difference

No.	d	Unit in SD	Unit in TD1	Unit in TD2	Syn	Sem	Pra
1	2	Payment of the fee must accompany the form.	手数料の支払は、用紙を添付する必要があります。	料金の支払いには、申請書を添付しなければなりません。	g4	NA	p100
2	3	payment of the fee	手数料の支払	料金の支払い	g100	PEQ	PEQ
3	4	the fee	手数料	料金	g100	s6	p9
4	4	payment	支払	支払い	g12	s2	p9
5	3	ϕ	、	、	EQ	EQ	EQ
6	3	the form	用紙	申請書	g100	s7	p7
7	3	must accompany	添付する必要があります	添付しなければなりません	g18	s10	p100
8	3	.	。	。	EQ	EQ	EQ

Table 2: Examples of extracted units for analysis labeled with their syntactic (Syn), semantic (Sem), and pragmatic (Pra) categories. d indicates the depth of the unit; for instance, the first unit with $d = 2$ means that this tuple of sentences has directly been extracted from a given ($d = 1$) parallel paragraphs.

SD. Here, functional words that are not mutually interchangeable are left unaligned, since such difference takes a part of the given pair of larger units. The identical functional expressions are also left unaligned, for the sake of simplicity in analyzing differences.

Note that this procedure is recursively applied to every pair of constituent units, in order to thoroughly decompose and extract the units for analysis in the given pair of TDs.

For a unit pair which has been decomposed into several constituent unit pairs, we analyze the differences between their constructions, ignoring the differences between the extracted constituent unit pairs. To this end, we decided to identify patterns for unit pairs that are decomposed. Given a unit pair, the pattern for each side is obtained by replacing the strings corresponding to each constituent unit with a unique symbol. For instance, the unit pair in line 1 in Table 2 ($d = 2$) is decomposed into unit pairs in lines 2, 5, 6, 7, and 8 ($d = 3$). By replacing the strings corresponding to each constituent with letters A to E, we obtain the patterns "AはBCをDE" for TD1 and "AにはBCをDE" for TD2. Note that, as explained in Step 4, some functional words, "は" (topic marker), "を" (accusative case), and "に" (dative case) in this case, are not extracted as a constituent unit pair and thus left lexicalized. For another instance, the pair in line 2 in Table 2 ($d = 3$) is further decomposed into pairs in lines 3 and 4 ($d = 4$), leaving aligned but identical function word "の" (genitive case) unextracted, and the patterns of the unit pair are both identified as "AのB."

4.2 Decision Lists for Classifying Differences

For each pair of units extracted from a pair of TDs, we separately analyze their syntactic, semantic, and pragmatic differences following the decision lists. Tables 3, 4, 5 show the categories of each group.[6] In each table, the categories with a check mark (✓) indicate that they do not exist in the scheme of Honda et al. (2022) and are newly added in our work. See Appendix A for their definitions.

Syntactic categories describe syntactic differences, such as structures and forms, not involving content. Note that some syntactic categories in Table 3 are only applicable to certain types of unit pairs, e.g., "g9 Clause structure difference" never happens when analyzing pairs of paragraphs.

Semantic categories describe differences of contents or meanings and are applied only to linguistic units. In the categories shown in Table 4, "NA Not applicable" is assigned to a unit pair that (a) both of the units are paragraphs or sentences, or (b) at least one of the units is non-linguistic unit. "PEQ Pattern equivalence" is used for unit pairs whose patterns are identical, e.g., the unit pair in line 2 in Table 2 both of which are identified as "AのB" as patterns.

Pragmatic categories describe pragmatic differences, such as relationships between the sender and receivers, and language use or structures considering the purposes of documents. "PEQ Pattern equivalence" in Table 5 is the same as "PEQ" in the semantic categories.

[6]We defined the decision list of syntactic categories for each pair of unit types. Thus, unlike Tables 4 and 5, Table 3 does not serve as a decision list.

Label	New	Category name
EQ	✓	Exact match
g1	✓	Paragraph structure difference
g2	✓	Sentence type difference
g3	✓	Voice difference
g4	✓	Topic difference
g5		Sentence structure difference
g6	✓	Segment structure difference
g7	✓	Clause type difference
g8	✓	Ellipsis/Repetition difference
g9	✓	Clause structure difference
g10	✓	Quotation difference
g11	✓	Original spelling difference
g12	✓	Orthography difference
g13		Loan difference
g14	✓	Acronym difference
g15		Phrase structure difference
g16	✓	Reference expression difference
g17		Part of speech difference
g18	✓	Predicate difference
g19	✓	Affix difference
g20		Function word difference
g21	✓	Presence of translation
g22	✓	Analysis unit difference
g23		Unit difference
g99	✓	Other syntactic difference
g100	✓	Syntactic equivalence

Table 3: Syntactic categories.

Label	New	Category name
EQ	✓	Exact match
NA	✓	Not applicable
PEQ	✓	Pattern equivalence
s1	✓	Conjugated form difference
s2	✓	Spelling difference
s3	✓	Polysemy difference
s4	✓	Causal difference
s5	✓	Trope difference
s6	✓	Hyponymy difference
s7		Abstraction difference
s8		Emphasis difference
s9		Perspective difference
s10	✓	Predicate meaning difference
s11		Synonym
s99	✓	Other semantic difference

Table 4: Semantic categories.

4.3 Instructional Materials for Annotators

In order for annotators to appropriately apply our scheme, we prepared four types of instructional materials. Two of them are documents for decomposition and classification, which are described in Sections 4.1 and 4.2.

In addition, we also assembled the following two materials about decomposition procedure in order to guide the annotators in the complicated decomposition process: (a) a document describing detailed procedure of decomposition with some examples, and (b) a video material showing the procedure of decomposition in a step by step manner.

All of the materials include some examples, such as those collected from Doc1-Doc7 in Table 1 during development of the scheme.

Label	New	Category name
EQ	✓	Exact match
PEQ	✓	Pattern equivalence
p1	✓	Translation error
p2	✓	Transediting difference
p3	✓	Structure-awareness difference
p4		Cultural filtering difference
p5	✓	Interpersonal difference
p6	✓	Cohesion difference
p7	✓	Explicitness/Implicitness difference
p8		Domain adaptation difference
p9	✓	Register difference
p10	✓	Readability difference
p99	✓	Other pragmatic difference
p100	✓	Pragmatic equivalence

Table 5: Pragmatic categories.

5 Intrinsic Evaluation

We evaluated whether our scheme meets the criteria of metalanguage of translation (Kageura et al., 2022), in particular, consistency of decomposition, consistency of classification, and coverage of categories. The two engaged in the development (A and B) and another one of the authors (C) participated in the evaluation as annotators. Annotator A is a graduate student in pedagogy, Annotator B is a Ph.D in computational linguistics, and Annotator C is an MA in translation studies. The annotators first read instructional materials of the scheme described in Section 4. They then independently annotated the two pairs of TDs reserved unseen for this purpose (Doc8 and Doc9 in Table 1) following the two-step annotation workflow: decomposition of the TD pairs into constituent unit pairs and classification of each pair into categories. In the classification step, they completed annotation for each of syntactic, semantic, and pragmatic categories for all the extracted TD pairs in this order.

As a result, they extracted 471, 466, and 443 pairs of units from Doc8, and 463, 456, and 451 from Doc9, respectively. Tables 6, 7, and 8 respectively show the frequencies of syntactic, semantic, and pragmatic categories labeled by each annotator.

5.1 Consistency of Decomposition

To gauge the inter-annotator consistency of unit decomposition, we computed recall, precision, and F1 score of each annotator's result regarding another

Category	Doc8			Doc9		
	A	B	C	A	B	C
EQ	129	139	131	166	161	164
g1	0	0	1	0	0	0
g2	0	0	0	1	0	0
g3	2	2	1	3	2	0
g4	7	7	3	2	1	3
g5	1	1	2	1	0	0
g6	0	1	1	3	1	3
g7	0	0	0	0	0	0
g8	1	0	1	0	0	0
g9	3	1	0	3	5	0
g10	0	0	0	0	0	0
g11	13	12	23	10	7	6
g12	47	44	39	37	33	26
g13	8	4	11	5	4	3
g14	0	0	0	0	0	0
g15	3	5	2	10	9	4
g16	1	1	3	0	1	1
g17	12	16	10	11	8	17
g18	15	14	14	18	10	17
g19	6	3	0	2	0	0
g20	4	5	9	8	7	6
g21	18	14	26	21	27	49
g22	0	0	1	4	7	0
g23	55	52	35	37	47	32
g99	0	11	18	6	3	15
g100	146	134	112	115	122	105
Other*	0	0	0	0	1	0
Total	471	466	443	463	456	451

Table 6: Frequency of syntactic categories. "Other*" indicates that the annotator judged that a pair of units could not be classified to any category.

Category	Doc8			Doc9		
	A	B	C	A	B	C
EQ	129	139	131	166	161	164
NA	48	49	49	52	55	14
PEQ	100	89	70	88	89	96
s1	3	4	2	9	7	10
s2	24	18	17	10	13	14
s3	1	3	2	0	1	7
s4	1	3	5	1	6	1
s5	0	0	0	0	0	0
s6	2	9	0	1	2	1
s7	15	35	44	15	25	26
s8	30	12	10	45	14	9
s9	9	10	6	9	15	4
s10	3	11	5	3	13	5
s11	101	73	68	62	46	43
s99	5	11	34	2	9	57
Total	471	466	443	463	456	451

Table 7: Frequency of semantic categories.

annotator's result as a gold standard. We excluded the original units given for annotation, i.e., 36 and 32 segments for Doc8 and Doc9, respectively, as they were consistent by definition.

Category	Doc8			Doc9		
	A	B	C	A	B	C
EQ	129	139	131	166	161	164
PEQ	126	115	69	112	115	96
p1	1	5	3	2	5	2
p2	0	0	0	0	1	0
p3	1	0	13	11	0	1
p4	33	24	24	9	10	8
p5	23	13	19	6	8	14
p6	10	2	10	10	2	11
p7	7	22	34	17	26	13
p8	4	1	3	8	10	27
p9	86	67	2	74	47	1
p10	27	13	26	30	37	10
p99	4	5	0	4	0	8
p100	20	60	109	14	34	96
Total	471	466	443	463	456	451

Table 8: Frequency of pragmatic categories.

Test	Gold	Doc8			Doc9		
		R	P	F1	R	P	F1
A	B	84.0	83.0	83.5	73.6	72.4	73.0
B	C	80.8	76.5	78.6	70.9	70.0	70.5
C	A	75.9	81.1	78.4	67.5	69.5	68.5

Table 9: Inter-annotator consistency of decomposition (%): R, P, F1 stand for recall, precision, and F1 score, respectively, computed regarding the result of one annotator as reference (Gold). For reversed pairs of test and gold annotators, consider R and P flipped.

Table 9 summarizes the results. The F1 scores span 78.4–83.5 for Doc8 and 68.5–73.0 for Doc9. While the F1 scores for each document were relatively stable ($\leq$ 5.1 points), there were larger gaps between Doc8 and Doc9 ($\geq$ 8.1 points).

We consider that our scheme has enabled the annotators to decompose unit pairs relatively consistently, but the lower F1 scores for Doc9 suggest that linguistic complexity in TDs and/or the similarity between independently produced TDs can affect the decomposition process.

Retrospective interview with the annotators revealed that the most typical disagreement was due to the different recognition of syntactic structure. For instance, see the following example of a noun phrase that the three annotators decomposed in different ways, where brackets indicate the constituent units extracted from the phrase.

SD: Types of Submissions Subject to eCTD Requirement

MT+PE: eCTD要件の対象となる申請の種類

A: [eCTD要件の対象となる][申請の種類]

Pair	Doc8				Doc9			
	# unit	Syntactic	Semantic	Pragmatic	# unit	Syntactic	Semantic	Pragmatic
A–B	280	79.6 (0.73)	70.4 (0.63)	66.1 (0.56)	218	71.1 (0.61)	61.9 (0.53)	63.3 (0.51)
B–C	255	71.4 (0.64)	65.5 (0.59)	39.6 (0.29)	198	69.2 (0.59)	46.0 (0.34)	51.5 (0.38)
C–A	263	74.1 (0.67)	65.4 (0.58)	38.8 (0.30)	196	73.5 (0.66)	48.5 (0.39)	45.4 (0.34)

Table 10: Inter-annotator agreement ratio (%) and Cohen's κ (in parenthesis) on classification, excluding "EQ Exact match." "# unit" indicates the number of unit pairs obtained by both of each pair of annotators.

B: [eCTD要件の対象となる][申請][の][種類]

C: [eCTD要件の対象となる申請][の][種類]

Annotator A recognized that the phrase comprises an adnominal clause and a head noun phrase, while Annotator B further detached the genitive modifier, "申請" (application), and genitive case marker, "の" (of), considering that the single noun, "種類" (type), is the shared modificand. Annotator C identified an adnominal noun phrase as a genitive modifier of the single head noun. This example illustrates that structural ambiguities in TDs affect the decomposition procedure.

5.2 Consistency of Classification

We computed inter-annotator agreement ratio and Cohen's κ (Cohen, 1960) for the set of unit pairs shared by each pair of annotators, excluding units annotated with "EQ," i.e., the identical pair of units in HT and MT+PE.

Table 10 summarizes the results. Compared to κ values for syntactic categories spanning 0.59–0.73, those for semantic and pragmatic categories were low: 0.34–0.63 and 0.29–0.56, respectively. This indicates that semantic and pragmatic categories are more difficult to consistently classify.

See, for instance, the pair of bracketed expressions in the following example.

SD: Submissions [for] blood and blood components

HT: 血液および血液成分[に関する]申請

MT+PE: 血液及び血液成分[の]申請

The three annotators labeled this pair with different semantic categories: "s7 Abstraction difference," "s8 Emphasis difference," and "s11 Synonym." Through discussion, the annotators agreed that this example should be classified as s7, since "に関する" (regarding) is more specific compared to "の" (of/for). Such discussion calls for the clarity of the definition of s7 in the decision list for classification.

5.3 Coverage of Categories

Relatively low frequency of p99 (Table 8) suggests that the scheme ensures the coverage of pragmatic categories. In contrast, the higher frequencies of g99 (up to 18 in Table 6) and s99 (up to 57 in Table 7) reveal the necessity of refining our scheme. For instance, see the following example.

SD: Products that [are intended] to be distributed commercially

HT: 商業的に流通することを[目的とした]製品

MT+PE: 市販されることを[意図した]製剤

Two of the annotators identified the syntactic differences between the idiomatic phrase in HT "目的とした" (are regarded as the goal) and the literal translation in MT+PE. We consider that we need a new category for this type of differences.

6 Discussion

Our intrinsic evaluation confirmed that our scheme enables us to analyze the differences between independently produced translations at a certain level of consistency and coverage. Toward improving the consistency of classification further, we plan to refine intensional definitions and enrich examples to delineate extensional definitions. External references, such as lists of functional expressions and named entities, terminology, and style specifications, should also help improve consistency. To ensure the coverage, we plan to introduce new categories.

Even though the present scheme does not achieve perfect consistency and coverage, we consider that the disagreed examples do not necessarily suggest the defects of the scheme. Such examples represent fundamental difficulties in understanding the notions indispensable for analyzing translations, and are thus useful in the practical use of the scheme. For instance, in educational settings, the scheme itself is a subject to learn. Through exercises of annotating the same TD pairs and discussing discrepancies of the annotation results, learners should be able to improve their competence in translation and grasp underlying concepts, such as syntax, semantics, and pragmatics, referred to in the scheme. The scheme will also help learners explain their specific choice of expressions in the target language.

Our scheme subsumes the categories of translation strategies (Chesterman, 2016; Yamamoto and Yamada, 2022) and enables comparisons of arbitrary pair of entire TDs. It is thus worth investigating that our scheme can also be used to analyze translation strategies.

7 Conclusion

This paper presented a scheme for analytically and systematically assessing the differences between independently produced translations for the same SD. On the basis of the work in Honda et al. (2022), we adopted nine types of linguistic/non-linguistic units for analysis and refined the decision lists with a wide variety of categories through annotation and discussion using substantially heterogeneous translations, i.e., HT and MT+PE. Unlike previous work in analytic assessment (Chesterman, 2016; Yamamoto and Yamada, 2022; Honda et al., 2022), we also conducted an intrinsic evaluation of the scheme, employing multiple annotators. The results show that classification of semantic and pragmatic differences is more difficult compared to decomposing unit pairs and classifying syntactic differences. Nevertheless, we believe that our scheme is useful, since it covers a wide range of translation-related concepts and thus can be a useful metalanguage to talk about differences in translation.

Our scheme is partly dependent on the target language, i.e., Japanese. We thus plan to examine its applicability to translations from other languages than English into Japanese. To analyze differences between translations in other target languages than Japanese, we need to adapt our scheme to them.

Acknowledgments

We would like to thank the anonymous reviewers, including those for past submissions, for their valuable comments and suggestions. This work was partly supported by JSPS KAKENHI Grant-in-Aid for Scientific Research (S)19H05660.

References

Mona Baker. 1993. Corpus linguistics and translation studies—implications and applications. In Mona Baker, Gill Francis, and Elena Tognini-Bonelli, editors, *Text and technology: In honour of John Sinclair*, pages 233–250. John Benjamins.

Steven Bird, Ewan Klein, and Edward Loper. 2009. *Natural language processing with Python*. O'Reilly Media.

Yuri Bizzoni and Ekaterina Lapshinova-Koltunski. 2021. Measuring translationese across levels of expertise: Are professionals more surprising than students? In *Proceedings of the 23rd Nordic Conference on Computational Linguistics (NoDaLiDa)*, pages 53–63.

Sheila Castilho, Stephen Doherty, Federico Gaspari, and Joss Moorkens. 2018. Approaches to human and machine translation quality assessment. In Joss Moorkens, Sheila Castilho, Federico Gaspari, and Stephen Doherty, editors, *Translation quality assessment from principles to practice*, pages 9–38. Springer International Publishing.

Andrew Chesterman. 2016. *Memes of translation: The spread of ideas in translation theory*. John Benjamins.

Jacob Cohen. 1960. A coefficient of agreement for nominal scales. *Educational and Psychological Measurement*, 20(1):37–46.

European Master's in Translation. 2022. European master's in translation competence framework.

Markus Freitag, George Foster, David Grangier, Viresh Ratnakar, Qijun Tan, and Wolfgang Macherey. 2021. Experts, errors, and context: A large-scale study of human evaluation for machine translation. *Transactions of the Association for Computational Linguistics*, 9:1460–1474.

Gert De Sutter Ghent, Bert Cappelle, Orphée De Clercq, Rudy Loock, and Koen Plevoets. 2018. Towards a corpus-based, statistical approach to translation quality: Measuring and visualizing linguistic deviance in student translations. *Linguistica Antverpiensia, New Series—Themes in Translation Studies*, 16:25–39.

Tomono Honda, Mayuka Yamamoto, and Kyo Kageura. 2022. Construction of a scheme for describing differences between translations. *Invitation to Interpreting and Translation Studies*, 24:1–21. (In Japanese).

ISO/TC37. 2015. ISO 17100:2015 translation services — requirements for translation services.

ISO/TC37. 2017. ISO 18587:2017 translation services — post-editing of machine translation output — requirements.

Kyo Kageura, Rei Miyata, and Masaru Yamada. 2022. Metalanguages and translation studies. In Rei Miyata, Masaru Yamada, and Kyo Kageura, editors,

Metalanguages for dissecting translation processes: Theoretical development and practical applications, pages 15–26. Routledge.

Geoffrey S. Koby, Paul Fields, Daryl Hague, Arle Lommel, and Alan Melby. 2014. Defining translation quality. *Tradumática*, 12:413–420.

Taku Kudo, Kaoru Yamamoto, and Yuji Matsumoto. 2004. Applying conditional random fields to Japanese morphological analysis. In *Proceedings of the 2004 Conference on Empirical Methods in Natural Language Processing*, pages 230–237.

Ekaterina Lapshinova-Koltunski. 2015. Exploration of inter- and intralingual variation of discourse phenomena. In *Proceedings of the Second Workshop on Discourse in Machine Translation*, pages 158–167.

Ekaterina Lapshinova-Koltunski, Maja Popović, and Maarit Koponen. 2022. DiHuTra: A parallel corpus to analyse differences between human translations. In *Proceedings of the Thirteenth Language Resources and Evaluation Conference*, pages 1751–1760.

Sara Laviosa-Braithwaite. 1998. Universals of translation. In Mona Baker, editor, *Routledge encyclopedia of translation studies*, pages 288–291. Routledge.

Arle Lommel, Hans Uszkoreit, and Aljoscha Burchardt. 2014. Multidimensional quality metrics (MQM): A framework for declaring and describing translation quality metrics. *Tradumática*, 12:455–463.

Takashi Masuoka and Yukinori Takubo. 1992. *Basic Japanese grammar*. Kurosio Publishers. (in Japanese).

Charles W. Morris. 1938. Foundations of the theory of signs. In Otto Neurath, Rudolf Carnap, and Charles W. Morris, editors, *International encyclopedia of unified science*, pages 1–59. Chicago University Press.

Gloria Corpas Pastor, Ruslan Mitkov, Naveed Afzal, and Viktor Pekar. 2008. Translation universals: do they exist? A corpus-based NLP study of convergence and simplification. In *Proceedings of the 8th Conference of the Association for Machine Translation in the Americas: Research Papers*, pages 75–81.

Raphael Rubino, Ekaterina Lapshinova-Koltunski, and Josef van Genabith. 2016. Information density and quality estimation features as translationese indicators for human translation classification. In *Proceedings of the 2016 Conference of the North American Chapter of the Association for Computational Linguistics: Human Language Technologies*, pages 960–970.

SIG for Descriptive Grammar in Japanese, editor. 2003. *Modern Japanese grammar*, volume 4. Kurosio Publishers. (in Japanese).

SIG for Descriptive Grammar in Japanese, editor. 2008. *Modern Japanese grammar*, volume 6. Kurosio Publishers. (in Japanese).

SIG for Descriptive Grammar in Japanese, editor. 2009a. *Modern Japanese grammar*, volume 2. Kurosio Publishers. (in Japanese).

SIG for Descriptive Grammar in Japanese, editor. 2009b. *Modern Japanese grammar*, volume 5. Kurosio Publishers. (in Japanese).

SIG for Descriptive Grammar in Japanese, editor. 2009c. *Modern Japanese grammar*, volume 7. Kurosio Publishers. (in Japanese).

SIG for Descriptive Grammar in Japanese, editor. 2010. *Modern Japanese grammar*, volume 1. Kurosio Publishers. (in Japanese).

Antonio Toral. 2019. Post-editese: An exacerbated translationese. In *Proceedings of Machine Translation Summit XVII: Research Track*, pages 273–281.

Mayuka Yamamoto and Masaru Yamada. 2022. Translation strategies for English-to-Japanese translation. In Rei Miyata, Masaru Yamada, and Kyo Kageura, editors, *Metalanguages for dissecting translation processes: Theoretical development and practical applications*, pages 80–91. Routledge.

A Definitions of Categories

Tables 11, 12, and 13 give the lists of categories and their definitions for each primary category group. The lists of semantic and pragmatic categories in Tables 12 and 13 also serve as decision lists.

Label	Category name	Definition
EQ	Exact match	Identical units; the character strings exactly match
g1	Paragraph structure difference	Differences in the order of translation at sentence level
g2	Sentence type difference	Differences in sentence types (e.g., simple sentences, complex sentences, declarative sentences, interrogative sentences, or imperative sentences)
g3	Voice difference	Differences in voice expressions which often lead to the differences in case structures
g4	Topic difference	Differences in salience and/or markedness of topic (e.g., presence or absence of the topic or the use of particles expressing the topic, differences of the words expressed as the topic, or differences of particles expressing the topic)
g5	Sentence structure difference	Differences in sentence structures, such as the relationship between a main clause and a subordinate clause, the order of translation at clause level, or modification relationships
g6	Segment structure difference	Differences in the structures (e.g., order of translation) in non-linguistic units (e.g., headlines, items, or footnotes)
g7	Clause type difference	Differences in clause types (e.g., interrogative, quotation, adnominal, and adverbial clauses)
g8	Ellipsis/Repetition difference	Differences in the ways of translation, such as repetition or ellipsis of a modifier or a modificand
g9	Clause structure difference	Differences in clause structures, such as modification relationships
g10	Quotation difference	Differences in the ways of translating quotations, including the uses of quotation marks
g11	Original spelling difference	Differences in the use of original spelling in SD
g12	Orthography difference	Differences in orthography
g13	Loan difference	Differences in the use of loan words (e.g., transliteration)
g14	Acronym difference	Differences in the use of acronym
g15	Phrase structure difference	Differences in phrase structures, such as word order or modification relationships
g16	Referring expression difference	Differences in the use of referring expressions
g17	Part of speech difference	Differences in parts of speech
g18	Predicate difference	Differences in predicates, such as tense, aspect, and mood
g19	Affix difference	Differences in types of affix or presence/absence of affix
g20	Function word difference	Differences in function words (e.g., particles, auxiliary verbs) or functional expressions
g21	Presence of translation	Differences in presence of translation
g22	Analysis unit difference	Differences between non-linguistic and linguistic units
g23	Unit difference	Differences in the types of linguistic units
g99	Other syntactic difference	Other syntactic differences that are not applicable to above categories
g100	Syntactic equivalence	No syntactic differences

Table 11: The list of syntactic categories and definitions.

Label	Category name	Definition
EQ	Exact match	Identical units; the character strings exactly match
NA	Not applicable	Not applicable in semantic categories; both of the units are paragraphs or sentences, or at least one of the units is non-linguistic unit
PEQ	Pattern equivalence	Identical pattern in both units
s1	Conjugated form difference	Differences only in conjugated form
s2	Spelling difference	Differences only in the orthography in Japanese writing system
s3	Polysemy difference	Differences in transferring different meanings of an ambiguous word in SD
s4	Causal difference	Causal relationships between the meanings of units
s5	Trope difference	Differences in the use of trope expressions or styles of trope expressions
s6	Hyponymy difference	Hyponym and hypernym relationships between the meanings of units
s7	Abstraction difference	Differences in the degrees of abstraction
s8	Emphasis difference	Differences in the ways of emphasis or focuses of the description
s9	Perspective difference	Differences in the perspectives of stating the same content
s10	Predicate meaning difference	Differences in the meanings of predicate expressions
s11	Synonym	Synonymous relationships between the meanings of the units
s99	Other semantic difference	Other semantic differences that are not applicable to above categories

Table 12: The decision list and definitions of semantic categories.

Label	Category name	Definition
EQ	Exact match	Identical units; the character strings exactly match
PEQ	Pattern equivalence	Identical pattern in both units
p1	Translation error	Differences in translating contents of SD wrongly in either one or both of TDs
p2	Transediting difference	Differences in the degrees of transediting the badly written SD (e.g., errors or ambiguities)
p3	Structure-awareness difference	Differences in the ways of adapting expressions and constructions to the functional roles of SD element (e.g., titles, items, footnotes, captions, and citations)
p4	Cultural filtering difference	Differences in whether domesticating to the target culture or not (e.g., translating a feature in source culture by using expressions that adapt to the target culture)
p5	Interpersonal difference	Differences in the degrees of reflecting the relationships between the sender and receivers (e.g., politeness, feeling, or intervention)
p6	Cohesion difference	Differences in the degrees of cohesiveness (e.g., those exhibited by the use of ellipsis, repetition, or conjunction words)
p7	Explicitness/Implicitness difference	Either one of TDs adds new information that does not exist in SD, or explicitly expresses information originally implicit in SD, for the purpose of explicitness of sender's intention or supplement of readers' understanding (e.g., differences in modifications, notes, explanation with parenthesis, or the use of words adapting to context)
p8	Domain adaptation difference	Differences in the use of expressions specific in the content domain of SD
p9	Register difference	Differences in the use of expressions adopted to the text type or register
p10	Readability difference	Differences in readability (considering the supposed readers)
p99	Other pragmatic difference	Other pragmatic differences that are not applicable to above categories
p100	Pragmatic equivalence	No pragmatic differences

Table 13: The decision list and definitions of pragmatic categories.

The 2023 ReproNLP Shared Task on Reproducibility of Evaluations in NLP: Overview and Results

Anya Belz
ADAPT/DCU, Ireland
and University of Aberdeen, UK
anya.belz@adaptcentre.ie

Craig Thomson
University of Aberdeen
Aberdeen, UK
c.thomson@abdn.ac.uk

Abstract

This paper presents an overview of, and the results from, the 2023 Shared Task on Reproducibility of Evaluations in NLP (ReproNLP'23), following on from two previous shared tasks on reproducibility of evaluations in NLG, ReproGen'21 and ReproGen'22. This shared task series forms part of an ongoing research programme designed to develop theory and practice of reproducibility assessment in NLP and machine learning, all against a background of an interest in reproducibility that continues to grow in the two fields. This paper describes the ReproNLP'23 shared task, summarises results from the reproduction studies submitted, and provides comparative analysis of the results.

1 Introduction

Reproducibility continues to be a topic dividing and troubling the Natural Language Processing (NLP) community (Belz et al., 2021a, 2023a). Despite a growing body of work on the topic, we still do not understand well enough what makes evaluations easier or harder to reproduce, and reproduction studies often reveal alarmingly low degrees of reproducibility not only for human evaluations but also for automatically computed metrics (Belz et al., 2023a).

With this fourth reproduction-focused shared task in NLP, following REPROLANG'20 (Branco et al., 2020), ReproGen'21 (Belz et al., 2021b) and ReproGen'22 (Belz et al., 2022), our aim is to continue to add to the body of reproduction studies in NLP and machine learning (ML) in order to increase the data points available for investigating reproducibility, and to begin to identify properties of evaluations that are associated with better reproducibility.

We start in Section 2 with a description of the organisation and structure of the shared task, followed by details of Track C and the participating teams (Section 3). Next, we present per-experiment results for each experiment in Track C, in terms of the reproduction task, degree of reproducibility assessments, and confirmation of findings (Section 4). We next look at the quality criteria assessed by evaluations and the properties of the ReproNLP evaluation studies in standardised terms as facilitated by HEDS datasheets, and explore if any properties appear to have an effect on degree of reproducibility (Section 5). We conclude with some discussion (Section 6) and a look to future work (Section 7).

2 ReproNLP 2023

ReproNLP 2023[1] consisted of three tracks. Tracks A and B were identical to the tracks in predecessor event ReproGen 2022: Track A a shared task in which teams try to reproduce the same previous evaluation results, Track B an 'unshared task' in which teams attempt to reproduce their own previous evaluation results.

Track C forms part of the ReproHum project[2] and the studies reproduced in it were selected according to criteria of suitability and balance to form part of a larger coordinated multi-lab multi-test reproduction study, as described in detail elsewhere (Belz et al., 2023a). The three tracks in overview were as follows:

A ***Main Reproducibility Track:*** For a shared set of selected evaluation studies, participants repeat one or more studies, and attempt to reproduce the results, using published information plus additional information and resources provided by the authors, and making common-sense assumptions where information is still incomplete.

[1] All information and resources relating to ReproNLP are available at https://repronlp.github.io/.

[2] https://reprohum.github.io/

Proceedings of the Third Workshop on Human Evaluation of NLP Systems, pages 35–48, Varna, Bulgaria, Sep 7, 2023.
https://doi.org/10.26615/978-954-452-088-5_004

B ***RYO Track:*** *R*eproduce *Y*our *O*wn previous evaluation results, and report what happened. Unshared task.

C ***ReproHum Track:*** For one or more of the set of papers selected for ReproHum Round 0, and for the specific experiments selected only, repeat one or more studies, and attempt to reproduce the results, using information provided by the ReproNLP organisers only.

There were no submissions for Tracks A and B this year. For the ReproHum Track (C), the specific experiments that are listed and described below were the subject of two reproduction studies each in the ReproHum project, and were also open to ReproNLP'23 participants. The original authors agreed to us using their experiments in the ReproHum project as well as in ReproNLP, and provided very detailed information about the experiments. The experiments, with many thanks to the authors for supporting ReproHum and ReproNLP, are:

1. Vamvas and Sennrich (2022): *As Little as Possible, as Much as Necessary: Detecting Over and Undertranslations with Contrastive Conditioning.* 1 human evalution study (of 2 in paper); English to German; 2 evaluators; 1 quality criteria; 1 system; approx. 1000 outputs; reproduction target: primary scores.
2. Lin et al. (2022): *Other Roles Matter! Enhancing Role-Oriented Dialogue Summarization via Role Interactions.* 1 human evaluation study; Chinese; 3 evaluators; 3 quality criteria; 200 outputs per system; 4 systems; reproduction target: primary scores.
3. Lux and Vu (2022): *Language-Agnostic Meta-Learning for Low-Resource Text-to-Speech with Articulatory Features.* 1 human evaluation; German; Student evaluators; 1 quality criterion; 12 outputs per system; 2 systems; reproduction target: primary scores.
4. Chakrabarty et al. (2022): *It's not Rocket Science: Interpreting Figurative Language in Narratives.* 2 human evaluation studies (of 4 in paper); English; MTurk; 1 quality criterion; 25 outputs per system, 5/8 systems (including human reference texts); reproduction target: primary scores.
5. Puduppully and Lapata (2021) A: *Data-to-text Generation with Macro Planning.* First human evaluation (relative); English; MTurk; 3 quality criteria; 20 outputs (summaries) per system; 5 systems, reproduction target: primary scores.
6. Puduppully and Lapata (2021) B: *Data-to-text Generation with Macro Planning.* Second human evaluation (absolute); English; MTurk; 2 quality criteria; 80 outputs (sentences) per system; 5 systems; reproduction target: primary scores.

For Track C, the ReproHum project team gathered all code and other resources needed for repeating the study, and acted as a go-between in those cases were there were additional questions from the reproducing teams; this was to avoid using more of the original authors' time than was absolutely necessary. Authors of reproduction papers were also asked to complete a HEDS datasheet.[3] (Shimorina and Belz, 2022).

We issued a call for participation in one or more tracks, and made available broad guidelines[4] to participating teams about how to report reproduction results, and provided light-touch review with comments and feedback on papers. In addition, for Track C, the ReproHum team and partners agreed a common approach to reproduction which ReproHum participants were expected to follow.

3 ReproHum Track (C) in Detail

3.1 Paper Selection

The papers in Track C, or rather the six specific experiments from the five papers in Track C, were selected by a systematic process to achieve balanced and diverse distribution over three properties. The process is described in full detail in a previous paper, coauthored by all participants at the ReproHum partner labs (Belz et al., 2023a).

The three properties and their associated value ranges are shown in Table 1 in the column headings. The cells show property-value counts split across the three most common NLP tasks evaluated and an Other category. The counts are for the larger set of 20 experiments which we deemed to have sufficiently clear properties for reproduction, and from which we selected the subset of six for ReproNLP Track C.

[3] https://forms.gle/MgWiKVu7i5UHeMNQ9
[4] https://repronlp.github.io

Task	Num. Evaluators		Cognitive Complexity			Training and/or Expertise		
	small	not small	low	medium	high	neither	either	both
Dialogue	1	0	0	1	0	0	1	0
Generation	6	5	4	5	2	4	5	2
Summarisation	3	1	2	1	1	1	3	0
Other	2	2	1	0	3	2	0	2

Table 1: Counts of control property values by NLP task for 20 experiments (from 15 papers) with clear properties, from which the ReproNLP Track C experiments were selected to cover as many property combinations as possible.

3.2 Common Approach to Reproduction

In order to ensure comparability between studies, we agreed the following common-ground approach to carrying out reproduction studies:

1. Plan for repeating the original experiment in a form that is as far as possible identical to the original experiment, ensuring you have all required resources in place, then apply to research ethics committee for approval.
2. If participants were paid during the original experiment, determine pay in accordance with the ReproHum common procedure for calculating fair pay (Belz et al., 2023a).
3. Following ethical approval start the reproduction study following the steps below. Contact the ReproHum team with any questions rather than the original authors, as they have already provided us with all the resources and information they have. Don't communicate with other ReproHum teams about their reproduction studies. This is to avoid inadvertently affecting outcomes.
4. Complete HEDS datasheet.
5. Identify the following types of results reported in the original paper for the experiment:
    (a) Type I results: single numerical scores, e.g. mean quality rating, error count, etc.
    (b) Type II results: sets of numerical scores, e.g. set of Type I results .
    (c) Type III results: categorical labels attached to text spans of any length.
    (d) Qualitative conclusions/findings stated explicitly in the original paper.[5]
6. Carry out the allocated experiment exactly as described in the HEDS sheet.
7. Report the results in the following form:
    (a) Description of the original experiment.
    (b) Description of any differences in your repeat experiment.
    (c) Side-by-side presentation of all results (8a-d above) from original and repeat experiments, in tables.
    (d) Report quantified reproducibility assessments as follows:
        i. Type I results: Small-sample oefficient of variation CV* (Belz, 2022).
        ii. Type II results: Pearson's r, Spearman's ρ.
        iii. Type III results: Multi-rater: Fleiss's κ; Multi-rater, multi-label: Krippendorff's α.
        iv. Conclusions/findings: Side-by-side summary of conclusions/findings that are / are not confirmed in the repeat experiment.

[5]We now call these Type IV results.

3.3 Participants and Submissions

Table 2 provides an overview of the NLP labs that participated in Track C, alongside the papers from which they reproduced an experiment.

4 Per-Experiment Results

By design, each of the six experiments in Track C was repeated by two ReproHum partner labs, and in this section we take a look at how results achieved in the two repeat experiments compare to each other and to results from the original experiment, for each of the six experiments.

4.1 Vamvas and Sennrich (2022) *As Little as Possible, as Much as Necessary: Detecting Over and Undertranslations with Contrastive Conditioning*

4.1.1 Reproduction task

The reproduction task for this experiment was to repeat one human evaluation (of two in the paper) of an English-to-German MT post-processing system that checks translations for content additions and omissions as compared to the source text (a

Original paper	Experiment for reproduction						Labs
	#exps	language(s)	#ev-ors	#qc	#sys	#out-s	
Vamvas and Sennrich (2022)	1 (of 2)	En to Ger	2	1	1	1000	(a) **ADAPT/Tech Univ Dublin** (b) **UFAL/Charles Uniersity**
Lin et al. (2022)	1	Chinese	3	3	4	200	(a) **WICT/Peking Uniersity** (b) **Utrecht Uniersity**
Lux and Vu (2022)	1	German	34	1	2	12	(b) **ZHAW (Zurich)** (a) **Darmstadt University**
Chakrabarty et al. (2022)	2 (of 4)	English	MTurk	1	4	25	(a) **Groningen University** (b) **Trivago**
Puduppully and Lapata (2021) A	1	English	MTurk	2	5	20	(a) **Uni Illinois Chicago** (b) **TiCC/Tilburg**
Puduppully and Lapata (2021) B	1	English	MTurk	3	5	80	(a) **Napier University** (b) **Uni Santiago de Compostela**

Table 2: Overview of reproduced papers, experiments, and the 12 labs participating in ReproNLP 2023 (#=number of, ev-ors=evaluators, qc=quality criteria, sys=systems, out-s=outputs.

form of semantic consistency checking). The evaluation involved two evaluators, one quality criterion, one system, and about 1000 system outputs per evaluator.

Each evaluator was shown about 800 system outputs randomly sampled from development and test data, where outputs are word-spans of over/undertranslation errors (aka additions and omissions) detected in translations. The evaluation interface showed source text, translation and the detected error span. The evaluation task was to judge whether the error span marked up by a system was in fact a bad translation, or whether it was ok (there was a second step which was not a reproduction target).

4.1.2 Notable issues

Plátek et al. (2023) (Reproduction 2) used the evaluation tool/interface provided by the original authors as a Docker image, whereas Klubička and Kelleher (2023) (Reproduction 1) who had trouble running it used a Google spreadsheet which made for a very different interface, e.g. without repeated questions.

The script used by the original authors for producing results was found to have a bug in it. Klubička and Kelleher (2023) used only a corrected version of the script provided by the authors, whereas Plátek et al. (2023) corrected the script themselves and produced results with both the buggy and the corrected versions.

4.1.3 Degree of Reproducibility

The table below shows overtranslation (OT) and undertranslation (UT) precision scores. OT precision is the proportion of word spans annotated as an overtranslation (containing incorrectly added content) which were correct. UT precision is the same for undertranslations. The human evaluation was for the proposed system only. The following table shows the word-span-level OT and UT precision scores from the Original human evaluation (which used the script with the bug), Repro 1 (corrected script), and Repro 2 (which used both buggy and non-buggy versions of the script); the last two columns show two three-way CV* scores, one including results obtained with the buggy version of Repro 2, the other with the non-buggy version.

	Orig (+bug)	Repro 1 (-bug)	Repro 2 +bug	Repro 2 -bug	CV* (n=3) +bug	CV* (n=3) -bug
OT Prec	0.0742	0.0948	0.0678	0.0691	21.85	20.96
UT Prec	0.3941	0.3529	0.2209	0.2256	34.28	33.12

We can see that the buggy and non-buggy versions of Repro 2 produced very similar precision scores (even though there are notable differences in the raw counts). At the same time, the (buggy) original results are closer to the non-buggy Repro 1 results, all of which makes for a confusing picture.

We do know from the raw counts that the two corrected versions of the script do not produce the same (corrected) counts for the original experiment. This combined with the fact that we do not have buggy results for Orig and Repro 1 *as reported by Repro 1*, means we do not have sufficient comparability to draw conclusion from this pair of reproductions. In the table above, we use the buggy original results as reported by the Repro 2 authors because we do not have raw counts for the original results, whereas the Repro 2 authors calculated them with the script they corrected themselves. Moreover, they report both buggy and non-buggy results for their reproduction.

All in all, it is hard to interpret the three-way CV* numbers above, given the above obervations, which is why we have greyed them out here, and do not include them in the comparative overview of results in Table 4.

Unlike for the other experiments below, we do not report correlations between score sets as there are only two scores in each set.

4.2 Lin et al. (2022) *Other Roles Matter! Enhancing Role-Oriented Dialogue Summarisation via Role Interactions*

4.2.1 Reproduction task

For this experiment, the task was to repeat one human evaluation of a Chinese role-oriented dialogue summariser. There were three evaluators, three quality criteria (Informativeness, Non-redundancy, and Fluency; an Overall aggregated metric was also reported), four systems (two baseline systems without role interaction, PGN-multi and BERT-multi, and two tested systems, PGN-both and BERT-both), and 200 outputs per system. The dataset was CSDS (Lin et al., 2021), a Chinese customer service dialogue summarisation dataset, from the test set of which 100 dialogues were randomly sampled for the human evaluation. Evaluators were asked to rate each sentence in a summary on a scale from 0 to 2 for each of the three quality criteria.

4.2.2 Notable issues

An interesting aspect of this pair of reproductions is that the original study triple-evaluated the first 10 evaluation items in order to assess IAA, which meant there are three scores for each of these items, compared to one score for the remaining 90. Rather than excluding the first ten items from aggregated results, the original authors decided to use the scores from the 'most experienced' evaluator only, discarding the others.

This was impossible to repeat as the assessment of experience was not explained (experience in terms of what?), and both reproducing teams (Gao et al., 2023; Ito et al., 2023) report results for keeping the first 10 scores of each of the evaluators, as well as for the mean of all three evaluators. The different variants reveal interesting differences in results and system rankings purely as the result of essentially arbitrary preferences for one evaluator over others.

4.2.3 Reproducibility

The following table shows 3-way reproducibility assessments for the original experiment (Lin et al., 2022), Repro 1 (Gao et al., 2023), and Repro 2 (Ito et al., 2023) in terms of CV* values (each computed over the three corresponding scores from the original, Repro 1 and Repro 2 experiments) for each of the four systems and each of the three quality criteria plus the overall aggregated measure (user=user-oriented, agent=agent-oriented, m=multi, b=both):

	CV* (n=3)							
	Inform		Non-Red		Fluency		Overall	
	user	agent	user	agent	user	agent	user	agent
PGN-m	5.89	5.91	5.67	1.28	11.1	15.37	6.01	6.54
PGN-b	5.72	4.61	3.53	0	12.5	12.07	6.58	5.72
BERT-m	2.14	13.29	3.76	5.95	6.74	6.77	1.75	5.72
BERT-b	6.22	13.66	0	2.41	6.93	7.61	3.72	6.98

Non-Redundancy has particularly good reproducibility, in fact the best reproducibility in ReproNLP 2023 of any quality criteria (see Table 4). CV* for for all system/measure combinations ranges from excellent to good for the most part.

4.2.4 Correlations

Table 3 shows Pearson's correlations between the PGN-* and BERT-* systems in (i) the original study compared to reproduction 1, (ii) the original study compared to reproduction 2, and (iii) reproduction 1 compared to reproduction 2, for each of the two modes user-oriented and agent-oriented. Correlations are > 0.9 for the user-oriented mode for all three criteria, for the agent-oriented mode for Informativeness, and (just) between Orig and Repro 2 for Fluency/agent-oriented.

Repro 1 has strikingly strong *negative* correlations for Fluency/agent-oriented mode, as well as weak to moderate correlations for Non-redundancy/agent-oriented. It is unclear why, but Repro 1 and agency-oriented mode are both associated with lower correlations. Finally, the Overall scores correlate less well with each other, especially when Repro 1 is involved.

4.2.5 Confirmation of findings

If we take the main findings to be the relative performance of the methods evaluated, and the reported ranks for the methods as the means of verification, then the following picture emerges. Ito et al. (2023) are unable to confirm the overall finding that the proposed approach really does improve the Fluency and Non-redundancy of summaries, while Gao et al. (2023) confirm the effectiveness of the proposed

	Informativeness		Non-Redundancy		Fluency		Overall	
	user-orient.	agent-orient.	user-orient.	agent-orient.	user-orient.	agent-orient.	user-orient.	agent-orient.
(i) Pearson's Orig v Repro 1								
PGN-*, BERT-*	0.943	1	0.948	0.486	0.908	-0.728	0.105	0.328
(ii) Pearson's Orig v Repro 2								
PGN-*, BERT-*	0.927	0.986	0.932	0.883	0.933	0.995	0.753	0.683
(iii) Pearson's Repro 1 v Repro 2								
PGN-*, BERT-*	0.984	0.984	0.999	0.263	0.96	-0.765	0.466	0.801

Table 3: Pearson's correlations between original study (Lin et al., 2022), reproduction 1 (Gao et al., 2023), and reproduction 2 (Ito et al., 2023), n=4, for each of the four quality criteria, for each of the two modes user-oriented and agent-oriented.

approach in terms of the Overall metric, but document slightly worse performance of the proposed method compared to the standard approach.

4.3 Lux and Vu (2022) *Language-Agnostic Meta-Learning for Low-Resource Text-to-Speech with Articulatory Features*

4.3.1 Reproduction task

The experiment that was the reproduction target from this paper was a human evaluation of a German text-to-speech (TTS) system. Evaluators were students, 34 responses were collected, one quality criterion (Naturalness) was assessed, using 6 audio outputs each for four system variants: the proposed approach and a baseline each combined with two different TTS systems (Tacotron and FastSpeech). The primary score for each system was the percentage of times that the system was preferred (counts of no preference were also collected).

4.3.2 Notable issues

One issue with this pair of reproductions was that the original authors had reported and confirmed that the order of audio files[6] had been randomised in the original experiment on Google Forms. However, at the time of reproduction there was no option to randomise the order of Google Form questions while at the same time preserving the connection between audios and evaluation response. We provided both reproducing teams with the same random order of items. Each participant in both reproductions was shown items in this order.

Another interesting issue arose: while both reproducing teams (Hürlimann and Cieliebak, 2023; Mieskes and Benz, 2023) found very low reproducibility in terms of CV* and Pearson's r, Hürlimann and Cieliebak (2023) found much better reproducibility when the system labels were swapped (i.e. when treating Tacotron as FastSpeech and vice versa). However, even if such an accidental transposition is assumed, the preference percentages reported by Mieskes and Benz (2023) in their reproduction study still do not confirm the original results, as we will see below.

4.3.3 3-way degree of reproducibility

The following table shows percentages of times that each baseline and proposed system version (*-base, *-prop) was preferred and where there was no preference (*-equal),[7] alongside three-way CV* values for scores from the three experiments (Original, Reproduction 1 (Hürlimann and Cieliebak, 2023), Reproduction 2 (Mieskes and Benz, 2023)):

Preferred system	Preference strength (% preferred) Orig	Repro 1	Repro 2	CV* (n=3)
FS-base	31.3	12.0	13.1	70.48
FS-prop	25.3	50.0	40.5	39.46
FS-equal	43.4	38.0	46.4	12.21
Taco-base	11.0	29.3	22.5	54.02
Taco-prop	52.0	29.3	25.7	48.87
Taco-equal	37.0	41.4	51.8	21.41

From this we can see that there is very little agreement (CV* is very high) among the three experiments, except for the *-equal percentages; Pearson's r values (Section 4.3.5) also confirm this. If instead we switch FS and Taco scores around in the two repeat evaluations (as indicated by the shading in the table) we get substantially improved reproducibility, again except for the *-equal percentages which remain similar:

[6]To be precise, the audio files were converted to audio-only video files.

[7]Note that the numbers in the three tables in this section may differ very slightly from those reported by Mieskes and Benz (2023) and (Hürlimann and Cieliebak, 2023), because we normalised percentages to add up to 100 excluding any skipped items.

Preferred system	Preference strength (% preferred			CV* (n=3)
	Orig	Repro 1 T	Repro 2 T	
FS-base	31.3	29.3	22.5	20.36
FS-prop	25.3	29.3	25.7	10.06
FS-equal	43.4	41.4	51.8	14.82
Taco-base	11.0	12.0	13.1	10.67
Taco-prop	52.0	50.0	40.5	15.81
Taco-equal	37.0	38.0	46.4	15.6

4.3.4 2-way degree of reproducibility

If we look at pairwise CV* (n=2) we can see that after transposition, Repro 1 T matches the original experiment much more closesly than Repro 2 T:

Preferred system	CV* of each Repro* with Orig (n=2)			
	Repro 1	Repro 2	Repro 1 T	Repro 2 T
FS-base	88.88	81.74	6.58	32.62
FS-prop	65.41	46.06	14.61	1.56
FS-equal	13.23	6.66	4.7	17.59
Taco-base	90.55	68.45	8.67	17.38
Taco-prop	55.68	67.49	3.91	24.79
Taco-equal	11.19	33.23	2.66	22.47

While it seems likely that some mixup has happened in the audio files that makes the transposed results match the original experiment better than the non-transposed results, we don't know exactly what has happened, and in fact we don't know for sure which scores belong to which system.

Something that might go some way towards explaining what has caused Repro 1 (T) to be a better match for the original scores is that in Repro 1, 157 evaluators were used, whereas the original used 34 and Repro 2 used 37, as more evaluators means better reliability (better representativeness of the sample relative to the population).

4.3.5 Correlations between score sets

The pairwise r coefficients (between the combined FastSpeech and Tacotron scores) below confirm that Repro 1 T tracks the original percentages more closely than Repro 2 T:

	O v R1	O v R2	R1 v R2	O v R1T	O v R2T	R1T v R2T
Pearson's	0.001	0.259	0.845	0.989	0.83	0.845

While there is no correlation at all between Orig and Repro 1, there is a mild positive correlation between Orig and Repro 2. Orig vs. the transposed Repro 1 (R1T) results is very strongly correlated (0.99), while Orig vs. R2T, and R1T vs. R2T are not much less strong. (We include the identical r for both Repro 1 vs. Repro 2 and Repro 1 T vs. Repro 2 T for ease of reference.)

4.3.6 Confirmation of findings

In terms of findings (Type IV results), on the basis of the non-transposed results, both reproducing teams are unable to confirm the original findings. On the basis of transposed results, Hürlimann and Cieliebak (2023) obtain the same system ranks in all cases (albeit in one case with a very small margin), showing Taco-prop > Taco-base, *but* FS-prop < FS-base (second table above). However, in Repro 2 T (created for this paper above) the proposed approach is found to be better in both FastSpeech and Tacotron.

4.4 Chakrabarty et al. (2022) *It's not Rocket Science: Interpreting Figurative Language in Narratives*

4.4.1 Reproduction task

The task here was to repeat two human evaluation studies (of four in the paper) of an English prompted text generator. The evaluation was carried out on MTurk, there was one quality criterion (Plausibility) evaluated in absolute mode, 25 outputs per system, and four systems addressing two tasks, namely continuation after idiom, and continuation after simile.

25 narratives ending in either an idiom or a simile were randomly sampled for each task. Each narrative was paired with (a) human-written continuations (5 for the similes, 3 for the idioms), and (b) automatically generated continuations, one by the baseline GPT2-XL model, one by a context-enhanced model, and one by a 'literal-enhanced' model. Each continuation was categorised as either plausible or not by evaluators.

4.4.2 3-way degree of reproducibility

The table below is a three-way comparison of percentages of plausible continuations for each of the four systems, separately for continuations after Idioms, and after Similes, obtained in the three experiments (Repro 1 is by Li et al. (2023), Repro 2 by Mahamood (2023)).[8] Three-way CV* values for the three experiments are shown in the last column:

Type	Model	% of plausible continuations			CV*
		Orig	Repro 1	Repro 2	(n=3)
Idioms	GPT2-XL	56	76	58	21.26
	+Context	68	92	83.33	18.32
	+Literal	48	68	66.66	22.45
	Human	80	68	80.55	11.38
Similes	GPT2-XL	60	68	64	7.64
	+Context	68	72	48	25.08
	+Literal	76	80	64	13.88
	Human	88	68	84	16.17

All CV* values are medium good, with GPT2-XL/Similes better on average.

[8]The number in red/bold was recalculated by Li et al. (2023) as 60; the original paper reports 76.

4.4.3 2-way degree of reproducibility

The 3-way CV* scores showed a medium degree of reproducibility, and a first indication that Repro 2 tracks the Orig scores more closely than Repro 1. This is supported by the pairwise CV* scores, except for +Context/Similes where Repro 1 is closer:

Type	Model	CV* of each Repro* with Orig (n=2)	
		Repro 1	Repro 2
Idioms	GPT2-XL	30.21	3.5
	+Context	29.91	20.2
	+Literal	34.38	32.45
	Human	16.17	0.68
Similes	GPT2-XL	12.46	6.43
	+Context	5.7	34.38
	+Literal	28.49	5.11
	Human	25.56	4.64

4.4.4 Correlations between score sets

The pairwise Pearson's r values show clearly that Repro 2 tracks the Orig scores much more closely than Repro 1, with which Orig has no correlation for idioms, and a medium *negative* correlation for Similes (note that none of the r values reach significance at $\alpha = 0.05$):

	Idioms			Similes		
	Orig	Repro 1	Repro 2	Orig	Repro 1	Repro 2
Orig	1	0.13	0.76	1	-0.5	0.68
Repro 1	0.13	1	0.38	-0.5	1	-0.32
Repro 2	0.76	0.38	1	0.68	-0.32	1

4.4.5 Confirmation of findings

In terms of main findings (Type IV results), the following picture emerges. The ranks determined by Orig, Repro 1 and Repro 2 are all different, for both Idioms and Similes. Repro 2 achieves closer similarity of ranks with Orig. Repro 1 has completely different ranks from Orig for Idioms and Similes.

4.5 Puduppully and Lapata (2021) A: *Data-to-text Generation with Macro Planning*

4.5.1 Reproduction task

In this experiment, five data-to-text methods (3 neural systems, one template, and human (gold) reference texts) were evaluated by relative human evaluations involving three quality criteria (Grammaticality, Coherence, and Conciseness), and 20 items from the Rotowire dataset (Wiseman et al., 2017). Pairs of systems were compared, with 10 combinations per input record, for a total of 200 evaluation items.

Each evaluation item was shown to 3 distinct workers on Amazon Mechanical Turk; there was no limit in the number of items a worker could complete. Evaluators were asked to select the best summary within the pair. Best-worst scaling was then applied (Louviere et al., 2015) to provide per-system scores ranging from -100 to 100.

4.5.2 Notable Issues

The authors of the original study performed attention checks whereby participants, if they failed, were excluded from future tasks (but the work they had done so far was retained). No process for these checks, or details of which output pairs were involved in a check were recorded. Following discussion with the original author, we created a method for systematic attention checks that was then used in both reproductions.

4.5.3 3-way degree of reproducibility

The table below shows the best-worst scores and CV* for the Grammaticality criterion:[9]

best-worst score (Grammaticality)				CV* (n=3)
System	Orig	Repro 1	Repro 2	
Gold	38.33	14.17	9.17	15.81
Templ	-61.67*	-23.33*	17.08*	62.23
ED+CC	5.00	-8.33	-19.58	16.28
RBF	13.33	9.17	-9.58	14.30
Macro	5.00	8.33	2.92	3.16

From this we can see that whilst CV* was low (good) for the Macro system, and moderate for others, the Templ (template) system score varied greatly between experiments and has a very high (bad) CV* value. In fact, the Templ system came out worst overall for the original experiment and Repro 1, yet best overall for the other Repro 2.

The next table shows results for Coherence, in the same format:

best-worst score (Coherence)				CV* (n=3)
System	Orig	Repro 1	Repro 2	
Gold	46.25*	12.50	-0.42	24.66
Templ	-52.92*	-20.00*	25.42	57.13
ED+CC	-8.33	-7.50	-15.00	5.60
RBF	4.58	9.17	-10.42	12.39
Macro	10.42	5.83	0.42	5.80

The same issue with the template system is observed, with CV* for other systems being low to moderate. Finally, the same is also seen for Conciseness:

[9]Note that because the measure used for assessing it ranges $-100..+100$, CV can't be applied directly. We have therefore shifted scores to the range 0..200, which is acceptable here as we have an interval (with fixed endpoints).

best-worst score (Conciseness)				CV* (n=3)
System	Orig	Repro 1	Repro 2	
Gold	30.83	5.83	-1.67	18.63
Templ	-36.67	-5.83	43.75*	49.39
ED+CC	-4.58	-5.00	-25.83	16.84
RBF	3.75	0.83	-14.58	12.45
Macro	6.67	4.17	-1.67	5.08

In all above tables, the asterisk indicates that the system was significantly different from the Macro system.

4.5.4 Correlations between score sets

Spearman's rank correlation (ρ) for each study pair looks as follows for the three quality criteria, with the caveat that the sample size is small:

Grammaticality	Orig	Repro 1	Repro 2
Orig	1	0.975	-0.205
Repro 1	0.975	1	-0.100
Repro 2	-0.205	-0.100	1

Coherence	Orig	Repro 1	Repro 2
Orig	1	0.900	-0.100
Repro 1	0.900	1	-0.300
Repro 2	-0.100	-0.300	1

Conciseness	Orig	Repro 1	Repro 2
Orig	1	1	-0.051
Repro 1	1	1	-0.051
Repro 2	-0.051	-0.051	1

As expected, this shows near perfect alignment of system ranks between Orig and Repro 1, but no correlation at all between Repro 2 and either of the other two.[10]

4.5.5 Confirmation of findings

We saw in the preceding section that the original study and Repro 1 have close rank correlations. This was also reported by the Repro 1 authors (Arvan and Parde, 2023) who reported an overall ρ of 0.83 when concatenating scores for the three criteria.

In terms of statistical significance, no study (original or reproduction) found any difference, for any criteria, between the proposed (Macro) system and either of the other neural systems. Some differences were seen between Macro and either the human reference or the template, but whether these differences were significant varied greatly between experiments. Like van Miltenburg et al. (2023), we are unable to explain why there are such fundamental differences between their reproduction on the one hand, and Orig and Repro 1 on the other, e.g. why the template system is judged best for all criteria in their reproduction whilst being worst in the other studies. This difference has a large impact on both CV* and Spearman's ρ.

[10] This is so striking a finding that we will investigate it further in future work, something that wasn't possible in the short time we had to write this report.

4.6 Puduppully and Lapata (2021) B: *Data-to-text Generation with Macro Planning*

4.6.1 Reproduction task

In this experiment, an absolute human evaluation of the same data-to-text system as in the last section was performed to obtain the mean number of facts in the output text that are (i) supported by the input (#Supp) and (ii) contradicted by the input (#Cont). For this, 20 input records from the Rotowire dataset and corresponding verbalisations (summaries) generated by the same five systems as in Section 4.5 were selected. From each summary, 4 sentences were selected as evaluation items, for a total of 400 evaluation items. Reproduction 1 was carried out by Watson and Gkatzia (2023), Reproduction 2 by González-Corbelle et al. (2023).

Experiments were carried out on Amazon Mechanical Turk, participants were shown the four sentences from a given summary on a form and asked to provide counts for both #Supp and #Cont on the same form. Three participants scored each sentence. Other than the above, there was no restriction on the total number of tasks each participant could undertake.

4.6.2 3-way degree of reproducibility

The following table shows the mean #Supp counts for the original experiment and the two reproductions, alongside three-way CV* values:

System	Orig	Repro 1	Repro 2	CV* (n=3)
Gold	3.63	4.000	3.36	10.72
Templ	7.57*	6.3167*	6.27*	13.42
ED+CC	3.92	5.100	4.42	16.16
RBF	5.08*	4.9458	4.31	10.52
Macro	4.00	4.5458	4.08	8.56

For all systems, CV* is moderate, indicating some consistency between the three studies. The below table shows the same for #Cont counts:

System	Orig	Repro 1	Repro 2	CV* (n=3)
Gold	0.07	1.525	0.66	119.01
Templ	0.08	1.3583	0.90	101.57
ED+CC	0.91*	1.9042	1.95*	45.24
RBF	0.67*	1.7583	1.22	54.70
Macro	0.27	1.5333	0.55	103.39

In both the above tables, the asterisk indicates that the system was significantly different from the Macro system at $\alpha = 0.05$.

For #Cont counts, we see *much* higher (worse) values for CV* for all systems. Since the experiment design only has participants provide a count for supported or contradicted facts, rather than annotating error spans in the text, it is not easy to determine whether there are differences between facts annotated as Supp and as Cont that might explain this very substantial difference.

However, we do know that there were far more Supp facts than there were Cont facts found (roughly 20–30 times as many), which would make the former far more stable than the latter.

This may be compounded by the fact that facts are overwhelmingly numeric in nature in this dataset, and it is particularly difficult to achieve acceptable agreement among evaluators regarding what counts as a numeric fact (Thomson et al., 2023). When annotating individual errors in system outputs for the same dataset, Thomson et al. noted that participants had to be specifically instructed as to what should be classed as a number, since ordinals, cardinals, determiners, and number-based phrases would otherwise be considered numeric by some annotators but not others.

4.6.3 Correlations between score sets

Shown below are the Pearson correlations between the studies for both the count of supporting facts (#Supp) and the count of contradicted facts (#Cont):

#Supp	Orig	Repro 1	Repro 2
Orig	1.000	0.912	0.942
Repro 1	0.912	1.000	0.989
Repro 2	0.942	0.989	1.000

#Cont	Orig	Repro 1	Repro 2
Orig	1.000	0.958	0.887
Repro 1	0.958	1.000	0.826
Repro 2	0.887	0.826	1.000

This shows strong correlations between all experiments, obscuring the fact that the raw counts in the reproduction studies being, in many cases, an order of magnitude higher than in the original study. Repro 2 has lower correlation with both Orig and Repro 1.

4.6.4 Confirmation of findings

The original study found there to significantly more supported facts (#Supp) in the template system compared with the proposed (Macro) system. Both reproduction studies confirm this. It also found significantly more supported facts in the RBF system compared to Macro, although this was not confirmed by either reproduction. For contradicted facts (#Cont), the original study showed the Macro system to have significantly fewer than the two other neural systems (ED+CC and RBF). Reproduction 1 found no significant differences, and Reproduction 2 confirmed Macro to have significantly fewer than ED+CC only.

5 Results by Quality Criterion

Table 4 provides an overview of the six ReproNLP experiments in terms of the quality criteria (measurands) assessed in the evaluations and the properties of the evaluation design (Shimorina and Belz, 2022). The first column identifies the studies and criteria, the last column shows the corresponding mean criterion-level CV*. The remaining columns show seven properties of each study/criterion, as per the HEDS datasheets; column headings identify HEDS question number (for brief explanation of each see table caption). Note that for property 3.2.1 (number of evaluators) we don't always have the information for both reproductions.

Note we are not including CV* for (Vamvas and Sennrich, 2022) because of the issues noted above. The experiment originally reported by Lin et al. (2022), and reproduced by Gao et al. (2023) and Ito et al. (2023), stands out for having good reproducibility for all three criteria assessed (all below 10), Non-redundancy having particularly low CV* (2.83). If we assume transposition of system outputs has indeed accidentally occurred, then the Naturalness evaluation from Lux and Vu (2022) is only slightly worse (14.55).

The evaluation from Chakrabarty et al. (2022) has the next best degrees of reproducibility, mean CV* for Plausibility after Idiom and Plausibility after Simile both being medium (in the 15-20 range). The assessments of Grammaticality, Coherence and Conciseness for the experiment from Puduppully and Lapata (2021) (A) have slightly worse reproducibility at just above 20 for all three criteria.

Finally, the second experiment from Puduppully and Lapata (2021) (B) has good reproducibility for the mean number of facts supported by the input (#Supp), but the worst reproducibility by far for the mean number of facts contradicted by the input (#Cont).

For comparison, in the ReproGen'22 studies, annotation-based evaluation (4.3.8=Anno) was clearly associated with lower reproducibility. Evaluations which involved assessment of content alone (4.1.2=Cont) also tended to have worse reproducibility. Assessing evaluation items relative to a system input (4.1.3=RtI) was also associated with

ReproNLP 2023									
Orig Study // *Repro 1 / Repro 2*, **measurands**	**3.1.1**	**3.2.1**	**4.3.4**	**4.3.8**	**4.1.1**	**4.1.2**	**4.1.3**	**scores /item**	**mean CV***
Vamvas and Sennrich (2022) // *Klubička and Kelleher (2023) / Plátek et al. (2023)*									
Correctly Identified Omissions	~1000	2	Yes,No	Cl/Lab	Corr	Both	RtI	1-2	N/A
Correctly Identified Additions	~1000	2	Yes,No	Cl/Lab	Corr	Both	RtI	1-2	N/A
Lin et al. (2022) // *Gao et al. (2023) / Ito et al. (2023)*									
Informativeness	100	3	0,1,2	DQE	Feature	Cont	iiOR	1	7.18
Non-Redundancy	100	3	0,1,2	DQE	Good	Cont	iiOR	1	2.83
Fluency	100	3	0,1,2	DQE	Good	Form	iiOR	1	9.89
Lux and Vu (2022) // *Hürlimann and Cieliebak (2023) / Mieskes and Benz (2023)*									
Naturalness (speech)	12	34/157/37	A,B,Tie	RQE	Good	Form	iiOR	34/157/37	41.08
Naturalness (speech) transposed	12	34/157/37	A,B,Tie	RQE	Good	Form	iiOR	34/157/37	14.55
Chakrabarty et al. (2022) // *Li et al. (2023) / Mahamood (2023)*									
Plausibility (continuation idiom)	150	4/?/35	Yes,No	Cl/Lab	Good	Both	RtI	3	18.35
Plausibility (continuation simile)	200	7/?/45	Yes,No	Cl/Lab	Good	Both	RtI	3	15.69
Puduppully and Lapata (2021) A // *Arvan and Parde (2023) / van Miltenburg et al. (2023)*									
Grammaticality	200	206/262/?	A,B	RQE	Corr	Form	iiOR	3	22.36
Coherence	200	206/262/?	A,B	RQE	Good	Cont	iiOR	3	21.12
Conciseness	200	206/262/?	A,B	RQE	Good	Both	iiOR	3	20.48
Puduppully and Lapata (2021) B // *Watson and Gkatzia (2023) / González-Corbelle et al. (2023)*									
Mean # Supported Facts	400	131/167/144	0-20	Count	Corr	Content	RtI	3	11.88
Mean # Contradicted Facts	400	131/167/144	0-20	Count	Corr	Content	RtI	3	84.78

Table 4: Summary of some properties of ReproNLP experiments, alongside mean CV* (n=3). 3.1.1 = number of items assessed per system; 3.2.1 = number of evaluators in original/reproduction experiment; 4.3.4 = List/range of possible responses; 4.3.8 = Form of response elicitation (DQE: direct quality estimation, RQE: relative quality estimation, Cl/Lab: classification/labelling, Count: counting occurrences in text); 4.1.1 = Correctness/Goodness/Features; 4.1.2 = Form/Content/Both; 4.1.3 = each output assessed in its own right (iiOR) / relative to inputs (RtI) / relative to external reference (EFoR); scores/item = number of evaluators who evaluate each evaluation item.

lower reproducibility for three of the studies (where comparison of outputs to inputs was far more complex than a straightforward is-it-simpler decision as in e.g. (Nisioi et al., 2017). Finally, correctness assessment (4.1.1=Corr) was also associated with lower reproducibility. For those of these properties that were present in ReproGen'21, the tendencies were the same.

6 Discussion

In terms of general tendencies found in ReproNLP reproductions, there were quite a few issues (see Notable Issues sections above) that made carrying out a repeat experiment difficult. These were discussed in detail in a previous paper (Belz et al., 2023a).

In some cases, there were striking differences between the two paired reproduction studies: for example, Repro 2 for Chakrabarty et al. (2022) achieved much closer results to the original study than Repro 1 in terms of both pairwise CV* and Pearson's, and while Repro 1 for (Puduppully and Lapata, 2021) (A) achieved very similar results to the original study, Repro 2 results had very little in common with either the original study or Repro 1. This very clearly highlights the importance of carrying out more than one reproduction study to get a rounded picture of an evaluation's degree of reproducibility.

None of the reproductions produced the same system ranks for all quality criteria evaluated, although in some cases it was close. Given that system ranks are the single most important result from the above types of evaluations, this is concerning.

In terms of patterns emerging about what properties make an evaluation more or less reproducible, we can glean two tendencies from the properties examined in Table 4: (i) there is some indication that Goodness-type criteria[11] are associated with better degree of reproducibility than Correctness-type criteria (see column 4.1.1 in Table 4); and (ii) sets of experiments that use the same number of evaluators (see column 3.2.1 in Table 4) tend to have better reproducibility than those that have different numbers.

7 Conclusions

Our intention in Track C had been to create a situation where we would have more than one reproduction of the same original study to analyse, in order to obtain truer estimates of the original study's reproducibility. Moreover, all three studies were supposed to be identical for as close as possible to ideal comparability. Two main problems arose: (a) the flaws, errors and bugs reported previously (Belz et al., 2023a,b) were in some cases fixed differently by reproducing authors, leading to different raw results; (b) reproducing authors in some cases chose different results to reproduce and compare, resulting in non-comparability; and (c) reproducing authors did not always manage to stick as closely as we had intended to the original experimental details, e.g. using different interfaces, revealing that the experiment was a reproduction, and most significantly, using very different numbers of evaluators. The latter is particularly significant, because it appears to be associated with worse reproducibility (see preceding section).

Our next step will be to fully standardise analysis and other scripts, and ask reproducing authors to both provide the same fully standardised set of results (something we did not have time for within the ReproNLP schedule). This will then provide the basis for more detailed analysis to be carried out and reported in future work.

We will also run another round of paired reproductions in the ReproHum project, using a different set of experiments for which we have corrected any issues prior to sharing them with the reproducing partners and where we are relaxing the strict-repetition requirement somewhat. We will again open up reproductions to any additional reproducing teams in ReproNLP 2024.

[11]From HEDS (Shimorina and Belz, 2022): "Goodness: select this option if, in contrast to correctness criteria, there is no single, general mechanism for deciding when outputs are maximally good, only for deciding for two outputs which is better and which is worse. E.g. for Fluency, even if outputs contain no disfluencies, there may be other ways in which any given output could be more fluent."

Acknowledgments

We thank the authors of the original papers that were up for reproduction in ReproNLP 2023. And of course the authors of the reproduction papers, without whom there would be no ReproHum project and no ReproNLP shared task.

Our work was carried out as part of the ReproHum project on Investigating Reproducibility of Human Evaluations in Natural Language Processing, funded by EPSRC (UK) under grant number EP/V05645X/1. In particular, we thank our numerous collaborators from NLP labs across the world who carried out the reproductions in Track C as part of the first batch of coordinated reproductions in the ReproHum project.

The ReproNLP work also benefits from the work being carried out in association with the ADAPT SFI Centre for Digital Media Technology which is funded by Science Foundation Ireland through the SFI Research Centres Programme and is co-funded under the European Regional Development Fund (ERDF) through Grant 13/RC/2106.

References

Mohammad Arvan and Natalie Parde. 2023. Human evaluation reproduction report for data-to-text generation with macro planning. In *Proceedings of the 3rd Workshop on Human Evaluation of NLP Systems*.

Anya Belz. 2022. A metrological perspective on reproducibility in NLP. *Computational Linguistics*, 48(4):1125–1135.

Anya Belz, Shubham Agarwal, Anastasia Shimorina, and Ehud Reiter. 2021a. A systematic review of reproducibility research in natural language processing. In *Proceedings of the 16th Conference of the European Chapter of the Association for Computational Linguistics: Main Volume*, pages 381–393, Online. Association for Computational Linguistics.

Anya Belz, Anastasia Shimorina, Shubham Agarwal, and Ehud Reiter. 2021b. The reprogen shared task on reproducibility of human evaluations in nlg: Overview and results. *INLG 2021*, page 249.

Anya Belz, Anastasia Shimorina, Maja Popovic, and Ehud Reiter. 2022. The 2022 reprogen shared task on reproducibility of evaluations in nlg: Overview and results. *INLG 2022*, page 43.

Anya Belz, Craig Thomson, Ehud Reiter, Gavin Abercrombie, Jose M Alonso-Moral, Mohammad Arvan, Jackie Cheung, Mark Cieliebak, Elizabeth Clark, Kees van Deemter, Tanvi Dinkar, Ondřej Dušek, Steffen Eger, Qixiang Fang, Albert Gatt, Dimitra Gkatzia, Javier González-Corbelle, Dirk Hovy, Manuela Hürlimann, Takumi Ito, John D. Kelleher, Filip Klubička, Huiyuan Lai, Chris van der Lee, Emiel van Miltenburg, Yiru Li, Saad Mahamood, Margot Mieskes, Malvina Nissim, Natalie Parde, Ondřej Plátek, Verena Rieser, Pablo Mosteiro Romero, Joel Tetreault, Antonio Toral, Xiaojun Wan, Leo Wanner, Lewis Watson, and Diyi Yang. 2023a. Missing information, unresponsive authors, experimental flaws: The impossibility of assessing the reproducibility of previous human evaluations in NLP. In *The Fourth Workshop on Insights from Negative Results in NLP*, pages 1–10.

Anya Belz, Craig Thomson, Ehud Reiter, and Simon Mille. 2023b. Non-repeatable experiments and non-reproducible results: The reproducibility crisis in human evaluation in NLP. In *Findings of the Association for Computational Linguistics: ACL 2023*, pages 3676–3687.

António Branco, Nicoletta Calzolari, Piek Vossen, Gertjan Van Noord, Dieter van Uytvanck, João Silva, Luís Gomes, André Moreira, and Willem Elbers. 2020. A shared task of a new, collaborative type to foster reproducibility: A first exercise in the area of language science and technology with REPROLANG2020. In *Proceedings of The 12th Language Resources and Evaluation Conference*, pages 5539–5545, Marseille, France. European Language Resources Association.

Tuhin Chakrabarty, Yejin Choi, and Vered Shwartz. 2022. It's not rocket science: Interpreting figurative language in narratives. *Transactions of the Association for Computational Linguistics*, 10:589–606.

Mingqi Gao, Jie Ruan, and Xiaojun Wan. 2023. A reproduction study of the human evaluation of role-oriented dialogue summarization models. In *Proceedings of the 3rd Workshop on Human Evaluation of NLP Systems*.

Javier González-Corbelle, Jose M. Alonso-Moral, and A. Bugarín-Diz. 2023. Some lessons learned reproducing human evaluation of a data-to-text system. In *Proceedings of the 3rd Workshop on Human Evaluation of NLP Systems*.

Manuela Hürlimann and Mark Cieliebak. 2023. Reproducing a comparative evaluation of german text-to-speech systems. In *Proceedings of the 3rd Workshop on Human Evaluation of NLP Systems*.

Takumi Ito, Qixiang Fang, Pablo Mosteiro, Albert Gatt, and Kees van Deemter. 2023. Challenges in reproducing human evaluation results for role-oriented dialogue summarization. In *Proceedings of the 3rd Workshop on Human Evaluation of NLP Systems*.

Filip Klubička and John D. Kelleher. 2023. Humeval'23 reproduction report for paper 0040: Human evaluation of automatically detected over- and undertranslations. In *Proceedings of the 3rd Workshop on Human Evaluation of NLP Systems*.

Yiru Li, Huiyuan Lai, Antonio Toral, and Malvina Nissim. 2023. Same trends, different answers: Insights from a replication study of human plausibility judgments on narrative continuations. In *Proceedings of the 3rd Workshop on Human Evaluation of NLP Systems*.

Haitao Lin, Liqun Ma, Junnan Zhu, Lu Xiang, Yu Zhou, Jiajun Zhang, and Chengqing Zong. 2021. Csds: A fine-grained chinese dataset for customer service dialogue summarization. *arXiv preprint arXiv:2108.13139*.

Haitao Lin, Junnan Zhu, Lu Xiang, Yu Zhou, Jiajun Zhang, and Chengqing Zong. 2022. Other roles matter! enhancing role-oriented dialogue summarization via role interactions. In *Proceedings of the 60th Annual Meeting of the Association for Computational Linguistics (Volume 1: Long Papers)*, pages 2545–2558, Dublin, Ireland. Association for Computational Linguistics.

Jordan J. Louviere, Terry N. Flynn, and A. A. J. Marley. 2015. *Best-Worst Scaling: Theory, Methods and Applications*. Cambridge University Press.

Florian Lux and Thang Vu. 2022. Language-agnostic meta-learning for low-resource text-to-speech with articulatory features. In *Proceedings of the 60th Annual Meeting of the Association for Computational Linguistics (Volume 1: Long Papers)*, pages 6858–6868, Dublin, Ireland. Association for Computational Linguistics.

Saad Mahamood. 2023. Reproduction of human evaluations in: 'it's not rocket science: Interpreting figurative language in narratives'. In *Proceedings of the 3rd Workshop on Human Evaluation of NLP Systems*.

Margot Mieskes and Jacob Georg Benz. 2023. h da@reprohum – reproduction of human evaluation and technical pipeline. In *Proceedings of the 3rd Workshop on Human Evaluation of NLP Systems*.

Emiel van Miltenburg, Anouck Braggaar, Nadine Braun, Martijn Goudbeek Debby Damen, Chris van der Lee, Frédéric Tomas, and Emiel Krahmer. 2023. How reproducible is best-worst scaling for human evaluation? a reproduction of 'data-to-text generation with macro planning. In *Proceedings of the 3rd Workshop on Human Evaluation of NLP Systems*.

Sergiu Nisioi, Sanja Štajner, Simone Paolo Ponzetto, and Liviu P. Dinu. 2017. Exploring neural text simplification models. In *Proceedings of the 55th Annual Meeting of the Association for Computational Linguistics (Volume 2: Short Papers)*, pages 85–91, Vancouver, Canada. Association for Computational Linguistics.

Ondřej Plátek, Mateusz Lango, and Ondřej Dušek. 2023. With a little help from the authors: Reproducing human evaluation of an mt error detector. In *Proceedings of the 3rd Workshop on Human Evaluation of NLP Systems*.

Ratish Puduppully and Mirella Lapata. 2021. Data-to-text generation with macro planning. *Transactions of the Association for Computational Linguistics*, 9:510–527.

Anastasia Shimorina and Anya Belz. 2022. The human evaluation datasheet: A template for recording details of human evaluation experiments in NLP. In *Proceedings of the 2nd Workshop on Human Evaluation of NLP Systems (HumEval)*, pages 54–75, Dublin, Ireland. Association for Computational Linguistics.

Craig Thomson, Ehud Reiter, and Barkavi Sundararajan. 2023. Evaluating factual accuracy in complex data-to-text. *Computer Speech & Language*, 80.

Jannis Vamvas and Rico Sennrich. 2022. As little as possible, as much as necessary: Detecting over- and undertranslations with contrastive conditioning. In *Proceedings of the 60th Annual Meeting of the Association for Computational Linguistics (Volume 2: Short Papers)*, pages 490–500, Dublin, Ireland. Association for Computational Linguistics.

Lewis Watson and Dimitra Gkatzia. 2023. Unveiling nlg human-evaluation reproducibility: Lessons learned and key insights from participating in the ReproNLP challenge. In *Proceedings of the 3rd Workshop on Human Evaluation of NLP Systems*.

Sam Wiseman, Stuart Shieber, and Alexander Rush. 2017. Challenges in data-to-document generation. In *Proceedings of the 2017 Conference on Empirical Methods in Natural Language Processing*, pages 2253–2263, Copenhagen, Denmark. Association for Computational Linguistics.

Some lessons learned reproducing human evaluation of a data-to-text system

Javier González-Corbelle, Jose M. Alonso-Moral, A. Bugarín-Diz
Centro Singular de Investigación en Tecnoloxías Intelixentes (CiTIUS),
Universidade de Santiago de Compostela, Spain
{j.gonzalez.corbelle,josemaria.alonso.moral,alberto.bugarin.diz}@usc.es

Abstract

This paper presents a human evaluation reproduction study regarding the data-to-text generation task. The evaluation focuses in counting the supported and contradicting facts generated by a neural data-to-text model with a macro planning stage. The model is tested generating sport summaries for the ROTOWIRE dataset. We first describe the approach to reproduction that is agreed in the context of the ReproHum project. Then, we detail the entire configuration of the original human evaluation and the adaptations that had to be made to reproduce such an evaluation. Finally, we compare the reproduction results with those reported in the paper that was taken as reference.

1 Introduction

An experiment or study is reproducible when independent researchers can replicate it by following the documentation shared in the original report and draw the same conclusions, which is also a clear synonym of reliability. In Natural Language Processing (NLP), reproducibility is not limited to specifying the parameters chosen to train a model, but it goes beyond that and requires the specification of all the details of the evaluation process by which the reported results are obtained. In NLP, until recently, not too much attention has been paid to the reproducibility of neither automatic nor human evaluations. In the case of automatic metrics, there is a reproducibility checklist (Pineau, 2020), but in the case of human evaluations not so much progress has been made.

In addition, some papers have been published about reproducibility in NLP, regarding reproducibility tests based on the fulfillment of certain properties in human evaluations (Belz et al., 2020) but also proposing a template for recording the details of human evaluations in NLP experiments, with the aim of improving the replicability of these processes (Shimorina and Belz, 2022).

The work presented in this paper is part of the ReproHum[1] project, that investigates the factors that make a human evaluation more reproducible in NLP by launching multi-lab sets of reproductions of human evaluations. As members of one of the 21 partner labs in this project, we performed a reproduction of an NLP study in which a data-to-text system is assessed and compare the results obtained in the reproduction with the original ones.

The rest of the manuscript is organised as follows. In section 2 we introduce related work and the common approach defined as a global requirement for all the reproducibility experiments within ReproHum project. Section 3 describes the reproduction of the NLP evaluation, first, explaining the content of the paper chosen for reproduction and then, explaining all the details of the evaluation that is going to be reproduced. In section 4, the results of the reproduced evaluation compared to the original paper are reported and discussed. Finally, section 5 concludes with final remarks and future work.

2 Background

In the context of the shared task REPROLANG (Branco et al., 2020) a replication of a human evaluation of a neural text simplification system by Nisioi et al. (2017) was performed (Cooper and Shardlow, 2020), obtaining worse results in the reproduction study, in terms of Grammaticality and Meaning Preservation.

With the aim of developing theory and practice of reproducibility assessment, the ReproGen shared task arose and in its two editions (Belz et al., 2021, 2022) several studies involving the reproduction of different experiments were carried out. Popović

[1] https://reprohum.github.io/

Proceedings of the Third Workshop on Human Evaluation of NLP Systems, pages 49–68, Varna, Bulgaria, Sep 7, 2023.
https://doi.org/10.26615/978-954-452-088-5_005

and Belz (2021) replicated an evaluation of Machine Translation outputs where errors related to comprehensibility and meaning correctness were annotated in texts by marking up word involved in an error (Popović, 2020). They found that 4 out of 6 system rankings were the same in both studies, but error rates for minor error types have lower reproducibility than those classified as major error types.

Mahamood (2021) reproduced human evaluations of data-to-text systems. Despite differences in the number and type of raters, authors found poor reproducibility when assessing the effect of hedges on preference judgments between native and fluent English speakers. Mille et al. (2021) faced the evaluation reproduction of a stance-expressing football report generator (van der Lee et al., 2017), finding good reproducibility for stance identification accuracy, but lower reproducibility for Clarity and Fluency.

In addition, it is worth noting that in the context of the ReproHum project, adhering to the following guidelines is mandatory when reproducing experiments:

1. You are allocated an experiment in a paper.
2. Go to the resources folder which is prepared adhoc for the experiment. This folder contains all the information you will need to reproduce the experiment.
3. Familiarise yourself with the experiment that was assigned for reproduction and all the resources provided in the public repositories or by the authors.
4. Plan for repeating the allocated experiment in a form that is as far as possible identical to the original experiment, ensuring you have all required resources, and apply to your research ethics committee for approval.
5. If participants were paid during the original experiment, follow the project procedure to recalculate a fair pay to the workers (regarding minimum wage, original study wage, and so on).
6. Ask for ethical approval and wait until the project team confirms the payment to the workers.
7. Complete the Human Evaluation Datasheet (HEDS, see appendix A) provided by the project team with all the details about how the repetition of the experiment is going to be carried out and share the HEDS with the project before launching the experiment.
8. Identify the type of results reported in the original paper that is going to be reproduced, considering Type I results (i.e., single numerical scores), Type II results (i.e., sets of numerical scores), Type III results (i.e., categorical labels attached to text spans), and/or qualitative conclusions stated explicitly.
9. Once the project team have validated your HEDS, carry out the experiment exactly as described in the HEDS.
10. Report the results in a paper describing the original experiment, any differences in your reproduction experiment, presentation of the results and conclusions in the original vs. reproduction experiment, and finally draw overall conclusions and share the HEDS in the appendix.

It must be noted that during all the reproduction process described above is not allowed to contact the authors of the original paper or communicate with other project labs carrying out this or any other reproduction experiment to avoid affecting the reported outcomes. Thus, all the information and resources provided should be in the common resources folder provided by the project team and in case of any question we were asked to only contact the ReproHum project managers who act as a proxy with the authors of the work to be reproduced.

3 Reproduction of an NLP evaluation

In this section we describe how we applied the ReproHum guidelines previously introduced. For the purpose of human evaluation reproduction, we were assigned the paper published by Puduppully and Lapata (2021). Based on the evaluation details described in the paper, the appendices, the resources available in the associated public repository, and the resources provided by the ReproHum managers after contacting the authors, we reproduced the evaluation as close as possible to the original one.

3.1 Paper for reproduction

As described above, our experiment consisted in performing a reproduction as accurate as possible of a human NLP evaluation. In the reference paper taken for reproduction, Puduppully and Lapata (2021) propose a neural model with a macro-planning stage followed by a generation stage reminiscent of traditional methods comprising separate modules for planning and surface realization. The proposed model (Macro) is tested with two datasets for data-to-text from the sports field: ROTOWIRE (Wiseman et al., 2017) and MLB (Puduppully et al., 2019). The former consists of a dataset composed of tables with NBA basketball game statistics, aligned with summaries describing such data; while the later maintains the same format, but the data are about MLB baseball games. Therefore, the task of the generation model is, from the data tables, to generate sports summaries describing the game statistics.

To demonstrate that Macro improves the results of other architectures for data-to-text generation, they make a comparison against different systems, applying both automatic and human evaluation on the system outputs. On the one hand, the metrics used to automatically evaluate the texts generated by the different models are BLEU, and the set of Information Extraction (IE) metrics proposed in (Wiseman et al., 2017) to evaluate the relation generation (RG), content selection (CS) and content ordering (CO) stages of the systems. On the other hand, in terms of human evaluation, two experiments using the Amazon Mechanical Turk (AMT) crowd-sourcing platform were performed. First, the quality of the generated texts was evaluated in terms of grammar, coherence and conciseness. Second, quantifying how many of the facts mentioned in the generated texts supported or contradicted the data in the box score, i.e., the table provided as input to the system.

We reproduced the first experiment for the ROTOWIRE dataset, so all the details that will be mentioned in the following sections will be about this evaluation task, i.e., the count of supported/contradicting facts in automatic generation of NBA summaries.

3.2 Evaluation details & Changes

In the human evaluation of supported/contradicting facts, the following baseline systems were compared against the proposed Macro model (Puduppully and Lapata, 2021): (1) Templ, a template-based generator from (Wiseman et al., 2017) for ROTOWIRE; (2) ED+CC, a vanilla encoder-decoder model with an attention and copy mechanism (Wiseman et al., 2017); (3) RBF-2020 (Rebuffel et al., 2020), a Transformer encoder model, with a hierarchical attention mechanism over entities and records within entities, which represents the state of the art on ROTOWIRE dataset. In addition, the gold summaries were also included for comparison, i.e., summaries from the dataset.

Twenty summaries from the tested dataset (i.e., ROTOWIRE) were selected, which gave us a total of 100 summaries generated by the 5 different systems (including the gold summaries). For each summary, using the AMT platform, 3 different evaluators performed the task of counting the supported/contradicting facts on the texts, which yielded a total of 300 HITs (Human Intelligence Tasks). Each evaluator was presented a questionnaire with sentences randomly selected from one of the summaries under consideration along with their corresponding box scores. Then, he/she was asked to count the facts that support and contradict the data (ignoring hallucinations, i.e., unsupported facts).

To carry out the evaluation, the AMT crowd-sourcing tool was used. In order to ensure a minimum quality of the results, only crowd-workers with a minimum of 1,000 previously completed HITs were allowed to take part in the experiment. Furthermore, quality of work requirements were stated, such as only workers with an approval rate greater than 98% in the platform and from English-speaking countries (i.e., US, UK, Canada, Ireland, Australia, or NZ) were admitted.

All the details mentioned so far would allow us to perform an approximate reproduction of the evaluation, yet not as detailed as we aim in this work. We are aware that the general trend in the NLP field when writing a paper is to focus more on the analysis of the results than on exhaustively detailing the evaluation process. This is normal due to the strict length limit of papers. However, we wanted to make a faithful reproduction of the evaluation, so we asked the ReproHum project managers to contact the authors of the paper to obtain extra details on how to carry out the evaluation. They kindly replied to all the questions with full transparency and accordingly we received extra resources to carry out an evaluation as close as possible to the original one.

Regarding the way in which the questions or HITs were shown to the workers, a box score along with 4 sentences extracted from a longer system generated summary were shown in each of the HITs. These sentences could belong to any of the 5 systems that were compared in the evaluation. Thus, for each of the 4 sentences, the worker had to count the number of contradicting and supported facts with respect to the box score and indicate it by means of a dropdown menu in a range from 0 to 20. It must be noted that all the sentences used in the evaluation were provided in a .csv file, together with the corresponding HTML template of the questionnaire for each of the HITs. This way, the format of the survey and also the sentences evaluated were exactly the same as in the original paper. In figure 1 we show an example of a HIT with the already mentioned dropdowns to fill the count of supported/contradicting facts.

In AMT the tasks must be published in batches, so we followed the same strategy as the original study to publish the different batches in which the tasks were splitted. Each dataset was divided into 4 mini-batches, i.e., taking into account the ROTOWIRE dataset, we had 100 different HITs to evaluate, so there were 4 mini-batches of 25 HITs size. The order in which the mini-batches, HITs and sentences inside each HIT were presented was the same as in the original experiment. Each posted HIT had to be completed by 3 different evaluators and there were no restrictions on the maximum number of different HITs that an evaluator could perform. Therefore, the number of unique evaluators at the end of the experiment was variable depending on how many HITs each worker had decided to complete.

After the completion of each mini-batch and before publishing the next one, certain conditions had to be checked. Answers in which the sum of contradicting and supported facts was equal to or greater than 20 must be excluded. This is because none of the sentences under evaluation had so many contradicting + supported facts.

At the end of each mini-batch the following procedure was applied:

1. Compute *FC* as the total number of facts (contradicting + supported), given by the crowd-worker for each sentence (see figure 1).

2. If $FC \geq 20$:

   2.1 The response should be excluded from the final results and a replacement HIT posted on AMT. To do this, use custom qualifications to ensure a crowd-worker who has already done this HIT, is not assigned it again.

   2.2 This crowd-worker should be prevented from doing any future task (using custom qualifications).

   2.3 Keep records of both the original response and the repeated response, but mark the final one that passed the check, so that it can be included in the final results (it is possible for the HIT to be repeated multiple times before one crowd-worker finally passes the check and that response is marked as valid for inclusion in the final results).

   2.4 Still pay the crowd-workers even if $FC \geq 20$, accept their work but exclude them from future tasks. This way their reputation in the platform is not affected.

3. If *FC* for every sentence from the set of 4 within a HIT is < 20, the response is valid. This HIT must be marked for inclusion in the final results.

4. Once there are valid responses for the complete mini-batch, move to the next one.

We set the HIT expiration time the same as in the original study: each crowd-worker had 7 days to perform the task once accepted before sending it without completing it.

It is worth noting that we had to set some AMT settings which were not defined in the original study. Namely, the time limit to complete the task once started was determined empirically by us. Performing several tests with people performing the task for the first time, we estimated that 4 min was the average time to complete the HIT, however we set the maximum time allotted per crowd-worker to 4h, just to ensure that no crowd-worker ran out of time. In addition, regarding the pay-per-task to crowd-workers, we had the information of the approximated payment per task in the original study, but according to the project common approach for reproduction presented in section 2, we recalculated this payment following the procedure to calculate a fair payment (see appendix B). We adjusted the payment to the current minimum wage conditions, taking as reference the UK minimum living wage per hour, that was GBP10.90 in the date of the experiment. Considering that each

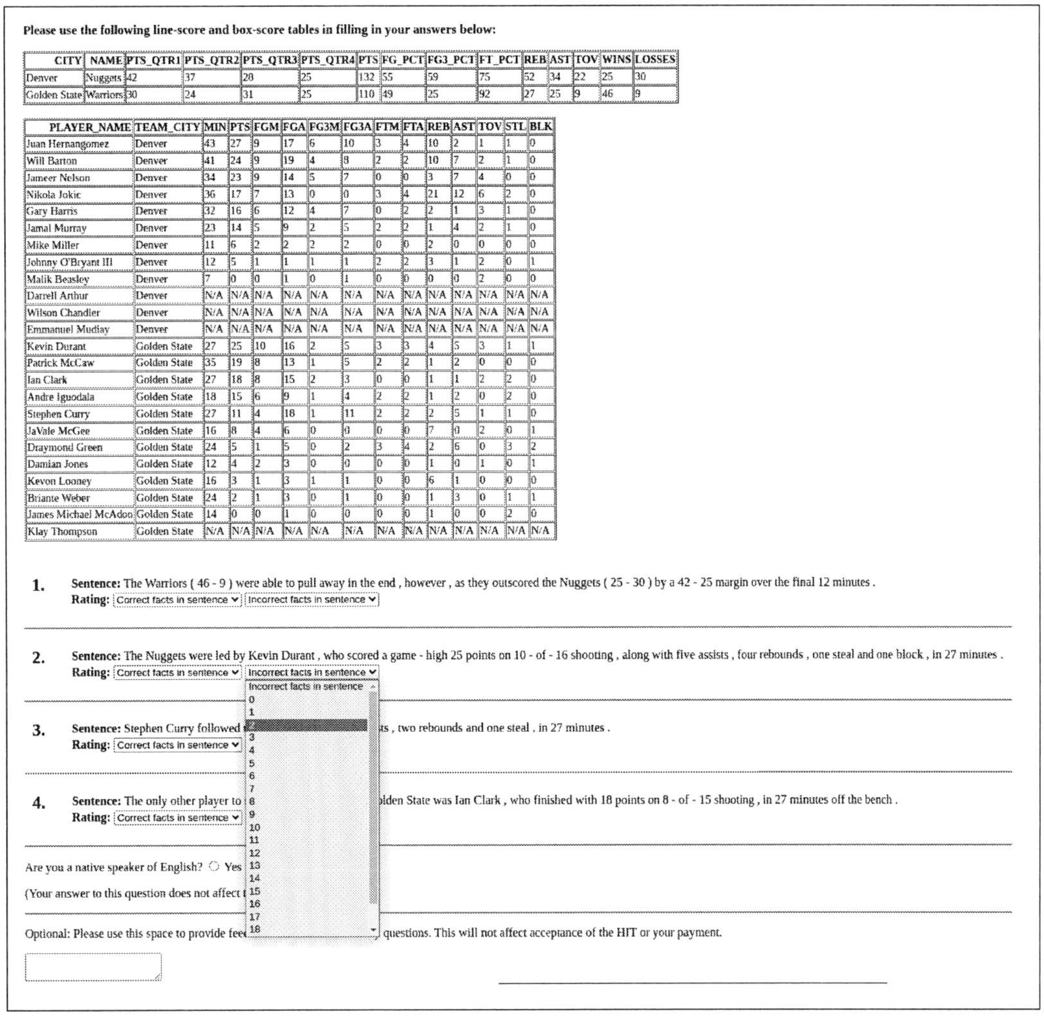

Please use the following line-score and box-score tables in filling in your answers below:

CITY	NAME	PTS_QTR1	PTS_QTR2	PTS_QTR3	PTS_QTR4	PTS	FG_PCT	FG3_PCT	FT_PCT	REB	AST	TOV	WINS	LOSSES
Denver	Nuggets	42	37	28	25	132	55	59	75	52	34	22	25	30
Golden State	Warriors	30	24	31	25	110	49	25	92	27	25	9	46	9

PLAYER_NAME	TEAM_CITY	MIN	PTS	FGM	FGA	FG3M	FG3A	FTM	FTA	REB	AST	TOV	STL	BLK
Juan Hernangomez	Denver	43	27	9	17	6	10	3	4	10	2	1	1	0
Will Barton	Denver	41	24	9	19	4	8	2	2	10	7	2	1	0
Jameer Nelson	Denver	34	23	9	14	5	7	0	0	3	7	4	0	0
Nikola Jokic	Denver	36	17	7	13	0	0	3	4	21	12	6	2	0
Gary Harris	Denver	32	16	6	12	4	7	0	2	2	1	3	1	0
Jamal Murray	Denver	23	14	5	9	2	5	2	2	1	4	2	1	0
Mike Miller	Denver	11	6	2	2	2	2	0	0	2	0	0	0	0
Johnny O'Bryant III	Denver	12	5	1	1	1	1	2	2	3	1	2	0	1
Malik Beasley	Denver	7	0	0	1	0	1	0	0	0	0	2	0	0
Darrell Arthur	Denver	N/A	N/A	N/A	N/A	N/A	N/A	N/A	N/A	N/A	N/A	N/A	N/A	N/A
Wilson Chandler	Denver	N/A	N/A	N/A	N/A	N/A	N/A	N/A	N/A	N/A	N/A	N/A	N/A	N/A
Emmanuel Mudiay	Denver	N/A	N/A	N/A	N/A	N/A	N/A	N/A	N/A	N/A	N/A	N/A	N/A	N/A
Kevin Durant	Golden State	27	25	10	16	2	5	3	3	4	5	3	1	1
Patrick McCaw	Golden State	35	19	8	13	1	5	2	2	1	2	0	0	0
Ian Clark	Golden State	27	18	8	15	2	3	0	0	1	1	2	2	0
Andre Iguodala	Golden State	18	15	6	9	1	4	2	2	1	2	0	2	0
Stephen Curry	Golden State	27	11	4	18	1	11	2	2	2	5	1	1	0
JaVale McGee	Golden State	16	8	4	6	0	0	0	0	7	0	2	0	1
Draymond Green	Golden State	24	5	1	5	0	2	3	4	2	6	0	3	2
Damian Jones	Golden State	12	4	2	3	0	0	0	0	1	0	1	0	1
Kevon Looney	Golden State	16	3	1	3	1	1	0	0	6	1	0	0	0
Briante Weber	Golden State	24	2	1	3	0	1	0	0	1	3	0	1	1
James Michael McAdoo	Golden State	14	0	0	1	0	0	0	0	1	0	0	2	0
Klay Thompson	Golden State	N/A	N/A	N/A	N/A	N/A	N/A	N/A	N/A	N/A	N/A	N/A	N/A	N/A

1. **Sentence:** The Warriors (46 - 9) were able to pull away in the end , however , as they outscored the Nuggets (25 - 30) by a 42 - 25 margin over the final 12 minutes .
Rating: Correct facts in sentence Incorrect facts in sentence

2. **Sentence:** The Nuggets were led by Kevin Durant , who scored a game - high 25 points on 10 - of - 16 shooting , along with five assists , four rebounds , one steal and one block , in 27 minutes .
Rating: Correct facts in sentence Incorrect facts in sentence

Incorrect facts in sentence
0
1
2
3
4
5
6
7
8
9
10
11
12
13
14
15
16
17
18

3. **Sentence:** Stephen Curry followed ts , two rebounds and one steal , in 27 minutes .
Rating: Correct facts in sentence

4. **Sentence:** The only other player to lden State was Ian Clark , who finished with 18 points on 8 - of - 15 shooting , in 27 minutes off the bench .
Rating: Correct facts in sentence

Are you a native speaker of English? Yes

(Your answer to this question does not affect t

Optional: Please use this space to provide fee questions. This will not affect acceptance of the HIT or your payment.

Figure 1: Example of a HIT from the survey. By checking the box score, evaluators must count how many correct/incorrect (i.e., supported/contradicting) facts are mentioned in each of the 4 sentences. Dropdowns allow to choose a value between 0 and 20 for each answer.

task takes about 4 minutes, a crowd-worker can do 15 tasks per hour, so the payment per HIT was set to GBP10.9/15 = GBP0.726 (i.e., 0.88USD = 0.80EUR) per completed task.

Finally, authors shared with the ReproHum project managers the script they used to process the results obtained from the evaluation. Given a file with the responses obtained from AMT, the mean of the scores for each system is automatically calculated and then tested by one-way ANOVA analysis of variance with Tukey posthoc to see if the results obtained for the baseline models and gold summaries show significant differences with respect to the Macro system that is evaluated.

4 Results

The evaluation process was organized in the above-mentioned 4 mini-batches to complete the total 300 tasks. Following the procedure explained in section 3.2, we had to repeat 59 HITs in order to obtain 300 valid responses. At the end, a total of 144 different crowd-workers participated in the evaluation. Notice that, in the original paper it is reported a total of 131 crowd-workers participating in the study, but for 600 tasks instead of 300, i.e., for both the ROTOWIRE and MLB datasets. Since we reproduced the experiment with the ROTOWIRE dataset, the number of unique participants is quite high, considering that we requested half of the HITs.

Furthermore, in the original paper it is reported

Table 1: Average number of Supported (#Supp) and Contradicting (#Contra) facts in game summaries for ROTOWIRE dataset, both for the original evaluation and the reproduction experiment (original results are extracted from Table 5 in Puduppully and Lapata (2021)). CV* column indicates the unbiased coefficient of variation of the reproduction scores for each system, computed following the method explained in Belz (2022). Systems significantly different from Macro are marked with an asterisk * (using one-way ANOVA with posthoc Tukey HSD tests; $p \leq 0.05$)

	Original		Reproduction			
	#Supp	#Contra	#Supp	CV*	#Contra	CV*
gold	3.63	0.07	3.36	52.17	0.66	175.7
Templ	7.57*	0.08	6.27*	42.86	0.90	234.26
ED+CC	3.92	0.91*	4.42	39.64	1.95*	119.23
RBF-2020	5.08*	0.67*	4.31	41.37	1.22	161.79
Macro	4.00	0.27	4.08	30.73	0.55	205.31

an inter annotator agreement of 0.44 for supported and 0.42 for contradicting facts, using Krippendorff's α. Of course, these values are calculated for the 600 tasks performed for both datasets, and the total of 131 crowd-workers. We calculated the same agreement measure, by adding the number of supported/contradicitng facts of each task, i.e., by adding the count of each of the four sentences in the HIT to have two scores per HIT: contradicting and supported facts scores. The results gave us an agreement of 0.188 for supported and 0.219 for contradicting facts. Therefore, the agreement in our evaluation is lower than in the original one, although we must take into account that the number of tasks and unique evaluators is different in our reproduction experiment, so a direct comparison is not really fair.

Looking at the original scores shown in Table 1 and as it is stated by Puduppully and Lapata (2021), the number of supported facts for Macro is comparable to gold and ED+CC (not statistically significant differences), but significantly smaller than Templ and RBF-2020. On the other hand, regarding the count of contradicting facts, Macro yields the smallest number among neural models. The number of contradicting facts for Macro is comparable to gold and Templ and significantly smaller than RBF-2020 and ED+CC.

Contrasting the original vs. reproduction results, we can see that for the Macro supported facts the score only differs in 0.08, but in the rest of the compared systems it differs more from the original study, reaching the largest difference in the Templ system (1.3, i.e., a 17% less supported facts in average). Comparing the results of the reproduction for the Macro supported facts with respect to the rest of the systems, Macro obtains significantly smaller values only with respect to the Templ system, while in the original study it is also significantly smaller compared with the RBF-2020 system.

Regarding the contradicting facts, for all the systems the reproduction scores are higher than in the original experiment, being the ED+CC system which yields the largest difference, with a 0.91 of counted contradicting facts in the original paper against a 1.95 in the reproduction experiment (i.e., an increase of the 114%). Surprisingly, the Macro system achieves the lowest score in terms of contradicting facts in our reproduction experiment, while in the original experiment the Templ system had the best performance. Looking at Macro results against the other systems, we can say that Macro achieves only significantly lower scores respect to the ED+CC system, whilst in the original experiment also significantly differences with the RBF-2020 were concluded.

It must be noted that if we pay attention to the unbiased coefficient of variation (CV*) in table 1, there is a big difference between the scores of the supported and contradicting facts. While CV* for supported facts is more stable, ranging from 30.73 to 52.17, the CV* for contradicting facts shows higher values, ranging from 119.23 to 234.26. It denotes a higher level of dispersion around the mean in the scores for contradicting facts.

After analyzing the results shown in Table 1, we can say that the general tendency observed from the reproduction results is similar to that of the results reported in the original study, despite differences in the score values. Table 2 summarizes the main differences between the conclusions obtained in the original experiment vs. those of our reproduction experiment. On the one hand, regarding supported facts, the scores are not very different from those of the original study. Comparing the Macro system with the rest of the systems evaluated, in the original paper the results achieved by the Macro system are comparable with gold and ED+CC system (the difference is not statistically significant), and significantly lower than Templ and RBF-2020 systems. In the reproduction experiment, it is concluded that Macro is comparable to gold, ED+CC, and RBF-2020, while only significantly lower scores are reported with respect to the Templ system. Thus, the tendency observed for supported facts is similar to the original study,

Table 2: Comparison of the conclusions from the original experiment by Puduppully and Lapata (2021) and our reproduction experiment, regarding the Macro system performance. For each type of facts checked, i.e., supported or contradicting, it is indicated with respect to which systems the Macro model is comparable or, on the contrary, obtains significantly lower scores.

Original	**Reproduction**
Supported	*Supported*
Comparable to gold and ED+CC	Comparable to gold, ED+CC, and RBF-2020
Sign. lower than Templ and RBF-2020	Sign. lower than Templ
Contradicting	*Contradicting*
Comparable to gold and Templ	Comparable to Templ, gold, and RBF-2020
Sign. lower than ED+CC and RBF-2020	Sign. lower than ED+CC

except for the RBF-2020, which in the reproduction experiment is comparable to the Macro system, instead of being statistically different.

On the other hand, if we look at the contradicting facts, the original study concluded that Macro results were comparable to gold and Templ, but significant differences were detected only with respect to ED+CC and RBF-2020. In the reproduction experiment, only significantly smaller scores are reported for ED+CC, whereas RBF-2020, Templ and gold yield results which are comparable to Macro. As in the case of the supported facts, the observed tendency is similar in the reproduction and original experiments, but now only significant differences are concluded in one of the two systems for which significant differences were detected in the original study.

This analysis of the scores allows us to say that in terms of supported facts, the reproduction study reports slightly better results for Macro than the original study. Furthermore, compared to the baseline systems, in the reproduction experiment only significantly smaller scores are obtained compared with one of the systems (i.e., Templ), which means that the amount of supported facts generated by Macro is comparable to more systems than in the original study. In terms of contradicting facts, the situation is the opposite. Despite a general increase in the number of contradicting facts for all the systems, only significantly smaller scores are reported with respect to one of the systems (i.e., ED+CC), while in the original study Macro generated significantly less contradicting facts than two other systems. As less generated contradicting facts is better, in this case the results can be considered slightly worse than in the original study.

5 Concluding Remarks and Future Work

In this work we performed a reproduction experiment of a human evaluation in NLP. Following the work by Puduppully and Lapata (2021), in the reproduced evaluation, a data-to-text system with a macro planning stage (Macro) is assessed in terms of contradicting/supported facts generated in the sports domain, i.e., ROTOWIRE dataset.

When counting the supported facts of the different systems, there is not a clear change pattern in the reproduction scores respect to the original ones. All of the scores are slightly different from the original ones, whether higher or lower. But, considering that having more supported facts is better, the Macro system shows a mildly improvement in the reproduction study in terms of score and also obtaining less statistically significant smaller scores with respect to the rest of systems in the comparison. Despite of that, the Templ system (Wiseman et al., 2017) is still the best in terms of supported facts, mainly because, as it is also pointed in the original paper for reproduction, the system essentially parrot facts.

Regarding the count of contradicting facts, there is a clear increase in general for all the systems and, surprisingly the system with the smallest number of contradicting facts is the Macro system, instead of the Templ system which was the best system in the original study. However, the Macro system produces statistically significant smaller scores only with respect to the ED+CC system.

The reproduction results show a similar tendency regarding supported facts, where the Templ system still produces the bigger number of supported facts. However, the tendency changes regarding contradicting facts. In addition to the general increase of contradicting facts, Templ and gold summaries, which were the baselines with the less contradicting facts, are outperformed by Macro, being the model with the less contradicting facts generated.

There are certain factors in human evaluation that cause the results of a reproduction study, despite replicating all the settings, not to be exactly the same as those reported in the original study. One of the most distinguishing factors are the evaluators. In this case, the same AMT crowd-worker requirements were applied to select a profile of workers in the crowd-sourcing platform equal to that of the original study, but they will never be the same evaluators. Moreover, a different number of evaluators have participated than in the original study, since they could choose how many tasks to perform freely. This is obviously one of the reasons why a reproduction of a human evaluation can lead to a difference in the results.

In connection to the AMT crowd-worker requirements, the following experience with a worker from the platform is worth to be mentioned here. As mentioned in the section 3.2, following the original evaluation settings we indicated as a requirement to perform our task to have a minimum of 1,000 HITs completed. A few hours after launching the first mini-batch of the experiment, we received a message in which an experienced AMT crowd-worker welcomed us to the platform and very kindly told us the following: "If this is your first batch posted here, welcome to Mturk! Just a heads up, posting work with insufficient qualifications tends to yield some terrible results. I'd suggest making the qualifications 10,000 approved HITs". Since this was a reproducibility experiment, we had to stick to the conditions specified in the original paper and kept the minimum number of HITs at 1,000. Anyways, this advice is worth to be mentioned here for consideration in future experiments. Having seen that some of the results of the replicated experiment differed from the original, and that the agreement between the raters was poor, we believe that the minimum number of HITs required may have had an influence. When the original evaluation was launched (in 2021) this requirement was probably enough to achieve good results in the platform, but currently, as the worker recommended, probably we should increase the minimum number of required HITs to 10,000 in order to get equivalent results to those reported by Puduppully and Lapata (2021).

Taking advantage of the fact that this worker had contacted us, we asked him/her about a special qualification granted in AMT that we were curious about, despite not being used in our experiment: the so-called "Masters qualification". On the official AMT website there is no clear information about the requirements that crowd-workers must meet to obtain this qualification and what it exactly means, so we asked the worker what he/she knew about it and the worker told us that AMT is notoriously tight-lipped about the Masters qualification and even the workers of the platform do not know what is the criteria for granting this type of qualification. This fact made us think about the platform's lack of transparency even with workers and why sometimes AMT has bad reputation, despite being a powerful tool that so many people use.

In the light of these findings, this reproduction study emphasizes the critical importance of providing comprehensive details about human evaluations in NLP. The standarization of reporting practices for human evaluations by tools such as the Human Evaluation Datasheet (HEDS) in the framework of a common approach for reproduction, increases the reproducibility and, therefore reliability of any work. Thus, we encourage researchers to further document their NLP evaluations using these standards, with the aim of enhancing the quality of the works in the field.

As future work, we plan to repeat the evaluation for the MLB dataset with the aim of checking if reported results differ in a similar way as observed in the ROTOWIRE dataset. Also, we would like to reproduce the other human evaluation reported in the original paper, i.e., the quality of the generated texts in terms of grammar, conciseness and coherence, by comparing pairs of summaries.

Acknowledgments

This research was funded by MCIN/AEI/10.13039/501100011033 (grants PID2020-112623GB-I00, PID2021-123152OB-C21 and TED2021-130295B-C33), the Galician Ministry of Culture, Education, Professional Training, and University (grants ED431C2022/19 and ED431G2019/04). All grants were co-funded by the European Regional Development Fund (ERDF/FEDER program). It was also funded by the Univ. de Santiago de Compostela, Xunta de Galicia, and Spanish Ministry for Economic Affairs and Digital Transformation through the Nós (Ref. 2021-CP081) and ILENIA projects.

References

Anya Belz. 2022. A metrological perspective on reproducibility in NLP*. *Computational Linguistics*, 48(4):1125–1135.

Anya Belz, Simon Mille, and David M. Howcroft. 2020. Disentangling the properties of human evaluation methods: A classification system to support comparability, meta-evaluation and reproducibility testing. In *Proceedings of the 13th International Conference on Natural Language Generation*, pages 183–194, Dublin, Ireland. Association for Computational Linguistics.

Anya Belz, Anastasia Shimorina, Shubham Agarwal, and Ehud Reiter. 2021. The ReproGen shared task on reproducibility of human evaluations in NLG: Overview and results. In *Proceedings of the 14th International Conference on Natural Language Generation*, pages 249–258, Aberdeen, Scotland, UK. Association for Computational Linguistics.

Anya Belz, Anastasia Shimorina, Maja Popović, and Ehud Reiter. 2022. The 2022 ReproGen shared task on reproducibility of evaluations in NLG: Overview and results. In *Proceedings of the 15th International Conference on Natural Language Generation: Generation Challenges*, pages 43–51, Waterville, Maine, USA and virtual meeting. Association for Computational Linguistics.

António Branco, Nicoletta Calzolari, Piek Vossen, Gertjan Van Noord, Dieter van Uytvanck, João Silva, Luís Gomes, André Moreira, and Willem Elbers. 2020. A shared task of a new, collaborative type to foster reproducibility: A first exercise in the area of language science and technology with REPROLANG2020. In *Proceedings of the Twelfth Language Resources and Evaluation Conference*, pages 5539–5545, Marseille, France. European Language Resources Association.

Michael Cooper and Matthew Shardlow. 2020. CombiNMT: An exploration into neural text simplification models. In *Proceedings of the Twelfth Language Resources and Evaluation Conference*, pages 5588–5594, Marseille, France. European Language Resources Association.

Chris van der Lee, Emiel Krahmer, and Sander Wubben. 2017. PASS: A Dutch data-to-text system for soccer, targeted towards specific audiences. In *Proceedings of the 10th International Conference on Natural Language Generation*, pages 95–104, Santiago de Compostela, Spain. Association for Computational Linguistics.

Saad Mahamood. 2021. Reproducing a comparison of hedged and non-hedged NLG texts. In *Proceedings of the 14th International Conference on Natural Language Generation*, pages 282–285, Aberdeen, Scotland, UK. Association for Computational Linguistics.

Simon Mille, Thiago Castro Ferreira, Anya Belz, and Brian Davis. 2021. Another PASS: A reproduction study of the human evaluation of a football report generation system. In *Proceedings of the 14th International Conference on Natural Language Generation*, pages 286–292, Aberdeen, Scotland, UK. Association for Computational Linguistics.

Sergiu Nisioi, Sanja Štajner, Simone Paolo Ponzetto, and Liviu P. Dinu. 2017. Exploring neural text simplification models. In *Proceedings of the 55th Annual Meeting of the Association for Computational Linguistics (Volume 2: Short Papers)*, pages 85–91, Vancouver, Canada. Association for Computational Linguistics.

Joelle Pineau. 2020. The machine learning reproducibility checklist v2.0.

Maja Popović. 2020. Informative manual evaluation of machine translation output. In *Proceedings of the 28th International Conference on Computational Linguistics*, pages 5059–5069, Barcelona, Spain (Online). International Committee on Computational Linguistics.

Maja Popović and Anya Belz. 2021. A reproduction study of an annotation-based human evaluation of MT outputs. In *Proceedings of the 14th International Conference on Natural Language Generation*, pages 293–300, Aberdeen, Scotland, UK. Association for Computational Linguistics.

Ratish Puduppully, Li Dong, and Mirella Lapata. 2019. Data-to-text generation with entity modeling. In *Proceedings of the 57th Annual Meeting of the Association for Computational Linguistics*, pages 2023–2035, Florence, Italy. Association for Computational Linguistics.

Ratish Puduppully and Mirella Lapata. 2021. Data-to-text generation with macro planning. *Transactions of the Association for Computational Linguistics*, 9:510–527.

Clément Rebuffel, Laure Soulier, Geoffrey Scoutheeten, and Patrick Gallinari. 2020. A hierarchical model for data-to-text generation. In *Advances in Information Retrieval*, pages 65–80, Cham. Springer International Publishing.

Anastasia Shimorina and Anya Belz. 2022. The human evaluation datasheet: A template for recording details of human evaluation experiments in NLP. In *Proceedings of the 2nd Workshop on Human Evaluation of NLP Systems (HumEval)*, pages 54–75, Dublin, Ireland. Association for Computational Linguistics.

Sam Wiseman, Stuart Shieber, and Alexander Rush. 2017. Challenges in data-to-document generation. In *Proceedings of the 2017 Conference on Empirical Methods in Natural Language Processing*, pages 2253–2263, Copenhagen, Denmark. Association for Computational Linguistics.

Appendices

A Human Evaluation Datasheet (HEDS)

Here we provide an adapted version of the HEDS that shows all the preregistration details of the experiment. A copy of the original HEDS .json file and all the additional files mentioned below to reproduce the experiment are also shared as supplementary material in the submission of the paper.

Section 1: Paper and supplementary resources

Sections 1.1–1.3 record bibliographic and related information. These are straightforward and don't warrant much in-depth explanation.

Section 1.1: Details of paper reporting the evaluation experiment

Question 1.1.1: Link to paper reporting the evaluation experiment. Enter a link to an online copy of the the main reference (e.g., a paper) for the human evaluation experiment. If the experiment hasn't been run yet, and the form is being completed for the purpose of submitting it for preregistration, simply enter 'for preregistration'.
Answer: For preregistration.

Question 1.1.2: Which experiment within the paper is this form being completed for? Enter details of the experiment within the paper for which this sheet is being completed. For example, the title of the experiment and/or a section number. If there is only one human human evaluation, still enter the same information. If this is form is being completed for pre-registration, enter a note that differetiates this experiment from any others that you are carrying out as part of the same overall work.
Answer: This form is being completed to reproduce the human-based evaluation from the Section 6 of the paper "Data-to-text Generation with Macro Planning" available at `https://arxiv.org/abs/2102.02723`. Namely, we pay attention here only to the first study, that is "the count of supported and contradicting facts on the generated texts".

Section 1.2: Link to resources

Question 1.2.1: Link(s) to website(s) providing resources used in the evaluation experiment.Enter the link(s). Such resources include system outputs, evaluation tools, etc. If there aren't any publicly shared resources (yet), enter 'N/A'.
Answer: There is a public github repository in the arxiv paper, in which you can find the models and datasets (`https://github.com/ratishsp/data2text-macro-plan-py`) and the authors also provided by email a repository with the files needed to reproduce the evaluation (`https://github.com/ratishsp/data2text-human-evaluation`). All the material used to reproduce the evaluation and the details of the procedure will be available at `https://drive.google.com/drive/folders/1ZySFzvZh-_2H8iJlBrkemG-9bJOCFSFH?usp=sharing`

Section 1.3: Contact details

This section records the name, affiliation, and email address of person completing this sheet, and of the contact author if different.

Section 1.3.1: Details of the person completing this sheet.

Question 1.3.1.1: Name of the person completing this sheet.
Answer: Javier González Corbelle, Jose María Alonso Moral

Question 1.3.1.2: Affiliation of the person completing this sheet.
Answer: Universidade de Santiago de Compostela, Spain

Question 1.3.1.3: Email address of the person completing this sheet.
Answer: j.gonzalez.corbelle@usc.es, josemaria.alonso.moral@usc.es

Section 1.3.2: Details of the contact author

Question 1.3.2.1: Name of the contact author. Enter the name of the contact author, enter N/A if it is the same person as in Question 1.3.1.1
Answer: N/A

Question 1.3.2.2: Affiliation of the contact author. Enter the affiliation of the contact author, enter N/A if it is the same person as in Question 1.3.1.2
Answer: N/A

Question 1.3.2.3: Email address of the contact author. Enter the email address of the contact author,

enter N/A if it is the same person as in Question 1.3.1.3
Answer: N/A

Section 2: System Questions

Questions 2.1–2.5 record information about the system(s) (or human-authored stand-ins) whose outputs are evaluated in the Evaluation experiment that this sheet is being completed for. The input, output, and task questions in this section are closely interrelated: the value for one partially determines the others,as indicated for some combinations in Question 2.3.
Question 2.1: What type of input do the evaluated system(s) take?
This question is about the type(s) of input, where input refers to the representations and/or data structures shared by all evaluated systems. This question is about input type, regardless of number. E.g. if the input is a set of documents, you would still select text: document below. Select all that apply. If none match, select 'other' and describe.

1. **raw/structured data**
2. deep linguistic representation (DLR)
3. shallow linguistic representation (SLR)
4. text: subsentential unit of text
5. text: sentence
6. text: multiple sentences
7. text: document
8. text: dialogue
9. text: other (please describe)
10. speech
11. visual
12. multi-modal
13. control feature
14. no input (human generation)
15. other (please describe)

Please describe:
Please provide further details for your above selection(s)
Question 2.2: What type of output do the evaluated system(s) generate? This question is about the type(s) of output, where output refers to the and/or data structures shared by all evaluated systems. This question is about output type, regardless of number. E.g. if the output is a set of documents, you would still select *text: document* below. Note that the options for outputs are the same as for inputs except that the *no input (human generation) option* is replaced with *human-generated 'outputs'*, and the *control feature* option is removed. Select all that apply. If none match, select 'other' and describe.

1. raw/structured data
2. deep linguistic representation (DLR)
3. Shallow linguistic representation (SLR)
4. text: subsentential unit of text
5. text: sentence
6. **text: multiple sentences**
7. text: document
8. text: dialogue
9. text: other (please describe)
10. speech
11. visual
12. multi-modal
13. human generated 'outputs'
14. other (please describe)

Please describe:
Please provide further details for your above selection(s)
Question 2.3: How would you describe the task that the evaluated system(s) perform in mapping the inputs in Q2.1 to the outputs in Q2.2? This question is about the task(s) performed by the system(s) being evaluated. This is independent of the application domain (financial reporting, weather forecasting, etc.), or the specific method (rule-based, neural, etc.) implemented in the system. We indicate mutual constraints between inputs, outputs and task for some of the options below. Occasionally, more than one of the options below may apply. Select all that apply. If none match, select 'other' and describe.

1. content selection/determination
2. content ordering/structuring
3. aggregation
4. referring expression generation
5. lexicalisation
6. deep generation
7. surface realisation (SLR to text)
8. feature-controlled text generation
9. **data-to-text generation**
10. dialogue turn generation
11. question generation
12. question answering
13. paraphrasing/lossless simplification

14. compression/lossy simplification
15. machine translation
16. summarisation (text-to-text)
17. end-to-end text generation
18. image/video description
19. post-editing/correction
20. other (please describe)

Please describe:
Please provide further details for your above selection(s)
Question 2.4: What are the input languages that are used by the system? This question is about the language(s) of the inputs accepted by the system(s) being evaluated. Select any language name(s) that apply, mapped to standardised full language names in ISO 639-1 (2019). E.g. English, Herero, Hindi. If no language is accepted as (part of) the input, select 'N/A'. Select all that apply. If any languages you are using are not covered by this list, select 'other' and describe.

1. Abkhazian
2. Afar
...
41. English
...
185. N/A (please describe)

Please describe:
Please provide further details for your above selection(s)
Question 2.5: What are the output languages that are used by the system? This field question the language(s) of the outputs generated by the system(s) being evaluated. Select any language name(s) that apply, mapped to standardised full language names in ISO 639-1 (2019). E.g. English, Herero, Hindi. If no language is generated, select 'N/A'.Select all that apply. If any languages you are using are not covered by this list, select 'other' and describe.

1. Abkhazian
2. Afar
...
41. English
...
185. N/A (please describe)

Please describe:
Please provide further details for your above selection(s)

Section 3: Sample of system outputs, evaluators, and experimental design

Section 3.1: Sample of system outputs

Questions 3.1.1–3.1.3 record information about the size of the sample of outputs (or human-authored stand-ins) evaluated per system, how the sample was selected, and what its statistical power is.
Question 3.1.1: How many system outputs (or other evaluation items) are evaluated per system in the evaluation experiment? Enter the number of system outputs (or other evaluation items) that are evaluated per system by at least one evaluator in the experiment. For most experiments this should be an integer, although if the number of outputs varies please provide further details here.
Answer: In the experiment, a total of 100 items are evaluated by at least one evaluator. Each of the items is composed of 4 summaries that must be rated. These 100 items are generations from the ROTOWIRE dataset. There are outputs generated by 5 different systems (20 from each). So, a total of 100 items are evaluated, from 5 different systems.

Question 3.1.2: How are system outputs (or other evaluation items) selected for inclusion in the evaluation experiment? Select one option. If none match, select 'other' and describe:

1. by an automatic random process
2. by an automatic random process but using stratified sampling over given properties
3. by manual, arbitrary selection
4. by manual selection aimed at achieving balance or variety relative to given properties
5. other (please describe)

Answer: We replicate the evaluation from the original paper, so we manually choose the same system outputs for evaluation. In the original paper these outputs were randomly selected.
Please describe: Please provide further details for your above selection(s)

Section 3.1.3: Statistical power of the sample size.

Question 3.1.3.1: What method was used to determine the the statistical power of the sample size?

Answer: In the paper taken as reference, no method, or criteria to determine the sample size ismentioned. In our reproduction we will evaluate the same number of summaries.

Question 3.1.3.2: What is the statistical power of the sample size? Enter the numerical results of a statistical power calculation on the output sample.
Answer: No method to determine the statistical power of the sample size was used.

Question 3.1.3.3: Where can other researchers find details of the script used? Enter a link to the script used (or another way of identifying the script). See, e.g., Card et al. (2020), Howcroft & Rieser (2021).
Answer: No method to determine the statistical power of the sample size was used.

Section 3.2: Evaluators

Questions 3.2.1–3.2.5 record information about the evaluators participating in the experiment.
Question 3.2.1: How many evaluators are there in this experiment? Enter the total number of evaluators participating in the experiment, as an integer.
Answer: N/A

Section 3.2.2: Evaluator Type

Questions 3.2.2.1–3.2.2.5 record information about the type of evaluators participating in the experiment.
Question 3.2.2.1: What kind of evaluators are in this experiment?

Select one option. These options should be valid for most experiments, but if not, select 'N/A' and describe why:

1. experts
2. non-experts
3. N/A (please describe)

Answer: The raters are crowdworkers required to be from English speaking countries, have a minimum of 1,000 previously completed tasks and have an approval rating in AMT greater than 98%.

Please describe:

Please provide further details for your above selection(s)
Question 3.2.2.2: Were the participants paid or unpaid? Select one option. These options should be valid for most experiments, but if not, select 'N/A' and describe why:

1. paid (monetary compensation)
2. paid (non-monetary compensation such as course credits)
3. not paid
4. N/A (please describe)

Question 3.2.2.3: Were the participants previously known to the authors? Select one option. These options should be valid for most experiments, but if not, select 'N/A' and describe why:

1. previously known to authors
2. not previously known to authors
3. N/A (please describe)

Please describe:
Question 3.2.2.4: Were one or more of the authors among the participants? Select one option. These options should be valid for most experiments, but if not, select 'N/A' and describe why:

1. evaluators include one or more of the authors
2. evaluators do not include any of the authors
3. N/A (please describe)

Please describe:
Question 3.2.2.5: Further details for participant type. Please use this field to elaborate on your selections for questions 3.2.2.1 to 3.2.2.4 above.
Answer: We take as reference the ReproHum global minimum wage per hour (UK living wage), that is GBP 10.90. Considering that each task will take about 4 minutes, an annotator can do 15 tasks per hour, so the payment per HIT will be GBP 10.9/15 = GBP 0.726 (0.88 USD = 0.8 EUR).

Question 3.2.3: How are evaluators recruited? Please explain how your evaluators are recruited. Do you send emails toa given list? Do you post invitations on social media? Posters on university walls? Were there any gatekeepers involved? What are the exclusion/inclusion criteria?
Answer: To recruit evaluators, we use the AMT

platform. The requisites for workers to be selected as valid are as follows: they are from English speaking countries, they have a minimum of 1,000 previously completed tasks and an approval rating greater than 98%.

Question 3.2.4: What training and/or practice are evaluators given before starting on the evaluation itself? Use this space to describe any training evaluators were given as part of the experiment to prepare them for the evaluation task, including any practice evaluations they did. This includes any introductory explanations they're given, e.g. on the start page of an online evaluation tool.
Answer: Before entering each task, evaluators are shown online the informed consent, the instructions of the task, how to read the different tables that will be shown, and an example task.

Question 3.2.5: What other characteristics do the evaluators have? Known either because these were qualifying criteria, or from information gathered as part of the evaluation. Use this space to list any characteristics not covered in previous questions that the evaluators are known to have, either because evaluators were selected on the basis of a characteristic, or because information about a characteristic was collected as part of the evaluation. This might include geographic location of IP address, educational level, or demographic information such as gender, age, etc. Where characteristics differ among evaluators (e.g. gender, age, location etc.), also give numbers for each subgroup.
Answer: The characteristics that evaluators have are the mentioned before: being from English speaking countries, having a minimum of 1,000 previously completed tasks and an approval rating greater than 98%.

Section 3.3: Experimental Design

Sections 3.3.1–3.3.8 record information about the experimental design of the evaluation experiment.
Question 3.3.1: Has the experimental design been preregistered? If yes, on which registry? Select 'Yes' or 'No'; if 'Yes' also give the name of the registry and a link to the registration page for the experiment.

1. yes
2. no

Please provide the name for, and link to the registration page for the experiment:
Please provide further details for your above selection(s)
Question 3.3.2: How are responses collected? Describe here the method used to collect responses, e.g. paper forms, Google forms, SurveyMonkey, Mechanical Turk, CrowdFlower, audio/video recording, etc.
Answer: Responses are collected via AMT.

Section 3.3.3: Quality assurance

Questions 3.3.3.1 and 3.3.3.2 record information about quality assurance.
Question 3.3.3.1: What quality assurance methods are used to ensure evaluators and/or their responses are suitable?

If any methods other than those listed were used, select 'other', and describe why below. If no methods were used, select *none of the above* and enter 'No Method' Select all that apply:

1. evaluators are required to be native speakers of the language they evaluate.
2. automatic quality checking methods are used during/post evaluation
3. manual quality checking methods are used during/post evaluation
4. evaluators are excluded if they fail quality checks (often or badly enough)
5. some evaluations are excluded because of failed quality checks 6. other (please describe)
7. none of the above

Please describe:
Question 3.3.3.2: Please describe in detail the quality assurance methods that were used. If no methods were used, enter 'N/A'
Answer: The task of the evaluators is to count the supported and contradicted facts on the generated texts. They are given two dropdowns to select the number of supported and contradicted facts detected, ranging from 0 to 20. So, when the sum of the supported and contradicted facts in a question is equal or higher than 20, the response is excluded, as there are no more than 20 facts to consider per sentence in none of the tasks

presented to the evaluators. Also, the ID of the evaluator that failed this quality check is saved in order to do not accept more HITs from this worker.

Section 3.3.3: Form/Interface

Questions 3.3.4.1 and 3.4.3.2 record information about the form or user interface that was shown to participants.

Question 3.3.4.1: Please include a link to online copies of the form/interface that was shown to participants. Please record a link to a screenshot or copy of the form if possible. If there are many files, please create a signpost page (e.g., on GitHub that contains links to all applicable resouces). If there is a separate introductory interface/page, include it under Question 3.2.4.

Answer: The HTML that will be used as template in AMT is available in the following link: `https://drive.google.com/drive/folders/1ZySFzvZh-_2H8iJlBrkemG-9bJOCFSFH?usp=share_link`.

Question 3.3.4.2: What do evaluators see when carrying out evaluations? Describe what evaluators are shown, in addition to providing the links in 3.3.4.1.

Answer: Evaluators are shown first the informed consent they must fill due to ethic reasons and, then they can read the instructions of the task they must perform, together with an illustrative example, to get them familiarized with the task. Finally, they go into the questionnaire where they can accomplish the required task.

Question 3.3.5: How free are evaluators regarding when and how quickly to carry out evaluations?

Select all that apply:

1. evaluators have to complete each individual assessment within a set time

2. evaluators have to complete the whole evaluation in one sitting

3. neither of the above (please describe)

Please describe:

Please provide further details for your above selection(s)

Question 3.3.6: Are evaluators told they can ask questions about the evaluation and/or provide feedback?

Select all that apply.

1. evaluators are told they can ask any questions during/after receiving initial training/instructions, and before the start of the evaluation

2. evaluators are told they can ask any questions during the evaluation

3. evaluators are asked for feedback and/or comments after the evaluation, e.g. via an exit questionnaire or a comment box

4. other (please describe)

5. None of the above

Please describe:

Question 3.3.7: What are the experimental conditions in which evaluators carry out the evaluations?

Multiple-choice options (select one). If none match, select 'other' and describe.

1. evaluation carried out by evaluators at a place of their own choosing, e.g. online, using a paper form, etc.

2. evaluation carried out in a lab, and conditions are the same for each evaluator

3. evaluation carried out in a lab, and conditions vary for different evaluators

4. evaluation carried out in a real-life situation, and conditions are the same for each evaluator

5. evaluation carried out in a real-life situation, and conditions vary for different evaluators

6. evaluation carried out outside of the lab, in a situation designed to resemble a real-life situation, and conditions are the same for each evaluator

7. evaluation carried out outside of the lab, in a situation designed to resemble a real-life situation, and conditions vary for different evaluators

8. other (please describe)

Please describe:

Question 3.3.8: Briefly describe the (range of different) conditions in which evaluators carry out the evaluations. Use this space to describe the variations in the conditions in which evaluators carry out the evaluation, for both situations where those variations are controlled,and situations where they are not controlled. If the evaluation is carried out at a place of the evaluators' own choosing, enter 'N/A'

Answer: N/A

Section 4: Quality Criteria – Definition and Operationalisation

Questions in this section collect information about each quality criterion assessed in the single human evaluation experiment that this sheet is being completed for.

Many Criteria : Quality Criterion - Definition and Operationalisation

In this section you can create named subsections for each criterion that is being evaluated. The form is then duplicated for each criterion. To create a criterion type its name in the field and press the *New* button, it will then appear on tab that will allow you to toggle the active criterion. To delete the current criterion press the *Delete current* button.

Fact-checking

Section 4.1: Quality Criteria

Questions 4.1.1–4.1.3 capture the aspect of quality that is assessed by a given quality criterion in terms of three orthogonal properties. They help determine whether or not the same aspect of quality is being evaluated in different evaluation experiments. The three properties characterise quality criteria in terms of (i) what type of quality is being assessed; (ii) what aspect of the system output is being assessed; and (iii) whether system outputs are assessed in their own right or with reference to some system-internal or system-external frame of reference. For full explanations see Belz et al. (2020).

Question 4.1.1: What type of quality is assessed by the quality criterion?

1. Correctness

2. Goodness

3. Feature

Please describe:

Please provide further details for your above selection(s)

Question 4.1.2: Which aspect of system outputs is assessed by the quality criterion?

1. Form of output

2. Content of output

3. Both form and content of output

Please describe:

Please provide further details for your above selection(s)

Question 4.1.3: Is each output assessed for quality in its own right, or with reference to a system-internal or external frame of reference?

1. Quality of output in its own right

2. Quality of output relative to the input

3. Quality of output relative to a system-external frame of reference

Please describe:

Please provide further details for your above selection(s)

Section 4.2: Evaluation mode properties

Questions 4.2.1–4.2.3 record properties that are orthogonal to quality criteria (covered by questions in the preceding section), i.e. any given quality criterion can in principle be combined with any of the modes (although some combinations are more common than others).

Question 4.2.1: Does an individual assessment involve an objective or a subjective judgment?

1. Objective

2. Subjective

Please describe:

Question 4.2.2: Are outputs assessed in absolute or relative terms?

1. Absolute

2. Relative

Please describe:

Question 4.2.3: Is the evaluation intrinsic or extrinsic?

1. Intrinsic

2. Extrinsic

Please describe:

Section 4.3: Response elicitation

The questions in this section concern response elicitation, by which we mean how the ratings or other measurements that represent assessments for the quality criterion in question are obtained, covering what is presented to evaluators, how they select response and via what type of tool, etc. The eleven questions (4.3.1–4.3.11) are based on the information annotated in the large scale survey of human evaluation methods in NLG by Howcroft et al. (2020).

Question 4.3.1: What do you call the quality criterion in explanations/interfaces to evaluators? Enter 'N/A' if no definition given. The name you use to refer to the quality criterion in explanations and/or interfaces created for evaluators. Examples of quality criterion names include Fluency, Clarity, Meaning Preservation. If no name is used, state 'N/A'.

Answer: Correctness of output relative to input (content)

Question 4.3.2: What definition do you give for the quality criterion in explanations/interfaces to evaluators? Enter 'N/A' if no definition given. Copy and past the verbatim definition you give to evaluators to explain the quality criterion they're assessing. If you don't explicitly call it a definition, enter the nearest thing to a definition you give them. If you don't give any definition, state 'N/A'.

Answer: In the form provided the task to perform is described as "For each sentence, your task is to determine how many of the facts in the sentence are actually supported by the tables, and how many are contradicted by the tables". Also, some examples are provided.

Question 4.3.3: Are the rating instrument response values discrete or continuous? If so, please also indicate the size. Is the rating instrument discrete or continuous? When discrete, also record the number of different response values for this quality criterion. E.g. for a 5-point Likert scale, select *Discrete* and record the size as 5 in the box below. For two-way forced-choice preference judgments, the size would be 2; if there's also a no-preference option, enter 3. For a slider that is mapped to 100 different values for the purpose of recording assessments select discrete and record the size as 100. If no rating instrument is used (e.g. when evaluation gathers post-edits or qualitative feedback only), select *N/A*.

1. Discrete

2. Continuous

3. N/A

Please record the size of the instrument here: 21

Question 4.3.4: List or range of possible values of the scale or other rating instrument. Enter 'N/A', if there is no rating instrument. List, or give the range of, the possible values of the rating instrument. The list or range should be of the size specified in Question 4.3.3. If there are too many to list, use a range. E.g. for two-way forced-choice preference judgments, the list entered might be *A better, B better*; if there's also a no-preference option, the list might be *A better, B better, neither*. For a slider that is mapped to 100 different values for the purpose of recording assessments, the range *1–100* might be entered. If no rating instrument is used (e.g. when evaluation gathers post-edits or qualitative feedback only), enter 'N/A'.

Answer: 0-20

Question 4.3.5: How is the scale or other rating instrument presented to evaluators? If none match, select 'Other' and describe.

1. Multiple-choice options

2. Check-boxes

3. Slider

4. N/A (there is no rating instrument)

5. Other (please describe)

Please describe:

Question 4.3.6: If there is no rating instrument, describe briefly what task the evaluators perform (e.g. ranking multiple outputs, finding information, playing a game, etc.), and what information is recorded. Enter 'N/A' if there is a rating instrument. If (and only if) there is no rating instrument, i.e. you entered 'N/A' for Questions 4.3.3–4.3.5, describe the task evaluators perform in this space. Otherwise, here enter 'N/A' if there *is* a rating instrument.

Answer: N/A

Question 4.3.7: What is the verbatim question, prompt or instruction given to evaluators (visible to them during each individual assessment)? Copy and paste the verbatim text that evaluators see during each assessment, that is intended to convey the evaluation task to them. E.g. *Which of these texts do you prefer?* Or *Make any corrections to this text that you think are necessary in order to improve it to the point where you would be happy to provide it to a client.*

Answer: Correct facts in sentence: dropdown.

Incorrect facts in sentence: dropdown.

Question 4.3.8: Form of response elicitation. If none match, select 'Other' and describe.

Explanations adapted from Howcroft et al. (2020).
1. (dis)agreement with quality statement
2. direct quality estimation
3. relative quality estimation (including ranking)
4. counting occurrences in text
5. qualitative feedback (e.g. via comments entered in a text box)
6. evaluation through post-editing/annotation
7. output classification or labelling
8. user-text interaction measurements
9. task performance measurements
10. user-system interaction measurements
11. Other (please describe)

Please describe:
Question 4.3.9: How are raw responses from participants aggregated or otherwise processed to obtain reported scores for this quality criterion? Normally a set of separate assessments is collected from evaluators and is converted to the results as reported. Describe here the method(s) used in the conversion(s). E.g. macro-averages or micro-averages are computed from numerical scores to provide summary, per-system results. If no such method was used, enter 'N/A'.
Answer: An average of the correct and incorrect facts is calculated for each system evaluated.

Question 4.3.10: Method(s) used for determining effect size and significance of findings for this quality criterion. Enter a list of methods used for calculating the effect size and significance of any results, both as reported in the paper given in Question 1.1, for this quality criterion. If none calculated, state 'None'.
Answer: The results of the different systems wil be compared using a one-way ANOVA with posthoc Tukey HSD tests to determine the significance of the results.

Section 4.3.11: Inter-annotator agreement

Questions 4.3.11.1 and 4.3.11.2 record information about inter-annotator agreement.

Question 4.3.11.1: Has the inter-annotator agreement between evaluators for this quality criterion been measured? If yes, what method was used? Select one option. If Yes, enter the methods used to compute any measures of inter-annotator agreement obtained for the quality criterion. If N/A, explain why.

1. yes
2. no
3. N/A

Please describe: Once the experiment finishes, the Krippendorff's agreement will be calculated.
Question 4.3.11.2: What was the inter-annotator agreement score? Enter N/A if there was none.
Answer: We expect an inter-annotator agreement score similar to the one reported in the paper that we took as reference: 0.44 for supported facts and 0.42 for contradicting facts.

Section 4.3.12: Intra-annotator agreement

Questions 4.3.12.1 and 4.3.12.2 record information about intra-annotator agreement.
Question 4.3.12.1: Has the intra-annotator agreement between evaluators for this quality criterion been measured? If yes, what method was used? Select one option. If Yes, enter the methods used to compute any measures of intra-annotator agreement obtained for the quality criterion. If N/A, explain why.

1. yes
2. no
3. N/A

Please describe: We only run the experiment once. To calculate the intra-annotator agreement the same evaluators must evaluate twice the same sentences.

Question 4.3.12.2: What was the intra-annotator agreement score? Enter N/A if there was none.
Answer: N/A

Section 5: Ethics

The questions in this section relate to ethical aspects of the evaluation. Information can be entered in the text box provided, and/or by linking to a source where complete information can be found.

Question 5.1: Has the evaluation experiment this sheet is being completed for, or the larger study it is part of, been approved by a research ethics committee? If yes, which research ethics committee? Typically, research organisations, universities and other higher-education institutions require some form ethical approval before experiments involving human participants, however innocuous, are permitted to proceed. Please provide here the name of the body that approved the experiment, or state 'No' if approval has not (yet) been obtained.
Answer: This experimental evaluation is approved by the ethics committee of the University of Santiago de Compostela (Approval Date: December 22, 2022; Approval Ref.: USC 56/2022). The approval certificate was issued by D. José Manuel Cifuentes Martínez, the Head of the USC Ethics Committee.

Question 5.2: Do any of the system outputs (or human-authored stand-ins) evaluated, or do any of the responses collected, in the experiment contain personal data (as defined in GDPR Art. 4, §1: `https://gdpr.eu/article-4-definitions`)? If yes, describe data and state how addressed. State 'No' if no personal data as defined by GDPR was recorded or collected, otherwise explain how conformity with GDPR requirements such as privacy and security was ensured, e.g. by linking to the (successful) application for ethics approval from Question 5.1.
Answer: No.

Question 5.3: Do any of the system outputs (or human-authored stand-ins) evaluated, or do any of the responses collected, in the experiment contain special category information (as defined in GDPR Art. 9, §1 [2]? If yes, describe data and state how addressed. State 'No' if no special-category data as defined by GDPR was recorded or collected, otherwise explain how conformity with GDPR requirements relating to special-category data was ensured, e.g. by linking to the (successful) application for ethics approval from Question 5.1.
Answer: No.

Question 5.4: Have any impact assessments been carried out for the evaluation experiment, and/or any data collected/evaluated in connection with it? If yes, summarise approach(es) and outcomes. Use this box to describe any *ex ante* or *ex post* impact assessments that have been carried out in relation to the evaluation experiment, such that the assessment plan and process, well as the outcomes, were captured in written form. Link to documents if possible. Types of impact assessment include data protection impact assessments, e.g. under GDPR. Environmental and social impact assessment frameworks are also available.
Answer: No.

B Fair Payment Calculation Method

1. Determine the original wage and minimum wage hourly values (if there is no minimum wage in a given location, set the value to 0). Please refer to the appropriate government sources of information (such as government websites) to determine minimum wages. Please consider regional variations of minimum wage within a country when applicable.
   1.1 *min_wage_your_lab*: the minimum wage in the country/region where your lab is based.
   1.2 *min_wage_your_participant*: the minimum wage in the country/region where your participants are based, converted to the same currency as *min_wage_your_lab*. For crowdsource work (such as Mechanical Turk) set this to 0.
   1.3 *original_study_wage*: what participants were paid in the original study.
   1.4 *original_study_min_wage*: the minimum wage where the original study was carried out, at the time when it was conducted. (*original_study_** variables should both be in the same currency as each other, but need not be converted to the same currency as used by your lab).
   1.5 *uk_living_wage*: set to the equivalent in your currency of £10.90 GBP, this is the project global minimum.
2. Calculate the $reproduction\_wage$ by following the below steps:
   2.1 *min_wage = MAX(min_wage_your_lab, min_wage_your_participant)*
   2.2 IF *original_study_min_wage* == NONE; THEN *original_study_min_wage = original_study_wage*

[2] urlhttps://gdpr.eu/article-9-processing-special-categories-of-personal-data-prohibited

2.3 *multiplier = (original_study_wage / original_study_min_wage)*
2.4 *wage = min_wage * multiplier*
2.5 *reproduction_wage = MAX(wage, min_wage, uk_living_wage)*

3. Round the final value (*reproduction_wage*) up to the smallest denomination of your currency (pence, cent, etc.)

Unveiling NLG Human-Evaluation Reproducibility: Lessons Learned and Key Insights from Participating in the ReproNLP Challenge

Lewis Watson and **Dimitra Gkatzia**
School of Computing, Engineering & The Built Environment
Edinburgh Napier University, UK
{l.watson, d.gkatzia}@napier.ac.uk

Abstract

Human evaluation is crucial for NLG systems as it provides a reliable assessment of the quality, effectiveness, and utility of generated language outputs. However, concerns about the reproducibility of such evaluations have emerged, casting doubt on the reliability and generalisability of reported results. In this paper, we present the findings of a reproducibility study on a data-to-text system, conducted under two conditions: (1) replicating the original setup as closely as possible with evaluators from AMT, and (2) replicating the original human evaluation but this time, utilising evaluators with a background in academia. Our experiments show that there is a loss of statistical significance between the original and reproduction studies, i.e. the human evaluation results are not reproducible. In addition, we found that employing local participants led to more robust results. We finally discuss lessons learned, addressing the challenges and best practices for ensuring reproducibility in NLG human evaluations.

1 Introduction

Human evaluations have long been considered the appropriate method for reliably evaluating NLG systems, due to the shortcomings of automatic evaluation metrics (Gehrmann et al., 2022). Notwithstanding the popularity and acceptance of human evaluations in the NLG community, the reproducibility of human evaluations has not been thoroughly documented. It is widely accepted that replicating human evaluation results can be really hard due to insufficient documentation (Belz et al., 2023a,b), variability in the generated text that leads to varying assessment results due to evaluator preferences, background, or other characteristics (Gkatzia et al., 2014, 2016), confusion and diversity in defining evaluation criteria (Howcroft et al., 2020), high costs (Thomson and Reiter, 2021) or even difficulty in identifying factual errors (Thomson et al., 2023).

The *ReproGen/ReproNLP challenges* led by Belz et al. (2020) aim to address the lack of understanding surrounding the reproducibility of human evaluations in NLG research by facilitating and encouraging research on the reproducibility of current evaluation methods, and the factors leading to irreproducibility. It involves a global multi-lab shared task study aimed at assessing the reproducibility of human evaluations conducted in selected published NLG research papers. The challenge organisers initially selected studies to be reproduced and allocated them to each participating lab. Each lab is then tasked with reproducing the results of the allocated human evaluation study, allowing for an assessment of the reproducibility of human evaluations across different methods, tasks, and participant characteristics. Labs were also allowed to explore additional research questions or perform further analyses of the results.

Our lab was tasked with reproducing one of the human evaluations reported in Puduppully and Lapata (2021), which aims to identify supporting and contradictory facts in text grounded on tabular data[1], namely basketball and baseball reports generated from game statistics tables. Here, we explore two research questions: (1) whether we can reproduce a human evaluation study on Amazon Mechanical Turk (AMT) following as closely as possible the original design as presented by the authors of the study; and (2) explore the impact of using local evaluators instead of AMT evaluators for this task. Our contributions are as follows:

- We present the results from our effort to reproduce the human evaluation presented by Puduppully and Lapata (2021).

[1]The paper presents two human evaluation studies - here we only reproduce the first, another lab is tasked with reproducing the second.

Proceedings of the Third Workshop on Human Evaluation of NLP Systems, pages 69–74, Varna, Bulgaria, Sep 7, 2023.
https://doi.org/10.26615/978-954-452-088-5_006

- We present results from an additional study that draws evaluators from a pool of colleagues and students with experience in AI and we demonstrate that using local evaluators results in more robust results (as measured through Inter-Annotator Agreement).
- We discuss the implications of our results to NLG evaluation studies.

The rest of the paper is shaped as follows: Section 2 presents the original human evaluation study, Section 3 presents our effort to reproduce the original study, Section 4 discusses our results in comparison to the original study, and Section 5 discusses an additional study we performed with local evaluators, and finally, Section 6 discusses the results and implications for reproducibility studies in NLG.

2 Original Study

The original study selected for our reproduction is "Data-to-text Generation with Macro Planning" by Puduppully and Lapata (2021) which proposed a new macro planning phase for data-to-text generation. This new phase aims to enhance the structure and accuracy of the generated content by emphasising higher-level content organisation, including entities, events, and their interactions. These high-level features, termed macro plans, are learned from the provided data and are then used as inputs to guide text generation. The authors employed both automatic and human evaluations to obtain accurate assessments of their model's performance. The human evaluations conducted in the original study compared the model's performance on two datasets: MLB (MLB dataset consisting of baseball games' box line-score tables, and play-by-play tables) (Puduppully et al., 2019) and RotoWire (RotoWire dataset consisting of NBA basketball games' box and line-score boxes) (Wiseman et al., 2017). The model's performance on both datasets was compared to four different NLG systems: Gold, Template (Template-based generators from Wiseman et al. (2017)), ED+CC (encoder-decoder with attention and copy mechanism), and ENT (Entity-based model) for the MLB dataset, and RBF-2020 for the RotoWire dataset.

The original paper reports two human evaluation studies: a fact-counting study and the quality of generated summaries. Here, we reproduce the **fact-counting study**. In this study, human evaluators were asked to count the number of supporting and contradicting facts in the outputs of the NLG systems by comparing them with the input data. For the MLB dataset, the input consisted of a baseball game box, line-score, and play-by-play tables, while for the RotoWire dataset, participants were provided with an NBA basketball game box- and line-score tables.

The fact-counting study involved a total of 600 evaluations or Human Intelligence Tasks (HITs) that required human evaluators. To facilitate these evaluations, the authors utilised Amazon Mechanical Turk (MTurk) to crowdsource the completion of the HITs. Specific qualifications were set for workers to be eligible to participate, including having an MTurk approval rating greater than 98%, a minimum of 1000 previously completed HITs on MTurk, and being based in one of the following English-speaking countries: US, UK, Canada, Ireland, Australia, or New Zealand.

In the original study, the authors reported that human evaluators were not required to have prior knowledge of basketball or baseball, as they were provided with a cheatsheet explaining the semantics of the box score tables. Each summary was evaluated by three different workers, and there were a total of 131 distinct MTurk workers involved in the evaluations. The 600 HITs were divided into eight mini-batches (four per dataset), and attention checks were employed to ensure the quality of the responses. If a worker reported more than 20 total facts, their response was rejected and rerun. The agreement among the three responses for each distinct HIT was calculated using Krippendorff's alpha, resulting in 0.44 for supported facts and 0.42 for contradicting facts.

3 Reproduced Study

In the reproduced study, we followed the design and methodology of the original study as closely as possible, however, we only reproduced the tasks for the RotoWire dataset due to the less complex task and cheat-sheets provided, which allowed for better control over the cognitive complexity of the HITs. This decision aligned with the recommendations by Belz et al. (2023a) in controlling factors such as the number of evaluators, the cognitive complexity of the task, and the level of training/expertise of the evaluators. By narrowing down these factors, our goal was to improve the accuracy and effectiveness of reproducing the results.

We obtained the necessary model outputs and

Original Study - Rotowire		
System	#Supp	#Contra
Gold	3.63	0.07
Templ	7.57*	0.08
ED+CC	3.92	0.91*
RBF-2020	5.08*	0.67*
Macro	4.00	0.27

Reproduction Study - Rotowire		
System	#Supp	#Contra
Gold	4.000	1.525
Template	6.3167*	1.3583
ED+CC	5.100	1.9042
RBF-2020	4.9458	1.7583
Macro	4.5458	1.5333

Table 1: Mean counts of supported (#Supp) and contradicting (#Contra) facts in game summaries (one-way ANOVA with posthoc Tukey HSD tests, * denotes significance with $p \leq 0.05$, when comparing each result to Macro).

Human Evaluation Datasheet (HEDs) from the original authors and filled out our own HEDs for reproduction. Then using the Amazon Mechanical Turk (MTurk) platform, we set up HITs for the fact-counting evaluation. Workers were asked to count the supporting and contradicting facts in summaries generated by different NLG systems, using the exact same UI and cheatsheet as the original study. We conducted multiple mini-batches of HITs with attention checks in between.

A total of 167 distinct workers participated in the study, and we ran 300 HITs divided into 4 batches (agreement using Krippendorff's α was -0.12 for supported and 0.12 for contradicting facts, as opposed to 0.44 and 0.42 respectively in the original study). We reran several batches where workers had failed the attention checks outlined in the original paper, resulting in 121 failed attention check tasks. Including paying for reruns, the total cost for the study came to \$665.18. Workers received compensation at UK's Living Wage[2] level.

To analyse the results, we mirrored the original study by using the exact same code for statistical analysis using a one-way ANOVA test with posthoc Tukey HSD test. This analysis helped us identify significant differences in the performance of the NLG systems for comparison with the proposed macro system.

4 Results

In this section, we compare the results from the fact-counting HIT on the RotoWire dataset for both the original and reproduced studies (see Table 1).

In the original study, the template-based generator (Template) showed a statistically significant higher number of reported supporting facts (7.57) when compared to the Macro system (4.00). Similarly, the RBF-2020 system showed a statistically significant increase in supporting facts (5.08). In terms of contradicting facts, ED+CC and RBF-2020 reported higher numbers, with statistical significance underlined at 0.91 and 0.67 respectively.

The reproduced study results demonstrated a different pattern. The Template system once again recorded a statistically significant higher number of supporting facts (when compared to the macro system) at 6.3167, but the differences in the contradicting facts were less pronounced across the systems, without statistical significance against macro.

4.1 Comparative Analysis

Comparing both studies, it is evident that there are inconsistencies between the original and reproduced results. While the Template system consistently showed a higher number of supporting facts in both studies, the magnitude of this difference was reduced in the reproduction. The number of contradicting facts, in particular, exhibited a notable increase in the reproduced study across all systems.

5 Additional study with local evaluators

In addition to the above reproduction study, we conducted a supplementary study **on a smaller scale** with a selected pool of academic evaluators. This study aimed to provide further insights into the reproducibility of human evaluations as well as the impact of sampling participants with different characteristics.

To carry out this additional study, we adapted the HTML task interface to work locally without relying on the MTurk platform. The interface was modified to allow participants to save their answers to a JSON file, which they would then email back to us. For each of the five NLG systems, two tasks were randomly selected from both the RotoWire

[2]https://www.livingwage.org.uk/what-real-living-wage

and MLB datasets (total of 20 HITS). Unlike the large-scale reproduction, each task in the additional study was completed by two distinct participants instead of three.

To gather respondents for the study, we allocated the individual HIT HTML files to participants and asked them to submit the JSON file once they completed the task(s). The participants were instructed to count the number of supporting and contradicting facts in the summary, following the same approach as the original and large-scale reproduction studies.

A total of 17 distinct evaluators, including 4 non-native English speakers (who however live and work/study in the UK), participated in the additional study (agreement using Krippendorff's α was 0.65 for supported and 0.56 for contradicting facts). We ran 40 HITs in total, with each task having two participants. There were no failed attention checks in this study. The collected responses from the additional study were analysed using the same statistical analysis Python script used for the original and large-scale reproduction studies. This allowed us to compare the performance of the different NLG systems in the additional study as well.

5.1 Results

5.1.1 RotoWire Dataset

The results of the additional study on RotoWire are shown in Table 2.

Additional Study - RotoWire		
System	#Supp	#Contra
Gold	<u>6.9375*</u>	0.0625
Template	4.125	0.25
ED+CC	<u>5.0625*</u>	0.5625
RBF-2020	<u>5.5*</u>	0.0
Macro	2.625	0.125

Table 2: Mean counts of supported (#Supp) and contradicting (#Contra) facts in game summaries (one-way ANOVA with posthoc Tukey HSD tests, * denotes significance with $p \leq 0.05$, when comparing each result to Macro).

Compared with the original study shown in Table 1, the Gold standard reported statistically higher supporting facts and maintained low contradicting facts. The Template system showed a decrease in supporting facts however, lost statistical significance in the additional study. Compared to the original study, ED+CC displayed an increase in supporting facts and gained statistical significance compared to the macro system. The RBF-2020 system maintained statistical significance against the macro system found in the original study. **We should note, however, that this additional study evaluates a smaller pool of system outputs and therefore there is an expected natural discrepancy in the number of supporting and contradictory facts. As such, the results should not be interpreted as definitive indicators of individual system performance.** However, when looking at the Inter-Annotator Agreement, we see that the participants in the local study score higher than the AMT participants, indicating that the results are more robust.

5.1.2 MLB Dataset

In addition to the RotoWire dataset, the supplementary study also evaluated task agreeability using the MLB dataset. The results are summarised in Table 3.

The Gold system exhibited an increase in supporting facts and a higher number of contradicting facts. The Template system reported a decrease in both supporting and contradicting facts, while ED+CC showed an increase in supporting facts with lower contradicting facts. The ENT system displayed lower supporting facts but higher contradicting facts, whereas the Macro system maintained similar levels. Similarly to the previous experiment, the outputs evaluated here are a subset of the ones used in the original study.

5.2 Feedback Insights

Feedback received from participants unveiled other critical aspects that might have impacted the studies. Many disagreed with the notion that prior knowledge of basketball or baseball was unnecessary, leading to confusion and the need to look up specific phrases. Some suggested layout changes to minimise scrolling, while others were unclear about what qualified as a "fact." Interestingly, unnecessary feedback was common in the larger study, possibly due to different incentives for paid workers trying to quickly fill out tasks versus unpaid student and academic participants - this is supported by the absence of failed attention checks in the additional study. The smaller sample size in the local study could also be argued as an explanation for the absence of such feedback, although it's unlikely to be the sole reason.

Original Study - MLB		
System	#Supp	#Contra
Gold	3.59	0.14
Templ	4.21	0.04
ED+CC	3.42	0.72*
ENT	3.71	0.73*
Macro	3.76	0.25

Additional Study - MLB		
System	#Supp	#Contra
Gold	4.375	0.75
Template	2.6875	0.5
ED+CC	4.875	0.25
ENT	2.875	0.875
Macro	3.0	0.8125

Table 3: Mean counts of supported (#Supp) and contradicting (#Contra) facts in game summaries (one-way ANOVA with posthoc Tukey HSD tests, * denotes significance with $p \leq 0.05$, when comparing each result to Macro).

6 Discussion & Conclusions

The attempt to reproduce the results of the original study yielded mixed outcomes, with substantial differences observed in the reproduction studies. While the original study showcased certain statistical significance in the reported performance of the systems against the macro system, this significance was often lost in reproduction studies, particularly concerning the number of contradicting facts.

The full, large-scale reproduction exhibited a noticeable increase in the number of contradicting facts across various systems, and the alignment between the original and reproduced studies was limited. Strikingly, the local study displayed more consistency with the original study but also brought forth its unique variations. As expected the local study resulted in higher annotator agreement than the AMT study.

Across different NLG systems, there was a clear fluctuation in the number of reported supporting and contradicting facts. This variation, although intriguing, added to the complexity of drawing definitive conclusions regarding the reproducibility of human evaluations in these contexts.

6.1 Contributing Factors

Several factors emerged as potential contributors to the observed discrepancies between the studies. Differences in evaluator opinions, missing information, and the evaluators' understanding of the task likely played significant roles in the outcomes. Additionally, inconsistencies in the evaluation criteria, the make-up of the evaluator pool, biases in the evaluation process, and the inherent subjectivity of human judgement cannot be overlooked as influencing factors.

The local study, being conducted in a more controlled environment, and with an evaluator pool where incentives are better aligned and not tied to financial gain, may have mitigated some of these confounding variables, showing more consistency with the original study. However, the human-centric nature of the evaluations leaves room for unpredictable variations.

6.2 Moving Forward

The findings of this research underscore the intricate nature of human evaluations and the challenges in reproducing such studies. While the reproduction attempt was not entirely successful, the insights gleaned from the process are invaluable.

Future work should aim to incorporate these insights, focusing on minimising biases, clarifying evaluation criteria, and possibly developing standardised protocols for human evaluations. The collaboration between AI and human judgement must be tuned, recognising the complex interaction between objectivity and subjectivity, to advance the field in a meaningful and responsible manner.

Acknowledgements

Dimitra Gkatzia's work is supported under the EPSRC projects NLG for low-resource domains (EP/T024917/1) and CiViL (EP/T014598/1).

References

Anya Belz, Shubham Agarwal, Anastasia Shimorina, and Ehud Reiter. 2020. ReproGen: Proposal for a shared task on reproducibility of human evaluations in NLG. In *Proceedings of the 13th International Conference on Natural Language Generation*, pages 232–236, Dublin, Ireland. Association for Computational Linguistics.

Anya Belz, Craig Thomson, Ehud Reiter, Gavin Abercrombie, Jose M. Alonso-Moral, Mohammad Arvan, Jackie Cheung, Mark Cieliebak, Elizabeth Clark, Kees van Deemter, Tanvi Dinkar, Ondřej Dušek, Steffen Eger, Qixiang Fang, Albert Gatt, Dimitra Gkatzia,

Javier González-Corbelle, Dirk Hovy, Manuela Hürlimann, Takumi Ito, John D. Kelleher, Filip Klubicka, Huiyuan Lai, Chris van der Lee, Emiel van Miltenburg, Yiru Li, Saad Mahamood, Margot Mieskes, Malvina Nissim, Natalie Parde, Ondřej Plátek, Verena Rieser, Pablo Mosteiro Romero, Joel Tetreault, Antonio Toral, Xiaojun Wan, Leo Wanner, Lewis Watson, and Diyi Yang. 2023a. Missing information, unresponsive authors, experimental flaws: The impossibility of assessing the reproducibility of previous human evaluations in nlp.

Anya Belz, Craig Thomson, Ehud Reiter, and Simon Mille. 2023b. Non-repeatable experiments and non-reproducible results: The reproducibility crisis in human evaluation in NLP. In *Findings of the Association for Computational Linguistics: ACL 2023*, pages 3676–3687, Toronto, Canada. Association for Computational Linguistics.

Sebastian Gehrmann, Elizabeth Clark, and Thibault Sellam. 2022. Repairing the cracked foundation: A survey of obstacles in evaluation practices for generated text. *ArXiv*, abs/2202.06935.

Dimitra Gkatzia, Helen Hastie, and Oliver Lemon. 2014. Finding middle ground? multi-objective natural language generation from time-series data. In *Proceedings of the 14th Conference of the European Chapter of the Association for Computational Linguistics, volume 2: Short Papers*, pages 210–214, Gothenburg, Sweden. Association for Computational Linguistics.

Dimitra Gkatzia, Oliver Lemon, and Verena Rieser. 2016. Natural language generation enhances human decision-making with uncertain information. In *Proceedings of the 54th Annual Meeting of the Association for Computational Linguistics (Volume 2: Short Papers)*, pages 264–268, Berlin, Germany. Association for Computational Linguistics.

David M. Howcroft, Anya Belz, Miruna-Adriana Clinciu, Dimitra Gkatzia, Sadid A. Hasan, Saad Mahamood, Simon Mille, Emiel van Miltenburg, Sashank Santhanam, and Verena Rieser. 2020. Twenty years of confusion in human evaluation: NLG needs evaluation sheets and standardised definitions. In *Proceedings of the 13th International Conference on Natural Language Generation*, pages 169–182, Dublin, Ireland. Association for Computational Linguistics.

Ratish Puduppully, Li Dong, and Mirella Lapata. 2019. Data-to-text generation with entity modeling. In *Proceedings of the 57th Annual Meeting of the Association for Computational Linguistics*, pages 2023–2035, Florence, Italy. Association for Computational Linguistics.

Ratish Puduppully and Mirella Lapata. 2021. Data-to-text generation with macro planning. *CoRR*, abs/2102.02723.

Craig Thomson and Ehud Reiter. 2021. Generation challenges: Results of the accuracy evaluation shared task. In *Proceedings of the 14th International Conference on Natural Language Generation*, pages 240–248, Aberdeen, Scotland, UK. Association for Computational Linguistics.

Craig Thomson, Ehud Reiter, and Barkavi Sundararajan. 2023. Evaluating factual accuracy in complex data-to-text. *Computer Speech Language*, 80:101482.

Sam Wiseman, Stuart Shieber, and Alexander Rush. 2017. Challenges in data-to-document generation. In *Proceedings of the 2017 Conference on Empirical Methods in Natural Language Processing*, pages 2253–2263, Copenhagen, Denmark. Association for Computational Linguistics.

How reproducible is best-worst scaling for human evaluation? A reproduction of 'Data-to-text Generation with Macro Planning'

Emiel van Miltenburg, Anouck Braggaar, Nadine Braun, Debby Damen, Martijn Goudbeek, Chris van der Lee, Frédéric Tomas, Emiel Krahmer
Department of Communication and Cognition
TiCC - Tilburg center for Cognition and Communication
Tilburg University
C.W.J.vanMiltenburg@tilburguniversity.edu

Abstract

This paper is part of the larger ReproHum project, where different teams of researchers aim to reproduce published experiments from the NLP literature. Specifically, ReproHum focuses on the reproducibility of human evaluation studies, where participants indicate the quality of different outputs of Natural Language Generation (NLG) systems. This is necessary because without reproduction studies, we do not know how reliable earlier results are. This paper aims to reproduce the second human evaluation study of Puduppully and Lapata (2021), while another lab is attempting to do the same. This experiment uses best-worst scaling to determine the relative performance of different NLG systems. We found that the *worst* performing system in the original study is now in fact the *best* performing system across the board. This means that we cannot fully reproduce the original results. We also carry out alternative analyses of the data, and discuss how our results may be combined with the other reproduction study that is carried out in parallel with this paper.

1 Introduction

Although human evaluation remains the gold standard for determining the quality of a text, little is known about the reproducibility of evaluation methods that are used to determine the quality of texts generated by Natural Language Generation (NLG) systems (Belz et al., 2020). To be sure, there are many different ways to assess NLG output. As van der Lee et al. (2019) and Howcroft et al. (2020) showed: different authors tend to focus on different quality dimensions (e.g. *grammaticality, coherence, conciseness*) and they also differ in the way they elicit quality judgments (e.g. using Likert scales or ranking tasks). If we want to understand how reliable these methods are, we need to carry out multiple reproduction studies to establish the amount of variance we may expect between different studies (Belz, 2022).

1.1 The ReproHum project

Establishing the reproducibility of human evaluation metrics is a relatively slow and incremental process, as it takes a great deal of time and resources to exactly reproduce even a single study. However, with a collective effort, we are currently making headway to achieve this goal. As part of the ReproHum project (Belz et al., 2023), this paper aims to reproduce an experiment from a published NLG study, while another lab (identity unknown to us) is attempting to do the same. Yet more labs are reproducing other studies, yielding a rich dataset of closely matched reproductions.

1.2 Target paper

Our target paper is Puduppully and Lapata 2021. This paper proposed a neural data-to-text model with a macro-planning stage (determining the high-level organisation of the text-to-be-generated, based on the provided input) followed by a generation stage (where the text is produced). This model is trained and evaluated on both the RotoWire and the MLB datasets (Wiseman et al., 2017; Puduppully et al., 2019). We refer to this model as *Macro*.

The authors carried out an automatic evaluation and two human evaluations. We focus solely on the latter. Experiment 1 asked crowd workers to count supported and contradicting facts in the generated texts (compared to the input data). Experiment 2 asked crowd workers to compare pairs of generated texts in terms of different quality dimensions (discussed in more detail below). In these evaluations, the Macro system was compared to the reference data (referred to as *Gold*), Template-based systems from Wiseman et al. (2017) and Puduppully et al. (2019), ED+CC (again from Wiseman et al.) and Hier (the hierarchical model from Rebuffel et al. 2020, also referred to as RBF-2020 in the original paper). The overall results of these evaluations are highly favourable to the Macro system.

Proceedings of the Third Workshop on Human Evaluation of NLP Systems, pages 75–88, Varna, Bulgaria, Sep 7, 2023.
https://doi.org/10.26615/978-954-452-088-5_007

1.3 Reproduction target & research question

This paper aims to reproduce Experiment 2 of Puduppully and Lapata (2021). The authors asked crowdworkers to inspect pairs of summaries, and to choose which summary is better in terms of three different quality dimensions (original definitions):

1. **Grammaticality** "Is the summary written in well- formed English?"

2. **Coherence** "Is the summary well structured and well organized and does it have a natural ordering of the facts?"

3. **Conciseness/repetition** "Does the summary avoid unnecessary repetition including whole sentences, facts or phrases?"[1]

The authors used Best-worst scaling (Louviere et al., 2015, BWS) to obtain scores for the three different quality dimensions. In the context of human evaluation of dialogue system output, Santhanam and Shaikh (2019) show that human ratings for coherence and readability are more reliable with magnitude estimation than with BWS. This result was replicated by Braggaar et al. (2022), who obtained similar results. Also in other domains, BWS has been shown to be more reliable than rating scales (e.g. Kiritchenko and Mohammad 2017 for sentiment annotations). In the domain of data-to-text, we are not aware of any studies looking into the reliability of BWS for human evaluations of NLG output. Thus, the main question we aim to answer in this study is: **How reproducible is best-worst scaling for human evaluation of NLG output?**

This question comes with the immediate disclaimer that we are only looking at one implementation of a human evaluation experiment using best-worst scaling, but as noted above: we need to start somewhere. Future studies may alter different parameters of the experiment under consideration, and show if and how these affect the results.

1.4 Contributions

This paper presents a reproduction study answering the research question outlined above. Beyond that, we offer additional analyses of the responses, providing more insight into participant behavior. Finally, we offer reflections on the reproduction process and a proposal for a future study using the data from both reproduction studies targeting experiment 2 of Puduppully and Lapata (2021). Our code and data are available online.[2]

[1]The original authors seem to use the two terms interchangeably in their paper and materials. In the remainder of this paper we use the term *repetition* because *conciseness* is a more general term, typically indicating a preference for brevity while communicating all relevant information.

2 Method

Next to the original paper and materials,[3] we also have the support of the original authors. Because multiple labs are all reproducing individual experiments from each paper-to-be-reproduced, we contacted the authors through the coordinator of the ReproHum project, who collated all answers in a shared online document. For the current paper under investigation, this meant that four labs (and the ReproHum coordinator) critically read the paper and asked questions about the methodology. Although this resulted in useful additional documentation, some details about the original study were still missing (as documented below).

Design. We tried to match the original experiment as closely as possible. The original authors used a classical crowdsourcing design, where each ranking decision (indicating which summary is better in terms of a given quality dimension) was distributed as a separate Human Intelligence Task (HIT) on the Mechanical Turk platform. Figure 1 provides an example HIT (without the information letter or informed consent form).

Materials. The original study compared the outputs of four systems with gold-standard summaries generated by humans. For each of the five groups (four systems plus humans), there were 20 summaries. Originally the comparison was made for two separate datasets (MLB and Rotowire), but our reproduction focuses on the outputs for the Rotowire dataset.[6] This means that there are 20 summaries × 10 combinations = 200 items to be

[2]https://github.com/evanmiltenburg/ReproHum-D2T

[3]The lead author of the original paper shared relevant code and data via public GitHub repositories[4,5] and we also obtained the original crowdsourcing templates for use on the Mechanical Turk platform. Details about the evaluation are also provided in the lead author's PhD dissertation (Puduppully, 2022, Appendix B).

[4]https://github.com/ratishsp/data2text-macro-plan-py

[5]https://github.com/ratishsp/data2text-human-evaluation

[6]There was an error in the instructions to prepare the data for the MLB experiment. This error was introduced as the code, data, and instructions were prepared for the ReproHum project and uploaded to GitHub. We do not know what the actual original script looked like. This uncertainty makes the comparison between any replication and the original study unreliable, since we do not know whether the replication corresponds to what was done for the original study. Thus, we leave out the MLB dataset.

Summaries

System Summaries

A: The Golden State Warriors (43 - 7) defeated the Los Angeles Clippers (31 - 19) 133 - 120 on Saturday. The Warriors came into this game as one of the best defenses in the NBA this season, but they were able to prevail with a huge road win. [...11 more sentences]

B: The Golden State Warriors defeated the Los Angeles Clippers, 133 - 120, at Staples Center on Wednesday. The Warriors (43 - 7) came into this game as a sizable favorite and they showed why in this clincher. Golden State (31 - 19) came into this game as a huge favorite and they showed some resiliency here with this win. [...11 more sentences]"

Ranking Criteria

Coherence: How coherent is the summary? How natural is the ordering of the facts? The summary should be well structured and well organized and have a natural ordering of the facts.

Answers

Best: [ ] Worst: [ ]

Figure 1: Example item showing the ranking task for Coherence. Summaries were manually shortened for presentation in this paper.

rated. With three ratings per item and three quality criteria, there are thus $9 \times 200 = 1800$ ratings to be collected. For these ratings, we use the original HTML interface provided by the authors (see the supplementary materials for the files). This interface contains some (Javascript-based) input validation to ensure that participants can only respond using the characters 'A' or 'B' to indicate their preference.

Participants. Participant location was restricted to English-speaking countries (United States of America, United Kingdom, Canada, Ireland, Australia, or New Zealand). In the general task instructions, participants were told to "attempt HITs if you are a native speaker of English or a near-native speaker who can comfortably comprehend summaries of NBA basketball games written in English." Because of the task's design, for each quality dimension, the participants were able to rate between 1 and 200 items. This also means there is a variable number of unique participants for each quality dimension (see §5.1 for discussion).

Payment. Based on earlier experience with a similar task, we estimate that the average time to complete a HIT would be about 90 seconds. Using a standard wage of \$13.59 per hour, this results in a compensation per HIT of \$0.34.[7] This is over twice the original amount of \$0.15 per HIT, but results from Buhrmester et al. (2011) indicate that compensation level does not seem to influence data quality. A later study from Litman et al. (2015) found similar results for US workers, but noted that greater compensation increased the internal consistency of workers from India. If anything, based on these results we should expect our results to be at least as reliable as the original study.

Procedure. Upon opening the HIT, participants are presented with an information letter and a description of the task. The task description contains the definition of the relevant quality criterion and an example item with an indication of the correct answer. If participants agree to participate, they are asked to provide their informed consent. Having done so, they are presented with two summaries and asked to indicate which summary is the best in terms of the relevant quality criterion. After finishing the HIT, they are optionally asked to indicate whether they are a native speaker of English, and to provide any feedback.

Quality control. Although the original paper made no mention of any quality control measures, these were carried out by the authors. The exact process was not recorded, so our approach is based on the recollection of the authors. This approach was standardised for both concurrent reproductions of the original paper.

For each of the three quality criteria, the HITs were sent out in four batches. The authors used attention checks for two criteria:

[7]Following the ReproHum guidelines, we determined the minimum wage based on Western European standards. We used the maximum of the UK hourly living wage (£10.91 = €12.51)[8] and the standard Dutch minimum wage for a 36-hour workweek (€12.40 per hour).[9] The UK living wage corresponds to \$13.59, which is greater than the minimum wages in Canada (CA\$16.55 = \$12.33), Ireland (€11.30 = \$12.24), and more than twice the US minimum wage of \$7.55. It is lower than the minimum wages in Australia (AU\$ 21.38 = \$14.21), New Zealand (NZ\$22.70 = \$14.17). Thus, the compensation level at least exceeds the median minimum wage for these countries. All wages were taken from government websites. All conversions here are computed using the rates on May 17, 2023.

[8]This amount takes into account the general cost of living in the UK, and exceeds the standard minimum wage. Source: https://www.livingwage.org.uk/what-real-living-wage

[9]The standard differs by sector, depending on the standard amount of hours for one workweek. These hours tend to range between 36 and 40, with fewer hours resulting in a higher wage per hour. Result computed using: https://www.rijksoverheid.nl/onderwerpen/minimumloon/rekenhulp-minimumloon-berekenen

1. *Conciseness* attention check: when considering Gold vs System (excluding template-based systems); if a participant selects a system output with a relatively high amount of repetitions as being more concise than Gold, then it is an exclusion trigger.[10]

2. *Coherence* attention check: when considering Gold vs Template; if a participant selects Template as being more coherent than Gold, then it is an exclusion trigger.

These attention checks were carried out after each batch. No checks were carried out for Grammaticality. The attention checks function as exclusion triggers: failing an attention check means that workers are excluded from working on future batches.[11] Because of the way the crowd sourcing task is set up, not all workers encounter attention checks. So it is possible that low-quality responses remain. Furthermore, following the original authors, we did not publish new HITs to replace the ones that were carried out by workers that were flagged by the exclusion triggers.

Analysis. To determine the inter-rater reliability, we first compute Krippendorff's (2011) alpha for the overall ratings. It is unclear how this was done in the original paper, since there are three different quality dimensions, but only one alpha score was reported. Thus we will report the alpha scores for all three quality dimensions, plus an average of those three values. (Alternatively, one *could* combine all data files for all quality dimensions and compute the overall reliability of participants' preferences, regardless of the relevant quality dimension. However, this misses the point of the alpha score, which is to determine how reliably different constructs can be coded.)

To compare system performance, we use the Best-Worst scaling approach as described in the original paper. For each summary, the output of all systems are compared to each other (for ease of exposition, use of the term 'system' includes Gold responses). This means that each system is compared to four others. For each system, we award a point for every win and we subtract a point for every loss, meaning that for every summary, every system receives a score in the range of [-12,12] (four comparisons per system, times three participants).[12] We use the authors' original scripts to first compute a one-way ANOVA to see if there are any significant differences between the systems, followed by Tukey's HSD to identify which systems differ significantly from each other.

Power analysis. Prior to carrying out our reproduction study, we computed a power analysis to determine the probability to detect a true effect (i.e. finding differences between the systems) if there is one. This turned out to be more difficult than we thought, since the original paper does not report any effect sizes, nor does it report enough information to compute Cohen's d (no standard deviations are reported). Using the available information about the experiment, we estimate that the original experiment had a power of 0.64 to detect a medium-sized effect or greater (≥ 0.3).[13,14] Our study uses the exact same parameters as the original study, and thus has the same power.

3 Results

We first provide some descriptive statistics (§3.1) to contextualise the results, before moving on to the inter-rater reliability (§3.2) and the system comparison (§3.3).

3.1 Descriptives

Table 1 shows the answer frequencies. We find that participants had an overall preference for the first system in the comparisons. Furthermore, despite JavaScript answer validation, some of the respondents provided invalid responses. These are simply

[10]This check was developed by the ReproHum coordinator, to make the original method (relying on human judgments) more reproducible and to keep the process the same between both concurrent reproduction attempts.

[11]We use a *soft block* for this: tagging workers with a custom qualification on Mechanical Turk, and setting a rule that tagged workers cannot take part in our study. This is preferable to a *hard block* (rejecting their work and negatively affecting their performance score) because the rating task is relatively subjective, and a hard block would punish the workers for having the 'wrong' opinion.

[12]Following Orme (2009), the reported scores in the original paper lie between -100 and 100. To obtain scores in this range, we simply carry out a linear transformation of the responses.

[13]We used the pwr library (Champely, 2020) in R (R Core Team, 2023) to run the following command: `pwr.anova.test(k=5,f=.3,sig.level=.05,n=20)` These numbers correspond to the number of different systems (5), desired effect size (0.3 or greater), significance level (0.05), and the number of summaries (20).

[14]One complication in the design of the current study is that it is not straightforward to discuss sample size. There were 206 participants in the original study, but they all provided different numbers of ratings. These were then aggregated to produce the scores for each ⟨system, summary⟩ pair. The reliability of the scores for each system depends on the number of binary judgments per combination of systems. The reliability of the statistical analysis depends on the number of summaries that the systems were evaluated on.

Category	A	B	5	19	Total
Grammaticality	319	277	4	0	600
Repetition	305	287	7	1	600
Coherence	320	277	3	0	600
Total	944	841	14	1	1800

Table 1: Answer frequencies per quality dimension. The answers '5' and '19' are wrongly provided.

skipped in the original best-worst scaling procedure. For other statistics, we do not know how invalid responses were dealt with. We will take up this issue in Section 3.2, when we discuss inter-rater reliability and Krippendorff's Alpha.

Table 2 shows the number of participants in our experiment. Overall, the number of unique respondents (216) is similar to the original experiment (206). We also see that participants carried out HITs for different quality criteria: one participant carried out 67 HITs overall, while the highest number of HITs for any participant on a single quality criterion is 36. We further find that Grammaticality has the lowest number of unique participants, which may be due to the fact that there were no attention checks for this criterion.

Table 3 shows the duration of each HIT. We observe that both mean and median times differ significantly between tasks, but we do not know why.[15] Given the extremely long times taken to complete each HIT, we believe the time to complete each HIT may reflect crowd working strategies of the participants more than they reflect task difficulty.

3.2 Inter-rater reliability

We computed separate Krippendorff's alpha scores for each construct, obtaining a score of α=0.131 for Coherence, α=0.0438 for Grammaticality, and α=0.203 for Repetition. The original authors did not specify (and could not remember) how Krippendorff's alpha was computed, but these were the highest scores after multiple different attempts. We computed Krippendorff's alpha:

1. using a sparse matrix where each row represents a worker and each column represents an item.
2. using a sparse matrix as before, but removing any responses that were not allowed. (For example, one worker responded with '5' while only the values A and B are allowed.) This gave the best result.
3. using a dense matrix where we have three rows representing the first, second, and third response for each item, and each column represents an item. The results from this approach were more or less equivalent to the first approach.

Our results are a far cry from the α=0.47 in the original paper. In Section 4.1 we will further investigate the annotator quality through two different percentage agreement scores.

[15]We initially wanted to run an ANOVA to determine whether there are any significant differences between the three groups. Since this analysis assumes equality of variance, we first ran Levene's test. This test was significant ($F(2,1797)=27.91$, $p<0.05$), indicating that this assumption of the ANOVA was not satisifed, so we ran a Kruskal-Wallis test instead of the ANOVA. This test was significant ($H(2)=136.26$, $p<0.05$), indicating that the time per HIT differs between groups.

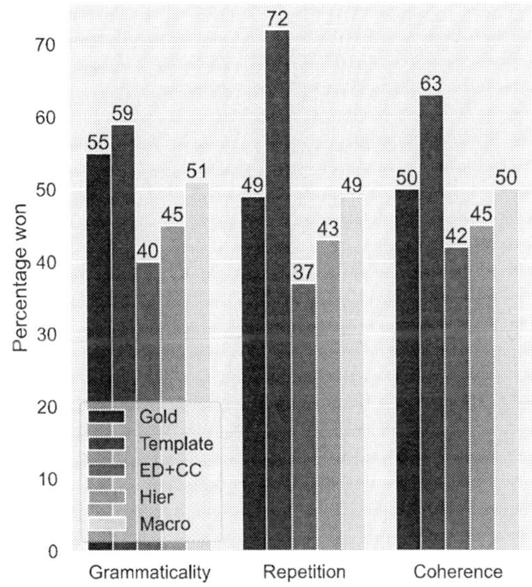

Figure 2: Percentage of system wins across all system comparisons, separated by task. Since we do not have the original data, we cannot compare our results to the original study.

3.3 System comparison

Figure 2 shows the percentage of system wins across all system comparisons, separated by task. We observe that, using this metric, the template-based approach beats all other systems, including the gold standard summaries. This is surprising, to say the least, since in the original paper the template-based approach is actually the *worst* system across the board.

We now turn to the Best-Worst Scaling (BWS) approach used in the original paper. Given the initial results in Figure 2, it is to be expected that

Category	Total	Min	Max	Mean	Stdev	Attention check
Overall	216	1	67	8.33	12.24	Mixed
Coherence	119	1	36	5.04	6.46	Yes
Repetition	135	1	33	4.44	6.37	Yes
Grammaticality	80	1	30	7.50	7.79	No

Table 2: Number of participants in our experiment. Total indicates the total number of unique participants per subset. Min, Max, Mean, and Std refer to the number of HITs per participant. The last column indicates the use of attention checks after each batch of 50 items.

Category	N	Mean	Median	Stdev	Min	Max
Overall	1800	73m49s	49m26s	65m19s	31s	239m56s
Coherence	600	73m26s	46m46s	70m0s	33s	239m56s
Repetition	600	52m36s	30m22s	56m17s	1m3s	234m38s
Grammaticality	600	95m25s	99m9s	61m50s	31s	237m59s

Table 3: Duration of each HIT. Times are cut off at the 4 hour mark, since we indicated that they should be completed within 4 hours. This differs from the 7 hours that were allotted to participants in the original experiment, but we doubt that this would have any effect on the results.

		Grammaticality	Coherence	Repetition
Replication	Gold	9.17	-0.42	-1.67
	Template	17.08	25.42	43.75*
	ED+CC	-19.58	-15.00	-25.83
	Hier	-9.58	-10.42	-14.58
	Macro	2.92	0.42	-1.67
		Grammaticality	Coherence	Repetition
Original	Gold	38.33	46.25*	30.83
	Template	−61.67*	−52.92*	−36.67*
	ED+CC	5.0	−8.33	−4.58
	Hier	13.33	4.58	3.75
	Macro	5.0	10.42	6.67

Table 4: Results using Best-Worst scaling. The asterisk indicates a significant difference between the system and Macro. The *Original* label refers to the original RotoWire results from Puduppully and Lapata (2021).

these results will also be different from the original paper. Table 4 shows that this is indeed the case. Whereas the original paper found multiple systems were significantly different from their system using Macro-planning (indicated by the asterisk), we now only find that the Template-based system is significantly better at avoiding repetitions than the system using Macro-planning. Full details about the statistics are provided in Appendix A.

3.4 Quantifying reproducibility

Now we can ask ourselves: how reproducible are the different measures that we aimed to reproduce? We might paraphrase this question as: how similar are our measures to the original measures of system quality? Given that the result of Best-Worst Scaling is a ranking with relative performance scores, the Spearman correlation is a natural fit.[16] For each of the three quality dimensions, we obtain low (and even negative) correlation values, meaning that our Best-Worst Scaling results do not seem associated with the original scores:

Grammaticality: $\rho = -0.21$
Coherence: $\rho = -0.1$
Repetition: $\rho = -0.05$

See Appendix B for a discussion of the CV* metric to quantify the reproducibility of the current experiment.

4 Additional/alternative analyses

4.1 Annotator quality

Next to Krippendorff's alpha, we can also compute other agreement metrics. For example, we can compute proportions for how often each participant agrees with the majority (i.e., at least 2 out of 3 ratings, for any given item). Table 5 shows the mean agreement for all workers (ranging between 0.72 and 0.74). To compensate for the variation in the number of items that were rated by each participant, we also compute a weighted mean where the agreement scores per participant is weighed

[16]With the caveat that the sample size is very small, leading to a less reliable measure of association.

Category	Mean	Weighted Mean
Coherence	0.72	0.78
Repetition	0.73	0.79
Grammaticality	0.74	0.76

Table 5: Mean agreement and weighted mean agreement of workers with the majority response for each item. The mean is computed based using the scores for all individual workers, even if they only carried out one HIT. The weighted mean multiplies each worker's agreement by the total number of HITs they performed, and divides the sum of all scores by the total number of HITs.

by the number of items rated by that participant. The resulting weighted agreement score is higher (between 0.76 and 0.78).

4.2 Mixed effects analysis

To control for possible random item effects of the individual summaries and to explore the extent to which the order in which the summaries were presented to workers influenced their ratings, we performed an additional generalized linear mixed effects analysis for each of the criteria (Coherence, Grammaticality, Repetition). We used the GLMER function from the *lme4* package in R (version 4.3.1.; R Core Team, 2023; Bates et al., 2015).[17] Since comparisons between Macro and the other systems were the main aim of the original authors, we set Macro as the reference category to which the other systems were compared for all three models. We first constructed a maximal model (Barr et al., 2013) that included a random intercept for *Items* and a random slope for *Order*. We started each criterion analysis by construing a maximal model that included the *System*Order* interaction in the fixed effects structure and a random slope for *Order*. For none of the criteria, the maximal model converged (presumably due to sparsity of the data). After removing the random slope for *Order*, the adjusted models converged. However, Likelihood Ratio Tests that compared the model with *Order* in the fixed effects structure to the random intercept for Summary model showed that adding the order in which the summaries were presented to workers did not improve the models' fit for any of the criteria:

Coherence: $\chi^2(5) = 8.97, p = .110$
Grammaticality: $\chi^2(5) = 4.87, p = .432$
Repetition:[18] $\chi^2(7) = 6.42, p = .491$

In other words: presentation order does not significantly influence the results; there is no evidence for a systematic preference for either the first or the second summary. See Appendix D for further discussion of our mixed effects analysis.

4.3 TrueSkill

Next to best-worst scaling, we also carried out a system comparison using the TrueSkill algorithm (Herbrich et al., 2007).[19] Since the performance of some systems may be very similar and a total ordering would not reflect this, we adopt the practice used in machine translation of presenting a partial ordering into significance clusters established by bootstrap resampling (Sakaguchi et al., 2014). In this case, the TrueSkill algorithm is run 1000 times, producing slightly different rankings each time as pairs of system outputs for comparison are randomly sampled. This way we can determine the range of ranks where each system is placed 95% of the time or more often. Clusters are then formed of systems whose rank ranges overlap.

Figure 3 shows the results. We find that only the Template-based and ED+CC system have non-overlapping confidence intervals, for one criterion, namely *Repetition*. Though robust (because of the bootstrapping procedure), this approach does find fewer differences between the systems than the original approach using an ANOVA and Tukey HSD test.

5 Discussion

5.1 Alternative design

One of the challenges of the design used in the original experiment is that for each quality dimension, the raters individually provided between 1 and 200 ratings. This makes it harder to assess inter-rater reliability, and also means that not all raters were presented with an attention check (providing grounds to exclude raters based on their performance). The design of this study could be improved by using larger sets of items, for example asking each participant to rate 50 items. This would allow us to

[17]We restructured the dataset by items (unique generated summaries) and coded the winning system in the comparison with "1" and the other system with "0", meaning that each HIT was represented by two rows, each focused on one of the two compared systems. We added an extra *Order* column, in which we coded whether the target system was the first (0) or second (1) system in the comparison.

[18]Here, the random slope for Order was included in the bigger model in the comparison.

[19]We used the Python implementation available through PyPI.

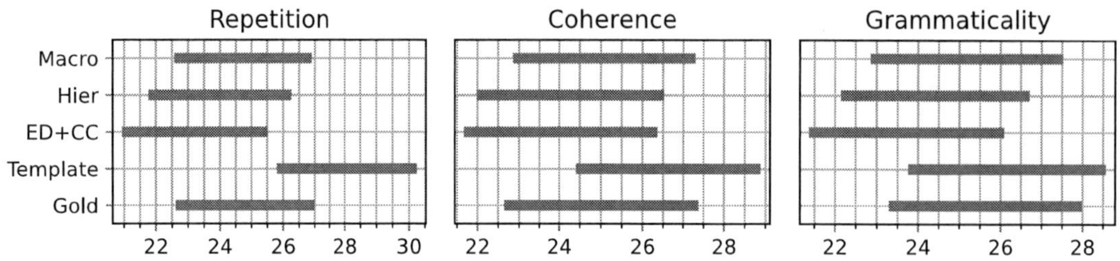

Figure 3: 95%-confidence intervals for the TrueSkill results. When the confidence intervals between two systems do not overlap, we can say that the system outputs are significantly different from each other. This is only the case for the repetition judgments for ed_cc and Template.

validate the performance of each participant, and to assess both inter- and intra-rater reliability.

In the original design, participants rank a pair of summaries but in the end four systems are compared to a gold standard. This is not the only possible implementation of Best-Worst Scaling. For example, Santhanam and Shaikh (2019) asked participants to rank all items at the same time. Presumably the original authors did not do this because the task may have become overwhelming, given the size of the texts. As another option, one could also introduce ties, to indicate that two summaries are roughly of the same quality. Finally, the order of presentation was not randomised in the original study. For each pair of summaries-to-be-assessed, $\langle A, B \rangle$, A was always presented before B.

Alternative design choices may or may not yield more reliable results, but the point is that there is a large parameter space that is ready to be explored. It would be useful for future studies to acknowledge this observation, and to motivate their design choices in more detail. Preregistration may be useful to specify the research methodology early on in the process (van Miltenburg et al., 2021).

5.2 On sample size fidelity

The guidelines for the ReproHum project indicated that we should copy the original set-up as closely as possible, including the number of participants (or in this case: HITs). However, Simonsohn (2015) suggests that the sample size for a replication should be 2.5 times bigger than the sample size estimated for the initial study, to be able to draw reliable conclusions about the reproducibility of the originally observed effects.[20,21] Discussing this idea in full goes beyond the scope of this paper, so for now we simply propose to consider the question: how can we ensure that reproduction studies in NLP provide a reliable estimate of the effects that are demonstrated in the original studies? This question is to some extent complementary to the one posed by Belz (2022): how variable are the human evaluation metrics that are used in NLP/NLG?

5.3 Exceptional circumstances

This reproduction took place in exceptional circumstances, where there were (1) responsive authors (2) who were able to share their original materials, *and* (3) multiple teams of investigators asking critical questions about implementation details for the original study (lowering the chance of overlooking important information, at the expense of time and effort). Thus, our study describes *the best case scenario* for reproduction studies in NLP, which is not representative of reproduction attempts in general. Even in the best scenario, some elements to be reproduced still raise questions. It is now even clearer to us that thorough documentation at publication time is essential, because otherwise many details about the original study may not be recovered.

6 Proposal for follow-up studies

Within the ReproHum project, another lab has simultaneously reproduced the same experiment as

[20]Furthermore, if the difference between systems is truly robust, we should be able to observe the difference through different methods as well. In other words: we might also try to carry out *conceptual* rather than *direct* replications, particularly if the original study is flawed. (See Zwaan et al. 2017; Derksen and Morawski 2022 for a discussion.)

[21]Van Zwet and Goodman (2022) go even further, and argue that the sample size for a replication study should depend on the original p-value. To be able to detect the original effect with high power, one might need a study with a sample size up to sixteen (!) times larger than the original study.

Claim	Reproduced?
Macro is the best system in comparison to the other systems	No
Template is the worst system across the board	No
Multiple systems are significantly different from Macro	No

Table 6: Original claims and their status in our paper.

in this paper. When the data for both experiments are released, this gives us the opportunity to run follow-up studies. Some ideas to consider are: (1) A more in-depth analysis of annotator reliability. (2) A reproduction of the original data analysis using the combined datasets —this at least gets us closer to Simonsohn's proposed sample size for reproduction studies. (3) A simulation study where ratings for the experiment are drawn from a larger pool of ratings and we can determine the amount of variation between different samples. This is similar to the bootstrap resampling strategy we used in the TrueSkill analysis (§4.3), but here we would run the original data analysis multiple times to estimate the range of possible scores for each model using Best-Worst Scaling approach.

7 Conclusion

We carried out a reproduction of Experiment 2 from Puduppully and Lapata (2021), with support from the original authors. We were not able to reproduce the exact results, instead finding opposite trends. For example, the Template-based approach seems to achieve the *best* performance across the board, where it was actually the *worst* performing system in the original paper. (See Table 6 for more.) It is not clear why the results differ from the original study, but we believe that both our study and the original study may be underpowered. Future reproduction studies should probably increase their sample size to make the results more reliable.

Next to the reproduction of the original study, we also provide an extensive selection of descriptive statistics, as well as a set of alternative analyses of the results. With these alternative approaches, we hope to have shown the possibilities and limitations of the experimental design. One key takeaway here is that it is important to have a sufficient amount of ratings per annotator (and ideally the same amount for each annotator). This enables us to dive deeper into the variation within and between ratings from different annotators. Understanding this variation also brings us closer to understanding the replicability of different research results.

Acknowledgments

We would like to thank Craig Thomson for coordinating the ReproHum project and assisting with our study. We also thank Ratish Puduppully for his responses to our inquiries about the original paper. The ReproHum project (and thus our evaluation experiment) is funded by EPSRC grant EP/V05645X/1. Our study was approved by the Research Ethics and Data management Committee (REDC) at the Tilburg School for Humanities and Digital Sciences (TSHD), reference REDC2019.40d.

References

Dale J Barr, Roger Levy, Christoph Scheepers, and Harry J Tily. 2013. Random effects structure for confirmatory hypothesis testing: Keep it maximal. *Journal of Memory and Language*, 68(3).

Douglas Bates, Martin Mächler, Ben Bolker, and Steve Walker. 2015. Fitting linear mixed-effects models using lme4. *Journal of Statistical Software*, 67(1):1–48.

Anya Belz. 2022. A Metrological Perspective on Reproducibility in NLP*. *Computational Linguistics*, 48(4):1125–1135.

Anya Belz, Shubham Agarwal, Anastasia Shimorina, and Ehud Reiter. 2020. ReproGen: Proposal for a shared task on reproducibility of human evaluations in NLG. In *Proceedings of the 13th International Conference on Natural Language Generation*, pages 232–236, Dublin, Ireland. Association for Computational Linguistics.

Anya Belz, Craig Thomson, and Ehud Reiter. 2023. Missing information, unresponsive authors, experimental flaws: The impossibility of assessing the reproducibility of previous human evaluations in NLP. In *The Fourth Workshop on Insights from Negative Results in NLP*, pages 1–10, Dubrovnik, Croatia. Association for Computational Linguistics.

Anouck Braggaar, Frédéric Tomas, Peter Blomsma, Saar Hommes, Nadine Braun, Emiel van Miltenburg, Chris van der Lee, Martijn Goudbeek, and Emiel Krahmer. 2022. A reproduction study of methods for evaluating dialogue system output: Replicating santhanam and shaikh (2019). In *Proceedings of the 15th International Conference on Natural Language*

Generation: Generation Challenges, pages 86–93, Waterville, Maine, USA and virtual meeting. Association for Computational Linguistics.

Michael Buhrmester, Tracy Kwang, and Samuel D. Gosling. 2011. Amazon's mechanical turk: A new source of inexpensive, yet high-quality, data? *Perspectives on Psychological Science*, 6(1):3–5.

Stephane Champely. 2020. *pwr: Basic Functions for Power Analysis*. R package version 1.3-0.

Maarten Derksen and Jill Morawski. 2022. Kinds of replication: Examining the meanings of "conceptual replication" and "direct replication". *Perspectives on Psychological Science*, 17(5):1490–1505. PMID: 35245130.

Ralf Herbrich, Tom Minka, and Thore Graepel. 2007. Trueskill(tm): A bayesian skill rating system. In *Advances in Neural Information Processing Systems 20*, pages 569–576. MIT Press.

David M. Howcroft, Anya Belz, Miruna-Adriana Clinciu, Dimitra Gkatzia, Sadid A. Hasan, Saad Mahamood, Simon Mille, Emiel van Miltenburg, Sashank Santhanam, and Verena Rieser. 2020. Twenty years of confusion in human evaluation: NLG needs evaluation sheets and standardised definitions. In *Proceedings of the 13th International Conference on Natural Language Generation*, pages 169–182, Dublin, Ireland. Association for Computational Linguistics.

Svetlana Kiritchenko and Saif Mohammad. 2017. Best-worst scaling more reliable than rating scales: A case study on sentiment intensity annotation. In *Proceedings of the 55th Annual Meeting of the Association for Computational Linguistics (Volume 2: Short Papers)*, pages 465–470, Vancouver, Canada. Association for Computational Linguistics.

Klaus Krippendorff. 2011. Computing krippendorff's alpha-reliability. Retrieved from https://repository.upenn.edu/asc_papers/43.

Leib Litman, Jonathan Robinson, and Cheskie Rosenzweig. 2015. The relationship between motivation, monetary compensation, and data quality among us- and india-based workers on mechanical turk. *Behavior Research Methods*, 47(2):519–528.

Jordan J Louviere, Terry N Flynn, and A A J Marley. 2015. *Best-Worst Scaling: Theory, Methods and Applications*. Cambridge University Press, Cambridge.

Bryan Orme. 2009. Maxdiff analysis: Simple counting, individual-level logit, and hb. Technical report, Sawtooth Software.

Ratish Puduppully, Li Dong, and Mirella Lapata. 2019. Data-to-text generation with entity modeling. In *Proceedings of the 57th Annual Meeting of the Association for Computational Linguistics*, pages 2023–2035, Florence, Italy. Association for Computational Linguistics.

Ratish Puduppully and Mirella Lapata. 2021. Data-to-text generation with macro planning. *Transactions of the Association for Computational Linguistics*, 9:510–527.

Ratish Surendran Puduppully. 2022. *Data-to-text generation with neural planning*. Ph.D. thesis, The University of Edinburgh.

R Core Team. 2023. *R: A Language and Environment for Statistical Computing*. R Foundation for Statistical Computing, Vienna, Austria.

Clément Rebuffel, Laure Soulier, Geoffrey Scoutheeten, and Patrick Gallinari. 2020. A hierarchical model for data-to-text generation. In *Advances in Information Retrieval*, pages 65–80, Cham. Springer International Publishing.

Keisuke Sakaguchi, Matt Post, and Benjamin Van Durme. 2014. Efficient elicitation of annotations for human evaluation of machine translation. In *Proceedings of the Ninth Workshop on Statistical Machine Translation*, pages 1–11, Baltimore, Maryland, USA. Association for Computational Linguistics.

Sashank Santhanam and Samira Shaikh. 2019. Towards best experiment design for evaluating dialogue system output. In *Proceedings of the 12th International Conference on Natural Language Generation*, pages 88–94, Tokyo, Japan. Association for Computational Linguistics.

Uri Simonsohn. 2015. Small telescopes: Detectability and the evaluation of replication results. *Psychological science*, 26(5):559–569.

Chris van der Lee, Albert Gatt, Emiel van Miltenburg, Sander Wubben, and Emiel Krahmer. 2019. Best practices for the human evaluation of automatically generated text. In *Proceedings of the 12th International Conference on Natural Language Generation*, pages 355–368, Tokyo, Japan. Association for Computational Linguistics.

Emiel van Miltenburg, Chris van der Lee, and Emiel Krahmer. 2021. Preregistering NLP research. In *Proceedings of the 2021 Conference of the North American Chapter of the Association for Computational Linguistics: Human Language Technologies*, pages 613–623, Online. Association for Computational Linguistics.

Erik W. van Zwet and Steven N. Goodman. 2022. How large should the next study be? predictive power and sample size requirements for replication studies. *Statistics in Medicine*, 41(16):3090–3101.

Sam Wiseman, Stuart Shieber, and Alexander Rush. 2017. Challenges in data-to-document generation. In *Proceedings of the 2017 Conference on Empirical Methods in Natural Language Processing*, pages 2253–2263, Copenhagen, Denmark. Association for Computational Linguistics.

Rolf A Zwaan, Alexander Etz, Richard E Lucas, and M Brent Donnellan. 2017. Making replication mainstream. *Behavioral and Brain Sciences*, 41:1–61.

A Detailed statistics

We find the following results:

- For Grammaticality, the ANOVA result was significant: F(4,95)=4.027, p=0.005. The Tukey HSD results are provided in Table 7.
- For Coherence, the ANOVA result was significant: F(4,95)=4.313, p=0.003. The Tukey HSD results are provided in Table 8.
- For Repetition, the ANOVA result was significant: F(4,95)=9.802, p<0.001. The Tukey HSD results are provided in Table 9.

Note that, as in the original study, these results were computed before re-scaling the scores to values between -100 and 100.

B Applying CV*

Belz (2022) suggests to use CV* as a general measure of reproducibility, but it is unclear to us whether CV* can or should be applied in this situation. If it can be applied in this case, then we can only compute CV* over two values at a time. For example: comparing the Grammaticality score of a particular system (e.g. Macro) between the original study and our reproduction. With only two data points, the CV* value is probably not very reliable. Having that said, we did run the CV* analysis for completeness' sake.

Because CV* requires all values to be greater than zero, we need to transform the scale from [-100,100] to [0, 200]. For Macro, this results in:

Grammaticality: CV*([102.92, 105])=1.995
Coherence: CV*([100.42, 110.42])=9.457
Repetition: CV*([98.33, 106.67])=8.112

It is not clear how to interpret these values.

C A brief qualitative look at the summaries

The most striking difference we found is the one between template and macro for repetition (as can be seen in Table 4. We take a brief look at two summaries for both macro and template to see if we can detect any patterns that might explain the difference.

The first summary (Figure 4 shows clear repetition in the macro case, but surprisingly only two

System summaries

Template: The San Antonio Spurs (25 - 16) defeated the Portland Trail Blazers (30 - 10) 110 - 96 . LaMarcus Aldridge scored 24 points (9 - 18 FG , 0 - 0 3PT , 6 - 6 FT) to go with 8 rebounds . Damian Lillard scored 23 points (9 - 17 FG , 0 - 5 3PT , 5 - 6 FT) to go with 2 rebounds . Kawhi Leonard scored 20 points (8 - 18 FG , 1 - 4 3PT , 3 - 4 FT) to go with 4 rebounds . Danny Green scored 19 points (6 - 8 FG , 4 - 5 3PT , 3 - 3 FT) to go with 5 rebounds . Patty Mills scored 18 points (7 - 14 FG , 3 - 7 3PT , 1 - 1 FT) to go with 4 rebounds . CJ McCollum scored 17 points (7 - 10 FG , 2 - 2 3PT , 1 - 4 FT) to go with 2 rebounds . The San Antonio Spurs ' next game will be at home against the Dallas Mavericks, while the Portland Trail Blazers will travel to play the Bulls .

Macro: The San Antonio Spurs defeated the Portland Trail Blazers , 110 - 96 , at AT & T Center on Wednesday . The Spurs (25 - 16) came into this game as one of the best defenses in the NBA , but they were able to prevail with a huge road win . The Spurs (30 - 10) have now won five of their last six games , as they continue to slide down the stretch . LaMarcus Aldridge scored a team - high 24 points on 9 - of - 18 shooting to go with eight rebounds , three assists , one steal and one block on 9 - of - 18 shooting . Damian Lillard finished with 23 points on 9 - of - 17 shooting , along with five assists and two rebounds , in 36 minutes . C. J. McCollum chipped in 17 points on 7 - of - 10 shooting , in 20 minutes off the bench . The Trail Blazers shot 50 percent from the field and 32 percent from three - point range . The Spurs shot 45 percent from the field and 38 percent from three - point range . Kawhi Leonard led the way with 20 points , four rebounds , five assists and three steals . Danny Green added 19 points , five rebounds , two assists and two steals , in 34 minutes . Tim Duncan chipped in 11 points , 12 rebounds , six assists , two blocks and one steal , in 30 minutes . Patty Mills chipped in 18 points on 7 - of - 14 shooting , in 22 minutes off the bench . The Spurs shot 45 percent from the field and 38 percent from three - point range , as they shot 45 percent from the field and 38 percent from three - point range . Up next , the Spurs will travel to New Orleans to take on the Pelicans on Friday .

Figure 4: Macro and template example 1.

group1	group2	meandiff	p-adj	lower	upper	reject
0	1	0.95	0.9396	-2.4979	4.3979	False
0	2	-3.45	0.0498	-6.8979	-0.0021	True
0	3	-2.25	0.3713	-5.6979	1.1979	False
0	4	-0.75	0.974	-4.1979	2.6979	False
1	2	-4.4	0.0053	-7.8479	-0.9521	True
1	3	-3.2	0.0821	-6.6479	0.2479	False
1	4	-1.7	0.6475	-5.1479	1.7479	False
2	3	1.2	0.8689	-2.2479	4.6479	False
2	4	2.7	0.1971	-0.7479	6.1479	False
3	4	1.5	0.7457	-1.9479	4.9479	False

Table 7: Grammaticality: Multiple Comparison of Means - Tukey HSD, FWER=0.05

group1	group2	meandiff	p-adj	lower	upper	reject
0	1	3.1	0.1178	-0.4564	6.6564	False
0	2	-1.75	0.6492	-5.3064	1.8064	False
0	3	-1.2	0.8812	-4.7564	2.3564	False
0	4	0.1	1.0	-3.4564	3.6564	False
1	2	-4.85	0.0024	-8.4064	-1.2936	True
1	3	-4.3	0.0096	-7.8564	-0.7436	True
1	4	-3.0	0.1398	-6.5564	0.5564	False
2	3	0.55	0.9928	-3.0064	4.1064	False
2	4	1.85	0.5994	-1.7064	5.4064	False
3	4	1.3	0.8472	-2.2564	4.8564	False

Table 8: Coherence: Multiple Comparison of Means - Tukey HSD, FWER=0.05.

group1	group2	meandiff	p-adj	lower	upper	reject
0	1	5.45	0.0023	1.4621	9.4379	True
0	2	-2.9	0.2635	-6.8879	1.0879	False
0	3	-1.55	0.8159	-5.5379	2.4379	False
0	4	0.0	1.0	-3.9879	3.9879	False
1	2	-8.35	0.0	-12.3379	-4.3621	True
1	3	-7.0	0.0	-10.9879	-3.0121	True
1	4	-5.45	0.0023	-9.4379	-1.4621	True
2	3	1.35	0.88	-2.6379	5.3379	False
2	4	2.9	0.2635	-1.0879	6.8879	False
3	4	1.55	0.8159	-2.4379	5.5379	False

Table 9: Repetition: Multiple Comparison of Means - Tukey HSD, FWER=0.05

System summaries

Template: The Portland Trail Blazers (2 - 2) defeated the Minnesota Timberwolves (2 - 1) 106 - 101 . Damian Lillard scored 34 points (14 - 25 FG , 4 - 9 3PT , 2 - 3 FT) to go with 2 rebounds . Kevin Martin scored 24 points (7 - 12 FG , 2 - 4 3PT , 8 - 11 FT) to go with 2 rebounds . CJ McCollum scored 18 points (7 - 18 FG , 2 - 6 3PT , 2 - 2 FT) to go with 6 rebounds . Al-Farouq Aminu scored 17 points (7 - 12 FG , 2 - 5 3PT , 1 - 2 FT) to go with 9 rebounds . Andrew Wiggins scored 16 points (5 - 17 FG , 0 - 3 3PT , 6 - 7 FT) to go with 6 rebounds . Gorgui Dieng scored 12 points (6 - 9 FG , 0 - 0 3PT , 0 - 1 FT) to go with 5 rebounds . The Portland Trail Blazers ' next game will be at home against the Dallas Mavericks, while the Minnesota Timberwolves will travel to play the Bulls .

Macro: The Portland Trail Blazers (2 - 2) defeated the Minnesota Timberwolves (2 - 1) 106 - 101 on Friday . Damian Lillard had a game - high 34 points on 14 - of - 25 shooting , to go along with seven assists , two rebounds , two steals and one block , in 38 minutes . C. J. McCollum added 18 points , six rebounds , four assists , one steal and one block , in 36 minutes . Al-Farouq Aminu chipped in 17 points , nine rebounds , one assist and one block , in 32 minutes . The Trail Blazers shot 46 percent from the field and 30 percent from three - point range . The Timberwolves , who shot 43 percent from the field and 23 percent from beyond the arc . Kevin Martin led the team in scoring , putting up 24 points on 7 - of - 12 shooting in 35 minutes off the bench . Andrew Wiggins struggled shooting , going 5 - of - 17 from the field and 0 - of - 3 from three - point range . Ricky Rubio added 12 points , nine assists , nine rebounds and three steals in 32 minutes . The Timberwolves shot just 43 percent from the field and 23 percent from three - point range .

Figure 5: Macro and template example 2.

out of three wins are given to template (while template does not show obvious repetitions). In the macro summary there is repetition both between and within sentences ('(...) The Spurs shot 45 percent from the field and 38 percent from three - point range . (...) The Spurs shot 45 percent from the field and 38 percent from three - point range , as they shot 45 percent from the field and 38 percent from three - point range . (...)')

The example in Figure 5 shows no such obvious repetitions. It is clear that macro is quite a bit longer than the summary generated by a template. The template text looks more concise (without fully describing all game statistics, only showing them briefly), focusing more on the key details and briefly describing the next game (which does not happen in macro). In this case template wins three out of three times. Surprisingly not because there are obvious repetitions, but maybe the short text without too many details and only showing the most essential facts is appreciated.

D Further results from the Mixed Effects analysis

We set the probability distribution on binomial with a logit link function and we used parametric bootstrapping over 100 iterations to estimate the confidence intervals and p-values. The complete results can be found in Table 10.

At 95% CI, the results of our mixed effects analyses largely confirm the findings of Section 3.3 in that Macro is significantly different, but worse, for Coherence and Repetition. However, in this analysis, we also find that Macro performs significantly better than Ed+CC for Grammaticality and Repetition.

	System	*B*	*SE* b	99% CI
Coherence	Macro	0.01	0.15	-0.42, 0.39
	Gold	-0.02	0.21	-0.59, 0.53
	Template*	0.53	0.21	0.10, 0.94
	Ed+CC	-0.33	0.19	-0.84, 0.16
	RBF-2020	-0.21	0.22	-0.78, 0.37
	System	*B*	*SE* b	99% CI
Grammat.	Macro	0.03	0.16	-0.36, 0.48
	Gold	0.13	0.21	-0.47, 0.66
	Template	0.31	0.21	-0.28, 0.84
	Ed+CC*	-0.44	0.23	-0.91, -0.009
	RBF-2020	-0.23	0.21	-0.79, 0.29
	System	*B*	*SE* b	99% CI
Repetition	Macro	-0.03	0.17	-0.46, 0.41
	Gold	-0.004	0.25	-0.64, 0.68
	Template**	1.06	0.25	0.46, 1.74
	Ed+CC*	-0.55	0.24	-1.05, -0.08
	RBF-2020	-0.30	0.25	-1.01, 0.33

Table 10: The estimated coefficients and standard errors for the GLMER models that were fitted to workers' ratings of Coherence, Grammaticality, and Repetitio; Macro represents the intercept for all models. Significant at 95% CI = *, at 99% CI = **.

Human Evaluation Reproduction Report for *Data-to-text Generation with Macro Planning*

Mohammad Arvan and **Natalie Parde**
University of Illinois Chicago, USA
{marvan3,parde}@uic.edu

Abstract

This paper presents a partial reproduction study of *Data-to-text Generation with Macro Planning* by Puduppully and Lapata (2021). This work was conducted as part of the ReproHum project, a multi-lab effort to reproduce the results of NLP papers incorporating human evaluations. We follow the same instructions provided by the authors and the ReproHum team to the best of our abilities. We collect preference ratings for the following evaluation criteria in order: conciseness, coherence, and grammaticality. Our results are highly correlated with the original experiment. Nonetheless, the presented results may be insufficient to conclude that the system proposed and developed by the original paper is superior compared to other systems. We suspect that combining our results with the three other reproductions of this paper through the ReproHum project will paint a clearer picture. Overall, we hope that our work is a step towards a more transparent and reproducible research landscape.

1 Introduction

Recent efforts have advanced the quality of automatic evaluation metrics, but these metrics still suffer from many shortcomings and flaws (e.g., a lack of correlation between scores and human judgments, such as that reported by Belz and Reiter (2006), Reiter and Belz (2009), Schluter (2017), Novikova et al. (2017), Post (2018), and van der Lee et al. (2019), among others) that render reliance on them less than ideal. Human evaluation eliminates most of these concerns, making it central to evaluating many machine learning, and in particular natural language processing (NLP), approaches. Nevertheless, evaluating the quality of algorithms and models using human raters still raises several unique challenges that can discourage researchers from doing so. For example, one prohibiting factor is cost: while automated metrics can be used repeatedly, essentially free of charge, human evaluations require the recruitment of paid raters with appropriate background knowledge or skillsets. The costs associated with this often force researchers only to evaluate a limited number of samples when conducting human evaluations, using crowd-sourcing platforms such as Amazon Mechanical Turk (AMT).[1] The use of crowd-sourcing platforms as a primary vehicle for subject recruitment can raise its own issues, as has been extensively documented by others even outside of the NLP research community (Goodman et al., 2013; Zhou and Fishbach, 2016; Arditte et al., 2016).

There have been many efforts to understand and mitigate the risks associated with human evaluation. Common practices include measuring inter-annotator agreement, calculating the power laws to select an appropriate sample size, and using statistical tests to measure the significance of the results (Wiebe et al., 1999; Snow et al., 2008; Pustejovsky and Stubbs, 2012; Dror et al., 2018; van der Lee et al., 2019). Undoubtedly, these practices further boost confidence in the results of human evaluation. However, they focus on pre-and post-analysis without providing insight into the human evaluation process. The lack of a systematic process for human evaluation has become a major concern in the last few years (Shimorina and Belz, 2021). Therefore, one may suggest that efforts to document and evaluate the human evaluation process are the next logical step to further improve the quality of human evaluation results without introducing any additional cost. This increased transparency and scrutiny is aligned with the goals of open science, will improve reproducibility, and will help the community to conduct higher-quality research.

From a broader perspective, concerns regarding scientific reproducibility are not new. In fact,

[1] https://www.mturk.com

Proceedings of the Third Workshop on Human Evaluation of NLP Systems, pages 89–96, Varna, Bulgaria, Sep 7, 2023.
https://doi.org/10.26615/978-954-452-088-5_008

the term *reproducibility crisis* has been used to describe the widespread barriers and inattention to reproducibility in many scientific fields (Baker, 2016; Wieling et al., 2018; Pineau et al., 2019; Belz et al., 2021; Pineau et al., 2021). With the increasing prominence of supervised machine learning methods that rely on empirical evidence in contemporary research, the importance of having reproducible results has become more important than ever. A global movement to promote increased reproducibility standards is gaining momentum (UNESCO, 2021), with the United Nations Educational, Scientific and Cultural Organization (UNESCO) taking a prominent role by underlining the value of open science with increased scrutiny and reproducibility as one of its main pillars. Ultimately, we can address reproducibility concerns by actively and systematically analyzing the current state of affairs, finding flaws, and proposing solutions (Belz et al., 2020; Sinha et al., 2021; Nature, 2022; Belz et al., 2022; ACL, 2022; Deutsch et al., 2022).

Over the last few years, many researchers have attempted to address the reproducibility crisis in NLP, often through meta-analyses and reproducibility studies of papers using automated metrics (Olorisade et al., 2017; Raff, 2019; Arvan et al., 2022a,b). Much less attention has been given to reproducibility studies of papers using human evaluations, mainly due to the additional complications of doing so (Belz et al., 2023). The ReproHum project aims to address this by conducting a large-scale, multi-lab reproducibility study of 50+ NLP papers incorporating human evaluations. As a participating lab in the ReproHum project, we were assigned a human evaluation experiment from *Data-to-text Generation with Macro Planning* by Puduppully and Lapata (2021). In this paper, we present our attempt to reproduce the results of that experiment. Thanks to the efforts of Puduppully and Lapata (2021) and the organizers of ReproHum, we were able to access most of the information required to reproduce our assigned experiment.

2 Background

Reproduction approaches were standardized across the ReproHum project, as summarized in this section (§2.1). We also present relevant evaluation details from the paper itself (§2.2), and we provide additional information from the paper's authors that was not included in the original paper itself but was necessary for reproducing the results (§2.3).

2.1 Common Approach to Reproductions

As a participating lab in the ReproHum project, we were provided with the following materials: (a) a document containing a common approach to reproduction, (b) the paper and the data required to reproduce the given experiment, and (c) a document containing all other additional information. We did not communicate with the authors directly. Instead, all communication was done through the ReproHum organizers. This decision was made to ensure consistency across reproductions and prevent authors from inadvertently influencing the reproduction process. It also enabled complete documentation of the process.

The document providing the common approach to reproductions offered a general overview of the process of reproducing a human evaluation experiment. The document was divided into two sections: one containing information for processes prior to the reproduction, and the other containing information for processes during and after the reproduction. The first section instructed us to familiarize ourselves with the paper and the experiment, and to calculate the amount of compensation required for crowd workers.[2] We were also asked to follow our own institutional guidelines regarding conducting human evaluation experiments. In our case, this involved applying for Institutional Review Board (IRB) approval at our own university (the University of Illinois Chicago). All outcomes of our reproduction were then achieved adhering to our approved IRB protocol.

The second section of the common approach focused on the reproduction process itself and subsequent data analyses. We were asked to fill out a Human Evaluation Data Sheet (HEDS) for each task. The HEDS is a spreadsheet that contains information about the task, the crowd workers, and the collected responses. Using this spreadsheet, we identified error types and created a side-by-side presentation of the results, findings, and conclusions to further assess the degree to which the reproduced outcomes matched the paper's original findings.

2.2 Evaluation Details from the Paper

Paper Summary. In our assigned paper, *Data-to-text Generation with Macro Planning*, Puduppully and Lapata (2021) augment a neural model

[2]Crowd workers providing annotations for ReproHum reproductions were all recruited from AMT using a single, centralized account.

with a macro planning stage for the task of data-to-text generation. This task aims to generate natural language that describes input data such as tabular data (e.g., databases of records or accounting spreadsheets) or structured data (e.g., knowledge graphs or semantic networks). The performance of end-to-end neural models has effectively rendered older techniques obsolete, but more modern models are far from perfect. The authors report that major issues including imprecision, hallucination, and poor context selection and document structuring plague modern models for this task. To address these issues, the authors propose the usage of macro planning, the high-level organization of information and how it should be presented. The authors highlight the current limitation of existing datasets for data-to-text generation using this approach, but note that nonetheless the expected output of these datasets is structured into several paragraphs, which can be used to define paragraph plans. Methodologically, the authors present a two-step pipeline for implementing their approach: first, a macro plan is generated using the training data, and then the plan is fed to a text generation model.

The authors use the RotoWire (Wiseman et al., 2017) and MLB (Puduppully et al., 2019) datasets to train and evaluate their proposed approach. Both datasets contain structured data about basketball and baseball games, respectively, with information pertaining to game statistics and summaries. They conducted human evaluation alongside automatic evaluation and empirically demonstrated that their generated text was more factual, coherent, and fluent compared to existing state-of-the-art models. Although their evaluation consists of both automatic evaluation and human evaluation, our focus is on the human evaluation part of their work. The human evaluation was performed through a comparative study of gold-standard output and four other systems, including theirs. Besides the model proposed by the authors (Macro), the other systems were: 1) a template-based generator (Templ), 2) ED+CC, which was the best performing system from an earlier study (Wiseman et al., 2017), and 3) the state-of-the-art model (RBF-2020) at the time of publication of the original paper (Rebuffel et al., 2020).

Human Evaluation. To conduct their human evaluation, Puduppully and Lapata (2021) used AMT. To ensure the acceptable quality of received responses, the authors required that workers had at

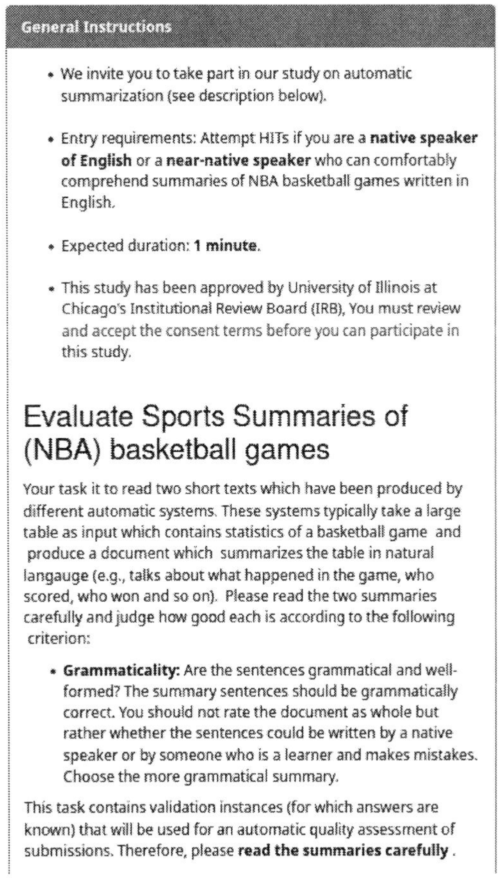
General Instructions

- We invite you to take part in our study on automatic summarization (see description below).
- Entry requirements: Attempt HITs if you are a **native speaker of English** or a **near-native speaker** who can comfortably comprehend summaries of NBA basketball games written in English.
- Expected duration: **1 minute**.
- This study has been approved by University of Illinois at Chicago's Institutional Review Board (IRB). You must review and accept the consent terms before you can participate in this study.

Evaluate Sports Summaries of (NBA) basketball games

Your task it to read two short texts which have been produced by different automatic systems. These systems typically take a large table as input which contains statistics of a basketball game and produce a document which summarizes the table in natural langauge (e.g., talks about what happened in the game, who scored, who won and so on). Please read the two summaries carefully and judge how good each is according to the following criterion:

- **Grammaticality:** Are the sentences grammatical and well-formed? The summary sentences should be grammatically correct. You should not rate the document as whole but rather whether the sentences could be written by a native speaker or by someone who is a learner and makes mistakes. Choose the more grammatical summary.

This task contains validation instances (for which answers are known) that will be used for an automatic quality assessment of submissions. Therefore, please **read the summaries carefully**.

Figure 1: Instructions given to AMT workers for this task.

least a 98% approval rate across at least 1000 previously completed tasks. Furthermore, they limited the locations of crowd workers to English-speaking countries (US, UK, Canada, Ireland, Australia, and New Zealand). The human evaluation was split into two tasks, with the first focusing on the number of supporting and contradicting facts in the game summaries and the second evaluating the quality of the generated text based on coherence, grammar, and conciseness. Our main objective was to reproduce the second task.

The second task elicited workers' preferences by asking them to compare two randomly selected summaries. Figures 1 and 2 illustrate the instructions and the input regions that the crowd workers used to respond. We used exact replicas of these in our reproduction (described later). The authors used Best-Worst Scaling (Louviere and Woodworth, 1991; Louviere et al., 2015) to present the results. The score for each system was calculated

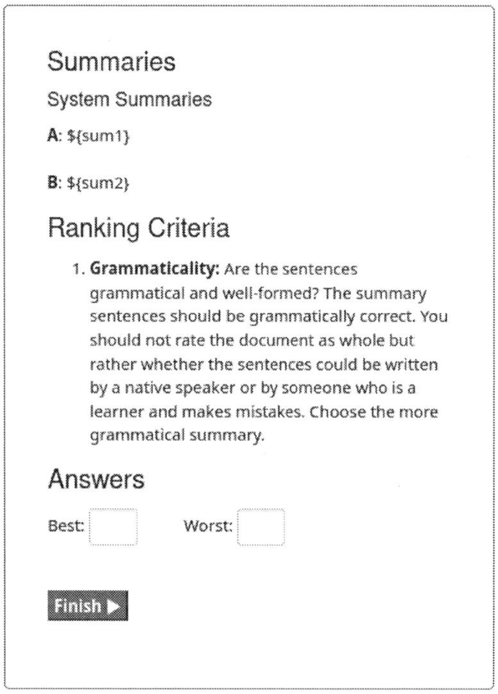

Figure 2: Specific input regions that AMT workers used to rank criteria associated with system summaries.

by subtracting the number of times the system was selected as the worst from the number of times it was selected as the best, divided by the total number of appearances of the system. The output of the four competing systems and gold output were divided into ten pairs of summaries. The evaluation criteria were grammar, coherence, and conciseness. Each pair was presented to three crowd workers to collect three distinct preference ratings per pair. Overall, the authors evaluated the system on the basis of 40 summaries (20 per dataset) and ten system pairs. With three evaluation criteria and three raters for each task, this meant that 3,600 preference ratings were solicited overall. The authors reported that 206 crowd workers overall participated in this task.

2.3 Additional Evalution Details from the Authors

Although we did not communicate with the authors directly, we were provided with a document containing additional information about the human evaluation process to support our reproduction. This information was acquired through correspondence between the authors and the ReproHum project team. The document contained information about the task setup, the instructions provided to the crowd workers, and the quality control measures that were employed. The ReproHum organizers mediated these correspondences to prevent undue influences to the reproduction process and to ensure that any communication between the authors and the reproduction team was documented. An additional practical motivation for this was that, as previously mentioned, two teams were assigned to reproduce each experiment—in requiring individual teams to refer to this document rather than correspond with the authors directly, the ReproHum organizers sought to maintain a level of consistency between the two teams.

The original authors were exceptional in providing additional information required to reproduce the experiments. For example, they granted us access to the original forms used in AMT to collect the responses. They also noted that while each task was assigned to three distinct crowd workers, the crowd workers had the option to accept multiple tasks. The authors also mentioned an exclusion criterion for the crowd workers to ensure the quality of the collected responses.

3 Methods

Our methods for reproducing the paper were as follows. We followed the same instructions provided by the ReproHum team to the best of our abilities, even following the exact same order of evaluation criteria as the other team. Specifically, we collected preference ratings for our evaluation criteria in the following order:

1. Conciseness
2. Coherence
3. Grammar

Each criterion was split into four mini-batches, each of which contained a quarter of the total number of tasks. The original authors incorporated attention checks to ensure the quality of received responses, by defining a set of conditions that (if met) would signal that the crowd worker should be excluded from the rest of the tasks. These exclusionary conditions were limited to the first two criteria (conciseness and coherence). For conciseness, they annotated and excluded the comparisons between all pairs except those involving the output generated by the template-based system. Since they

Model	Original			Ours		
	Gram	*Coher*	*Concis*	*Gram*	*Coher*	*Concis*
Gold	38.33	46.25*	30.83	14.17	12.50	5.83
Templ	-61.67*	-52.92*	-36.67*	-23.33*	-20.00*	-5.83
ED+CC	5.0	-8.33	-4.58	-8.33	-7.50	-5.00
RBF-2020	13.33	4.58	3.75	9.17	9.17	0.83
Macro	5.0	10.42	6.67	8.33	5.83	4.17

Table 1: Comparison of ROTOWIRE performance metrics. *Gram*, *Coher*, and *Concis* correspond to grammar, coherence, and conciseness, respectively. * indicates a statistically significant difference ($p < 0.05$) between Macro and the other systems. Note that the **Original** column numbers are from Table 5 of the original paper, while the **Ours** column numbers are from our reproduction.

no longer had access to the annotated exclusion criteria, we had to slightly diverge from the original process. As an alternative, we followed the instructions provided by the ReproHum team and limited the exclusion to pairs involving the gold output and one of the systems other than the template-based system. Specifically, the ReproHum team utilized NLTK[3] to compute an n-gram-based similarity score. The difference between the gold score and the system score was used to select 12 pairs with the highest difference. If any of the crowd workers rated one of these very different system outputs as superior to gold output, they were excluded from the rest of the tasks.

The exclusion process based on ratings of coherence was simpler than that used for ratings of conciseness. For coherence, if a crowd worker selected the template system output as superior to the gold output they were excluded from the rest of the tasks. Since we conducted our experiment after the other team assigned to this paper had finished their reproduction, workers excluded from the first team's study were also excluded from ours. Workers were paid for all tasks that they completed regardless of whether they were excluded. We paid workers $0.22 per task, compared to $0.15 in the original paper. This difference was due to adjustments for inflation and local minimum wage.

4 Results

Our results are summarized in Table 1. The results were computed using 1800 responses collected through twelve mini-batches (four for each of the three evaluation criteria). Each batch took approximately a day to finish collecting all responses. Overall, 262 crowd workers participated in this task.

[3]https://www.nltk.org

While the original study reported Krippendorff's $\alpha = 0.47$, ours was much worse ($\alpha = -0.011$). Note that the original authors calculated this coefficient using the results on both datasets; however, we computed our results using half the number of responses they used. The feedback we received from the crowd workers was positive.

We can observe from the results that the magnitude of difference reported between conditions in the original study's results is much higher than ours. For example, when evaluating grammaticality, the original study reports a best-worst scaling (BWS) score of -61.67 for the template system (the lowest score reported among all conditions), while ours is -23.33 (the lowest score reported among all conditions in our reproduction). Similarly, for coherence, our BWS score of 12.50 is much smaller than the reported BWS=46.25. We utilized the same statistical significance test as the original study (a one-way ANOVA with post-hoc Tukey HSD tests). The results of this test suggest that only two conditions (the Template system's scores for grammar and coherence) yield results with statistically significant differences from the Macro system. This is a different finding from the original study, which reported statistically significant different results for four measures. These measures were Templ for grammar, coherence, and conciseness, and Gold for coherence.

In our analyses of the observed errors, we found a high level of similarity between the original experiment and our reproduction. We used Pearson's r and Spearman's ρ to measure the correlation between the two experiments. With Pearson's $r = 0.90$ and Spearman's $\rho = 0.83$, we can conclude that the outcomes from the two experiments are highly correlated. In other words, in spite of the differences explained and observed between the two studies, our results do not invalidate the original study's findings.

5 Discussion

To discuss the implications of our findings, we first reiterate the contributions of the original study and the scope of our reproduction. Puduppully and Lapata (2021) presented a novel technique with the goal of improving the quality of data-to-text generation. They used a combination of automatic and human evaluation methods to show that their approach was superior to existing state-of-the-art models on two datasets, RotoWire and MLB. The scope of our reproduction was limited to the second human evaluation task reported in their paper, examining the quality of generated text based on coherence, grammaticality, and conciseness. Furthermore, we only reproduced the results on the RotoWire dataset. To provide a better perspective, MLB dataset, is larger (nearly ten times as many tokens) than the RotoWire dataset. Hence, we cannot form conclusive judgments based on a full reproduction of this experiment; rather, we focus on a subset of it.

Thus, our outcomes are currently inconclusive but promising, with evidence of a high level of similarity between our findings and those originally reported. Through our focus on the results that are available, we do not believe that there is enough evidence to claim that the Macro system proposed and developed by the original paper is superior compared to other systems. However, we believe that combining our results with the three other reproductions of this paper through the ReproHum project will paint a clearer picture. Therefore, we leave the final judgment to the ReproHum team.

Regarding the reproduction process itself, we found that many details required to successfully reproduce the original work were missing from the paper. We believe that this is likely due to many factors associated with the current NLP research climate, including an overemphasis on novelty, formatting, and paper length, that are all beyond the original authors' control. Thanks to the cooperation of the authors, we were able to find answers to the most important questions. We underscore that this level of communication is hard to find. Unfortunately, there are still little to no guidelines regarding the long-term support of research artifacts and files once studies have been published. It is hard to imagine the contemporary machine learning and natural language processing research landscapes without empirical studies driving them forward. At the same time, perhaps conferences and journals should consider potential avenues for collecting technical details beyond what has been made available in the paper itself. Another option is to further encourage the publication of reproduction studies in primary publication venues.

6 Conclusion

In this work, we have presented our attempt to reproduce the human evaluation of one experiment from *Data-to-text Generation with Macro Planning* by Puduppully and Lapata (2021). Overall, with Pearson's $r = 0.90$ and Spearman's $\rho = 0.83$ when comparing outcomes of the original study and our reproduction, we can conclude that when reproducing the experiment as described in the paper we observe highly correlated results. Nonetheless, we believe that without the help and cooperation of the original authors, we might have observed a different outcome. We note that the reproduced results in this work are only a portion of the results presented in the original paper. Therefore, concluding that the claims made by the original study are valid at this point would be premature. We leave the final judgment to the ReproHum team.

Acknowledgments

We are immensely grateful to Ratish Puduppully and Mirella Lapata, the authors of the original paper, for their invaluable work and exceptional responsiveness in providing additional information and support throughout this reproduction project. Their cooperation and guidance have been instrumental in ensuring the accuracy and fidelity of our work. We also extend our appreciation to the ReproHum project team, including Anya Belz, Ehud Reiter, Craig Thomson, and Maja Popović, for their collaboration and expertise, which have enriched this endeavor. Furthermore, we would like to express our sincere thanks to the Engineering and Physical Sciences Research Council (EPSRC) for their generous grant support (EP/V05645X/1), without which this project would not have been possible. The collective efforts of all involved have been crucial in shaping the success of this reproduction, and we are truly thankful for their support and contributions.

References

ACL. 2022. ACL Responsible NLP Research.

Kimberly A Arditte, Demet Çek, Ashley M Shaw, and Kiara R Timpano. 2016. The importance of assessing clinical phenomena in mechanical turk research. *Psychological assessment*, 28(6):684.

Mohammad Arvan, Luís Pina, and Natalie Parde. 2022a. Reproducibility in computational linguistics: Is source code enough? In *Proceedings of the 2022 Conference on Empirical Methods in Natural Language Processing, EMNLP 2022, Abu Dhabi, United Arab Emirates, December 7-11, 2022*, pages 2350–2361. Association for Computational Linguistics.

Mohammad Arvan, Luís Pina, and Natalie Parde. 2022b. Reproducibility of exploring neural text simplification models: A review. In *Proceedings of the 15th International Conference on Natural Language Generation: Generation Challenges*, pages 62–70, Waterville, Maine, USA and virtual meeting. Association for Computational Linguistics.

Monya Baker. 2016. 1,500 scientists lift the lid on reproducibility. *Nature*, 533(7604).

Anja Belz and Ehud Reiter. 2006. Comparing automatic and human evaluation of NLG systems. In *EACL 2006, 11st Conference of the European Chapter of the Association for Computational Linguistics, Proceedings of the Conference, April 3-7, 2006, Trento, Italy*. The Association for Computer Linguistics.

Anya Belz, Shubham Agarwal, Anastasia Shimorina, and Ehud Reiter. 2020. ReproGen: Proposal for a shared task on reproducibility of human evaluations in NLG. In *Proceedings of the 13th International Conference on Natural Language Generation, INLG 2020, Dublin, Ireland, December 15-18, 2020*, pages 232–236. Association for Computational Linguistics.

Anya Belz, Shubham Agarwal, Anastasia Shimorina, and Ehud Reiter. 2021. A systematic review of reproducibility research in natural language processing. In *Proceedings of the 16th Conference of the European Chapter of the Association for Computational Linguistics: Main Volume, EACL 2021, Online, April 19 - 23, 2021*, pages 381–393. Association for Computational Linguistics.

Anya Belz, Maja Popovic, and Simon Mille. 2022. Quantified reproducibility assessment of NLP results. In *Proceedings of the 60th Annual Meeting of the Association for Computational Linguistics (Volume 1: Long Papers)*, pages 16–28, Dublin, Ireland. Association for Computational Linguistics.

Anya Belz, Craig Thomson, Ehud Reiter, Gavin Abercrombie, Jose M. Alonso-Moral, Mohammad Arvan, Jackie Cheung, Mark Cieliebak, Elizabeth Clark, Kees van Deemter, Tanvi Dinkar, Ondřej Dušek, Steffen Eger, Qixiang Fang, Albert Gatt, Dimitra Gkatzia, Javier González-Corbelle, Dirk Hovy, Manuela Hürlimann, Takumi Ito, John D. Kelleher, Filip Klubicka, Huiyuan Lai, Chris van der Lee, Emiel van Miltenburg, Yiru Li, Saad Mahamood, Margot Mieskes, Malvina Nissim, Natalie Parde, Ondřej Plátek, Verena Rieser, Pablo Mosteiro Romero, Joel Tetreault, Antonio Toral, Xiaojun Wan, Leo Wanner, Lewis Watson, and Diyi Yang. 2023. Missing information, unresponsive authors, experimental flaws: The impossibility of assessing the reproducibility of previous human evaluations in NLP. In *The Fourth Workshop on Insights from Negative Results in NLP*, pages 1–10, Dubrovnik, Croatia. Association for Computational Linguistics.

Daniel Deutsch, Yash Kumar Lal, Annie Louis, Pete Walsh, Jesse Dodge, and Niranjan Balasubramanian. 2022. 2022 North American Chapter of the Association for Computational Linguistics Reproducibility Track.

Rotem Dror, Gili Baumer, Segev Shlomov, and Roi Reichart. 2018. The hitchhiker's guide to testing statistical significance in natural language processing. In *Proceedings of the 56th Annual Meeting of the Association for Computational Linguistics, ACL 2018, Melbourne, Australia, July 15-20, 2018, Volume 1: Long Papers*, pages 1383–1392. Association for Computational Linguistics.

Joseph K. Goodman, Cynthia E. Cryder, and Amar Cheema. 2013. Data collection in a flat world: The strengths and weaknesses of mechanical turk samples. *Journal of Behavioral Decision Making*, 26(3):213–224.

Chris van der Lee, Albert Gatt, Emiel van Miltenburg, Sander Wubben, and Emiel Krahmer. 2019. Best practices for the human evaluation of automatically generated text. In *Proceedings of the 12th International Conference on Natural Language Generation, INLG 2019, Tokyo, Japan, October 29 - November 1, 2019*, pages 355–368. Association for Computational Linguistics.

Jordan J Louviere, Terry N Flynn, and Anthony Alfred John Marley. 2015. *Best-worst scaling: Theory, methods and applications*. Cambridge University Press.

Jordan J Louviere and George G Woodworth. 1991. Best-worst scaling: A model for the largest difference judgments. Technical report, Working paper.

Nature. 2022. Nature's Reporting standards and availability of data, materials, code and protocols.

Jekaterina Novikova, Ondrej Dusek, Amanda Cercas Curry, and Verena Rieser. 2017. Why we need new evaluation metrics for NLG. In *Proceedings of the 2017 Conference on Empirical Methods in Natural Language Processing, EMNLP 2017, Copenhagen, Denmark, September 9-11, 2017*, pages 2241–2252. Association for Computational Linguistics.

Babatunde Kazeem Olorisade, Pearl Brereton, and Peter Andras. 2017. Reproducibility of studies on text mining for citation screening in systematic reviews: Evaluation and checklist. *J. Biomed. Informatics*, 73:1–13.

Joelle Pineau, Koustuv Sinha, Genevieve Fried, Rosemary Nan Ke, and Hugo Larochelle. 2019. Iclr reproducibility challenge 2019. *ReScience C*, 5(2):5.

Joelle Pineau, Philippe Vincent-Lamarre, Koustuv Sinha, Vincent Larivière, Alina Beygelzimer, Florence d'Alché-Buc, Emily B. Fox, and Hugo Larochelle. 2021. Improving reproducibility in machine learning research(a report from the neurips 2019 reproducibility program). *J. Mach. Learn. Res.*, 22:164:1–164:20.

Matt Post. 2018. A call for clarity in reporting BLEU scores. In *Proceedings of the Third Conference on Machine Translation: Research Papers, WMT 2018, Belgium, Brussels, October 31 - November 1, 2018*, pages 186–191. Association for Computational Linguistics.

Ratish Puduppully, Li Dong, and Mirella Lapata. 2019. Data-to-text generation with entity modeling. In *Proceedings of the 57th Conference of the Association for Computational Linguistics, ACL 2019, Florence, Italy, July 28- August 2, 2019, Volume 1: Long Papers*, pages 2023–2035. Association for Computational Linguistics.

Ratish Puduppully and Mirella Lapata. 2021. Data-to-text generation with macro planning. *Trans. Assoc. Comput. Linguistics*, 9:510–527.

James Pustejovsky and Amber Stubbs. 2012. *Natural Language Annotation for Machine Learning - a Guide to Corpus-Building for Applications*. O'Reilly.

Edward Raff. 2019. A step toward quantifying independently reproducible machine learning research. In *Advances in Neural Information Processing Systems 32: Annual Conference on Neural Information Processing Systems 2019, NeurIPS 2019, December 8-14, 2019, Vancouver, BC, Canada*, pages 5486–5496.

Clément Rebuffel, Laure Soulier, Geoffrey Scoutheeten, and Patrick Gallinari. 2020. A hierarchical model for data-to-text generation. In *Advances in Information Retrieval - 42nd European Conference on IR Research, ECIR 2020, Lisbon, Portugal, April 14-17, 2020, Proceedings, Part I*, volume 12035 of *Lecture Notes in Computer Science*, pages 65–80. Springer.

Ehud Reiter and Anja Belz. 2009. An investigation into the validity of some metrics for automatically evaluating natural language generation systems. *Comput. Linguistics*, 35(4):529–558.

Natalie Schluter. 2017. The limits of automatic summarisation according to ROUGE. In *Proceedings of the 15th Conference of the European Chapter of the Association for Computational Linguistics, EACL 2017, Valencia, Spain, April 3-7, 2017, Volume 2: Short Papers*, pages 41–45. Association for Computational Linguistics.

Anastasia Shimorina and Anya Belz. 2021. The human evaluation datasheet 1.0: A template for recording details of human evaluation experiments in NLP. *CoRR*, abs/2103.09710.

Koustuv Sinha, Jesse Dodge, Sasha Luccioni, Jessica Forde, Sharath Chandra Raparthy, François Mercier, Joelle Pineau, and Robert Stojnic. 2021. ML Reproducibility Challenge 2021.

Rion Snow, Brendan O'Connor, Daniel Jurafsky, and Andrew Y. Ng. 2008. Cheap and fast - but is it good? evaluating non-expert annotations for natural language tasks. In *2008 Conference on Empirical Methods in Natural Language Processing, EMNLP 2008, Proceedings of the Conference, 25-27 October 2008, Honolulu, Hawaii, USA, A meeting of SIGDAT, a Special Interest Group of the ACL*, pages 254–263. ACL.

UNESCO. 2021. UNESCO recommendation on open science.

Janyce Wiebe, Rebecca F. Bruce, and Thomas P. O'Hara. 1999. Development and use of a gold-standard data set for subjectivity classifications. In *27th Annual Meeting of the Association for Computational Linguistics, University of Maryland, College Park, Maryland, USA, 20-26 June 1999*, pages 246–253. ACL.

Martijn Wieling, Josine Rawee, and Gertjan van Noord. 2018. Reproducibility in computational linguistics: Are we willing to share? *Comput. Linguistics*, 44(4).

Sam Wiseman, Stuart M. Shieber, and Alexander M. Rush. 2017. Challenges in data-to-document generation. In *Proceedings of the 2017 Conference on Empirical Methods in Natural Language Processing, EMNLP 2017, Copenhagen, Denmark, September 9-11, 2017*, pages 2253–2263. Association for Computational Linguistics.

Haotian Zhou and Ayelet Fishbach. 2016. The pitfall of experimenting on the web: How unattended selective attrition leads to surprising (yet false) research conclusions. *Journal of personality and social psychology*, 111(4):493.

Challenges in Reproducing Human Evaluation Results for Role-Oriented Dialogue Summarization

Takumi Ito
Tohoku University
Sendai, Japan;
Utrecht University
the Netherlands
t-ito@tohoku.ac.jp

Qixiang Fang
Utrecht University
the Netherlands
q.fang@uu.nl

Pablo Mosteiro
Utrecht University
the Netherlands
p.mosteiro@uu.nl

Albert Gatt
Utrecht University
the Netherlands
a.gatt@uu.nl

Kees van Deemter
Utrecht University
the Netherlands
c.j.vandeemter@uu.nl

Abstract

There is a growing concern regarding the reproducibility of human evaluation studies in NLP. As part of the ReproHum campaign, we conducted a study to assess the reproducibility of a recent human evaluation study in NLP. Specifically, we attempted to reproduce a human evaluation of a novel approach to enhance Role-Oriented Dialogue Summarization by considering the influence of role interactions. Despite our best efforts to adhere to the reported setup, we were unable to reproduce the statistical results as presented in the original paper. While no contradictory evidence was found, our study raises questions about the validity of the reported statistical significance results, and/or the comprehensiveness with which the original study was reported. In this paper, we provide a comprehensive account of our reproduction study, detailing the methodologies employed, data collection, and analysis procedures. We discuss the implications of our findings for the broader issue of reproducibility in NLP research. Our findings serve as a cautionary reminder of the challenges in conducting reproducible human evaluations and prompt further discussions within the NLP community.

1 Introduction

Natural Language Processing (NLP) has witnessed remarkable advances in recent years. Human evaluation plays a pivotal role in assessing the effectiveness of NLP systems and their performance in meeting specific task requirements. However, concerns have arisen regarding the reproducibility of human evaluation studies in the NLP community (Belz et al., 2022; Huidrom et al., 2022). Reproducibility is defined as the ability of other researchers to repeat the experiments under identical conditions and obtain consistent results.

As part of the ReproHum campaign (Belz and Reiter, 2022), which strives to systematically assess the reproducibility of human evaluation studies in NLP, we conducted a rigorous reproduction study of Lin et al. (2022), with the title *Other Roles Matter! Enhancing Role-Oriented Dialogue Summarization via Role Interactions.*

Dialogue summarization aims to distil relevant information from conversations while preserving their context, presenting a concise and informative summary. The quality of such summarization systems is critical in real-world applications, and a careful evaluation of said quality is a prerequisite to the application of summarization systems.

Lin et al. (2022) start from the idea that, when a system summarises a dialogue between a user (e.g., a customer) and an agent (e.g., someone who answers the customer's questions), it can be helpful to attend to each of these two roles (user, agent) separately. When a user's utterance is summarised, some information from the agent should be taken into account, and the other way around. The authors hypothesise that cross-attention and self-attention can help create an optimal combination of both roles, and they investigate various neural mechanisms for doing so, in particular BERT (Devlin et al., 2019) and PGN (See et al., 2017). After an extensive metric-based evaluation, their human evaluation — on which our paper focuses — tests the hypothesis that, for both BERT and PNG, better summaries are generated when both cross-attention and self-attention are used (in Lin et al. (2022), the systems with these mechanisms are referred to as *BERT-both* and *PNG-both*), compared to settings where the dialogue is summarised as one whole without separating the two roles (settings referred to as *BERT-multi* and *PNG-multi*). They conclude

Proceedings of the Third Workshop on Human Evaluation of NLP Systems, pages 97–123, Varna, Bulgaria, Sep 7, 2023.
https://doi.org/10.26615/978-954-452-088-5_009

that adding both interactions increases performance with respect to the baseline case.

The objective of our reproduction study was to validate the reported statistical results from the original paper and to investigate the reproducibility of the human evaluation process as outlined by the authors. To achieve this, we meticulously replicated the experimental setup provided in the original work, while also seeking clarification from the authors regarding details of their experimental procedure.

In this paper, we present our findings from the reproduction study, shedding light on the challenges and implications of conducting reproducible human evaluations in the NLP domain.

Our study uncovers significant discrepancies between the statistical results reported in the original paper and those obtained in our reproduction attempt. While we did not find any contradicting evidence, our results raise questions about the validity of the original statistical-significance findings. We emphasise that our aim is not to undermine a valuable piece of work, but to contribute to the ongoing discussion on reproducibility, fostering a more transparent and reliable foundation for future advancements.

2 Data

For our evaluation, we used 100 sample dialogues from the same Chinese Sales Dialogue Summarization (CSDS) dataset used in Lin et al. (2022). The samples were provided to us by the ReproHum organizers. For each of the 100 dialogues, there are two kinds of summaries (user and agent) generated by each of the following four systems: PGN-multi, PGN-both, BERT-multi, BERT-both. Thus, there are 800 summaries in total. A sub-summary refers to a complete sentence in the role-oriented summary.

3 Experimental Setup

We closely follow the guidelines provided in the original paper by Lin et al. (2022). We asked participants to assess the summary quality of Role-Oriented Dialogue Summarization models on three aspects: informativeness, non-redundancy, and fluency. We sought to replicate the evaluation process as faithfully as possible, while also addressing certain details that were obtained from the original authors but were not explicitly mentioned in the original paper.

We treated each "sub-summary" (i.e. sentence) in the role-oriented summary as an individual unit to be scored by the annotators. The evaluation was carried out by three trained volunteers who were familiarised with the evaluation rules provided by the original authors. In the original study, annotators were graduate school-level students and spoke native Mandarin. They were recruited from among the members of the lab conducting the study. In a similar spirit, we recruited three PhD candidates from the department of Information and Computing Sciences at Utrecht University, all of whom self-reported Mandarin as their native language. Contrary to the original study where the annotators were not paid for their participation, we will pay each of our annotators 120 Euros for 12 hours of work.[1]

The annotators assessed each sub-summary according to three pre-defined aspects: informativeness, non-redundancy, and fluency. Each sub-summary received a score for each aspect based on the perceived quality of the summary with respect to that particular aspect.

As was done in the original paper, we first gave the three annotators the same ten summaries, and asked them to rate those summaries. To ensure the reliability of the obtained scores, we conducted an inter-annotator agreement analysis. This process involved comparing the scores given by the three volunteers for each sub-summary. We used Cohen's kappa coefficient as a measure of agreement. This was calculated by concatenating all values for each participant together.

We then gave each participant a different set of 30 summaries to rate. In total, there were 100 summaries: 10 were annotated by all three participants, while the remaining 90 were annotated by one participant each.

To represent the summary quality in general, we aggregated the scores for all three aspects (informativeness, non-redundancy, and fluency) into an "Overall" metric for each sub-summary. The overall score for a sub-summary was obtained by averaging the individual scores assigned by the annotators for that specific aspect.

The obtained scores were then normalised to a range between 0 and 1 to facilitate comparison and presentation. The normalised scores were compiled into a table, which is analogous to Table 4 in

[1]Payment is still being processed at the time of writing this article.

the original paper, showcasing the performance of different models across the evaluated aspects.

There is some ambiguity regarding how scores should be computed for the summaries that were evaluated by the three participants. In particular, every sub-summary evaluated by a single participant has a single score; but for the summaries evaluated by all participants (which was done for the purpose of computing the inter-annotator agreement), there are three scores per sub-summary. The original paper does not specify how the scores were computed for these *multi-annotated* summaries. We performed our analysis under four "cases". These are defined by the way we compute the score for each multi-annotated summary:

1. use the scores of participant 1
2. use the scores of participant 2
3. use the scores of participant 3
4. use the average score among participants

Although we felt that it was necessary to distinguish between these four cases, we will see in Section 4 that our overall conclusions do not depend on which case we focus on.

To ensure transparency and to facilitate reproducibility of our study, we have made our code and datasets publicly available on our GitHub repository[2]. The repository contains the necessary scripts and documentation to replicate our experimental procedures and results accurately.

4 Results and Discussion

4.1 Participant results

After the first 10 annotations, the results of the three annotators were compared, and we calculated the inter-annotator agreement using Cohen's kappa, as in the original paper. We computed κ for each pair of annotators, and computed the average of the three values. We obtained a κ_{average}=0.48. This was exactly the same – admittedly rather low (see Section 5 for a discussion) – value as the one reported in the original paper. We then gave 30 more summaries to each annotator, which resulted in a total of 100 summaries being evaluated.

The participants' results presented by Lin et al. (2022) are found in Table 1. These are found in Table 4 of the original paper, and copied here without modification. Table 1 also presents the results of our reproduction experiment. Each horizontal block represents a different case of whose values should be taken for the first 10 annotations; these are referred to as "cases" in Section 3.

4.2 Reproducibility assessment

To assess the reproducibility of the original result, we computed three scores:

1. The Pearson correlation coefficient
2. The fraction of matching both/multi pairs
3. The F1 score of statistical significance results

Further details about each of these follow.

Pearson correlation coefficient. If the results of our experiment reproduced the original experiment exactly, we would have a perfectly linear correlation between the two sets of results. To estimate how far we are from that, we have concatenated all the values in each of the 5 tables of results (the original paper, plus our 4 "cases"), from left to right and top to bottom, and computed the Pearson correlation coefficient between each of our 4 cases and the original paper. The results are shown on Table 2.

Fraction of matching both/multi pairs. The original paper reports a number in boldface if it is larger than its multi/both counterpart. In other words, it highlights the performance of multi vs both, or vice versa. Thus, we have computed, for each of the four cases, the fraction of multi-/both pairs that follow the same trend (lower/equal/higher) as in the original paper. We call this the *matching accuracy* A. It is reported on Table 2.

F1 score of statistical significance. The aforementioned matching accuracy penalises non-matches too harshly, because it does not account for near-matches. Indeed, we are often only interested in the difference between two values if they are statistically significant. To that end, we have computed the F1 score for statistical significance. We consider the original paper as the gold standard. For each value, we take the true label to be 1 if the value is statistically significantly larger than its multi/both counterpart, and 0 otherwise. The results are reported on Table 2. While there exists a reasonable degree of concordance between the numerical values in the original findings and our

[2]`https://github.com/taku-ito/reprohum-utrecht`

CSDS	Info	Non-Red	Flu	Overall
Lin et al. (2022)				
PGN-multi	**0.69**/0.65	0.54/0.55	0.70/0.79	0.64/0.66
PGN-both	0.66/**0.69**	**0.58**/**0.59***	**0.73**/**0.81**	**0.66**/**0.70***
BERT-multi	0.58/0.56	**0.66**/**0.61**	0.84/**0.87**	0.69/0.68
BERT-both	**0.62***/**0.60***	0.62/0.60	**0.85**/**0.87**	**0.70**/**0.69**
Case 1				
PGN-multi	**0.63**/0.59	0.58/0.55	**0.69**/0.70	0.63/0.61
PGN-both	0.62/**0.64***	**0.61**/**0.59**	0.68/**0.74**	**0.64**/**0.65***
BERT-multi	0.55/0.45	**0.69***/**0.61**	**0.82**/**0.80**	**0.69***/**0.62**
BERT-both	**0.56**/**0.47**	0.62/0.58	0.78/**0.80**	0.65/**0.62**
Case 2				
PGN-multi	**0.62**/0.58	0.57/0.56	**0.68**/0.69	0.62/0.61
PGN-both	0.61/**0.62**	**0.60**/**0.58**	0.67/**0.71**	**0.63**/**0.64***
BERT-multi	**0.55**/0.45	**0.70***/**0.60**	**0.82**/**0.78**	**0.69***/**0.61**
BERT-both	**0.55**/**0.47**	0.62/0.57	0.78/**0.78**	0.65/**0.61**
Case 3				
PGN-multi	**0.64**/0.60	0.59/0.58	**0.69**/0.72	**0.64**/0.63
PGN-both	0.63/**0.65***	**0.62**/**0.60**	0.68/**0.75**	**0.64**/**0.67***
BERT-multi	**0.57**/0.46	**0.72***/**0.62**	**0.83**/**0.81**	**0.71***/**0.63**
BERT-both	**0.57**/**0.49**	0.63/0.59	0.79/0.80	0.67/**0.63**
Case 4				
PGN-multi	**0.63**/0.59	0.58/0.56	**0.69**/0.70	0.63/0.62
PGN-both	0.62/**0.64***	**0.61**/**0.59**	0.68/**0.73**	**0.64**/**0.65***
BERT-multi	**0.56**/0.45	**0.71***/**0.61**	**0.82**/**0.80**	**0.70***/**0.62**
BERT-both	**0.56**/**0.48**	0.62/0.58	0.78/0.79	0.66/**0.62**

Table 1: Results of Lin et al. (2022), reproduced here without modification (above the double line), along with the results of the present human evaluation (below the double line) under the four "cases" (see Section 3). Each cell contains two numbers separated by a slash: the left number corresponds to the user, and the right number corresponds to the agent. A number for "multi" in boldface indicates that the performance is better than the corresponding number for "both", and vice versa; if both are the same, both appear in boldface. An asterisk indicates that the difference between the "both" and "multi" results is statistically significant.

Case	Pearson's r	A	F1
1	0.90	0.75	0.25
2	0.89	0.69	0.29
3	0.90	0.56	0.25
4	0.90	0.62	0.25

Table 2: Reproducibility scores between the results of the original experiment and our results. The "cases" refer to how the scores of the ten summaries that were rated by all three participants were aggregated. Pearson's r is computed across all 32 reported values. A: matching accuracy, the fraction of multi/both pairs that follow the same trend (lower/equal/higher) as in the original paper. F1 score is computed by taking the paper as gold standard, labelling a value as 1 if it is statistically significantly larger than its multi/both counterpart, 0 otherwise.

outcomes, as shown by the aforementioned r and A metrics, a notably weaker concurrence is evident when considering the statistical-significance F1 score. This indicates potential issues concerning the efficacy of the employed statistical significance testing methodology. Further elaboration on this matter will be provided in Section 5. We note that, despite the low agreement in the statistical significance of the results, none of the multi/both pairs deemed to be statistically significantly different in the original paper exhibited the opposite trend in our study.

4.3 Comparison of findings

In the original paper, the authors conclude from the human evaluations that applying interactions on the PGN architecture (i.e., using the "both" model) leads to improvements in all metrics except informativeness, where they deem the two options comparable. Meanwhile, for the BERT architecture, the "both" model is better on all metrics except non-redundancy, for which "multi" is better. They also conclude that, given that the "Overall" metric is higher for "both" in both architectures (PGN and BERT), the "both" option is better than "multi".

In our study, the most salient differences are:

- For Fluency+User, PGN-both was worse than PGN-multi in all four cases;
- For Fluency, BERT-both was worse than or equal to BERT-multi for both roles in all four cases;
- For Overall, BERT-both was worse than or equal to BERT-multi for both roles in all four cases

These differences suggest that we cannot reproduce the original paper's conclusion that "both" is generally better than "multi", at least based on the human evaluation alone.

5 Conclusions

In this paper, we conducted a reproduction study of the human evaluation in Lin et al. (2022), as part of the ReproHum campaign to assess the reproducibility of human evaluation in NLP (Belz et al., 2023). Our objective was to assess the reproducibility of the results reported in the original paper and thoroughly investigate the difference between our results and the original paper's, if any.

Throughout our study, we sought to adhere closely to the original experimental setup. However, our findings reveal notable discrepancies in the statistical results obtained, particularly in comparing the improvements of the "both" method with respect to the "multi" method. In the original paper, "multi" is a baseline method, while "both" adds cross-attention and self-attention interactions to the models (see Section 1). Unlike the original work, our experiments did not demonstrate clear improvements in summary quality when considering role interactions.

Despite the differences in our obtained results, we acknowledge the high Pearson correlation coefficient between the original paper's scores and our own, indicating a strong consistency in the relative ranking of models across the evaluation aspects. Furthermore, while our findings were different from the original results in terms of statistical significance, we acknowledge that they are not contradictory, i.e., there is no model for which the authors of the original paper claim statistically significantly better results for "both" or "multi", while we find the opposite to be true (i.e., statistically significantly worse results). We believe that the statistical significance analysis employed in the original paper may have certain flaws. Firstly, we maintain that a correction procedure for inflated type-1 error should have been applied, considering that multiple statistical significance tests were conducted on the same dataset. Failure to account for this potential bias might have resulted in too many false positives (i.e. results which appear to be statistically significant but are not). Secondly, the authors computed statistical significance tests, but then also drew conclusions from results that were not statistically significantly different. This should be avoided.

One significant observation from our study was the relatively low level of agreement among the annotators. This raises concerns about the consistency of the evaluation process and the potential for different interpretations of the instructions. It would have been valuable to closely scrutinise the reasons for such disagreement. If the disagreements stemmed from differing interpretations of the guidelines, an update to the instructions and a restart of the annotation process might have been necessary. Alternatively, if the disagreements were legitimate, the study could have been improved by having multiple annotators assess all the summaries, allowing for a better understanding of the inherent variability. This is along the lines of recent work that tries to account for inherent variability when training NLP models (Leonardelli et al., 2023).

Regarding the reproducibility experiment itself, the description provided in the original paper was insufficient for us to fully attempt a replication. Nonetheless, thanks to the cooperation of the authors, we were able to clarify the necessary procedures. Even so, we had to perform four studies under different "cases", which refer to the various ways we pooled together the results of the first 10 summaries, annotated by all participants.

Moreover, the data collection process posed significant challenges, largely due to the participants making multiple errors that needed to be corrected before statistical analysis became feasible. Namely, we observed several mismatches between the number of sentences and the number of annotations provided by participants. This was probably caused by the annotation being done in a spreadsheet. In those cases, we had to ask participants to correct their work. Ensuring data quality and accuracy is crucial in human evaluation studies, and these difficulties further underscore the importance of transparent reporting and careful handling of data.

Finally, we wish to clarify that our focus was on the parts of the original paper that dealt with human evaluations, particularly in terms of reproducibility. We do not make any general claims about the strength of the entire original paper, which included metric-based evaluations as well. The results of the metric-based evaluation in the original work may indeed be more convincing.

In conclusion, our reproduction study highlights the importance of carefully reporting the conditions under which a human evaluation was conducted to enhance reproducibility, and the need for thorough reporting of experimental details necessary for reproduction studies, as well as scrutiny of statistical significance analyses in NLP research. We also provide suggestions for future studies to enhance the reproducibility and transparency of human evaluation experiments. Despite the challenges we encountered, we commend the authors for their cooperation, which allowed us to perform a comprehensive reproduction of their work. We believe that open dialogue and collaborative efforts within the research community are essential for advancing the field of NLP and achieving meaningful progress in dialogue summarization and other language generation tasks.

References

Anya Belz, Maja Popovic, and Simon Mille. 2022. Quantified reproducibility assessment of NLP results. In *Proceedings of the 60th Annual Meeting of the Association for Computational Linguistics (Volume 1: Long Papers)*, pages 16–28, Dublin, Ireland. Association for Computational Linguistics.

Anya Belz and Ehud Reiter. 2022. ReproHum: Investigating Reproducibility of Human Evaluations in Natural Language Processing. `https://gow.epsrc.ukri.org/NGBOViewGrant.aspx?GrantRef=EP/V05645X/1`.

Anya Belz, Craig Thomson, and Ehud Reiter. 2023. Missing information, unresponsive authors, experimental flaws: The impossibility of assessing the reproducibility of previous human evaluations in NLP. In *The Fourth Workshop on Insights from Negative Results in NLP*, pages 1–10, Dubrovnik, Croatia. Association for Computational Linguistics.

Jacob Devlin, Ming-Wei Chang, Kenton Lee, and Kristina Toutanova. 2019. BERT: Pre-training of deep bidirectional transformers for language understanding. In *Proceedings of the 2019 Conference of the North American Chapter of the Association for Computational Linguistics: Human Language Technologies, Volume 1 (Long and Short Papers)*, pages 4171–4186, Minneapolis, Minnesota. Association for Computational Linguistics.

Rudali Huidrom, Ondřej Dušek, Zdeněk Kasner, Thiago Castro Ferreira, and Anya Belz. 2022. Two reproductions of a human-assessed comparative evaluation of a semantic error detection system. In *Proceedings of the 15th International Conference on Natural Language Generation: Generation Challenges*, pages 52–61, Waterville, Maine, USA and virtual meeting. Association for Computational Linguistics.

Elisa Leonardelli, Alexandra Uma, Gavin Abercrombie, Dina Almanea, Valerio Basile, Tommaso Fornaciari, Barbara Plank, Verena Rieser, and Massimo Poesio. 2023. SemEval-2023 Task 11: Learning With Disagreements (LeWiDi).

Haitao Lin, Junnan Zhu, Lu Xiang, Yu Zhou, Jiajun Zhang, and Chengqing Zong. 2022. Other Roles Matter! Enhancing Role-Oriented Dialogue Summarization via Role Interactions. In *Proceedings of the 60th Annual Meeting of the Association for Computational Linguistics (Volume 1: Long Papers)*, pages 2545–2558, Dublin, Ireland. Association for Computational Linguistics.

Abigail See, Peter J. Liu, and Christopher D. Manning. 2017. Get to the point: Summarization with pointer-generator networks. In *Proceedings of the 55th Annual Meeting of the Association for Computational Linguistics (Volume 1: Long Papers)*, pages 1073–1083, Vancouver, Canada. Association for Computational Linguistics.

A HEDS sheet


```
{
  "heds-criteria-criterion-response_elicitation-scale_presented_as-5": {
    "data": {
      "Informativeness": true,
      "Fluency": true,
      "Non-redundancy": true
    },
    "control": {},
    "text": {
      "Informativeness": "5. Other (please describe)",
      "Fluency": "5. Other (please describe)",
      "Non-redundancy": "5. Other (please describe)"
    }
  },
  "heds-criteria-criterion-response_elicitation-response_aggregation": {
    "data": {
      "Informativeness": "average the set of per-sentence values.",
      "Non-redundancy": "average the set of per-sentence values.",
      "Fluency": "average the set of per-sentence values."
    },
    "control": {}
  },
  "heds-criteria-criterion-evaluation_mode-objective_or_subjective-1": {
    "data": {
      "Informativeness": true,
      "Non-redundancy": true,
      "Fluency": true
    },
    "control": {},
    "text": {
      "Informativeness": "1. Objective",
      "Non-redundancy": "1. Objective",
      "Fluency": "1. Objective"
    }
  },
  "heds-paper_and_resources-names_and_affiliations-person_completing_this_sheet-affiliation": {
    "data": {
      "": "Utrecht University / Tohoku University"
    },
    "control": {}
  },
  "heds-paper_and_resources-names_and_affiliations-person_completing_this_sheet-name": {
    "data": {
      "": "Takumi Ito"
    },
    "control": {}
  },
  "heds-criteria-criterion-criteria-output_aspect-1": {
    "data": {
      "Informativeness": false,
      "Non-redundancy": false,
      "Fluency": true
    },
    "control": {},
    "text": {
      "Informativeness": "",
      "Non-redundancy": "",
      "Fluency": "1. Form of output"
```

```
    }
  },
  "heds-sample_evaluators_design-evaluators-evaluators-expertise-other_text": {
    "data": {
      "": ""
    },
    "control": {}
  },
  "heds-sample_evaluators_design-evaluators-evaluators-expertise-1": {
    "data": {
      "": false
    },
    "control": {},
    "text": {
      "": ""
    }
  },
  "heds-criteria-criterion-response_elicitation-form_of_response-10": {
    "data": {
      "Informativeness": false,
      "Non-redundancy": false,
      "Fluency": false
    },
    "control": {},
    "text": {
      "Informativeness": "",
      "Non-redundancy": "",
      "Fluency": ""
    }
  },
  "heds-criteria-criterion-response_elicitation-scale_presented_as-2": {
    "data": {
      "Informativeness": false,
      "Fluency": false,
      "Non-redundancy": false
    },
    "control": {},
    "text": {
      "Informativeness": "",
      "Fluency": "",
      "Non-redundancy": ""
    }
  },
  "heds-system-input_types-8": {
    "data": {
      "": true
    },
    "control": {},
    "text": {
      "": "8. text: dialogue"
    }
  },
  "heds-paper_and_resources-names_and_affiliations-contact_author-affiliation": {
    "data": {
      "": "Utrecht University"
    },
    "control": {}
  },
  "heds-criteria-criterion-response_elicitation-form_of_response-7": {
    "data": {
```

"Informativeness": false,
"Non-redundancy": false,
"Fluency": false
},
"control": {},
"text": {
"Informativeness": "",
"Non-redundancy": "",
"Fluency": ""
}
},
"heds-sample_evaluators_design-experimental_design-experimental_conditions-8": {
"data": {
"": false
},
"control": {},
"text": {
"": ""
}
},
"heds-system-input_languages-29": {
"data": {
"": true
},
"control": {},
"text": {
"": "29. Chinese"
}
},
"heds-criteria-criterion-response_elicitation-form_of_response-6": {
"data": {
"Informativeness": false,
"Non-redundancy": false,
"Fluency": false
},
"control": {},
"text": {
"Informativeness": "",
"Non-redundancy": "",
"Fluency": ""
}
},
"heds-sample_evaluators_design-evaluators-evaluators-payment-3": {
"data": {
"": false
},
"control": {},
"text": {
"": ""
}
},
"heds-criteria-criterion-response_elicitation-form_of_response-5": {
"data": {
"Informativeness": false,
"Non-redundancy": false,
"Fluency": false
},
"control": {},
"text": {
"Informativeness": "",

"Non-redundancy": "",
"Fluency": ""
}
},
"heds-sample_evaluators_design-sample-system_output_selection-1": {
"data": {
"": false
},
"control": {},
"text": {
"": ""
}
},
"heds-sample_evaluators_design-experimental_design-quality_assurance-description": {
"data": {
"": "N/A"
},
"control": {}
},
"heds-sample_evaluators_design-evaluators-evaluators-expertise-2": {
"data": {
"": true
},
"control": {},
"text": {
"": "2. non-experts"
}
},
"heds-sample_evaluators_design-experimental_design-experimental_conditions-1": {
"data": {
"": true
},
"control": {},
"text": {
"": "1. evaluation carried out by evaluators at a place of their own choosing, e.g. online, using a paper form, etc."
}
},
"heds-ethics-review_body": {
"data": {
"": "No"
},
"control": {}
},
"heds-criteria-criterion-response_elicitation-effect_size_method": {
"data": {
"Non-redundancy": ""
},
"control": {}
},
"heds-criteria-criterion-response_elicitation-verbatim_question": {
"data": {
"Informativeness": "N/A ",
"Non-redundancy": "N/A",
"Fluency": "N/A"
},
"control": {}
},
"heds-sample_evaluators_design-evaluators-evaluators-known_to_authors-2": {
"data": {

```
      "": false
    },
    "control": {},
    "text": {
      "": ""
    }
  },
  "heds-criteria-criterion-evaluation_mode-intrinsic_or_extrinsic-1": {
    "data": {
      "Informativeness": false,
      "Non-redundancy": true,
      "Fluency": true
    },
    "control": {},
    "text": {
      "Informativeness": "",
      "Non-redundancy": "1. Intrinsic",
      "Fluency": "1. Intrinsic"
    }
  },
  "heds-criteria-criterion-evaluation_mode-objective_or_subjective-other_text": {
    "data": {
      "Informativeness": "",
      "Non-redundancy": "",
      "Fluency": ""
    },
    "control": {}
  },
  "heds-criteria-criterion-response_elicitation-scale_presented_as-other_text": {
    "data": {
      "Informativeness": "fill in the cells on the spreadsheet",
      "Non-redundancy": "fill in the cells on the spreadsheet",
      "Fluency": "fill in the cells on the spreadsheet"
    },
    "control": {}
  },
  "heds-sample_evaluators_design-evaluators-evaluators-payment-1": {
    "data": {
      "": true
    },
    "control": {},
    "text": {
      "": "1. paid (monetary compensation)"
    }
  },
  "heds-sample_evaluators_design-evaluators-evaluators-description": {
    "data": {
      "": "Chinese PhD candidates in the same department as the authors."
    },
    "control": {}
  },
  "heds-sample_evaluators_design-sample-number_of_system_outputs": {
    "data": {
      "": "100"
    },
    "control": {}
  },
  "heds-system-output_types-4": {
    "data": {
      "": false
```

```
    },
    "control": {},
    "text": {
      "": ""
    }
  },
  "heds-criteria-criterion-evaluation_mode-objective_or_subjective-2": {
    "data": {
      "Informativeness": false,
      "Non-redundancy": false,
      "Fluency": false
    },
    "control": {},
    "text": {
      "Informativeness": "",
      "Non-redundancy": "",
      "Fluency": ""
    }
  },
  "heds-criteria-criterion-response_elicitation-form_of_response-4": {
    "data": {
      "Informativeness": false,
      "Non-redundancy": false,
      "Fluency": false
    },
    "control": {},
    "text": {
      "Informativeness": "",
      "Non-redundancy": "",
      "Fluency": ""
    }
  },
  "heds-criteria-criterion-response_elicitation-size_of_scale-2": {
    "data": {
      "Informativeness": false,
      "Non-redundancy": false,
      "Fluency": false
    },
    "control": {},
    "text": {
      "Informativeness": "",
      "Non-redundancy": "",
      "Fluency": ""
    }
  },
  "heds-sample_evaluators_design-evaluators-evaluators-known_to_authors-other_text": {
    "data": {
      "": ""
    },
    "control": {}
  },
  "heds-criteria-criterion-criteria-output_aspect-other_text": {
    "data": {
      "Informativeness": "",
      "Non-redundancy": "",
      "Fluency": ""
    },
    "control": {}
  },
  "heds-criteria-criterion-evaluation_mode-absolute_or_relative-1": {
```

```
  "data": {
    "Informativeness": false,
    "Non-redundancy": false,
    "Fluency": false
  },
  "control": {},
  "text": {
    "Informativeness": "",
    "Non-redundancy": "",
    "Fluency": ""
  }
},
"heds-sample_evaluators_design-experimental_design-quality_assurance-method-1": {
  "data": {
    "": true
  },
  "control": {},
  "text": {
    "": "1. evaluators are required to be native speakers of the language they evaluate."
  }
},
"heds-sample_evaluators_design-evaluators-evaluators-payment-other_text": {
  "data": {
    "": ""
  },
  "control": {}
},
"heds-sample_evaluators_design-experimental_design-experimental_conditions-other_text": {
  "data": {
    "": ""
  },
  "control": {}
},
"heds-criteria-criterion-criteria-quality_type-2": {
  "data": {
    "Informativeness": false,
    "Non-redundancy": false,
    "Fluency": true
  },
  "control": {},
  "text": {
    "Informativeness": "",
    "Non-redundancy": "",
    "Fluency": "2. Goodness"
  }
},
"heds-criteria-criterion-response_elicitation-form_of_response-9": {
  "data": {
    "Informativeness": false,
    "Non-redundancy": false,
    "Fluency": false
  },
  "control": {},
  "text": {
    "Informativeness": "",
    "Non-redundancy": "",
    "Fluency": ""
  }
},
"heds-criteria-criterion-evaluation_mode-intrinsic_or_extrinsic-2": {
```

"data": {
"Informativeness": true,
"Non-redundancy": false,
"Fluency": false
},
"control": {},
"text": {
"Informativeness": "2. Extrinsic",
"Non-redundancy": "",
"Fluency": ""
}
},
"heds-sample_evaluators_design-sample-system_output_selection-other_text": {
"data": {
"": "The same samples used in the original paper."
},
"control": {}
},
"heds-sample_evaluators_design-sample-system_output_selection-5": {
"data": {
"": true
},
"control": {},
"text": {
"": "5. other (please describe)"
}
},
"heds-sample_evaluators_design-experimental_design-evaluator_freedom-other_text": {
"data": {
"": "No restrictions."
},
"control": {}
},
"heds-criteria-criterion-criteria-quality_type-1": {
"data": {
"Informativeness": true,
"Non-redundancy": true,
"Fluency": false
},
"control": {},
"text": {
"Informativeness": "1. Correctness",
"Non-redundancy": "1. Correctness",
"Fluency": ""
}
},
"heds-criteria-criterion-evaluation_mode-absolute_or_relative-2": {
"data": {
"Informativeness": true,
"Non-redundancy": true,
"Fluency": true
},
"control": {},
"text": {
"Informativeness": "2. Relative",
"Non-redundancy": "2. Relative",
"Fluency": "2. Relative"
}
},
"heds-paper_and_resources-names_and_affiliations-contact_author-name": {

"data": {
  "": "Kees van Deemter"
},
"control": {}
},
"heds-system-output_types-8": {
  "data": {
    "": false
  },
  "control": {},
  "text": {
    "": ""
  }
},
"heds-ethics-special_category_data": {
  "data": {
    "": "No"
  },
  "control": {}
},
"heds-sample_evaluators_design-experimental_design-experimental_conditions-6": {
  "data": {
    "": false
  },
  "control": {},
  "text": {
    "": ""
  }
},
"heds-system-output_languages-29": {
  "data": {
    "": true
  },
  "control": {},
  "text": {
    "": "29. Chinese"
  }
},
"heds-criteria-criterion-response_elicitation-list_or_range": {
  "data": {
    "Informativeness": "0,1,2",
    "Non-redundancy": "0,1,2",
    "Fluency": "0,1,2"
  },
  "control": {}
},
"heds-criteria-criterion-response_elicitation-task_description": {
  "data": {
    "Informativeness": "N/A",
    "Non-redundancy": "N/A",
    "Fluency": "N/A"
  },
  "control": {}
},
"heds-criteria-criterion-response_elicitation-participant_criterion_name": {
  "data": {
    "Informativeness": "Informativeness",
    "Non-redundancy": "Non-redundancy",
    "Fluency": "Flunecy"
  },

```
    "control": {}
},
"heds-sample_evaluators_design-evaluators-recruitment_method": {
    "data": {
        "": "sent an email to those who met the requirements"
    },
    "control": {}
},
"heds-paper_and_resources-names_and_affiliations-contact_author-email": {
    "data": {
        "": "c.j.vandeemter@uu.nl"
    },
    "control": {}
},
"heds-sample_evaluators_design-evaluators-evaluators-known_to_authors-1": {
    "data": {
        "": true
    },
    "control": {},
    "text": {
        "": "1. previously known to authors"
    }
},
"heds-criteria-criterion-response_elicitation-form_of_response-2": {
    "data": {
        "Informativeness": true,
        "Non-redundancy": true,
        "Fluency": true
    },
    "control": {},
    "text": {
        "Informativeness": "2. direct quality estimation",
        "Non-redundancy": "2. direct quality estimation",
        "Fluency": "2. direct quality estimation"
    }
},
"heds-sample_evaluators_design-experimental_design-experimental_conditions-7": {
    "data": {
        "": false
    },
    "control": {},
    "text": {
        "": ""
    }
},
"heds-sample_evaluators_design-evaluators-evaluators-are_authors-2": {
    "data": {
        "": true
    },
    "control": {},
    "text": {
        "": "2. evaluators do not include any of the authors"
    }
},
"heds-sample_evaluators_design-experimental_design-evaluators_place_of_choosing": {
    "data": {
        "": "N/A"
    },
    "control": {}
},
```

"heds-sample_evaluators_design-sample-system_output_selection-3": {
  "data": {
    "": false
  },
  "control": {},
  "text": {
    "": ""
  }
},
"heds-criteria-criterion": {
  "data": {},
  "control": {
    "Informativeness": false,
    "Non-redundancy": false,
    "Fluency": true
  },
  "text": {}
},
"heds-sample_evaluators_design-evaluators-training_practice": {
  "data": {
    "": "ask the participants to read the task description provided by the original authors before starting the annotation."
  },
  "control": {}
},
"heds-criteria-criterion-criteria-quality_type-other_text": {
  "data": {
    "Informativeness": "",
    "Non-redundancy": "",
    "Fluency": ""
  },
  "control": {}
},
"heds-sample_evaluators_design-evaluators-evaluators-payment-4": {
  "data": {
    "": false
  },
  "control": {},
  "text": {
    "": ""
  }
},
"heds-criteria-criterion-criteria-quality_type-3": {
  "data": {
    "Informativeness": false,
    "Non-redundancy": false,
    "Fluency": false
  },
  "control": {},
  "text": {
    "Informativeness": "",
    "Non-redundancy": "",
    "Fluency": ""
  }
},
"heds-criteria-criterion-criteria-self_vs_external_frame-3": {
  "data": {
    "Informativeness": false,
    "Non-redundancy": false,
    "Fluency": false

```
    },
    "control": {},
    "text": {
      "Informativeness": "",
      "Non-redundancy": "",
      "Fluency": ""
    }
  },
  "heds-sample_evaluators_design-experimental_design-evaluator_freedom-2": {
    "data": {
      "": false
    },
    "control": {},
    "text": {
      "": ""
    }
  },
  "heds-sample_evaluators_design-evaluators-evaluators-are_authors-1": {
    "data": {
      "": false
    },
    "control": {},
    "text": {
      "": ""
    }
  },
  "heds-paper_and_resources-paper-link": {
    "data": {
      "": "https://aclanthology.org/2022.acl-long.182/"
    },
    "control": {}
  },
  "heds-criteria-criterion-evaluation_mode-intrinsic_or_extrinsic-other_text": {
    "data": {
      "Informativeness": "",
      "Non-redundancy": "",
      "Fluency": ""
    },
    "control": {}
  },
  "heds-ethics-personal_data": {
    "data": {
      "": "No"
    },
    "control": {}
  },
  "heds-sample_evaluators_design-experimental_design-experimental_conditions-4": {
    "data": {
      "": false
    },
    "control": {},
    "text": {
      "": ""
    }
  },
  "heds-sample_evaluators_design-sample-system_output_selection-2": {
    "data": {
      "": false
    },
    "control": {},
```

```
    "text": {
      "": ""
    }
  },
  "heds-criteria-criterion-response_elicitation-form_of_response-8": {
    "data": {
      "Informativeness": false,
      "Non-redundancy": false,
      "Fluency": false
    },
    "control": {},
    "text": {
      "Informativeness": "",
      "Non-redundancy": "",
      "Fluency": ""
    }
  },
  "heds-criteria-criterion-response_elicitation-size_of_scale-3": {
    "data": {
      "Informativeness": false,
      "Non-redundancy": false,
      "Fluency": false
    },
    "control": {},
    "text": {
      "Informativeness": "",
      "Non-redundancy": "",
      "Fluency": ""
    }
  },
  "heds-criteria-criterion-response_elicitation-scale_presented_as-3": {
    "data": {
      "Informativeness": false,
      "Fluency": false,
      "Non-redundancy": false
    },
    "control": {},
    "text": {
      "Informativeness": "",
      "Fluency": "",
      "Non-redundancy": ""
    }
  },
  "heds-sample_evaluators_design-experimental_design-collection_method": {
    "data": {
      "": "Excel spreadsheet"
    },
    "control": {}
  },
  "heds-criteria-criterion-response_elicitation-inter_annotator-agreement-other_text": {
    "data": {
      "Informativeness": "Cohen's kappa",
      "Non-redundancy": "Cohen's kappa",
      "Fluency": "Cohen's kappa"
    },
    "control": {}
  },
  "heds-system-tasks-16": {
    "data": {
      "": true
```

```
    },
    "control": {},
    "text": {
      "": "16. summarisation (text-to-text)"
    }
  },
  "heds-criteria-criterion-criteria-output_aspect-2": {
    "data": {
      "Informativeness": true,
      "Non-redundancy": false,
      "Fluency": false
    },
    "control": {},
    "text": {
      "Informativeness": "2. Content of output",
      "Non-redundancy": "",
      "Fluency": ""
    }
  },
  "heds-sample_evaluators_design-evaluators-number_of_evaluators": {
    "data": {
      "": "3"
    },
    "control": {}
  },
  "heds-sample_evaluators_design-experimental_design-preregistered-2": {
    "data": {
      "": true
    },
    "control": {},
    "text": {
      "": "2. no"
    }
  },
  "heds-criteria-criterion-criteria-self_vs_external_frame-1": {
    "data": {
      "Informativeness": false,
      "Non-redundancy": false,
      "Fluency": true
    },
    "control": {},
    "text": {
      "Informativeness": "",
      "Non-redundancy": "",
      "Fluency": "1. Quality of output in its own right"
    }
  },
  "heds-sample_evaluators_design-evaluators-evaluators-payment-2": {
    "data": {
      "": false
    },
    "control": {},
    "text": {
      "": ""
    }
  },
  "heds-sample_evaluators_design-experimental_design-preregistered-1": {
    "data": {
      "": false
    },
```

"control": {},
"text": {
"": ""
}
},
"heds-system-output_types-5": {
"data": {
"": true
},
"control": {},
"text": {
"": "5. text: sentence"
}
},
"heds-sample_evaluators_design-experimental_design-preregistered-other_text": {
"data": {
"": ""
},
"control": {}
},
"heds-paper_and_resources-resources-links": {
"data": {
"": "https://drive.google.com/drive/u/0/folders/1hevFqMAwx9qZpfvsYSar6e4IBgFuSVKw"
},
"control": {}
},
"heds-criteria-criterion-criteria-self_vs_external_frame-other_text": {
"data": {
"Informativeness": "",
"Non-redundancy": "",
"Fluency": ""
},
"control": {}
},
"heds-sample_evaluators_design-evaluators-evaluators-expertise-3": {
"data": {
"": false
},
"control": {},
"text": {
"": ""
}
},
"heds-sample_evaluators_design-sample-statistical_power-value": {
"data": {
"": "N/A"
},
"control": {}
},
"heds-criteria-criterion-response_elicitation-inter_annotator-agreement-3": {
"data": {
"Informativeness": false,
"Non-redundancy": false,
"Fluency": false
},
"control": {},
"text": {
"Informativeness": "",
"Non-redundancy": "",
"Fluency": ""

```
    }
  },
  "heds-sample_evaluators_design-evaluators-evaluators-are_authors-other_text": {
    "data": {
      "": ""
    },
    "control": {}
  },
  "heds-sample_evaluators_design-experimental_design-experimental_conditions-3": {
    "data": {
      "": false
    },
    "control": {},
    "text": {
      "": ""
    }
  },
  "heds-criteria-criterion-response_elicitation-form_of_response-1": {
    "data": {
      "Informativeness": false,
      "Non-redundancy": false,
      "Fluency": false
    },
    "control": {},
    "text": {
      "Informativeness": "",
      "Non-redundancy": "",
      "Fluency": ""
    }
  },
  "heds-criteria-criterion-response_elicitation-size_of_scale-other_text": {
    "data": {
      "Informativeness": "3",
      "Non-redundancy": "3",
      "Fluency": "3"
    },
    "control": {}
  },
  "heds-sample_evaluators_design-experimental_design-evaluator_freedom-3": {
    "data": {
      "": true
    },
    "control": {},
    "text": {
      "": "3. neither of the above (please describe)"
    }
  },
  "heds-criteria-criterion-response_elicitation-form_of_response-3": {
    "data": {
      "Informativeness": false,
      "Non-redundancy": false,
      "Fluency": false
    },
    "control": {},
    "text": {
      "Informativeness": "",
      "Non-redundancy": "",
      "Fluency": ""
    }
  },
```

"heds-sample_evaluators_design-sample-statistical_power-method": {
  "data": {
    "": "N/A"
  },
  "control": {}
},
"heds-sample_evaluators_design-sample-system_output_selection-4": {
  "data": {
    "": false
  },
  "control": {},
  "text": {
    "": ""
  }
},
"heds-criteria-criterion-response_elicitation-inter_annotator-agreement-2": {
  "data": {
    "Informativeness": false,
    "Non-redundancy": false,
    "Fluency": false
  },
  "control": {},
  "text": {
    "Informativeness": "",
    "Non-redundancy": "",
    "Fluency": ""
  }
},
"heds-criteria-criterion-response_elicitation-scale_presented_as-4": {
  "data": {
    "Informativeness": false,
    "Fluency": false,
    "Non-redundancy": false
  },
  "control": {},
  "text": {
    "Informativeness": "",
    "Fluency": "",
    "Non-redundancy": ""
  }
},
"heds-paper_and_resources-paper-experiment_identification": {
  "data": {
    "": "Human Evaluation (Section 4.3 and Section 5.2)"
  },
  "control": {}
},
"heds-sample_evaluators_design-evaluators-evaluators-are_authors-3": {
  "data": {
    "": false
  },
  "control": {},
  "text": {
    "": ""
  }
},
"heds-criteria-criterion-response_elicitation-form_of_response-other_text": {
  "data": {
    "Informativeness": "",
    "Non-redundancy": "",

"Fluency": ""
},
"control": {}
},
"heds-sample_evaluators_design-evaluators-characteristics": {
"data": {
"": "PhD candidates in computer science\n2 males, 1 female"
},
"control": {}
},
"heds-sample_evaluators_design-evaluators-evaluators-known_to_authors-3": {
"data": {
"": false
},
"control": {},
"text": {
"": ""
}
},
"heds-criteria-criterion-response_elicitation-inter_annotator-agreement-1": {
"data": {
"Informativeness": true,
"Non-redundancy": true,
"Fluency": true
},
"control": {},
"text": {
"Informativeness": "1. yes",
"Non-redundancy": "1. yes",
"Fluency": "1. yes"
}
},
"heds-criteria-criterion-criteria-self_vs_external_frame-2": {
"data": {
"Informativeness": true,
"Non-redundancy": true,
"Fluency": false
},
"control": {},
"text": {
"Informativeness": "2. Quality of output relative to the input",
"Non-redundancy": "2. Quality of output relative to the input",
"Fluency": ""
}
},
"heds-ethics-impact_assessments": {
"data": {
"": "No"
},
"control": {}
},
"heds-criteria-criterion-response_elicitation-size_of_scale-1": {
"data": {
"Informativeness": true,
"Non-redundancy": true,
"Fluency": true
},
"control": {},
"text": {
"Informativeness": "1. Discrete",

"Non-redundancy": "1. Discrete",
"Fluency": "1. Discrete"
}
},
"heds-criteria-criterion-response_elicitation-participant_criterion_definiiton": {
"data": {
"Informativeness": "Does the generated summary correctly cover the information in the ground truth summary?\n(标准答案是由多个子句组成的，这里我们想要判断标准答案中的每子句的信息是否被抽取到了。)",
"Non-redundancy": "Does the generated summary not contain repeated, meaningless or unnecessary information?\n(待测摘要文本也是由多个子句组成的，这里我们想要判断待测文本中的每个子句的信息是否是冗余的。)",
"Fluency": "Is the generated summary well-formed, semantically complete, and easy to understand?\n(我们想要判断待测文本中的每个子句的语言表达流畅性。)"
},
"control": {}
},
"heds-sample_evaluators_design-sample-statistical_power-script": {
"data": {
"": "N/A"
},
"control": {}
},
"heds-sample_evaluators_design-experimental_design-experimental_conditions-5": {
"data": {
"": false
},
"control": {},
"text": {
"": ""
}
},
"heds-criteria-criterion-criteria-output_aspect-3": {
"data": {
"Informativeness": false,
"Non-redundancy": true,
"Fluency": false
},
"control": {},
"text": {
"Informativeness": "",
"Non-redundancy": "3. Both form and content of output",
"Fluency": ""
}
},
"heds-criteria-criterion-response_elicitation-scale_presented_as-1": {
"data": {
"Informativeness": false,
"Fluency": false,
"Non-redundancy": false
},
"control": {},
"text": {
"Informativeness": "",
"Fluency": "",
"Non-redundancy": ""
}
},

```
  "heds-sample_evaluators_design-experimental_design-evaluators_can_ask_questions-1": {
    "data": {
      "": true
    },
    "control": {},
    "text": {
      "": "1. evaluators are told they can ask any questions during/after receiving initial training/
instructions, and before the start of the evaluation"
    }
  },
  "heds-criteria-criterion-response_elicitation-form_of_response-11": {
    "data": {
      "Informativeness": false,
      "Non-redundancy": false,
      "Fluency": false
    },
    "control": {},
    "text": {
      "Informativeness": "",
      "Non-redundancy": "",
      "Fluency": ""
    }
  },
  "heds-paper_and_resources-names_and_affiliations-person_completing_this_sheet-email": {
    "data": {
      "": "t-ito@tohoku.ac.jp"
    },
    "control": {}
  },
  "heds-criteria-criterion-evaluation_mode-absolute_or_relative-other_text": {
    "data": {
      "Informativeness": "",
      "Non-redundancy": "",
      "Fluency": ""
    },
    "control": {}
  },
  "heds-sample_evaluators_design-experimental_design-experimental_conditions-2": {
    "data": {
      "": false
    },
    "control": {},
    "text": {
      "": ""
    }
  }
}
```

A Reproduction Study of the Human Evaluation of Role-Oriented Dialogue Summarization Models

Mingqi Gao, Jie Ruan, Xiaojun Wan
Wangxuan Institute of Computer Technology, Peking University
{gaomingqi, wanxiaojun}@pku.edu.cn
ruanjie@stu.pku.edu.cn

Abstract

This paper reports a reproduction study of the human evaluation of role-oriented dialogue summarization models, as part of the ReproNLP Shared Task 2023 on Reproducibility of Evaluations in NLP. We outline the disparities between the original study's experimental design and our reproduction study, along with the outcomes obtained. The inter-annotator agreement within the reproduction study is observed to be lower, measuring 0.40 as compared to the original study's 0.48. Among the six conclusions drawn in the original study, four are validated in our reproduction study. We confirm the effectiveness of the proposed approach on the overall metric, albeit with slightly poorer relative performance compared to the original study. Furthermore, we raise an open-ended inquiry: how can subjective practices in the original study be identified and addressed when conducting reproduction studies?

1 Introduction

Reproducibility has gained significant attention within the field of Natural Language Processing (NLP) in recent years. This paper presents a reproduction study focused on the human evaluation of role-oriented dialogue summarization models. The study was conducted as part of the ReproNLP Shared Task 2023, which aims to foster reproducibility in NLP evaluations. Our participation in Track C involved conducting a reproduction study specifically targeting the human evaluation component described in the work by Lin et al. (2022), which is one of the five papers included in this track. The shared dataset used in this track originates from the ReproHum project [1], which employs a multi-lab paradigm to assess reproducibility in NLP.

Role-oriented dialogue summarization aims to generate summaries tailored to various roles within a conversation. For instance, in the context of a customer service chat, distinct summaries can be generated for the user's and the agent's utterances. The original research paper introduced an approach that leverages role interaction to effectively integrate the content of other roles into the summary pertaining to a specific role (Lin et al., 2022). The aforementioned study empirically demonstrated the effectiveness of the proposed approach in comparison to baseline methods through both automatic and human evaluations. In this study, we specifically concentrate on the human evaluation aspect.

2 Experimental Design

2.1 Original experiment

Lin et al. (2022) applied the proposed approach to two popular sequence-to-sequence models: PGN (See et al., 2017) and BERTAbs (Liu and Lapata, 2019). The baseline dialogue summarization models are denoted as **PGN-multi** and **BERT-multi**, and the models with the role interaction approach are noted as **PGN-both** and **BERT-both**. The human evaluation was conducted on CSDS (Lin et al., 2021), a Chinese customer service dialogue summarization dataset.

Selection of evaluation samples. From the test set of CSDS, 100 dialogues were randomly chosen as evaluation samples. Each dialogue is associated with two reference summaries, one for the user and one for the agent. A model also generated summaries for both the user and the agent. For each reference summary, four model-generated summaries (PGN-multi, BERT-multi, PGN-both, and BERT-both) were evaluated by human annotators. Notably, the source dialogues were excluded from the human evaluation process.

Participating annotators and compensation.

[1] https://reprohum.github.io/

Proceedings of the Third Workshop on Human Evaluation of NLP Systems, pages 124–129, Varna, Bulgaria, Sep 7, 2023.
https://doi.org/10.26615/978-954-452-088-5_010

Three Chinese graduate students, all proficient in Chinese, volunteered as annotators for this evaluation. These participants were not remunerated for their involvement.

Evaluation dimensions and criteria. Given a reference summary, a model-generated summary was evaluated on three dimensions: *Informativeness*, *non-redundancy*, and *fluency*. Specifically, the annotators were asked to rate each sentence in the summary on a Likert scale from 0 to 2.

Informativeness: The reference summary is composed of multiple sentences, and the annotators were asked to determine whether the information of each sentence in the reference summary is extracted by the model-generated summary. For each sentence in the reference summary, the rule is as follows:

- 0 if most of its content is not extracted by the model-generated summary.
- 1 if some of its content is extracted.
- 2 if basically all of its content is extracted.

Non-redundancy: The model-generated summary is also composed of multiple sentences, and the annotators were asked to determine whether the information of each sentence in the model-generated summary is redundant. For each sentence in the model-generated summary, the rule is as follows:

- 0 if its content is not in the reference summary.
- 1 if its content is in the reference summary but there is redundancy compared to the reference summary.
- 2 if the content is basically the same.

Fluency: For each sentence in the model-generated summary, the rule is as follows:

- 0 if it has more grammatical errors or misspellings, or if the statement is incomprehensible.
- 1 if it has minor grammatical errors or typos, or if the expression is more colloquial.
- 2 if the expression is fluent, free of grammatical errors and misspellings, and semantically completed.

Annotation interface. The reference summaries and model-generated summaries were presented to annotators using an Excel sheet, and they filled in the ratings in the specified places as shown in Figure 1. To ensure impartiality, the names of the summarization models were withheld from the annotators, and the order of the model-generated summaries was randomized.

Annotation procedure. Annotators were asked to read the evaluation instructions before annotation. Initially, all three annotators independently annotated the first 10 samples (ID 0-9). After a moderate level of inter-annotator agreement was attained, they were allowed to continue annotation. The remaining 90 samples were divided equally into thirds. The remaining 90 samples were evenly divided into thirds. Annotator #1 was assigned samples with ID 10-39, annotator #2 received samples with ID 40-69, and annotator #3 handled samples with ID 70-99.

Inter-annotator agreement. The results of the first 10 samples were used to compute inter-annotator agreement. All per-sentence scores given by an annotator on all three dimensions are flattened into a list. The Cohen's kappa (Cohen, 1960) was computed between every two annotators with the script in the scikit-learn library[2], and the average of the kappa scores was considered as the final inter-annotator agreement.

Post-processing, calculation, and significance testing. To normalize the scores to a range of 0 to 1, they were divided by 2. For the first 10 samples, the annotations of the annotator with the most expertise were selected as the final results. For each of the three dimensions, the per-sentence scores of the summary were averaged as the score of the summary. In addition, the average of the summary-level scores of the three dimensions was calculated as an "Overall" score for a summary. The model's score was obtained by averaging the scores of its generated summaries. A paired t-test was conducted to assess the significance between the scores of summaries generated by two models.

2.2 Reproduction experiment

The reproduction experiment utilized the same Excel sheet for annotation as the original study, which encompassed identical samples for evaluation. Furthermore, the evaluation instructions were also pro-

[2] `https://scikit-learn.org/stable/modules/generated/sklearn.metrics.cohen_kappa_score.html`

Dialogue ID	Reference Summary	The summary to be evaluated	Informativeness	Non-redundancy	Fluency
0	Users ask about methods other than cell phone verification to change their passwords. Users ask how they can log in with a password without cell phone number verification. Users ask if they can buy something without verification.	The user said that the previous cell phone number was canceled, the password was forgotten, and the cell phone verification code was needed to change the password.			
		The user said that the previous cell phone number was canceled, the password was forgotten, and the cell phone verification code was needed to change the password.			
		The user wants to change the password. The user asks if a verification code is required.	1,0,0	2,0	2,1
		The user says he has forgotten his previous cell phone number and wants to change his password. The user asks if he can buy something. The user says he can't change his password by email.			
	Customer service allows the user to provide the number and give it to the commissioner to call back to solve the problem. Customer service helps feedback the user's problem to the commissioner. Customer service asks the user to wait patiently.	Customer service helps the user upgrade the commissioner will be tomorrow [number] o'clock before the user calls back to facilitate the provision of the user to bind the cell phone number. Customer service answer has been feedback commissioner, please keep the user's phone open.			
		Customer service helps user upgrade specialist will call back before tomorrow [number] o'clock to facilitate the provision of the user to bind the cell phone number.			
		Customer service replied to help the user to upgrade the commissioner to deal with, and told the user that the commissioner will call the user back by tomorrow [number] o'clock. Customer service answers the user can see the previous cell phone number			
		Customer service answers to help the user feedback commissioner and call the user back by tomorrow [number] o'clock.			

Figure 1: Annotation interface. The text actually presented to annotators is in Chinese, and the translated version is shown here.

vided. With these materials, we were able to set up most of the experiment in the exact same way as the original. Nonetheless, certain variations were introduced in the reproduction experiment, which is outlined below. For more detailed information, please see the Human Evaluation Sheet (HEDS) file in supplementary materials.

Participating annotators and compensation. Recruiting unpaid volunteers as annotators proved to be challenging. Following discussions with the organizers of the ReproHum project, we recruited three participants who met the same requirements as those in the original experiment and provided them with compensation of 12.24 EUR per hour.

Annotation procedure. We cannot know what the original experiment would have done if the three annotators had not reached a moderate level of agreement on the first 10 samples because this did not actually happen. In consultation with the organizers of the ReproHum project, we determined that all annotators would continue with the annotation process, regardless of whether a moderate agreement was reached on the first 10 samples or not.

Post-processing, calculation, and significance testing. It is subjective to determine which participant was most knowledgeable on this task. Given the challenging nature of reproduction, the organizers of the ReproHum project asked us not to copy the original practices to post-process the first 10 samples. they proposed that we calculate separate results using each of the following five methods (referred to as different reproduction settings):

- Repr1: With only annotator #1 representing each sentence in the first 10 samples (as if #1 had been selected).
- Repr2: With only annotator #2 representing each sentence in the first 10 samples (as if #2 had been selected).
- Repr3: With only annotator #3 representing each sentence in the first 10 samples (as if #3 had been selected).
- Repr4: With the mean of annotator responses representing each sentence in the first 10 samples (i.e., [0,1,2] $\Rightarrow$ 1.00, [0,0,2] $\Rightarrow$ 0.67).
- Repr5: With the median of annotator responses representing each sentence in the first 10 samples (i.e., [0,1,2] $\Rightarrow$ 1, [0,0,2] $\Rightarrow$ 0).

In addition, our reproduction experiments began after the protocol was approved by the ethics committee.

3 Results and Discussion

3.1 Inter-annotator agreement (IAA)

The initial study reported an IAA of 0.48, while our reproduction experiment yielded a slightly lower IAA of 0.40. The IAA observed in the original study can be classified as moderate (0.41-0.60), and

Original					Repr3				
	Info	Non-Red	Flu	Overall		Info	Non-Red	Flu	Overall
PGN-multi	**0.69**/0.65	0.54/0.55	0.70/0.79	0.64/0.66	PGN-multi	0.68/0.62	0.60/0.56	0.82/**0.90**	0.70/0.69
PGN-both	0.66/**0.69**	**0.58/0.59***	**0.73/0.81**	**0.66/0.70***	PGN-both	0.68/**0.66***	**0.61/0.59**	**0.84**/0.89	**0.71/0.71**
BERT-multi	0.58/0.56	**0.66/0.61**	0.84/0.87	0.69/0.68	BERT-multi	0.57/0.52	**0.67**/0.56	**0.91**/0.89	**0.71**/0.66
BERT-both	**0.62*/0.60***	0.62/0.60	**0.85**/0.87	**0.70/0.69**	BERT-both	**0.59/0.56**	0.62/**0.58**	0.87/0.89	0.69/**0.68**
Repr1					Repr4				
	Info	Non-Red	Flu	Overall		Info	Non-Red	Flu	Overall
PGN-multi	0.68/0.62	0.60/0.55	0.80/0.89	0.69/0.69	PGN-multi	0.68/0.62	0.59/0.55	0.81/0.89	0.69/0.69
PGN-both	**0.69/0.68***	**0.61/0.60***	**0.83**/0.89	**0.71/0.72***	PGN-both	0.68/**0.67***	**0.60/0.59**	**0.83**/0.89	**0.71/0.72***
BERT-multi	0.57/0.51	**0.67**/0.57	**0.90**/0.88	**0.71**/0.66	BERT-multi	0.56/0.51	**0.67**/0.56	**0.90**/0.88	**0.71**/0.65
BERT-both	**0.60/0.56***	0.63/**0.58**	0.86/0.88	0.70/**0.68**	BERT-both	**0.59/0.56***	0.62/**0.58**	0.87/**0.89**	0.69/**0.67**
Repr2					Repr5				
	Info	Non-Red	Flu	Overall		Info	Non-Red	Flu	Overall
PGN-multi	0.67/0.62	0.58/0.55	0.80/**0.90**	0.68/0.69	PGN-multi	0.68/0.62	0.59/0.55	0.81/**0.90**	0.69/0.69
PGN-both	0.67/**0.66***	**0.60/0.58**	**0.83**/0.89	**0.70/0.71**	PGN-both	0.68/**0.67***	**0.61/0.59***	**0.83**/0.89	**0.70/0.72**
BERT-multi	0.56/0.51	**0.67**/0.56	**0.91**/0.89	**0.71**/0.65	BERT-multi	0.57/0.51	**0.67**/0.56	**0.90**/0.88	**0.71**/0.65
BERT-both	**0.58/0.55**	0.61/**0.57**	0.87/0.89	0.69/**0.67**	BERT-both	**0.59/0.56**	0.62/**0.58**	0.87/**0.89**	0.69/ **0.67**

Table 1: Human evaluation results in the original experiment and the reproduction experiment. Two values separated by a slash in a cell are scores for user-oriented summary and agent-oriented summary. * denotes that the enhancement achieved by utilizing role interactions, compared to the *multi* baseline, is statistically significant ($p < 0.05$). The original results are taken from Lin et al. (2022). "Repr#" is defined in Section 2.2.

	Original	Reproduction	Confirmation
1	For PGN models, applying role interactions could reduce redundancy.	For PGN models, applying role interactions could reduce redundancy.	Confirmed.
2	For PGN models, applying role interactions could maintain a comparable performance of informativeness.	For PGN model, applying role interactions could partially improve informativeness.	Confirmed. The relative performance of the proposed approach in the experiment is slightly better than the original.
3	For PGN models, applying role interactions could improve fluency.	For PGN models, applying role interaction could maintain a comparable performance of fluency.	Not confirmed. The relative performance of the proposed approach in the experiment is worse than the original.
4	For BERTAbs models, applying role interactions could improve informativeness.	For BERTAbs models, applying role interactions could improve informativeness.	Confirmed.
5	For BERTAbs models, applying role interactions could add redundancy.	For BERTAbs models, applying role interactions could maintain a comparable performance of non-redundancy.	Not confirmed. The relative performance of the proposed approach in the experiment is better than the original.
6	Applying role interactions is effective in terms of the overall metric.	For PGN models, applying role interactions is effective in terms of the overall metric.	Confirmed. The relative performance of the proposed approach in the experiment is slightly worse than the original.

Table 2: The conclusions in the original experiment and the reproduction experiment. The *Confirmation* column shows whether the conclusion is confirmed in the reproduction experiment or not and how the relative performance changed in the reproduction experiment. **Note** that relative performance refers to the results of the proposed approach relative to the baseline model.

All reproduction settings (Repr1, 2, 3, 4, 5)					Original vs. Repr3				
	Info	Non-Red	Flu	Overall		Info	Non-Red	Flu	Overall
PGN-multi	0.74/0.00	1.58/0.90	1.16/0.68	1.14/0.00	PGN-multi	1.46/4.71	10.49/1.80	15.74/12.98	8.93/4.43
PGN-both	1.16/1.40	1.01/1.34	0.60/0.00	0.87/0.85	PGN-both	2.98/4.43	5.03/0.00	13.97/9.38	7.28/1.41
BERT-multi	1.08/0.98	0.00/0.89	0.68/0.69	0.00/0.94	BERT-multi	1.73/7.39	1.50/8.52	7.98/2.27	2.85/2.98
BERT-both	1.34/0.90	1.27/0.86	0.58/0.56	0.72/0.91	BERT-both	4.94/6.88	0.00/3.38	2.32/2.27	1.43/1.46
Original vs. Repr1					Original vs. Repr4				
	Info	Non-Red	Flu	Overall		Info	Non-Red	Flu	Overall
PGN-multi	1.46/4.71	10.49/0.00	13.29/11.87	7.50/4.43	PGN-multi	1.46/4.71	8.82/0.00	14.53/11.87	7.50/4.43
PGN-both	4.43/1.46	5.03/1.68	12.78/9.38	7.28/2.81	PGN-both	2.98/2.93	3.38/0.00	12.78/9.38	7.28/2.81
BERT-multi	1.73/9.32	1.50/6.76	6.88/1.14	2.85/2.98	BERT-multi	3.50/9.32	1.50/8.52	6.88/1.14	2.85/4.50
BERT-both	3.27/6.88	1.60/3.38	1.17/1.14	0.00/1.46	BERT-both	4.94/6.88	0.00/3.38	2.32/2.27	1.43/2.93
Original vs. Repr2					Original vs. Repr5				
	Info	Non-Red	Flu	Overall		Info	Non-Red	Flu	Overall
PGN-multi	2.93/4.71	7.12/0.00	13.29/12.98	6.04/4.43	PGN-multi	1.46/4.71	8.82/0.00	14.53/12.98	7.50/4.43
PGN-both	1.50/4.43	3.38/1.70	12.78/9.38	5.86/1.41	PGN-both	2.98/2.93	5.03/0.00	12.78/9.38	5.86/2.81
BERT-multi	3.50/9.32	1.50/8.52	7.98/2.27	2.85/4.50	BERT-multi	1.73/9.32	1.50/8.52	6.88/1.14	2.85/4.50
BERT-both	6.65/8.67	1.62/5.11	2.32/2.27	1.43/2.93	BERT-both	4.94/6.88	0.00/3.38	2.32/2.27	1.43/2.93

Table 3: CV*s among all reproduction settings (Repr1, 2, 3, 4, 5) and CV*s between scores in the original experiment and scores in the reproduction experiment with a specific setting. Two values separated by a slash in a cell are scores for user-oriented summary and agent-oriented summary.

the slightly lower IAA in the reproduction study falls near the boundary between the moderate and fair levels. There is not much difference between the two. Nevertheless, it might be more reasonable to calculate the IAA independently for each of the three evaluation dimensions, but only an overall IAA was reported in the original study.

3.2 Side-by-side comparison of conclusions

Table 1 presents the human evaluation results of various models in both the original experiment and the reproduction experiment conducted under different settings (Repr1, 2, 3, 4, 5). It is evident that the outcomes of the reproduction experiment exhibit minor divergence across the different settings. The original paper posits six conclusions, each of which can be assessed for confirmation based on the results of the reproduction experiment, as depicted in Table 2. Notably, **four out of the six conclusions are substantiated**.

Furthermore, our analysis centers on the variations observed in the relative performance of the proposed approach between the reproduction experiment and the original experiment. In certain aspects, such as the informativeness of the summaries generated by PGN models, the reproduction experiment demonstrates an improvement over the original experiment. Conversely, in other aspects, the relative performance of the proposed approach is inferior to that of the original experiment. In particular, the fifth conclusion from the original experiment, as stated in Table 2, highlights a drawback of the proposed approach. However, this drawback is not supported by the findings of the reproduction experiment. As for the sixth conclusion from the original experiment, **the effectiveness of the proposed approach is confirmed in terms of the overall metric, although the relative performance in the reproduction experiment exhibits a slight decline in comparison to the original experiment.**

3.3 Quantifying the difference

To quantify the disparities between the outcomes of the original experiment and the reproduction experiment, as well as the variations in the results across different settings in the reproduction experiment, we employ two statistical measures: the small-sample coefficient of variation (CV*) and Spearman's ρ.

A lower value of CV* corresponds to a smaller discrepancy, rendering it a quantifiable metric for assessing the reproducibility of numerical scores (Belz et al., 2022). Table 3 demonstrates that **the CVs between scores obtained in the original experiment and those obtained in the reproduction experiment with a specific setting are considerably larger than the CVs observed among different reproduction settings.** This finding suggests that the variations introduced by distinct reproduction settings, specifically the methods employed for post-processing the initial 10 samples, have a relatively minor impact on the results.

In Table 4, we present the system-level Spearman's rank correlation between the original experiment and the reproduction experiment. The con-

	Info	Non-Red	Flu	Overall
Repr1	0.80/1.00	1.00/0.20	0.80/-0.94	0.32/0.40
Repr2	0.95/1.00	1.00/0.20	0.80/-0.82	0.40/0.40
Repr3	0.95/1.00	1.00/-0.11	0.80/-0.82	-0.32/0.40
Repr4	0.95/1.00	1.00/0.20	0.80/-0.54	0.00/0.40
Repr5	0.95/1.00	1.00/0.20	0.80/-0.83	0.11/0.40

Table 4: Spearman's ρ between the scores of four models in the original experiment and the reproduction experiment with a specific setting. Two values separated by a slash in a cell are scores for user-oriented summary and agent-oriented summary.

siderable variation across different dimensions can be attributed to the limited number of comparable systems in this study. Therefore, it is better to use CV* to measure the differences in this case.

4 Conclusion

We present a reproduction study focused on evaluating dialogue summarization models through human evaluation. The successful execution of our reproduction experiment was facilitated by the collaboration with ReproNLP organizers and the utilization of materials provided by the original authors. As a result, we have drawn the following conclusions:

- The inter-annotator agreement in our reproduction study was found to be lower, with a value of 0.40 compared to the original study's 0.48.
- Four out of the six conclusions reached in the original study were confirmed through our reproduction study.
- Our findings affirm the effectiveness of the proposed approach in terms of the overall metric; however, the relative performance was slightly inferior in the reproduction study.
- The utilization of different post-processing methods for the first 10 samples yielded minor variations in the final results.

One intriguing query that arises in the context of our reproduction study pertains to the identification and handling of subjective practices that may have been employed in the original study. Specifically, we explore the different post-processing methods of annotation results from the initial 10 samples in this experiment. Despite the limited impact of varying treatments on the ultimate outcome, the underlying concern persists. Notably, if subjective practices are embedded within the core of the original experiment, the potential simulation of multiple possibilities can significantly amplify the scale of the experiment. This matter merits further investigation and remains an avenue for future research.

References

Anya Belz, Maja Popovic, and Simon Mille. 2022. Quantified reproducibility assessment of NLP results. In *Proceedings of the 60th Annual Meeting of the Association for Computational Linguistics (Volume 1: Long Papers)*, pages 16–28, Dublin, Ireland. Association for Computational Linguistics.

Jacob Cohen. 1960. A coefficient of agreement for nominal scales. *Educational and Psychological Measurement*, 20:37 – 46.

Haitao Lin, Liqun Ma, Junnan Zhu, Lu Xiang, Yu Zhou, Jiajun Zhang, and Chengqing Zong. 2021. CSDS: A fine-grained Chinese dataset for customer service dialogue summarization. In *Proceedings of the 2021 Conference on Empirical Methods in Natural Language Processing*, pages 4436–4451, Online and Punta Cana, Dominican Republic. Association for Computational Linguistics.

Haitao Lin, Junnan Zhu, Lu Xiang, Yu Zhou, Jiajun Zhang, and Chengqing Zong. 2022. Other roles matter! enhancing role-oriented dialogue summarization via role interactions. In *Proceedings of the 60th Annual Meeting of the Association for Computational Linguistics (Volume 1: Long Papers)*, pages 2545–2558, Dublin, Ireland. Association for Computational Linguistics.

Yang Liu and Mirella Lapata. 2019. Text summarization with pretrained encoders. In *Proceedings of the 2019 Conference on Empirical Methods in Natural Language Processing and the 9th International Joint Conference on Natural Language Processing (EMNLP-IJCNLP)*, pages 3730–3740, Hong Kong, China. Association for Computational Linguistics.

Abigail See, Peter J. Liu, and Christopher D. Manning. 2017. Get to the point: Summarization with pointer-generator networks. In *Proceedings of the 55th Annual Meeting of the Association for Computational Linguistics (Volume 1: Long Papers)*, pages 1073–1083, Vancouver, Canada. Association for Computational Linguistics.

h_da@ReproHum – Reproduction of Human Evaluation and Technical Pipeline

Margot Mieskes
University of Applied Sciences
Darmstadt, Germany
margot.mieskes@h-da.de

Jacob Benz
University of Applied Sciences
Darmstadt, Germany
jacob.benz@stud.h-da.de

Abstract

How reliable are human evaluation results? Is it possible to replicate human evaluation? This work takes a closer look at the evaluation of the output of a Text-to-Speech (TTS) system. Unfortunately, our results indicate that human evaluation is not as straightforward to replicate as expected. Additionally, we additionally present results on reproducing the technical background of the TTS system and discuss potential reasons for the reproduction failure.

1 Introduction

Replication of research results in Natural Language Processing (NLP) has gained considerable attention in the past years. While quite some progress has been achieved with initiatives such as the Responsible Research Checklist[1] and the Reproduction Checklist [2] (Dodge et al., 2019), the question about the reproduction of human evaluation is widely unanswered. The work presented here is part of the ReproHum Project[3], which aimes to reproduce human evaluation. In our experiment, we tried to reproduce the evaluation of a low-resource Text-to-Speech (TTS) system for German. As the results of our reproduction indicated that we were unsuccessful, we also had a closer look at the technical aspects of the work and attempted to reproduce those elements for our study as well.

Our major contributions are therefore: 1) the results on the reproduction of the human evaluation of the TTS output, 2) the results of the reconstruction of the language data required for the TTS system and 3) the results of the reconstruction of the TTS model required to create the TTS output, which is then judged during the human evaluation.

[1]https://aclrollingreview.org/responsibleNLPresearch/

[2]https://2021.aclweb.org/calls/reproducibility-checklist/

[3]https://reprohum.github.io/

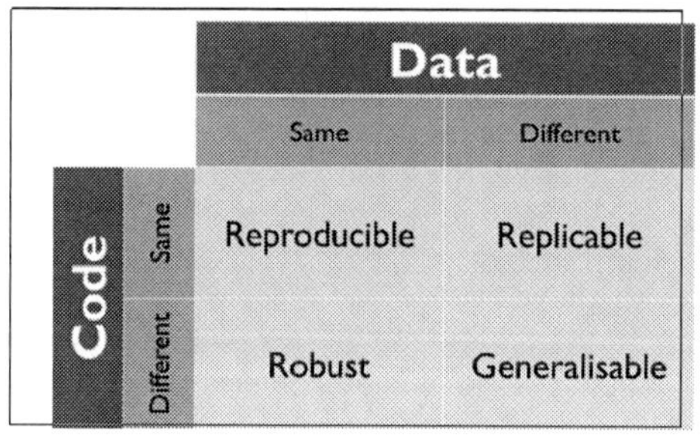

Figure 1: Dimensions of Reproducibility according to (Whitaker, 2017)

2 Background and Related Work

Replication is a topic that is being discussed in a wide range of fields. In NLP the primary focus so far has been on the technical reproduction – i.e. reproducing results based on quantitative evaluation. (Cohen et al., 2018) presented three dimensions of reproduction:

- Reproduction of a Conclusion
- Reproduction of Results
- Reproduction of a Value

But their focus has been on the technical reproduction.

Figure 1 shows another set of parameters for the reproduction: Whether the Code and the Data are the same or different allows for different conclusions with respect to Reproducibility, Replicability, Robustness and Generlizability.

This is also clear from the reproducibilty spectrum according to (Peng, 2011), which focuses heavily on code and data (see Figure 2, similar to (Whitaker, 2017)).

There are major differences between the technical reproduction and the reproduction of human evaluation results, although initially, the aim is also to reproduce a certain value, a certain result or a

Proceedings of the Third Workshop on Human Evaluation of NLP Systems, pages 130–135, Varna, Bulgaria, Sep 7, 2023.
https://doi.org/10.26615/978-954-452-088-5_011

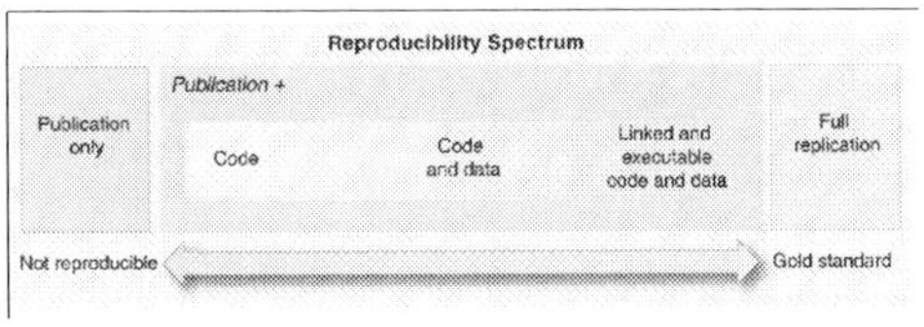

Figure 2: Spectrum of Reproducibility according to (Peng, 2011)

certain conclusion. But a look at other fields, where the reproduction of human input has been already evaluated, such as Psychology and Social Sciences, reveals that this is also far from straightforward. For Psychology it seems that only between 36 % and 68 % of the results were reproducible by an independent researcher (Open Science Collaboration, 2015), while in Social Sciences between 57 % and 67 % of the studies were reproducible (Camerer et al., 2018). Although what dimension of reproduction has been aimed for, is open.

There are various reasons for the lack of reproducibility of human generated results. One element is the lack in objectivity in humans and their individuality, as each human has individual experiences and opinions. Another element is the language, the instructions are presented in. Some languages distinguish between a formal address and an informal address. A person used to being addressed formally, might react negatively to an informal address and the other way around. When performing an evaluation using online tools or any form of technical equipment, this too can affect the results. A high-resolution screen will represent colours differently to a smartphone screen. When dealing with acoustical data, using a headset or speakers can make a vast difference and the quality of each can also influence the results, when asked to evaluate the quality of the presented sound.

3 The Original TTS Experiment

The basis for our work is the paper by (Lux and Vu, 2022). Its aim is to present the possibility to create TTS systems with little training data and reduced training time. This is achieved by using a large multilingual model, which is then fine-tuned towards the target language based on the reduced training data and reduced training time. A specific focus is put to model articulatory features of the language.

The technical basis for the model is Tacotron2 (Shen and Pang) and FastSpeech2 (Ren et al., 2020). Where Tacotron2 is based on a recurrent sequence-to-sequence network, FastSpeech2 is based on a Feed-Forward Transformer network.

The basis for the multilingual model is data from English, Greek, Spanish, Finnish, Russian, Hungarian, Dutch and French. The German data is derived from the HUI corpus (see Section 6 below).

While the multi-lingual model required lots of resources, both in time and hardware, the adaptation to German was performed using 30 minutes of speech and training for about 2 hours. In order to allow for a comparison and to verify the low-resource approach, the authors also trained both FastSpeech2 and Tacotron2 exclusively on German, using 29 hours of recorded speech.

4 Reproduction – Experimental Setup

Following the original study, we set up a Google Form survey, where each participant is presented with two stimuli and asked to judge, which of the two sounds more natural. Figure 3 shows the interface we used to conduct the survey. As we were dealing with German speech output and German students were asked to judge the TTS output, we also addressed participants in German. Participants could choose from three different options: Either one of the outputs is better than the other, or both are equally good.

Prior to starting the evaluation, we submitted all relevant information to the University of Aberdeen Ethics Board for evaluation, which approved of our experimental setup, the way we dealt with the data and the personal information collected from the participants.

The participants were recruited by email from our university. Other than sending out an email via a central email address, we did not collect any personal data from our participants.

5 Reproduction – Results

In the end, 37 participants took part in our experiment, which is comparable to the original study. In general, the output from the proposed Fastspeech2 model is considered better than the baseline system in 41 % of the cases, while the baseline system is considered better in 13 % of the cases. When comparing the two Fastspeech2 versions, 46 % of the participants did not hear any noticeable difference. This is comparable to the original evaluation, where 43 % of the participants did not hear a difference. See also Figure 4.

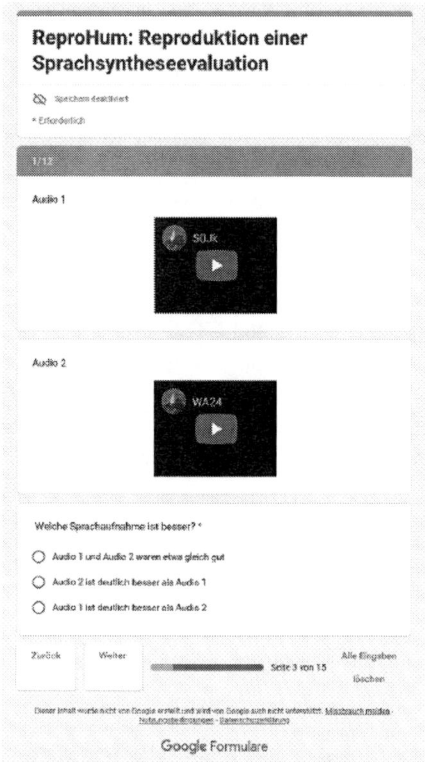

Figure 3: The survey interface.

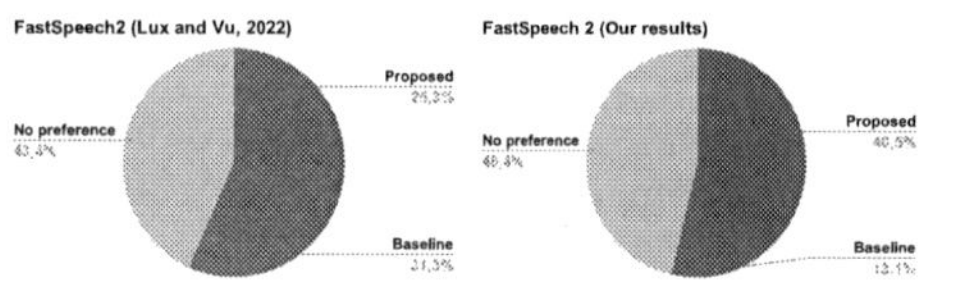

Figure 4: Human Evaluation for FastSpeech2 Low Resource and Baseline.

When evaluating Tacotron2, 26 % of the participants preferred the low-resource model, while 23 % preferred the original version. But, 51 % of the participants did not hear a difference between the two versions. Compared to the original evaluation, where 52 % of the participants preferred the low-resource version, while 11 % preferred the original system and only 37 % did not hear a difference. The results are also shown in Figure 5.

As shown in table 1, the coefficient of variation values for the pair-wise comparisons between the original results and our reproduction are with the exception of one value always in the double digits, further indicating that our reproduction resulted not only in rather different values but different results as well.

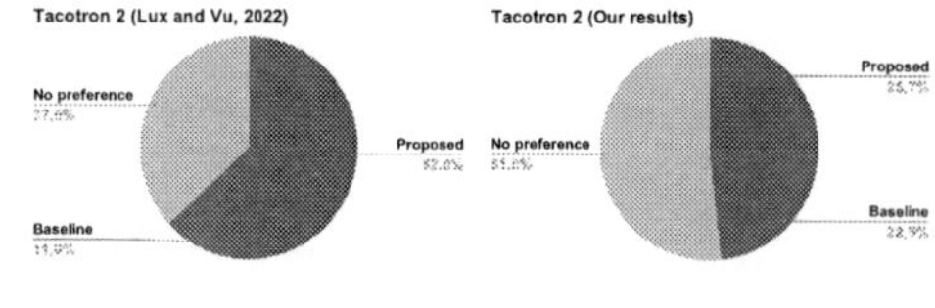

Figure 5: Human Evaluation for Tacotron2 Low Resource and Baseline.

6 Technical Reproduction

In light of these results for the reproduction of the human evaluation we had a closer look at the background of the TTS system. First, we tried to reproduce the data and then we aimed to reproduce the TTS model.

6.1 Reproducing the Data

The original corpus project, as presented in (Puchtler et al., 2021). The Hof Universität – Institut für Informationsysteme (HUI) Audio Corpus German aimed to create a high-quality, open source dataset for German TTS systems. Figure 6 schematically describes the approach.

The authors originally defined a range of parameters for choosing data for their speech synthesis system:

- at least 20 hours of audio per speaker
- minimal sampling rate of 22 kHz
- normalization of textual data
- normalization of loudness
- audios of between 5 and 10 seconds of length
- recording of punctuation

In the end, the original study had collected 326 hours of audio and processed them according to their pipeline in Figure 6. This included five speakers with between 32 and 96 hours of audio and another set of 97 hours of audio by 117 other speakers.

We tried to be very accurate with our reproduction, documenting all steps. Unfortunately, due to a range of errors described below, this reproduction proved to be unsuccessful in the limited time. Initially, the link for the German Deep Speech Model was faulty. Luckily, the original authors reacted quickly and fixed this.

Next, the textual representation of the spoken data had to be downloaded. This referred to a Gutenberg repository, where the mirror was hardcoded, but not valid anymore. Additionally, the URI was automatically created, but again, in the

Model	(Lux and Vu, 2022)	Our Reproduction	Coefficient of Variation
Tacotron2 Proposed preferred	52 %	25,7 %	33,9 %
Tacotron2 Baseline preferred	11 %	22,5 %	34,4 %
Tacotron2 No preference	37 %	51,8 %	16,6 %
FastSpeech2 Proposed preferred	25,3 %	40,5 %	23,7 %
FastSpeech2 Baseline preferred	31,3 %	13,1 %	40,7 %
FastSpeech2 No preference	43,4 %	46,4 %	3,8 %

Table 1: Comparison of the results of the original evaluation and our reproduction.

Modell	Hardware	Duration Preprocessing	Iterations	Time/Iteration	Total Duration
Tacotron2 Low Resource	GPU	1:13 min	10,020	1.25 It/sec	2:25 hrs
Tacotron2 full	GPU	50:32 min	100,224	1.4 It/sec	19:54 hrs
Tacotron2 Low Resource	CPU	NA	925	22 sec/It	6 hrs
FastSpeech2 Low Resource	GPU	NA	100,071	4.4 It/sec	6:27 hrs

Table 2: Retraining of the Low Resource and Full Models according to the specifications given in (Lux and Vu, 2022)

wrong format for the mirror we chose instead of the original one.

The next problem was linked to FFMPEG and NLTK packages that had to be added to the original installation.

Finally, we had to remove one speaker completely from the data set, as several files associated with that speaker could not be processed and this error could not be eliminated.

This resulted in the abortion of the replication attempt, as removing one of the five major speakers from the data set did not allow for a plausible further result.

6.2 Reproducing the TTS Model

Furthermore, we tried to replicate the initial speech synthesis model, as described by (Lux and Vu, 2022). Figure 7 represents the pipeline to create the TTS model, including the technical packages used. Theoretically, this reproduction attempt should have been straightforward, as most research artifacts have been made available to the research community. Unfortunately, the resulting model has not been provided and the TTS outputs are also only available in the context of this project.

Despite the seemingly straightforward problem, the availability of the research artifacts and an extensive `Readme` file, we came across a range of issues in the process. First of all, not all required packages are listed in the `requirements.txt` file. The biggest issue was a `Invalid render options` error during the data pre-processing, which occurred multiple times and only with some files, but not all. Identifying the specific files which caused issues, was quite time-consuming. It turned out, that the original problem is the `unsilence` package, that is used to skip over longer period of silence in the recorded data. With some of those, a parameter required for `ffmpeg` is set to an invalid value, which results in the `invalid render option` error. We extended the code to check for invalid values and set them to a default value, in cases where an invalid value was reached.

Another issue is the fact that the HUI-corpus is available in two versions: *clean* and *full*. Unfortunately, the authors did not report which version of the data has been used for the original experiments, so we decided to use the *full* version.

Finally, the number of training iterations has not been reported. We assume that the figures set in the original code represent these numbers, but it is unsure, if those are actually the figures used in the original experiments.

Table 2 shows the duration of training for the reproduced models. We retrained both the Low Resource models for Tacotron2 and FastSpeech2 and the full Tacotron model. As a proof-of-concept, we also retrained the Tacotron2 Low Resource model on a CPU rather than a GPU. Retraining the Fast Speech2 Full model was beyond the scope of our work. We can support the results from previous work, that indeed, low-resource models can be quickly trained. But we observed a notable difference in the sound quality, pronunciation and the prosody of the resulting output, leading to the conclusion that despite not changing any of the given parameters, the reproduction of the final results was only partially successful.

7 Discussion

Table 3 shows a summary of the different reproductions we attempted and the respective results.

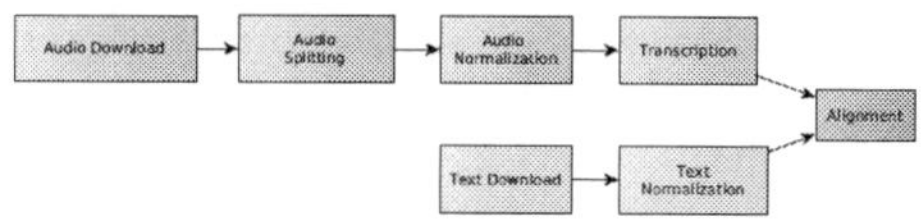

Figure 6: Pipeline for creating the Audio-Transcript Data according to (Puchtler et al., 2021)

Reproduction	Reproducibility	Remarks
Data set	Reproduction had to be abandoned	Mirrors unavailable, software issues
TTS Model	Partially, conclusions were reproduced	Different results, conclusion can be supported
Human Evaluation	Values and results not reproducible	Overall conclusion reproducible

Table 3: List of our attempted reproductions and the respective results.

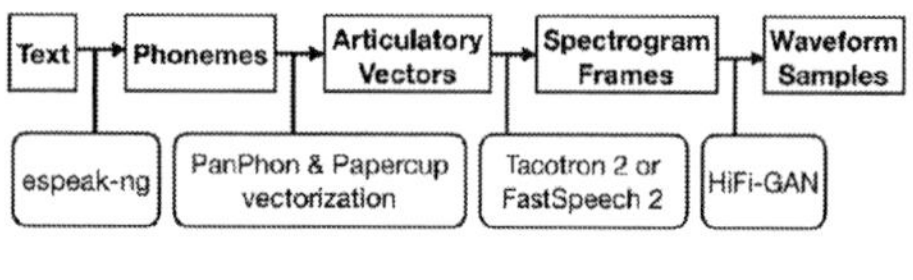

Figure 7: Pipline to create the TTS model according to (Lux and Vu, 2022)

These are quite baffling, since none of our approaches reached the same values or results. There are a number of potential reasons for this:

The differences in results when reproducing the TTS models could be explainable by different hardware or slightly different software versions, especially since we faced issues that the original authors obviously did not encounter.

Regarding the different results for the reproduction of the human evaluation, one reason could be the different group of people. While both studies employed students to evaluate the synthesis output, in the original study, the students are from the field of computational linguistics and natural language processing and as such more used to hearing and judging synthetic speech. In our study, the students did not have any particular training in judging synthetic speech.

Another reason could be that the stimuli were somehow mixed up. If that would be case, we would have to transpose the results and would have results that are more comparable to the original study.

The problem might be related to the problems with reproducing the original data set and/or the original TTS models, since the stimuli were recreated for the purpose of this study[4], which could have lead to a variance in sound quality compared to the original stimuli.

Comparing our results to the results of (Hürlimann and Cieliebak, 2023), who ran the exact same experiment, the chances that the stimuli were transposed somewhere in the process are increasing, as their results also indicate low reproducibility, except if a transposition is assumed. As their results are based on a larger number of participants, they are more pronounced than ours and statistically more reliable. The authors state a range of other potential error sources, which have to be taken into account in addition to our experiments. Additionally, it is certainly remarkable that in both reproductions the lowest coefficients of variation were achieved for the "no preference" option.

8 Conclusion

In general, we can support the conclusion of the previous study, that the low-resource speech synthesis (both using Tacotron2 and Fastspeech2) are viable approaches to produce reasonable TTS output based on limited resources (time, computing and available speech data). Our results also show, that the reproduction of human evaluation and possibly human annotation as well are important research areas. As quantitative results can only give so much information, while human evaluation in various domains (i.e. synthetic speech, but also text quality in Natural Language Generation) can provide a more detailed insight into the data.

Unfortunately, the way human evaluation is currently reported, the reproduction of human evaluation has not been successful.

With respect to the whole pipeline, of a technical reproduction based on which a human evaluation can take place, it is important to make sure, that research artifacts are stored properly, documented thoroughly and potential pitfalls (i.e. dying links) are noted.

Our results indicate that more research is necessary into the issue of human evaluation. Related to

[4]Florian Lux personal communication.

this, it would be interesting to study human annotation tasks, which are related to human evaluation and are the basis of a wide range of models built in the context of NLP.

Acknowledgments

We would like to thank Jonathan Baum for his experiments on the replication of the TTS model and Christian Stute for his support in the replication of the human evaluation replication study.

References

Colin F. Camerer, Anna Dreber, Felix Holzmeister, Teck-Hua Ho, Jürgen Huber, Magnus Johannesson, Michael Kirchler, Gideon Nave, Brian A. Nosek, Thomas Pfeiffer, Adam Altmejd, Nick Buttrick, Taizan Chan, Yiling Chen, Eskil Forsell, Anup Gampa, Emma Heikensten, Lily Hummer, Taisuke Imai, Siri Isaksson, Dylan Manfredi, Julia Rose, Eric-Jan Wagenmakers, and Hang Wu. 2018. Evaluating the replicability of social science experiments in nature and science between 2010 and 2015. 2(9):637–644.

K Bretonnel Cohen, Jingbo Xia, Pierre Zweigenbaum, Tiffany J Callahan, Orin Hargraves, Foster Goss, Nancy Ide, Aurelie Neveol, Cyril Grouin, and Lawrence E Hunter. 2018. Three dimensions of reproducibility in natural language processing. In *Proceedings of the Eleventh International Conference on Language Resources and Evaluation (LREC 2018)*, pages 156–65.

Jesse Dodge, Suchin Gururangan, Dallas Card, Roy Schwartz, and Noah A. Smith. 2019. Show your work: Improved reporting of experimental results. In *Proceedings of the 2019 Conference on Empirical Methods in Natural Language Processing and the 9th International Joint Conference on Natural Language Processing (EMNLP-IJCNLP)*, pages 2185–2194, Hong Kong, China. Association for Computational Linguistics.

Manuela Hürlimann and Mark Cieliebak. 2023. Reproducing a comparative evaluation of german text-to-speech systems. In *Proceedings of the 3rd Workshop on Human Evaluation of NLP Systems (HumEval'23)*.

Florian Lux and Thang Vu. 2022. Language-agnostic meta-learning for low-resource text-to-speech with articulatory features. In *Proceedings of the 60th Annual Meeting of the Association for Computational Linguistics. Volume 1: Long Papers*, pages 6858–6868.

Open Science Collaboration. 2015. Estimating the reproducibility of psychological science. *Science*, 349(6251):aac4716.

Roger D. Peng. 2011. Reproducible research in computational science. *Science*, 334(6060):1226–1227.

Pascal Puchtler, Johannes Wirth, and René Peinl. 2021. HUI-audio-corpus-german. a high quality TTS dataset.

Yi Ren, Chenxu Hu, Xu Tan, and Tao Qin. 2020. FastSpeech 2. fast and high-quality end-to-end text to speech. arXiv.

Jonathan Shen and Ruoming Pang. Tacotron 2: Generating human-like speech from text.

Kirstie Whitaker. 2017. Showing your working. a how to guide to reproducible research.

A Human Evaluation Datasheet (HEDS)

The Human Evaluation Datasheet (HEDS) is part of the supplemental material.

B Spreadsheet Results Evaluation

The spreadsheet that we used for analysing the results of our human evaluation is part of the supplemental material.

Reproducing a Comparative Evaluation of German Text-to-Speech Systems

Manuela Hürlimann
Centre for Artificial Intelligence,
Zurich University of Applied Sciences,
Winterthur, Switzerland
manuela.huerlimann@zhaw.ch

Mark Cieliebak
Centre for Artificial Intelligence,
Zurich University of Applied Sciences,
Winterthur, Switzerland
mark.cieliebak@zhaw.ch

Abstract

This paper describes the reproduction of a human evaluation in *Language-Agnostic Meta-Learning for Low-Resource Text-to-Speech with Articulatory Features* reported in Lux and Vu (2022). It is a contribution to the ReproNLP 2023 Shared Task on Reproducibility of Evaluations in NLP. The original evaluation assessed the naturalness of audio generated by different Text-to-Speech (TTS) systems for German, and our goal was to repeat the experiment with a different set of evaluators.

We reproduced the evaluation based on data and instructions provided by the original authors, with some uncertainty concerning the randomisation of question order. Evaluators were recruited via email to relevant mailing lists and we received 157 responses over the course of three weeks. Our initial results show low reproducibility, but when we assume that the systems of the original and repeat evaluation experiment have been transposed, the reproducibility assessment improves markedly. We do not know if and at what point such a transposition happened; however, an initial analysis of our audio and video files provides some evidence that the system assignment in our repeat experiment is correct.

1 Introduction

The work reported in this paper has been carried out as part of a multi-lab, multi-test study in the context of the ReproHum project (Belz et al., 2023) and the ReproNLP shared task. The goal of the project is to assess the reproducibility of human evaluations in Natural Language Processing and to find out which factors contribute to making human evaluations more or less reproducible. Our contribution attempts to reproduce an evaluation in a paper from Track C of ReproNLP 2023, Lux and Vu (2022), which presents a language-agnostic low-resource approach for Text-to-Speech (TTS). The human evaluation is carried out on German audios generated with four different Text-to-Speech systems.

We first (Section 2) describe the approaches of the original experiment and our reproduction in detail.

In Section 3, we present the answer distribution of our results (Section 3.1) and the reproduction targets (Section 3.2). In Section 3.3 we then compare the results of both studies in terms of the scores obtained by each model and report the coefficients of variation (CV*), which quantify the variability of original-reproduced measurement pairs. We also report Pearson's correlation coefficients between the original and the reproduction system measurement sets. These results show very low reproducibility (large CV* and low Pearson correlations) and we notice a strong cross-similarity between the system results, meaning that the original results for one system are very similar to repeat results for the other, and vice versa. Therefore, in Section 3.4 we also re-evaluate the results with an assumed system transposition and find improved reproducibility (lower CV* and very high Pearson correlations).

In the light of these results, after ruling out some error sources (Section 4), we compare the Mel-Frequency Cepstral Coefficients (MFCC) of the audio and video files used in the repeat evaluation (Section 4.1). The results indicate that the system assignments in our repeat experiment are likely to be correct. In Section 5, we discuss our findings and in Section 6 we briefly compare our results with those of another reproduction submitted to ReproNLP 2023.

All our resources are publicly available.[1]

[1] https://github.com/manhue/repronlp2023_lux_and_vu

Proceedings of the Third Workshop on Human Evaluation of NLP Systems, pages 136–144, Varna, Bulgaria, Sep 7, 2023.
https://doi.org/10.26615/978-954-452-088-5_012

2 Evaluation Experiments

In this section we first (Section 2.1) describe the original experiment and then (Section 2.2) our reproduction.

2.1 Original Evaluation

This section describes the original evaluation experiment as reported in Lux and Vu (2022), Section 4.2.2. The authors shared the details of their evaluation protocol with the ReproHum team in personal communication with the authors and the resources were subsequently provided to us.

Systems The original human evaluation was a preference study of four Text-to-Speech systems for German. The systems are based on two different models, FastSpeech 2 (Ren et al., 2021) and Tacotron 2 (Shen et al., 2018). For each model, there are two flavours: the baseline system (trained on 29 hours of German) and the proposed low-resource system (trained in a multilingual low-resource regime with 30 minutes of data for each of 8 languages,[2] then fine-tuned on 30 minutes of German). This results in a total of four different systems: FastSpeech-Baseline, FastSpeech-Proposed, Tacotron-Baseline and Tacotron-Proposed.

Data and Task The evaluation was done via a comparative evaluation of generated audio. There were six text prompts, which were chosen to be phonetically balanced. Each of these six prompts was synthesised using each of the four systems. In each judgement, evaluators were presented with two synthesised audio files, one from the baseline and one from the low-resource flavour of the same model. They then had to choose one of the following three responses:

- Audio 1 is significantly better than Audio 2
- Audio 2 is significantly better than Audio 1
- Audio 1 and Audio 2 are about equally good

Evaluators were not informed of the number or type of systems that were used to generate the audios but were simply asked to make a preference judgement as outlined above for each audio pair. As far as we can tell from the provided materials, "naturalness" was not mentioned to evaluators as an explicit criterion.

[2]English, Greek, Spanish, Finnish, Russian, Hungarian, Dutch and French

Survey Form The authors of the original paper conducted the evaluation using a Google Form survey[3]. Since Google Forms do not have any functionality to embed audio directly, they converted the audio files to videos with a black image as visual. They then uploaded these videos to YouTube and embedded them in the Google Form.

Not Reproducible: Randomised Question Order The original authors reported that they had randomised the order of the questions in the Google Form. When working on the repeat evaluation experiment, the authors of the current work and the ReproHum project team were not able to reproduce this functionality: there was no option to randomise the order of Google Form questions which preserved the video-response pairs. A randomisation option was available in the current version of Google Forms but its functionality proved unsuitable for the proposed setting since it jumbled all elements of the questionnaire, breaking the link between videos and questions. It remains unclear whether this feature has changed since the original authors did their evaluation or whether they in fact proceeded differently from what they reported. In Section 2.2 below, we describe how this was handled.

Evaluators The original survey was sent via email to students in speech-related courses at the original authors' university. 34 evaluators who self-identified as native speakers of German participated in the evaluation, leading to a total of 408 human judgements (6 prompts x 2 systems x 34 evaluators = 408 judgements).

Results The authors of the original evaluation aggregated the survey responses per system and found the preference distributions in Table 1 (from Figure 3 in Lux and Vu (2022)[4]).

Their results show a clear preference for the proposed low-resource system for the Tacotron model. For FastSpeech, the most frequently chosen option

[3]`https://www.google.com/intl/en/forms/about/`

[4]The numbers in Figure 3 of (Lux and Vu, 2022) do not agree completely with the text. In Section 4.2.2, the authors write "In 56% of the cases, the [Tacotron] model fine-tuned on 30 minutes of data was perceived to be as good or better than the model trained on 29 hours." During correspondence with the ReproHum project team, they said that this number should in fact be 69% (=52% + 37%) as in the figure.
Also note that the caption of Figure 3 in (Lux and Vu, 2022) mentions 102 judgements per system, but this number should be 204.

Label	%
Fastspeech-baseline	31%
Fastspeech-proposed	25%
Fastspeech-equal	43%
Tacotron-baseline	11%
Tacotron-proposed	52%
Tacotron-equal	37%

Table 1: Percentages of answers reported in the original study, from Figure 3 of (Lux and Vu, 2022). The number in each row indicates the proportion of responses for a specific option; for example, Tacotron-baseline was preferred over Tacotron-proposed in 11% of the cases and Tacotron-proposed over Tacotron-baseline in 52%.

was that both audios are equal, and the baseline was preferred more frequently than the proposed low-resource system.

2.2 Repeat Evaluation

For the repeat evaluation, the authors of the original paper provided us with the following:

- The introductory text, instructions, and set of answer options for the survey.
- The 24 audios that were presented to evaluators.
- An explanation of how they had created the survey.

We added a short consent screen, which evaluators saw first and had to agree to. We do not know if the original study also had a consent screen but we assume that it did not since this information was not provided to us. We then used the provided introductory text and instructions[5] and the provided answer options to create the survey.[6]

As explained in Section 2.1, it was not possible to reproduce the randomised order of the questions that the original authors reported. To standardise the question order of the different repeat evaluations, the ReproHum project team created a randomly shuffled order to be used in each repeat experiment. They used a Python script, *random_videos.py*[7] to shuffle the questions.

We applied the suggested process to create the videos that could be embedded in the Google Form and extended the *random_videos.py* script to generate a unique four-character identifier for each video in order not to reveal the system type.

We then sent the survey via email to different mailing lists within and outside our university. These included staff mailing lists for institutes and communities, as well as a dedicated mailing list of students who had consented to participate in research surveys. In the email, which was written in German, potential evaluators were told that they needed to speak German as their native language in order to participate.

3 Results

Below, we first (Section 3.1) present the results obtained in our reproduction study. We then show the reproduction targets (Section 3.2) and compare our results to the original study, assessing their reproducibility (Section 3.3). Since we find that the original results for FastSpeech are very similar to the repeat results for Tacotron and vice versa, we add Section 3.4, where we redo the comparisons and reproducibility assessments after *transposing* the system labels of our results. Note that we cannot be certain that such a transposition happened.

3.1 Results Obtained in the Reproduction Study

In this section, we present the results that we obtained in the repeat experiment. We show the distribution of answers and calculate the interrater agreement. We also run a Logistic Random-Effects Model to assess the preferences between the two systems, FastSpeech and Tacotron. Finally, we aggregate the preferences per evaluator per system, creating Per-Person Preference Data (PPPD), which allows to run a binomial test, testing against the mean preferences obtained in the original study - see Sections 3.3 and 3.1 for the tests and results.

Answer Distribution A total of 157 evaluators participated in our survey over the course of three weeks, creating 1878 individual judgements (6 prompts x 2 systems x 157 evaluators - 6 skipped questions[8] = 1878 judgements). Table 2 shows the distribution of the obtained answers.

[5] We only removed the final sentence from the original instructions which said that the order of answer options and audios could vary, since this was not the case in our survey.

[6] A PDF version of the Google Form survey is available in the project documentation: `https://github.com/manhue/repronlp2023_lux_and_vu/blob/main/google_form_pdf/GoogleForm_Evaluation%20von%20Text-zu-Sprache-Systemen%20-%20Google%20Formulare.pdf`

[7] `https://github.com/manhue/repronlp2023_lux_and_vu/blob/main/random_videos.py`

[8] Since the questions in our survey were not mandatory, it was possible to skip.

Label	n	%
Fastspeech-baseline	113	12%
Fastspeech-proposed	471	50%
Fastspeech-equal	358	38%
Fastspeech-skipped	0	-
Tacotron-baseline	274	29%
Tacotron-proposed	271	29%
Tacotron-equal	391	41 %
Tacotron-skipped	6	<1%

Table 2: Distribution of answers obtained in the reproduction study.

Interrater Agreement In order to assess the interrater agreement, we calculate Krippendorff's alpha on the evaluator judgements. We find rather low agreement: 0.12 overall, 0.18 for the FastSpeech questions, and 0.055 for the Tacotron questions.

Within-Rater Variability By survey design, our 157 evaluators rated both systems several times. The data therefore contains a between-rater variability (difference in judgements between the evaluators) as well as a within-rater variability (difference of an individual evaluator's judgement of the same system). There are several ways to address the within-rater variability, e.g., as a random effect in a mixed model or aggregating the data to obtain one judgement per person and system. We describe both below.

Logistic Random Effects Model We run a logistic random effects regression model with a random effect for person. The results show that the odds of the proposed model being perceived as better than the baseline is 0.385 times lower (95% confidence interval [0.315, 0.468]) for the Tacotron answers than the corresponding odds for the FastSpeech answers. In percentages, this means it is 61.5% less likely that Tacotron is perceived as better than the baseline in comparison to the same judgement for FastSpeech (95% CI [51.5%, 68.5%]). This constrasts with the results of Lux and Vu (2022), who found a much higher preference for Tacotron as opposed to FastSpeech.

Per-Person Preference Data (PPPD) If the data are aggregated per-label as in Table 2, we brush over potential effects of individual annotators. We therefore additionally create per-person preference data (we will refer to this as PPPD in the remainder of this paper). For this, we aggregate the raw counts from the survey into agreement ratios per system and per person, i.e. we count in how many questions about system X did person Y perceive the proposed system as better than the baseline. The PPPD will be used for binomial tests comparing against the mean preferences found in the original study in Sections 3.3 and 3.4 below.

3.2 Reproduction Targets

In line with the ReproNLP shared task guidelines, we attempt to reproduce the following type (i) and type (ii) results from Lux and Vu (2022).

(i) Single numeric values, i.e., the overall number of times each label was chosen.

(ii) Sets of related numeric values, i.e. sets of label counts per system.

Note that we cannot assess the reproducibility of type (iii) results since we do not have these from the original study. We reported our own type (iii) results (Krippendorff's alpha) above. The sets of labels are *Fastspeech-baseline*, *Fastspeech-proposed* and *Fastspeech-equal* for the FastSpeech system and *Tacotron-baseline*, *Tacotron-proposed* and *Tacotron-equal* for the Tacotron sytem.

3.3 Comparison to Original Study

Type (i) results In Table 3 we show the raw counts[9], the percentages of each answer category and the coefficient of variation (CV*) computed on the percentages for the original study and our reproduction.

The CV* in each row provides a measure of the dispersion of the original versus repeat percentages. A lower value means that the repeat result matches the original one more closely. The values in Table 3 show that the judgements of equality are more easily reproducible than the preference judgements for the baseline or proposed systems. Overall, the CV* values are rather high, indicating that the repeat results diverge from the original ones.

Type (ii) results In order to compare the full sets of results of the two studies, i.e. the sets of counts per label, we calculate Pearson's r. The results are shown in Table 4. The observed Pearson correlations are very low and none of them are significant, meaning that our repeat experiment does not confirm the original results.

[9]Lux and Vu (2022) (Figure 3) provide percentages but not raw counts per answer, so we calculated these. For FastSpeech, the counts add up to 202 instead of the expected 204, which could mean that two answers were skipped, or perhaps this is due to rounding the percentages.

	(Lux and Vu, 2022)		Current work		$CV*$
	n	%	n	%	
Fastspeech-baseline	63	31%	113	12%	88.1
Fastspeech-proposed	51	25%	471	50%	66.5
Fastspeech-equal	88	43%	358	38%	12.3
Tacotron-baseline	22	11%	274	29%	89.7
Tacotron-proposed	106	52%	271	29%	56.6
Tacotron-equal	76	37%	391	41%	10.2

Table 3: Comparison of original and repeat evaluation. The Coefficient of Variation ($CV*$) is calculated on the percentages.

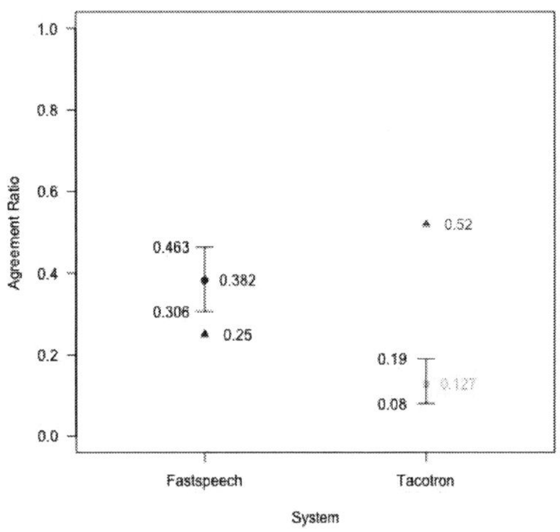

Figure 1: True preference confidence intervals from a binomial test on PPPD. The y-axis represents the percent of questions in which an evaluator agreed that the proposed system is superior to the baseline. The circles mark the estimated mean preference values from the binomial test and the whiskers show the 95% confidence intervals. The triangles indicate the values from the original study.

Comparison	Pearson's r	p-value
All labels	0.0019	0.997
Fastspeech	-0.113	0.928
Tacotron	0.141	0.910

Table 4: Pearson's r for label counts.

Binomial Test on PPPD We run a binomial test on the PPPD and test against the original study's reported preference outcomes. For both systems, we can reject the null hypothesis that our preference data leads to the preference outcomes reported in Lux and Vu (2022) (FastSpeech preferred in 25% of cases, Tacotron in 52%) with p-values < 0.05 for both systems (FastSpeech=0.00029, Tacotron<2.2e-16). This is visualised in Figure 1.

3.4 Comparison to Original Study - Transposed Systems

Since the analysis in Section 3.3 show a large similarity between the FastSpeech results of the original study and our Tacotron results, and vice versa. Therefore, in this section, we re-run the comparisons after transposing the labels of the two systems in our results. We do not know where the transposition happened, so this should not be taken as a statement regarding which system label corresponds to which set of results. The goal at this point is to see how the reproducibility assessment changes after the transposition.

Type (i) results In Table 5 we show the raw counts, the percentages of each answer category and the coefficient of variation computed on the percentages when the repeat results are transposed. We can see that the coefficients of variation are much lower for each original-repeated value pair than in Table 3. The Tacotron-Equal outcome is the easiest to reproduce and FastSpeech-proposed the most difficult.

Type (ii) results We also repeat the comparisons of type (ii) results with transposed labels. Table 6 shows the Pearson's r values. They show very high correlations of at least 0.95; the correlation for the combined set of labels (FastSpeech and Tacotron) as well as for FastSpeech on its own are significant, but not for Tacotron on its own. This indicates that our results broadly reproduce those of the original study when we transpose the system labels.

Binomial Test on PPPD We re-run the binomial test with transposed system labels on our PPPD. We find that also in the transposed scenario, we can reject the null hypotheses that we reproduce the mean preference of the original study with p-values < 0.05 for both systems (FastSpeech=0.00057, Tacotron=0.0002).

The identified 95% confidence intervals for the

	(Lux and Vu, 2022)		Current work **transposed**		*CV**
	n	%	n	%	
Fastspeech-baseline	63	31%	274	29%	6.7
Fastspeech-proposed	51	25%	271	29%	14.8
Fastspeech-equal	88	43%	391	41%	4.8
Tacotron-baseline	22	11%	113	12%	8.7
Tacotron-proposed	106	52%	471	50%	3.9
Tacotron-equal	76	37%	358	38%	2.7

Table 5: Comparison of original and **transposed** repeat evaluation. The Coefficient of Variation (*CV**) is calculated on the percentages.

Comparison	Pearson's r	p-value
All labels	0.991	0.00012
Fastspeech	0.999	0.0295
Tacotron	0.955	0.192

Table 6: Pearson's r for label counts with **transposition**.

true preference are [31%, 46%] for FastSpeech and [8%, 19%] for Tacotron. Note that our values of 50% and 29% also lie outside these intervals. All the per-label aggregated values are beyond the upper bound of the 95% confidence intervals on the PPPD. It thus appears that the per-label aggregation overestimates the preferences due to some effects of the evaluators.

Figure 2 visualises the outcomes of the binomial tests with transposed repeat results. We can see that the mean values from the original study now match the distributions better, but, as discussed above, they do not fall within the 95% confidence intervals of the PPPD.

4 Analysing Potential Error Sources

Our analysis show a more positive reproducibility assessment for system-transposed results. The current section is an attempt to assess potential sources of this supposed transposition error.

We were able to verify the following:

- The files provided to us match the corresponding ones in the possession of the original authors in terms of file size.

- The order of the videos in the Google Form[10] corresponds to the order created by the *random_videos.py* script, which is stored in *video2id.csv*.[11]

[10]Google Form: https://github.com/manhue/repronlp2023_lux_and_vu/blob/main/google_form_pdf/GoogleForm_Evaluation%20von%20Text-zu-Sprache-Systemen%20-%20Google%20Formulare.pdf

[11]https://github.com/manhue/repronlp2023_lux_and_vu/blob/main/

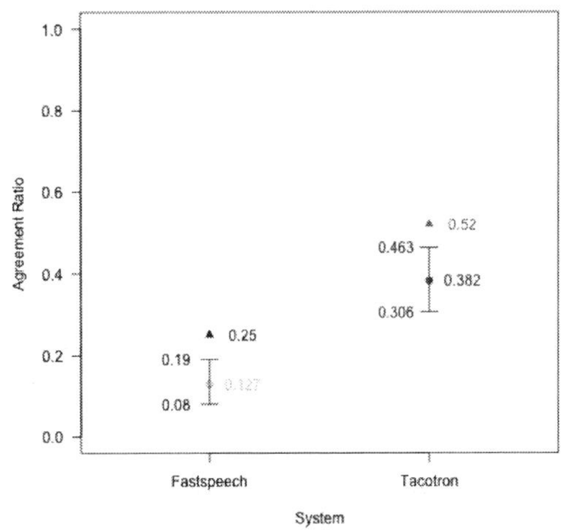

Figure 2: True preference confidence intervals from a binomial test on PPPD with **transposed** values from the repeat evaluation. The y-axis represents the percent of questions in which an evaluator agreed that the proposed system is superior to the baseline. The circles mark the estimated preference values from the binomial test and the whiskers show the 95% confidence intervals. The triangles indicate the values from the original study.

- The same order from *video2id.csv* is used to evaluate the results of the form and calculate the scores.[12]

This leaves us with the following potential sources of error:

1. The systems were transposed when creating the videos from the audio files
   (a) in the original experiment
   (b) in the repeat experiment
2. The results of the original survey were transposed when they were reported (due to the validation of the video order with *video2id.csv*, we can exclude this option for the repeat experiment.)

We cannot assess potential error sources (1a) and (2), since we do not have access to the required materials from the original study. Therefore, below we analyse the likelihood of option (1b) by comparing the audio files with the generated videos.

4.1 Audio Features Analysis

It is possible that systems were transposed when we create the videos from the audio files in order to embed them in the Google Form (option 1b above). We therefore want to verify if the created videos are similar to the audio files that they should correspond to. For this comparison, we use the Mel-Frequency Cepstral Coefficient (MFCC) audio features and cross-compare the audios and videos that correspond to each of the six text prompts.

We first generate the MFCC features of the audio and video using the Librosa Python library.[13]

For each audio-video pair with the same prompt (4x4=16 pairs per prompt) we then truncate the longer MFCC to the length of the shorter MFCC[14] and calculate the L2-norm of the difference between two MFCC-vectors as follows: $distance = \sqrt{\sum_1^n (a_i - b_i)^2}$, where a and b are the two vectors, x_i the element of vector x at index i and n is the length of the shorter MFCC-vector.

We visualise the resulting values as heatmaps in Figure 3: the x-axis shows the audios and the y-axis shows the videos that we presume to correspond to each audio. If our audio-video assignment is correct, the diagonal should display the lowest values. Indeed this is what we find: the diagonal is zero for all prompts, which makes it appear unlikely that there is a mistake in the audio-video assignment of our repeat experiment. Unfortunately, we cannot compare this to the audio-video assignment of Lux and Vu (2022) since their videos are no longer available.

5 Discussion and Conclusions

The positive aspects of this evaluation were that the original authors were able to provide the exact prompts, instructions, and questions used for the evaluation as well as information on how they set up the evaluation, so the setup was relatively straightforward. However, the question randomisation in the survey form could not be reproduced.

As for reproducibility, our initial assessment completely fails to confirm the results of the original study (see Section 3.3). Once we assume a transposition of systems (Section 3.4), we can paint a more positive picture with strong positive correlations and agreement. However, even in the transposed scenario, the per-label aggregation does not fully agree with the per-user preference data (PPPD): in a binomial test, we reject the null hypothesis that the per-label aggregated means could be drawn from the per-user preference data distribution. It appears that, when we aggregate on the question level, as opposed to the user level, we smooth over some within-rater variability. The low inter-annotator agreement (Krippendorff's alpha) further underscores that there are disagreements between the different evaluators. For both these assessments, the binomial tests and the inter-annotator agreement, we do not have any comparison to the original study since these data were not reported.

Table 7 summarises the findings of our repeat experiment for the originally obtained and transposed results.

Finally, it is unclear in which study the hypothesised transposition happened. We can only confirm that for one of the systems there is a relatively clear preference for the proposed low-resource model (as opposed to the baseline), but we do not know for certain whether this is FastSpeech or Tacotron.

video2id.csv

[12]See scripthttps://github.com/manhue/repronlp2023_lux_and_vu/blob/main/get_label_counts_from_raw_results.py

[13]https://librosa.org/doc/latest/generated/librosa.feature.mfcc.html

[14]This is necessary because we do not exactly truncate the videos to the audio length and there can be trailing silence

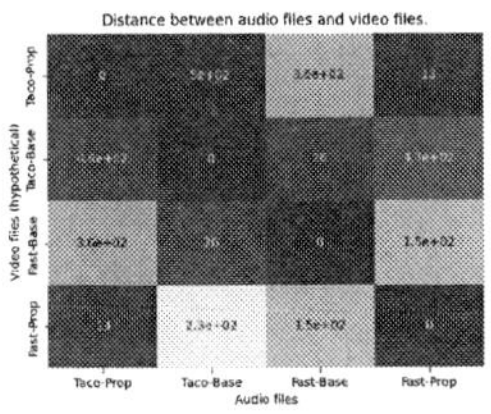

(a) Prompt 1

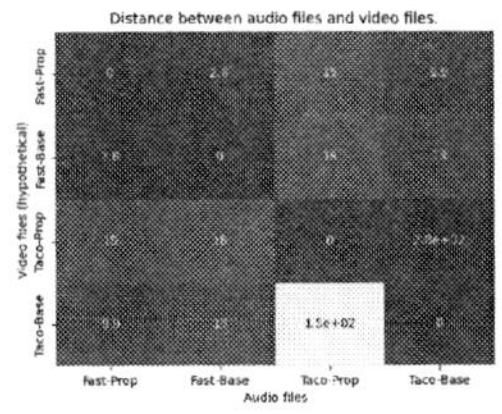

(b) Prompt 2

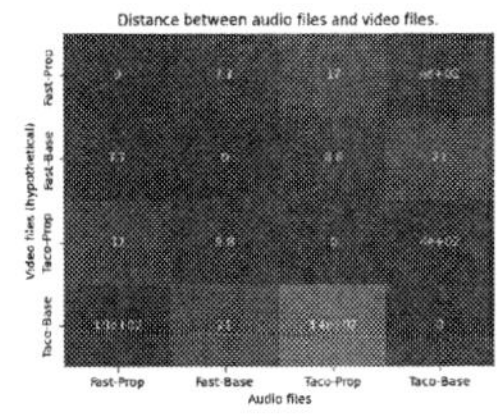

(c) Prompt 3

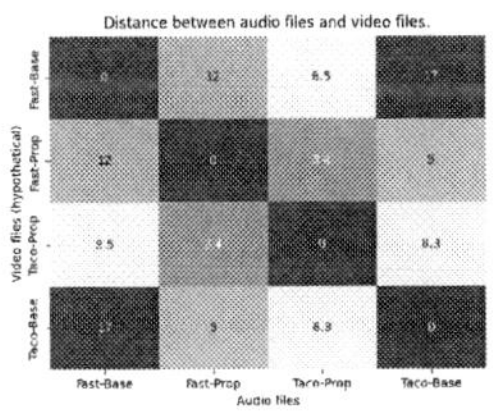

(d) Prompt 4

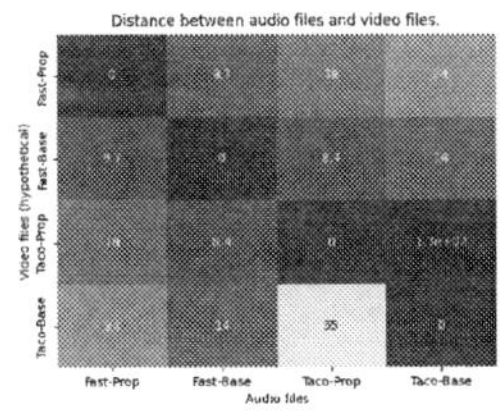

(e) Prompt 5

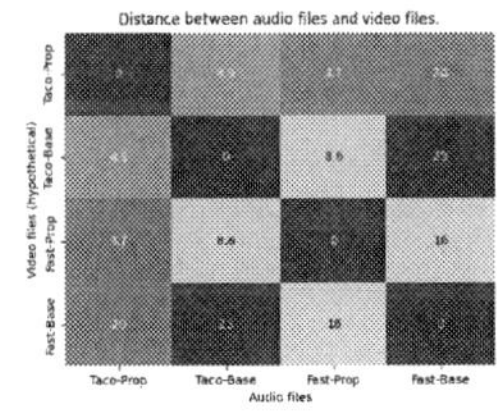

(f) Prompt 6

Figure 3: Heatmaps showing distance between audio and video files for each text prompt. Video labels are hypothetical and correspond to the ones used in the current study.

Test	Outcome	Reproducibility	Table/Figure Ref.
Type (i) results	High CV* values	Not reproduced	Table 3
Type (ii) results	Low Pearson correlations, not significant	Not reproduced	Table 4
Binomial Test	Reject null hypothesis	Not congruent	Figure 1

(a) Findings of repeat experiment

Test	Outcome	Reproducibility	Table/Figure Ref.
Type (i) results	Lower CV* values	Reproduced	Table 5
Type (ii) results	High Pearson correlations, some significant	Reproduced	Table 6
Binomial Test	Reject null hypothesis	Not congruent	Figure 2

(b) Findings of **transposed** repeat experiment

Table 7: Summary of findings and reproducibility assessment.

6 Post-reporting Comparison Between Reproductions

The ReproHum team gave us access to another study which reproduced the same evaluation after finalising our report. Here, we briefly comment on their approach and findings. Mieskes and Benz (2023) also reproduced the human evaluation from Lux and Vu (2022). As far as we can see, there are two differences between their reproduction and ours: they randomised the order of answer options for each survey (whereas we always had the same order) and they informed participants that the study is a reproduction (whereas we did not). They collected a somewhat smaller set of responses (n=37) and their results also show high Coefficients of Variation. This finding provides further evidence (in addition to our audio/video features comparison in Section 4.1) that the label transposition happened in the original paper, either when creating the videos or when reporting the results (cp. Section 4). Therefore, if one wanted to interpret the results of the human evaluation with respect to the two systems, one should likely use the system label assignment from our study. The conclusion would then be that there is a preference for the proposed low-resource model (as opposed to the baseline) for FastSpeech, while for Tacotron, there is no clear preference.

Acknowledgments

We would like to thank Jan Deriu for his careful proofreading of the manuscript and his helpful suggestions.

References

Anya Belz, Craig Thomson, Ehud Reiter, Gavin Abercrombie, Jose M Alonso-Moral, Mohammad Arvan, Jackie Cheung, Mark Cieliebak, Elizabeth Clark, Kees van Deemter, et al. 2023. Missing Information, Unresponsive Authors, Experimental Flaws: The Impossibility of Assessing the Reproducibility of Previous Human Evaluations in NLP. In *Proceedings of The Fourth Workshop on Insights from Negative Results in NLP*.

Florian Lux and Ngoc Thang Vu. 2022. Language-Agnostic Meta-Learning for Low-Resource Text-to-Speech with Articulatory Features. In *Proceedings of the 60th Annual Meeting of the Association for Computational Linguistics; Volume 1: Long Papers*, pages 6858–6868, Dublin, Ireland. Association for Computational Linguistics.

Margot Mieskes and Jacob Benz. 2023. h_da@ReproHum – Reproduction of Human Evaluation and Technical Pipeline. In *Proceedings of the 3rd Workshop on Human Evaluation of NLP Systems (HumEval'23)*.

Yi Ren, Chenxu Hu, Xu Tan, Tao Qin, Sheng Zhao, Zhou Zhao, and Tie-Yan Liu. 2021. Fastspeech 2: Fast and High-Quality End-to-End Text to Speech. In *International Conference on Learning Representations*.

Jonathan Shen, Ruoming Pang, Ron J Weiss, Mike Schuster, Navdeep Jaitly, Zongheng Yang, Zhifeng Chen, Yu Zhang, Yuxuan Wang, Rj Skerrv-Ryan, et al. 2018. Natural TTS Synthesis by Conditioning Wavenet on Mel Spectrogram Predictions. In *2018 IEEE International Conference on Acoustics, Speech and Signal Processing (ICASSP)*, pages 4779–4783. IEEE.

A Human Evaluation Datasheet (HEDS)

The Human Evaluation Datasheet (HEDS) for our evaluation can be accessed at `https://github.com/manhue/repronlp2023_lux_and_vu/blob/main/HEDS/datacard.json` and is also included in the supplementary materials of this paper.

With a Little Help from the Authors: Reproducing Human Evaluation of an MT Error Detector

Ondřej Plátek, Mateusz Lango and **Ondřej Dušek**
Charles University, Faculty of Mathematics and Physics
Institute of Formal and Applied Linguistics
Prague, Czech Republic
{oplatek,lango,odusek}@ufal.mff.cuni.cz

Abstract

This work presents our efforts to reproduce the results of the human evaluation experiment presented in the paper of Vamvas and Sennrich (2022), which evaluated an automatic system detecting over- and undertranslations (translations containing more or less information than the original) in machine translation (MT) outputs. Despite the high quality of the documentation and code provided by the authors, we discuss some problems we found in reproducing the exact experimental setup and offer recommendations for improving reproducibility. Our replicated results generally confirm the conclusions of the original study, but in some cases statistically significant differences were observed, suggesting a high variability of human annotation.

1 Introduction

Reproducibility of experimental results is a fundamental principle of scientific research that ensures the validity, credibility, and reliability of scientific findings. The NLP research community is increasingly interested in reproducibility, which leads to the organization of shared tasks (Belz et al., 2021, 2022b; Branco et al., 2020), the formulation of reproducibility guidelines (Pineau et al., 2021), and so on. However, most previous efforts are limited to the reproducibility of automatic measures, and reproducibility of human evaluation has received less attention (Belz et al., 2023). The ReproHum project,[1] which this paper is a part of, aims to improve this situation.

In this paper, we describe our efforts to reproduce the results of the human evaluation experiment conducted in (Vamvas and Sennrich, 2022) to evaluate the performance of their over- and undertranslation detection method for machine translation (MT). More specifically, the method detects phrases in the source texts whose meaning is not reflected in an MT output, or phrases in the MT output that are not supported by the source (see details in Sec. 2). The human annotators evaluated the detection accuracy and provided additional reasons for their evaluation by choosing from a list (see Figure 1). The original experiment was run for English-Chinese and English-German translation pairs, but our reproducibility study is limited to the English-German pair due to the availability of skilled human annotators.

Despite the precise description of the experiment in the original paper, we still encountered difficulties in running the study (see Section 4), and were only able to finish it successfully thanks to the strong support of the original authors. Our results overall support the main claims of Vamvas and Sennrich (2022)'s original paper, but we still found some discrepancies, despite using the same data, interface and guidelines for the annotation (see Section 5).

Our collected annotation outputs, reproduction code, and the filled HEDS sheet (Shimorina and Belz, 2022) for the reproduction study are available on Github.[2]

2 Original Experiment

The original paper (Vamvas and Sennrich, 2022) proposed an automatic method for detecting coverage errors in the output of MT systems. Coverage errors include *undertranslations*, i.e. the omission of important source content in the MT system output, and *overtranslations*, i.e. the addition of superfluous words to the translation that may not be supported by the source.

The method uses contrastive conditioning (Vamvas and Sennrich, 2021) and finds coverage errors

[1] https://reprohum.github.io/

[2] https://github.com/oplatek/reprohum-as-little-as-possible

Proceedings of the Third Workshop on Human Evaluation of NLP Systems, pages 145–152, Varna, Bulgaria, Sep 7, 2023.
https://doi.org/10.26615/978-954-452-088-5_013

by iteratively computing the probability of the generated translation with an MT system conditioned on an incomplete text source. If the probability of the generated translation increases when a particular phrase is deleted from the source, the method takes this as an indicator that the deleted phrase is not adequately reflected in the translation and treats it as an omission (undertranslation). Similarly, by reversing the source with the target, the method also detects overtranslations. To summarize, for a given input-translation pair, the output of the method is the type of problem detected (over- or undertranslation) and a phrase that has been omitted from the translation (in the case of undertranslation), or that is superfluous (in the case of overtranslation).

The corresponding human evaluation aimed to analyze in detail the predicted problematic text spans and assess their correctness. Human annotators were presented with a source sentence, the generated MT translation, and a highlighted passage. The annotator's task was to decide whether the highlighted passage was correctly translated and later to select additional feedback for fine-grained analysis from a given single-choice list. If the annotator confirmed that the highlighted span was incorrectly translated, they were asked to specify the type of error (e.g., fluency error, accuracy error, addition/omission of non-trivial information, etc). On the other hand, if the annotator considered the span to be correctly translated, they were asked to give a possible reason why one could think that it was translated incorrectly (e.g., syntactic differences, adding/removing trivial/obvious information). The full list of possible reasons can be seen in Figure 1.

The manual evaluation was carried out by two linguists who were provided with a two-page document containing annotation guidelines. The guidelines included the task description, instructions on using the annotation interface, and examples of three incorrect and three correct translations. Each annotator responded to approximately 700 randomly selected examples.

3 Differences in Our Reproduction Study

We aimed to conduct the reproduction as close as possible to the original study. We worked on the same set of system outputs, with the identical annotation interface and instructions.[3] However, there were some differences with respect to annotator hiring and to splitting the annotation between them.

Annotator hiring We hired two annotators who were university students and native speakers of German with high proficiency in English, same as in the original study. We used contacts arranged through ReproHum organizers at two German universities (Bielefeld and Munich), which means that the students spoke a different variety of German from the original study, which was conducted in Zurich, i.e., with Swiss German speakers. In addition, one of our annotators was from a different study field (public health) than the original study's annotators (NLP). The reason is that we could not find interested NLP students at the time of hiring. Each annotator was paid €180 for the approximate 10 hours of work. The €18 hourly wage differs from the original study (which reports ca. $30) but is in line with ReproHum recommendations (150% of German minimum wage).

Data split for annotation We used the same input data for the human evaluation, i.e., the same outputs of the machine translation (MT) system, together with error annotations. Similarly to the original study, the sentences with annotated errors were split randomly into two parts, for one annotator each. However, the original authors prepared for us a different random split of data since the reproduction of the study should not depend on how the original data are split among the annotators.

4 Implementation Issues

We found two implementation problems while running the study: one with setting up the annotation interface and the other with the script computing final statistics.

Annotation interface The authors of the original study used the popular open-source annotation software Doccano (Nakayama et al., 2018), which was customized to implement the interface required for their human evaluation experiment. The original open-source software has been updated over time, making the authors' customization incompatible with the toolkit. Even after downgrading Doccano to the version used by the authors, some of the dependencies were found to be no longer available. Our attempts to use newer versions of dependencies and/or Doccano were unsuccessful.

Finally, with the permission of the ReproHum organisers, we contacted the authors, who fortu-

[3] https://github.com/ZurichNLP/coverage-contrastive-conditioning

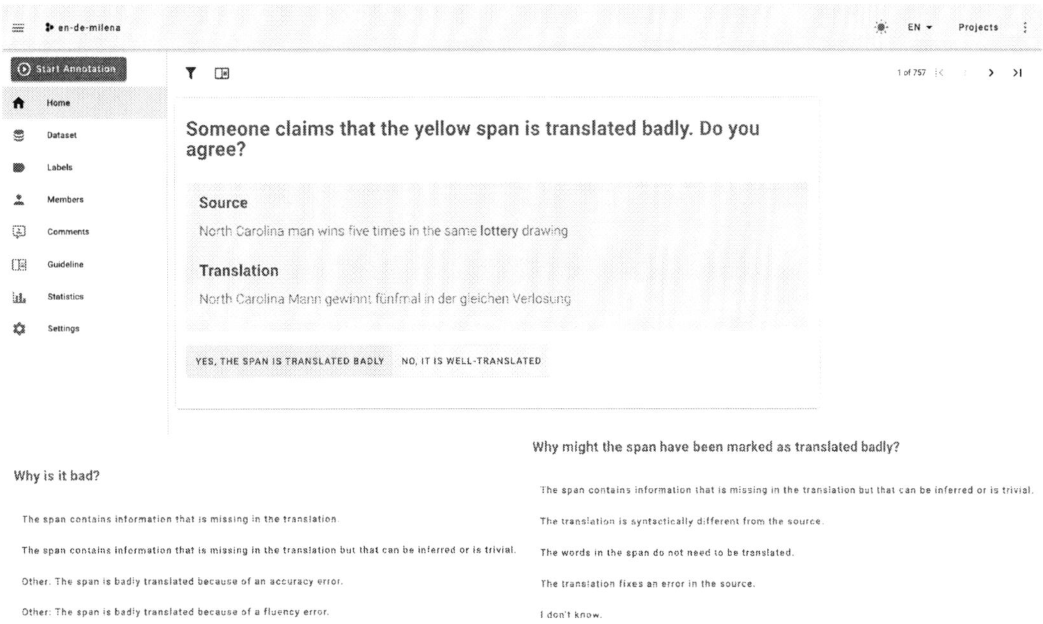

Figure 1: Screenshots of the Annotation Interface where the annotator needs to: (1) Top image; Select whether the source sentence is well translated. (2) Bottom left image; In the case of a bad translation, indicate the type of error. (3) Bottom right image; In the case of a correct translation, hypothesize why it was marked as an error.

nately kept the annotation interface in an easy-to-distribute form of a Docker snapshot (Merkel, 2014). With the Docker image provided, we were able to run the reproduction with the identical annotation interface.

Statistics computation To compute the necessary annotation statistics, we used the evaluation script provided by Vamvas and Sennrich (2022). During our data analysis, we noticed that the script did not correctly handle examples with multiple spans annotated within the same sentence. For such examples, the last annotation analysed by the script would override the previous ones, resulting in some annotations being unintentionally removed. We fixed this bug and ran the analysis with the original and corrected script on the annotation data from both the original and repeated study (see Table 1).

5 Results

A side-by-side presentation of all the results can be found in Table 1. We report results calculated using both the original script (Original, Reproduced) and the corrected script detailed in Section 4 (Original_v2, Reproduced_v2). The use of the corrected script increased the number of examples by 54 for the original results and by 56 for the reproduced results, which represents less than 4% of the total data size. In order to maintain a better reference to the results reported in the original paper, and since the difference is not large, the following discussion will analyse the results computed with the original script.

In both experiments, each annotator provided feedback on approximately 700 examples, which were similarly divided into examples of over- and under-translation. The inter-annotator agreement, measured with Cohen's κ, was higher in our reproduction for the simple evaluation of the correctness of highlighted spans, but the results were within the constructed 95% confidence interval for the original value. According to McHugh (2012), these κ values should be interpreted as weak/moderate agreement. On the other hand, the inter-annotator agreement for fine-grained responses was statistically significantly lower in our repeated study, but again, both values from the original and the repeated study should be interpreted as "minimal agreement" (McHugh, 2012).

In the original paper, the results of the experiments are reported in terms of word-level precision of the highlighted spans. The comparison of the original precision values with those obtained in our reproduction can be observed in Table 2. In addition, for each original value, we computed

Basic statistics	Orig	Repro	Orig_v2	Repro_v2
Annotator 1 no. of overtranslation examples	372	372	390	389
Annotator 1 no. of undertranslation examples	344	348	354	361
Annotator 1 total no. of examples	716	720	744	750
Annotator 2 no. of overtranslation examples	348	352	362	366
Annotator 2 no. of undertranslation examples	351	350	363	362
Annotator 2 total no. of examples	699	702	725	728
Inter-annotator agreement				
Number of overlapping samples	466	471	474	479
Cohen's κ for trans. correctness eval.	0.5343	0.6044	0.5593	0.6313
Cohen's κ for fine-grained answers	0.3186	0.2420	0.3328	0.2536
Precision of spans indicated by the method as incorrect				
Incorrectly translated spans detected as overtanslations	49	45	54	48
Correctly translated spans detected as overtanslations	611	619	638	647
Incorrectly translated spans detected as undertranslations	240	135	250	143
Correctly translated spans detected as undertranslations	369	476	379	491
Fine-grained analysis for overtranslations				
True overtranslations - addition of trivial or inferable information	10	2	10	2
True overtranslations - addition of unsupported information	5	11	5	12
True errors - accuracy errors	28	24	32	24
True errors - fluency errors	6	8	7	10
False errors - addition of redundant but fluent info.	113	120	117	124
False errors - addition of supported information	19	30	20	30
False errors - a syntactic difference	428	254	449	263
False errors - unknown reason	51	215	52	230
Fine-grained analysis for undertranslations				
True undertranslations - lack of important information	114	80	120	86
True undertranslations - lack of redundant information	107	7	110	7
True errors - accuracy errors	16	35	17	37
True errors - fluency errors	3	13	3	13
False errors - fluency errors in the source	72	107	72	110
False errors - addition of redundant but fluent info.	25	103	25	104
False errors - a syntactic difference	249	174	257	178
False errors - unknown reason	23	92	25	99

Table 1: The summary of the raw results obtained in the original and reproduced study. The columns with "v2" suffix are computed with the fixed evaluation script (see Sec. 4). Note that annotators for Original and Reproduced studies differ: Annotator 1 is a different different person for the Original(_v2) and Reproduced(_v2) studies. Similarly for Annotator 2.

		Original	95% CI	Reproduction	CV*
Target	Addition errors	2.3	(1.38; 3.71)	1.95	16.42
	Any errors	7.4	(5.66; 9.68)	6.77	8.86
Source	Omission errors	36.3	(32.57; 40.18)	* 14.23	19.56
	Any errors	39.4	(35.61; 43.34)	* 22.09	15.34

Table 2: Word-level precision (%) of the spans that were highlighted by the method (Vamvas and Sennrich, 2022, Table 2) in the original study and in our reproduction, together with 95% confidence intervals constructed for the original values (95% CI) and the small-sample coefficient of variation (CV*). Reproduced results that do not fall within the CI are marked with an asterisk.

		χ^2	p-value	V
Overtrans.	good trans.	355.77	<0.0001	0.50
	bad trans.	* 201.88	<0.0001	0.71
Undertrans.	good trans.	596.99	<0.0001	0.57
	bad trans.	* 15.8	0.0016	0.34

Table 3: The results of goodness-of-fit (GOF) tests of human answers in fine-grained analysis (types of error) in the original and our reproduced study. The effect size is measured with Cramér's V for GOF. For cases marked with an asterisk, the conditions to use χ^2 approximation were not met, thus the test statistics were estimated with Monte Carlo simulation (10k samples).

a 95% confidence interval using Wilson's score method (Wilson, 1927). The precision values obtained in our reproduction are generally lower than those reported in the original study. However, the differences in precision for the overtranslation spans are still within the confidence intervals. In contrast, the differences for under-translation are substantial, as the reproduced precision values are about 44-46% lower. This difference is also statistically significant at the significance level $\alpha = 5\%$.

To compare the results of the fine-grained analysis, we performed χ^2 goodness-of-fit tests between the answers provided by the original annotators and those provided by us, as well as calculating Cramér's V for goodness-of-fit. The results are presented in Table 3. We were able to reject the null hypothesis that the reproduced fine-grained responses follow the distribution of the original responses with low p-values for all four sets of results. All obtained values of Cramér's V exceed the 0.29 threshold suggested by Cohen (1988) as an indicator of a large discrepancy between the data distributions.

The differences are visible even to the naked eye, as our annotators selected unknown reasons for highlighting a correctly translated text span about four times more often than in the original study.

In the case of undertranslations, the annotators in the original study chose much more often that the translation is incorrect, but the missing information can be inferred or is trivial (107 vs. 7 counts). On the other hand, our annotators were much more likely to consider that the translation was correct but could be considered inaccurate because some trivial or easily inferable information was missing (25 vs. 103 counts). Our annotators also found more spans highlighted as under-translations as reasons for accuracy or fluency errors in the translation. These larger differences for examples of undertranslation may also indicate that this variant of the evaluation task is more difficult. Note that the annotators have a highlighted text span in the source text, but still have to answer questions about the final translation without any word/phrase alignment information.

6 Quantifying Reproducibility

Following the guidelines of the ReproHum shared task (Belz et al., 2023, Sect. A5), we identify reproduction targets in the following categories:

- Type I – numerical scores:
  - the precision of text spans labeled as over-/undertranslations to truly contain over-/undertranslation errors
  - the precision of text spans labeled as over-/undertranslations to contain some translation errors
- Type II – sets of numerical values:
  - the set of precision results for examples marked as overtranslations
  - the set of precision results for examples marked as undertranslations
- Type III – categorical labels attached to text spans:
  - Sets of spans annotated with the correct/incorrect translation label, separately for over- and under-translations.
  - Sets of fine-grained reasons given by annotators for marking a span as incorrect, separately for over- and under-translations and for correctly/incorrectly detected spans.

Type I For the numerical results, we followed the quantified reproducibility assessment by Belz et al. (2022a), which involves calculating the small sample coefficient of variation (CV*) as a measure of the degree of reproducibility. The results are given in the last column of Table 2. Three out of four CV* values are in the 15-20 range. Only for the precision of detecting a translation error in the text span marked as overtanslation, the CV* value is significantly lower (8.86).

	α	%Ident.
Overtranslation	0.6976	0.9558
Undertranslation	0.3762	0.7266
Joint	0.5109	0.8475

Table 4: Krippendorff's alpha coefficient (α) for assessment of bad/good translation using combined annotations for both original and replication studies. %Ident. is the percentage of identical answers between the original and replicated annotation. (The annotations of both annotators were combined into one list. For examples where both annotators provided an answer, half of the answers were taken from each annotator.)

		α	%Ident.
Overtranslation	Good translation	0.2238	0.5059
	Bad translation	0.1982	0.4687
	Joint	0.2607	0.5033
Undertranslation	Good translation	0.1427	0.3365
	Bad translation	0.1994	0.4468
	Joint	0.2084	0.3621
Joint		0.2664	0.4366

Table 5: Krippendorff's alpha coefficient (α) for fine-grained analysis using the combined annotations (see comment in Table 4). %Ident. is the percentage of identical answers between the original and replicated annotation.

Type II results are usually evaluated with Pearson's correlation (Huidrom et al., 2022), but there is little point in calculating it here. It is equal to 1 for both over- and under-translations, while the standard statistical test for correlation fails to reject the null hypothesis that the true correlation is 0.

Type III Finally, the reproducibility of categorical labels was assessed with Krippendorff's alpha. Since the aim of this analysis is not to measure the agreement between all four annotators (2 from the original study and 2 from the replication) but rather to measure the reproducibility, for the purpose of computing Krippendorff's alpha the annotations obtained from each pair of annotators were combined into one set. For the overlapping examples i.e. examples annotated by both annotators, the response of a randomly chosen annotator was retained.

The values of Krippendorff's alpha together with the percentage of identical evaluations in both the original and reproduced study for coarse-grained annotations (i.e. correct/incorrect translation label) are given in Tab. 4. The value for overtranslation is significantly higher than for undertranslations and is above the 2/3 threshold suggested by Krippendorff (2004) as the lowest limit to consider a good agreement between the raters. The high agreement between the original annotation and the reproduced one can also be observed in terms of the proportion of identical answers – almost 85% for the whole dataset.

Similar results for fine-grained annotations are provided in Tab. 5. All reported values of Krippendorff's alpha are relatively low, and the proportion of examples that are evaluated identically in both studies is below 51%. However, the ratio for overtranslation spans marked as correct translations is significantly higher than the same ratio for undertranslations (roughly 16 percentage points).

7 Findings

Based on the manual evaluation, the authors of the original paper present several findings/conclusions:

- Precision is higher for undertranslations, but still low for overtranslations
- Many of the highlighted spans are translation errors, but not over/undertranslations
- Fine-grained analysis suggests that syntactic differences contribute to the false positives for overtranslations.

All of the above findings roughly correspond to the results of our reproduced experiment. The precision for undertranslations is also higher than for overtranslations, but the difference between the two was considerably smaller in our experiment. For example, the difference in precision for true coverage errors is 34.0 percentage points in the original study but only 12.3 in ours. Similarly, our fine-grained analysis confirms that syntactic differences contribute to false positives, but they are reported about 40% less frequently than in the original study. However, as mentioned above, this is partly due to the fact that our annotators were much more likely to select the "unknown reason" response.

8 Conclusion

We carefully repeated a human evaluation study of paper (Vamvas and Sennrich, 2022). Despite the high-quality documentation and well-organized code provided by the authors, we encountered several problems that were difficult to overcome. In particular, we would not have been able to run the annotation interface and repeat the study without the authors' help. We also noticed a minor error in their evaluation script and suggested a modification. The reproduction process made us realise that it is almost impossible to publish a fully reproducible paper without actually trying to reproduce it end-to-end. We also advocate distributing annotation interfaces in the form of a Docker image containing all the dependencies.

Our overall results agree with the high-level conclusions made in the original paper. The reproduction of results of the coarse-grained analysis was successful for overtranslations, but the results for undertranslations were significantly lower than the reported in the original study. The results of the fine-grained analysis were even more difficult to reproduce – we observed significant differences in all analyzed groups of answers. This may suggest that when designing experiments with human judgments, setups with a very limited number of possible answers (especially binary questions) are easier to replicate and should be prioritized over more complex setups whenever possible.

Acknowledgments

This research was supported by Charles University projects GAUK 40222 and SVV 260575 and by the European Research Council (Grant agreement No. 101039303 NG-NLG). It used resources provided by the LINDAT/CLARIAH-CZ Research Infrastructure (Czech Ministry of Education, Youth, and Sports project No. LM2018101). The authors are very grateful to Jannis Vamvas and Rico Sennrich, as well as the ReproHum organizers, especially Craig Thomson, for assisting in this reproduction study. We also thank Steffen Eger and Ivan Habernal for helping us find annotators.

References

Anya Belz, Maja Popovic, and Simon Mille. 2022a. Quantified reproducibility assessment of NLP results. In *Proceedings of the 60th Annual Meeting of the Association for Computational Linguistics (Volume 1: Long Papers)*, pages 16–28, Dublin, Ireland. Association for Computational Linguistics.

Anya Belz, Anastasia Shimorina, Shubham Agarwal, and Ehud Reiter. 2021. The ReproGen shared task on reproducibility of human evaluations in NLG: Overview and results. In *Proceedings of the 14th International Conference on Natural Language Generation*, pages 249–258, Aberdeen, Scotland, UK. Association for Computational Linguistics.

Anya Belz, Anastasia Shimorina, Maja Popović, and Ehud Reiter. 2022b. The 2022 ReproGen shared task on reproducibility of evaluations in NLG: Overview and results. In *Proceedings of the 15th International Conference on Natural Language Generation: Generation Challenges*, pages 43–51, Waterville, Maine, USA and virtual meeting. Association for Computational Linguistics.

Anya Belz, Craig Thomson, Ehud Reiter, Gavin Abercrombie, Jose M. Alonso-Moral, Mohammad Arvan, Jackie Cheung, Mark Cieliebak, Elizabeth Clark, Kees van Deemter, Tanvi Dinkar, Ondřej Dušek, Steffen Eger, Qixiang Fang, Albert Gatt, Dimitra Gkatzia, Javier González-Corbelle, Dirk Hovy, Manuela Hürlimann, Takumi Ito, John D. Kelleher, Filip Klubicka, Huiyuan Lai, Chris van der Lee, Emiel van Miltenburg, Yiru Li, Saad Mahamood, Margot Mieskes, Malvina Nissim, Natalie Parde, Ondřej Plátek, Verena Rieser, Pablo Mosteiro Romero, Joel Tetreault, Antonio Toral, Xiaojun Wan, Leo Wanner, Lewis Watson, and Diyi Yang. 2023. Missing information, unresponsive authors, experimental flaws: The impossibility of assessing the reproducibility of previous human evaluations in nlp.

António Branco, Nicoletta Calzolari, Piek Vossen, Gertjan Van Noord, Dieter van Uytvanck, João Silva, Luís Gomes, André Moreira, and Willem Elbers. 2020. A shared task of a new, collaborative type to foster reproducibility: A first exercise in the area of language science and technology with REPROLANG2020. In *Proceedings of the Twelfth Language Resources and Evaluation Conference*, pages 5539–5545, Marseille, France. European Language Resources Association.

J. Cohen. 1988. *Statistical Power Analysis for the Behavioral Sciences*. Lawrence Erlbaum Associates.

Rudali Huidrom, Ondřej Dušek, Zdeněk Kasner, Thiago Castro Ferreira, and Anya Belz. 2022. Two reproductions of a human-assessed comparative evaluation of a semantic error detection system. In *Proceedings of the 15th International Conference on Natural Language Generation: Generation Challenges*, pages 52–61, Waterville, Maine, USA and virtual meeting. Association for Computational Linguistics.

Klaus Krippendorff. 2004. *Content analysis: An introduction to its methodology*. Sage publications.

Mary L McHugh. 2012. Interrater reliability: the kappa statistic. *Biochemia medica*, 22(3):276–282.

Dirk Merkel. 2014. Docker: lightweight linux containers for consistent development and deployment. *Linux journal*, 2014(239):2.

Hiroki Nakayama, Takahiro Kubo, Junya Kamura, Yasufumi Taniguchi, and Xu Liang. 2018. doccano: Text annotation tool for human. Software available from https://github.com/doccano/doccano.

Joelle Pineau, Philippe Vincent-Lamarre, Koustuv Sinha, Vincent Larivière, Alina Beygelzimer, Florence d'Alché Buc, Emily Fox, and Hugo Larochelle.

2021. Improving reproducibility in machine learning research (a report from the neurips 2019 reproducibility program). *The Journal of Machine Learning Research*, 22(1):7459–7478.

Anastasia Shimorina and Anya Belz. 2022. The human evaluation datasheet: A template for recording details of human evaluation experiments in NLP. In *Proceedings of the 2nd Workshop on Human Evaluation of NLP Systems (HumEval)*, pages 54–75, Dublin, Ireland. Association for Computational Linguistics.

Jannis Vamvas and Rico Sennrich. 2021. Contrastive conditioning for assessing disambiguation in MT: A case study of distilled bias. In *Proceedings of the 2021 Conference on Empirical Methods in Natural Language Processing*, pages 10246–10265, Online and Punta Cana, Dominican Republic. Association for Computational Linguistics.

Jannis Vamvas and Rico Sennrich. 2022. As little as possible, as much as necessary: Detecting over- and undertranslations with contrastive conditioning. In *Proceedings of the 60th Annual Meeting of the Association for Computational Linguistics (Volume 2: Short Papers)*, pages 490–500, Dublin, Ireland. Association for Computational Linguistics.

Edwin B. Wilson. 1927. Probable inference, the law of succession, and statistical inference. *Journal of the American Statistical Association*, 22(158):209–212.

HumEval'23 Reproduction Report for Paper 0040: Human Evaluation of Automatically Detected Over- and Undertranslations

Filip Klubička
ADAPT Centre
Technological University Dublin
filip.klubicka@adaptcentre.ie

John D. Kelleher
ADAPT Centre
Maynooth University
john.kelleher@mu.ie

Abstract

This report describes a reproduction of a human evaluation study evaluating automatically detected over- and undertranslations obtained using neural machine translation approaches. While the scope of the original study is much broader, a human evaluation is included as part of its system evaluation. We attempt an exact reproduction of this human evaluation, pertaining to translations on the the English-German language pair. While encountering minor logistical challenges, with all the source material being publicly available and some additional instructions provided by the original authors, we were able to reproduce the original experiment with only minor differences in the results.

1 Introduction

This report presents a reproduction of a human evaluation originally conducted and presented in the paper *As Little as Possible, as Much as Necessary: Detecting Over- and Undertranslations with Contrastive Conditioning* (Vamvas and Sennrich, 2022). The paper proposes an approach for detecting over- and under-translations using *contrastive conditioning* (Vamvas and Sennrich, 2021), a method that relies on hypothetical reasoning over the likelihood of partial sequences and thus has the advantage of not requiring access to the original translation system or to a quality estimation model. The authors evaluate their system based on real machine translations and show that the approach outperforms a supervised baseline in the detection of omissions.

While the scope of their original study is much broader, a human evaluation is included as part of the system evaluation and is described in Section 5.2 of their paper. In this evaluation step, the original authors employ expert annotators to determine whether the spans of text that their system predicts as mistranslated are indeed under- or overtranslations, and do this on the English-German and English-Chinese language pairs. In our reproduction study, we attempt to reproduce the evaluations of the English-German data, by employing expert annotators to evaluate the same data samples.

This reproduction study was conducted as part of the ReproHum project[1] (Belz et al., 2023), the aim of which is to build on existing work on recording properties of human evaluations datasheet-style (Shimorina and Belz, 2022), and assessing how close results from a reproduction study are to the original study (Belz et al., 2022), to systematically investigate what factors make human evaluations more—or less— reproducible. Our choice to reproduce this particular paper is motivated by our previous experience in related fields: both authors have previously worked in the space of machine translation (Popovic et al., 2023; Moslem et al., 2023; Klubička et al., 2022; Bago et al., 2022; Moslem et al., 2022; Toral et al., 2017; Popović et al., 2016; Salton et al., 2014a), have a track record of interest in human evaluation (Klubička et al., 2018b,a; Klubička et al., 2017; Salton et al., 2014b) and reproducibility (Klubička and Fernández, 2018), and are thus well-positioned to conduct this reproduction experiment.

2 Original Study Design

For the English-German language pair, the original study employed two linguistic experts as evaluators. As their annotation interface, the authors opted for Doccano[2] (Nakayama et al., 2018), an open-source text annotation tool which provides annotation features for text classification, sequence labeling, and sequence to sequence tasks. Each expert evaluator was shown 80+720 (dev+test set) randomly sampled positive predictions across both types of coverage errors. Evaluators were shown

[1] https://reprohum.github.io
[2] https://github.com/doccano/doccano

Proceedings of the Third Workshop on Human Evaluation of NLP Systems, pages 153–189, Varna, Bulgaria, Sep 7, 2023.
https://doi.org/10.26615/978-954-452-088-5_014

the source sequence, the machine translation, and the predicted error span. They were asked whether the highlighted span was indeed translated badly, and were asked to perform a fine-grained analysis based on a list of predefined answer options (see Appendix A). A subset of the samples (100 sentences) was annotated by both raters in order to calculate inter-annotator agreement.

The authors made all predictions, annotations and notebooks used for calculating the precision values available in the GitHub repository[3].

3 Reproduction Study Details

We used the exact same dataset as provided by (Vamvas and Sennrich, 2022) and had each annotator annotate the same set of instances as provided by the original authors. Once we obtained the evaluations, we used the original authors' evaluation script, as provided on their GitHub page. It is worth noting that during the reproduction phase, another team reproducing the same experiment noticed a possible bug in the authors' results processing script. After communication via the ReproHum team, the issues were clarified and corrected, and the authors uploaded a revised script to fix one of the errors that arose. The updated script is also included in their GitHub page and is the one we used for result processing[4].

3.1 Evaluators

Our selection criteria for evaluators required them to be proficient in German and English, with a background in linguistics or (machine) translation, which are all crucial for evaluating a MT-based task on the two languages. The evaluators were recruited via a colleague who teaches a translation studies course and highly recommended them as exceptional students in the course. They are both native German speakers who are fluent in English, currently attending a translation studies course in Ireland.

We sent the evaluators the annotation instructions and had an initial meeting to clear up any questions or uncertainties. We then gave them the smaller development sample to annotate to give them hands-on experience with the task and clear up any confusion that might arise. After this step they were given the full test set for annotation, but were told that they can ask any practical questions should they arise, but should not communicate with each other or ask for opinions on how to annotate questionable instances, but should rely on their own judgement.

We estimated that the annotation would take about 10 hours of work, which turned out to be the case and was consistent with the original authors' experience. Given that participants were paid during the original experiment, we aimed to do the same by following the shared ReproHum procedure for calculating fair pay. However, as the original study was conducted in Switzerland where a minimum wage is not defined, we opted to simply match the rates paid to the evaluators of the original experiment and paid our annotators the equivalent amount in euros, at a rate of €30/hour. This also exceeds the minimum wage in Ireland and would be considered fair pay for an annotation task.

3.2 Differences

Regarding the choice of annotation interface, we attempted to deploy Doccano to a virtual machine so that the participants could access the application over the web, just as the original authors had. However we faced a number of technical challenges in setting this up, and after a number of attempts had to abandon this direction. The original authors had noted that it is not strictly necessary to use a web application for the annotation, and give liberty to use other methods such as a spreadsheet. Given our difficulties with setting up Doccano, we opted for the spreadsheet option.

Specifically, we used the Google Sheets application and created a separate sheet that contained the data for each annotator individually. This approach made it straightforward to set up and more accessible to the annotators, as it was a familiar interface to them. The annotators were presented with a source sentence, target sentence, the candidate spans in the source and target sentence, and two drop-down menus to select annotation labels, in line with the original study's annotation guidelines. Additionally, we colour-coded the different error categories to reduce the cognitive load of choose from the many possible options. Image 1 shows the annotation interface.

In order to transform the data into the spread-

[3] https://github.com/ZurichNLP/coverage-contrastive-conditioning/tree/master/evaluation/human_evaluation

[4] https://github.com/ZurichNLP/coverage-contrastive-conditioning/blob/master/evaluation/human_evaluation/Human%20Evaluation%20ENDE.v2.ipynb

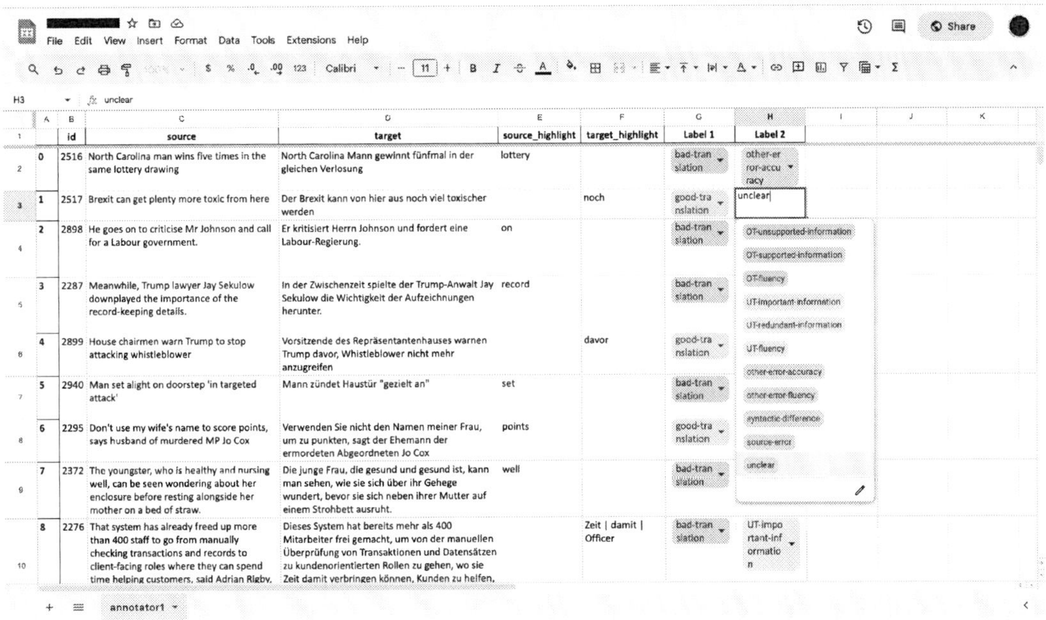

Figure 1: Screenshot of the annotation interface shown to the evaluators.

sheet annotation interface we had to extract it from the .jsonl format it was provided in. Additionally, given that the original authors' evaluation script relies on the .jsonl data format that is output by Doccano, we also had to convert the annotations from the spreadsheet format back to the required format. It was clear this conversion would be necessary once we opted for the spreadsheet-based approach, and performing the conversion was fairly straightforward, but still made for an added processing step which was not noted anywhere in the reproduction guidelines.

4 Reproduction Results

For the human evaluation aspect, the original paper reports three sets of results: (a) a table containing word-level precision scores of the spans that were highlighted by their automatic approach, based on the human evaluations (Table 2 in the original paper), (b) plots that display the results for the human evaluation of predicted addition and omission errors (Appendix G in the original paper) and (c) Cohen's Kappa scores for inter-annotator agreement (mentioned in the body of Section 5.2 of the original paper).

Above results (a) and (b) fall under **Type I** results as defined in the ReproHum reproduction guidelines, given that they are numerical error counts or precision calculations. Results (c) fall under **Type III**, as they are multi-rater categorical labels attached to text spans.

It should be noted that regarding (a), the original paper does not seem to mention how these precision values are calculated, nor does such a calculation seem to be included in the authors' annotation processing script or reproducibility guidelines, making these results difficult to reproduce without relying on guesswork.

Regarding (b), while the plots presented in the paper are indicative of general trends, precise error counts are difficult to infer from the graphics alone. Fortunately the authors do provide the full annotated data and the exact output of the calculations as part of the notebook on their GitHub page. The same notebook also includes a calculation for (c), making both (b) and (c) straightforward to reproduce. One could argue that the error counts and the Cohen's Kappa are the core reproduction values, as they constitute the raw outputs of the human evaluation. Tables 1 and 2 show the original values provided by (Vamvas and Sennrich, 2022) and our reproduced values side by side. It is worth noting that the original values were not provided in the paper itself, but rather in supplementary material, specifically the notebook on the original author's GitHub page (which is still publicly accessible, but requires some digging to acquire the data).

Type	Label 1	Original	Reproduced
OT	bad translation	54	67
OT	good translation	644	640
UT	bad translation	251	228
UT	good translation	382	418
Type	Label 2	Original	Reproduced
OT	bad+OT-supported-info	10	1
OT	bad+OT-unsupported-info	5	11
OT	bad+UT-important-info	0	19
OT	bad+UT-redundant-info	0	2
OT	bad+other-accuracy	32	28
OT	bad+other-fluency	7	3
OT	good+OT-fluency	117	77
OT	good+OT-supported-info	20	13
OT	good+UT-fluency	0	11
OT	good+UT-redundant-info	0	5
OT	good+syntactic-diff	455	443
OT	good+unclear	52	85
UT	bad+OT-supported-info	0	0
UT	bad+OT-unsupported-info	0	2
UT	bad+UT-important-info	120	109
UT	bad+UT-redundant-info	111	45
UT	bad+other-accuracy	17	61
UT	bad+other-fluency	3	11
UT	good+OT-fluency	0	4
UT	good+OT-supported-info	0	0
UT	good+UT-fluency	72	101
UT	good+UT-redundant-info	25	55
UT	good+syntactic-diff	260	198
UT	good+unclear	25	56

Table 1: Error annotation counts broken down by error type, comparing originally reported values (after the minor bug fix) and our own reproduced values.

Labels	Oκ	Rκ
Question 1	0.56	0.58
Question 1+2	0.33	0.46

Table 2: Cohen's Kappa values for inter-annotator agreement, comparing (O) originally reported values (after the minor bug fix) and (R) our own reproduced values.

4.1 Findings Comparison

The original results presented in the paper by (Vamvas and Sennrich, 2022) find that **(a)** fine-grained answers allow to quantify the word-level precision of the spans highlighted by their approach, both with respect to coverage errors in particular and to translation errors in general; **(b)** precision is higher than expected when detecting omission errors in English–German translations, but is still low for additions; **(c)** the distribution of the detailed answers suggests that syntactical differences between the source and target language contribute to the false positives regarding additions; **(d)** many of the predicted error spans are in fact translation errors, but not coverage errors in a narrow sense–e.g. more than 10% of the spans marked in English–German translations were classified by their raters as a different type of accuracy error, such as mistranslation.

Note that the authors frame their core findings as pertaining to the precision results, which they did not provide a way to calculate, so we are not able to verify their claims. They also do not go into detail discussing the distribution of human evaluations themselves, and say little about the obtained inter-annotator agreements. This is understandable, as the human annotation was only a small fraction of their work, but consequently there are few findings for us to compare in this regard. Still, we are able to note that based on the distribution of error types our annotators have achieved a similar distribution of errors on the same data, and have achieved comparable agreement on Label 1 (good/bad translation), while also having somewhat higher agreement on Label 1+2 than in the original study.

5 Conclusion

While we were not able to reproduce the core findings on model precision due to lack of information, we did manage to achieve similar Cohen's Kappa scores for our annotator agreement on one question, and a somewhat higher score on the more difficult question. We also reproduced the distribution of labels on Question 1 and on most categories in Question 2.

Acknowledgments

This research was conducted with the financial support of Science Foundation Ireland under Grant Agreements No. 13/RC/2106 and 13/RC/2106_P2 at the ADAPT SFI Research Centre at Technological University Dublin and Maynooth University. ADAPT, the SFI Research Centre for AI-Driven Digital Content Technology, is funded by Science Foundation Ireland through the SFI Research Centres Programme, and is co-funded under the European Regional Development Fund.

References

Petra Bago, Sheila Castilho, Edoardo Celeste, Jane Dunne, Federico Gaspari, Niels Runar Gislason, Andre Kasen, Filip Klubička, Gauti Kristmannsson, Helen McHugh, Roisin Moran, Orla Ni Loinsigh, Jon Arild Olsen, Carla Parra Escartin, Akshai Ramesh, Natalia Resende, Paraic Sheridan, and Andy Way. 2022. Sharing high-quality language resources in the legal domain to develop neural machine translation for under-resourced languages. *Revista de Llengua i Dret*, (78):9–34.

Anya Belz, Maja Popovic, and Simon Mille. 2022. Quantified reproducibility assessment of NLP results. In *Proceedings of the 60th Annual Meeting of the Association for Computational Linguistics (Volume 1: Long Papers)*, pages 16–28, Dublin, Ireland. Association for Computational Linguistics.

Anya Belz, Craig Thomson, and Ehud Reiter. 2023. Missing information, unresponsive authors, experimental flaws: The impossibility of assessing the reproducibility of previous human evaluations in NLP. In *The Fourth Workshop on Insights from Negative Results in NLP*, pages 1–10, Dubrovnik, Croatia. Association for Computational Linguistics.

Filip Klubička, Lorena Kasunić, Danijel Blazsetin, and Petra Bago. 2022. Challenges of building domain-specific parallel corpora from public administration documents. In *Proceedings of the BUCC Workshop within LREC 2022*, pages 50–55, Marseille, France. European Language Resources Association.

Filip Klubička, Giancarlo D. Salton, and John D. Kelleher. 2018a. Is it worth it? budget-related evaluation metrics for model selection. In *Proceedings of the Eleventh International Conference on Language Resources and Evaluation (LREC 2018)*, Miyazaki, Japan. European Language Resources Association (ELRA).

Filip Klubička, Antonio Toral, and Víctor M Sánchez-Cartagena. 2018b. Quantitative fine-grained human evaluation of machine translation systems: a case study on english to croatian. *Machine Translation*, 32(3):195–215.

Filip Klubička, Antonio Toral Ruiz, and M. Víctor Sánchez-Cartagena. 2017. Fine-grained human evaluation of neural versus phrase-based machine translation. *The Prague Bulletin of Mathematical Linguistics*, 108(1):121–132.

Filip Klubička and Raquel Fernández. 2018. Examining a hate speech corpus for hate speech detection and popularity prediction. In *Proceedings of 4REAL: 1st Workshop on Replicability and Reproducibility of Research Results in Science and Technology of Language*.

Yasmin Moslem, Rejwanul Haque, John Kelleher, and Andy Way. 2022. Domain-specific text generation for machine translation. In *Proceedings of the 15th biennial conference of the Association for Machine Translation in the Americas (Volume 1: Research Track)*, pages 14–30, Orlando, USA. Association for Machine Translation in the Americas.

Yasmin Moslem, Rejwanul Haque, John D. Kelleher, and Andy Way. 2023. Adaptive machine translation with large language models. *arXiv preprint arXiv:2301.13294*.

Hiroki Nakayama, Takahiro Kubo, Junya Kamura, Yasufumi Taniguchi, and Xu Liang. 2018. doccano: Text annotation tool for human. Software available from https://github.com/doccano/doccano.

Maja Popović, Mihael Arčan, and Filip Klubička. 2016. Language related issues for machine translation between closely related South Slavic languages. In *Proceedings of the Third Workshop on NLP for Similar Languages, Varieties and Dialects (VarDial3)*, pages 43–52, Osaka, Japan. The COLING 2016 Organizing Committee.

Maja Popovic, Vasudevan Nedumpozhimana, Meegan Gower, Sneha Rautmare, Nishtha Jain, and John Kelleher. 2023. Using mt for multilingual covid-19 case load prediction from social media texts. European Association for Machine Translation.

Giancarlo Salton, Robert Ross, and John Kelleher. 2014a. An empirical study of the impact of idioms on phrase based statistical machine translation of English to Brazilian-Portuguese. In *Proceedings of the 3rd Workshop on Hybrid Approaches to Machine Translation (HyTra)*, pages 36–41, Gothenburg, Sweden. Association for Computational Linguistics.

Giancarlo Salton, Robert Ross, and John Kelleher. 2014b. Evaluation of a substitution method for idiom transformation in statistical machine translation. In *Proceedings of the 10th Workshop on Multiword Expressions (MWE)*, pages 38–42, Gothenburg, Sweden. Association for Computational Linguistics.

Anastasia Shimorina and Anya Belz. 2022. The human evaluation datasheet: A template for recording details of human evaluation experiments in NLP. In *Proceedings of the 2nd Workshop on Human Evaluation of NLP Systems (HumEval)*, pages 54–75, Dublin, Ireland. Association for Computational Linguistics.

Antonio Toral, Miquel Esplá-Gomis, Filip Klubička, Nikola Ljubešić, Vassilis Papavassiliou, Prokopis Prokopidis, Raphael Rubino, and Andy Way. 2017. Crawl and crowd to bring machine translation to under-resourced languages. *Language resources and evaluation*, 51:1019–1051.

Jannis Vamvas and Rico Sennrich. 2021. Contrastive conditioning for assessing disambiguation in MT: A case study of distilled bias. In *Proceedings of the 2021 Conference on Empirical Methods in Natural Language Processing*, pages 10246–10265, Online and Punta Cana, Dominican Republic. Association for Computational Linguistics.

Jannis Vamvas and Rico Sennrich. 2022. As little as possible, as much as necessary: Detecting over- and undertranslations with contrastive conditioning. In *Proceedings of the 60th Annual Meeting of the Association for Computational Linguistics (Volume 2: Short Papers)*, pages 490–500, Dublin, Ireland. Association for Computational Linguistics.

A Annotator Guidelines

Annotation Guidelines

Thank you for taking part in this annotation project – we appreciate it! In case of questions, feel free to reach out to Jannis Vamvas (vamvas@cl.uzh.ch) at any time.

Task Description

You will be shown a series of source sentences and translations. One or several spans in the text are highlighted and it is claimed that the spans are translated badly. You are asked to determine whether the claim is true.

The highlighted spans can be either in the source sequence or in the translation. If a span is in the source sentence, check whether is has been correctly translated. If a span is in the translation, check whether it correctly conveys the source.
Sometimes, multiple spans are highlighted. In that case, focus your answer on the span that is most problematic for the translation.

In a second step, you are asked to select an explanation. On the one hand, if you agree that the highlighted span is translated badly, please explain your reasoning by selecting your explanation. On the other hand, if you disagree and think that the span is well-translated, please select an explanation why the span might have been marked as badly translated in the first place.
Should multiple explanations be equally plausible, select the first plausible explanation from the top.

Annotation Interface

Please sign in and click on the annotation project named after you, e.g. "Jannis' Annotations".
Click on the "Start Annotation" button.
You can use the arrow keys to move between samples, or the pagination on the upper right.
A sample is fully annotated if two labels have been selected. The first label is the general assessment (agree/disagree) and the second label is the explanation.
Your annotations are saved automatically.

Examples (English-German)

Examples for bad translations

The span contains information that is missing in the translation.
The government, reeling from low oil prices, says it hopes tourism will contribute up to 10 percent of the gross domestic product.
Die Regierung hofft, dass der Tourismus bis zu 10 Prozent des Bruttoinlandsprodukts ausmachen wird.

Other: The span is badly translated because of an accuracy error.
after millions of people joined a protest in the run-up to a U.N. climate summit.
... nachdem sich im Vorfeld eines Klimagipfels in den Vereinigten Staaten Millionen Menschen einem Protest angeschlossen hatten.

Other: The span is badly translated because of a fluency error.
after millions of people joined a protest in the run-up to a U.N. climate summit.
... nachdem sich im Vorfeld eines Vereinte Nationen Klimagipfels Millionen Menschen einem Protest angeschlossen hatten.

Examples for good translations

The span contains information that is missing in the translation but that can be inferred or is trivial.
... to ensure the country has an adequate supply of medical drugs.
... um sicherzustellen, dass das Land über eine ausreichende Versorgung mit Medikamenten verfügt.

The words in the span are redundant but fluent.
The way it was done ...
Die Art und Weise, wie es gemacht wurde, ...

The translation is syntactically different from the source.
During a conversation with the female tech founders ...
Während eines Gesprächs mit den Tech-Gründerinnen ...

Label explanations

bad-translation
- The span is badly translated.

good-translation
- The span is well translated.

OT-unsupported-information
- OverTranslation: The span adds unsupported information.
- applies only to bad translations

OT-supported-information
- OverTranslation: The span adds information that is supported by the context or trivial.
- applies to band and good translations

OT-fluency
- OverTranslation: The words in the span are redundant but fluent.
- applies only to good translations

- UT-important-information
- UnderTranslation: The span contains information that is missing in the translation.
- applies only to bad translations

UT-redundant-information
- UnderTranslation: The span contains information that is missing in the translation but that can be inferred or is trivial.
- applies to good and bad translations

UT-fluency
- UnderTranslation: The words in the span do not need to be translated.
- applies only to good translations

other-error-accuracy
- Other: The span is badly translated because of an accuracy error.
- this can be used both when the text is Over- and Under-Translated

other-error-fluency
- Other: The span is badly translated because of a fluency error.
- this can be used both when the text is Over- and Under-Translated

syntactic-difference
- The translation is syntactically different from the source.
- applies only to good translations, can use when the text is both Over- and Under Translated

source-error
- The translation fixes an error in the source.
- applies only to good translations, can use when the text is both Over- and Under Translated

unclear
- I don't know.
- applies only to good translations, can use when the text is both Over- and Under Translated

HEDS Form

Download to file

download json

Press the button to download your current form in JSON format.

Upload from file

Choose File no f

upload json

Press the button to upload a JSON file. Warning: This will clear your current form completely then upload the contents from the file.

Count of errors

Instructions

Instructions

This is the Human Evaluation Datasheet (HEDS) form. Within each section there are questions about the human evaluation experiment for which details are being recorded. There can be multiple subsections within each section and each can be expanded or collapsed.

This form is not submitted to any server when it is completed, instead please use the "download json" button in the "Download to file" section. This will download a file (in .json format) that contains the current values from each form field. You can also upload a json file (see the "Upload from file" section" on the left of the screen). Warning: This will delete your current form content, then populate the blank form with content from the file. It is advisable to download files as a backup when you are compelting the form. The form saves the field values in local storage of your browser, it will be deleted if you clear the local storage, or if you are in a private/incognito window and then close it.

The form will not prevent you from downloading your save file, even when there are error or warning messages. Yellow warning messages indicate fields that have not been completed. If a field is not relevant for your experiment, enter N/A, and ideally also explain why. Red messages are errors, for example if the form expects an integer and you have entered something else, a red message will be shown. These will still not prevent you from saving the form.

You can generate a list of all current errors/warnings, along with their section numbers, in the "all form errors" tab at the bottom of the form. A count of errors will also be refreshed every 60 seconds on the panel on the left side of the screen.

Section 4 should be completed for each criterion that is evaluated in the experiment. Instructions on how to do this are shown when at the start of the section.

Credits

Updates every 60 seconds.

Questions 2.1–2.5 relating to evaluated system, and 4.3.1–4.3.8 relating to response elicitation, are based on Howcroft et al. (2020), with some significant changes. Questions 4.1.1–4.2.3 relating to quality criteria, and some of the questions about system outputs, evaluators, and experimental design (3.1.1–3.2.3, 4.3.5, 4.3.6, 4.3.9–4.3.11) are based on Belz et al. (2020). HEDS was also informed by van der Lee et al. (2019, 2021) and by Gehrmann et al. (2021)'s[6] data card guide. More generally, the original inspiration for creating a 'datasheet' for describing human evaluation experiments of course comes from seminal papers by Bender & Friedman (2018), Mitchell et al. (2019) and Gebru et al. (2020). References

---

References

Banarescu, L., Bonial, C., Cai, S., Georgescu, M., Griffitt, K., Hermjakob, U., Knight, K., Koehn, P., Palmer, M., & Schneider, N. (2013). Abstract Meaning Representation for sembanking. Proceedings of the 7th Linguistic Annotation Workshop and Interoperability with Discourse, 178–186. https://www.aclweb.org/anthology/W13-2322

Belz, A., Mille, S., & Howcroft, D. M. (2020). Disentangling the properties of human evaluation methods: A classification system to support comparability, meta-evaluation and reproducibility testing. Proceedings of the 13th International Conference on Natural Language Generation, 183–194.

Bender, E. M., & Friedman, B. (2018). Data statements for natural language processing: Toward mitigating system bias and enabling better science. Transactions of the Association for Computational Linguistics, 6, 587–604. https://doi.org/10.1162/tacl_a_00041

Card, D., Henderson, P., Khandelwal, U., Jia, R., Mahowald, K., & Jurafsky, D. (2020). With little power comes great responsibility. Proceedings of the 2020 Conference on Empirical Methods in Natural Language Processing (Emnlp), 9263–9274. https://doi.org/10.18653/v1/2020.emnlp-main.745

Gebru, T., Morgenstern, J., Vecchione, B., Vaughan, J. W., Wallach, H., III, H. D., & Crawford, K. (2020). Datasheets for datasets. http://arxiv.org/abs/1803.09010

Gehrmann, S., Adewumi, T., Aggarwal, K., Ammanamanchi, P. S., Anuoluwapo, A., Bosselut, A., Chandu, K. R., Clinciu, M., Das, D., Dhole, K. D., Du, W.,

Durmus, E., Dušek, O., Emezue, C., Gangal, V., Garbacea, C., Hashimoto, T., Hou, Y., Jernite, Y., ... Zhou, J. (2021). The GEM benchmark: Natural language generation, its evaluation and metrics. http://arxiv.org/abs/2102.01672

Howcroft, D. M., Belz, A., Clinciu, M.-A., Gkatzia, D., Hasan, S. A., Mahamood, S., Mille, S., Miltenburg, E. van, Santhanam, S., & Rieser, V. (2020). Twenty years of confusion in human evaluation: NLG needs evaluation sheets and standardised definitions. Proceedings of the 13th International Conference on Natural Language Generation, 169–182. https://www.aclweb.org/anthology/2020.inlg-1.23

Howcroft, D. M., & Rieser, V. (2021). What happens if you treat ordinal ratings as interval data? Human evaluations in NLP are even more under-powered than you think. Proceedings of the 2021 Conference on Empirical Methods in Natural Language Processing, 8932–8939. https://doi.org/10.18653/v1/2021.emnlp-main.703

Kamp, H., & Reyle, U. (2013). From discourse to logic: Introduction to modeltheoretic semantics of natural language, formal logic and discourse representation theory (Vol. 42). Springer Science & Business Media.

Mitchell, M., Wu, S., Zaldivar, A., Barnes, P., Vasserman, L., Hutchinson, B., Spitzer, E., Raji, I. D., & Gebru, T. (2019). Model cards for model reporting. Proceedings of the Conference on Fairness, Accountability, and Transparency, 220–229. https://doi.org/10.1145/3287560.3287596

Shimorina, A., & Belz, A. (2022). The human evaluation datasheet: A template for recording details of human evaluation experiments in NLP. Proceedings of the 2nd Workshop on Human Evaluation of Nlp Systems (Humeval), 54–75. https://aclanthology.org/2022.humeval-1.6

van der Lee, C., Gatt, A., Miltenburg, E. van, Wubben, S., & Krahmer, E. (2019). Best practices for the human evaluation of automatically generated text. Proceedings of the 12th International Conference on Natural Language Generation, 355–368. https://www.aclweb.org/anthology/W19-8643.pdf

van der Lee, C., Gatt, A., van Miltenburg, E., & Krahmer, E. (2021). Human evaluation of automatically generated text: Current trends and best practice guidelines. Computer Speech & Language, 67, 101151. https://doi.org/10.1016/j.csl.2020.101151

Section 1: Paper and supplementary resources

Sections 1.1–1.3 record bibliographic and related information. These are straightforward and don't warrant much in-depth explanation.

Section 1.1: Details of paper reporting the evaluation experiment

Question 1.1.1: Link to paper reporting the evaluation experiment.

Enter a link to an online copy of the the main reference (e.g., a paper) for the human evaluation experiment. If the experiment hasn't been run yet, and the form is being completed for the purpose of submitting it for preregistration, simply enter 'for preregistration'.

https://aclanthology.org/2022.acl-short.53.pdf

Question 1.1.2: Which experiment within the paper is this form being completed for?

Enter details of the experiment within the paper for which this sheet is being completed. For example, the title of the experiment and/or a section number. If there is only one human human evaluation, still enter the same information. If this is form is being completed for pre-registration, enter a note that differetiates this experiment from any others that you are carrying out as part of the same overall work.

Human evaluation of precision for the English-German MT systems (described in section 5.2)

Section 1.2: Link to resources

Question 1.2.1: Link(s) to website(s) providing resources used in the evaluation experiment.

Enter the link(s). Such resources include system outputs, evaluation tools, etc. If there aren't any publicly shared resources (yet), enter 'N/A'.

https://github.com/ZurichNLP/coverage-contrastive-conditioning/blob/master/evaluation/human_evaluation/Human%20Evaluation%20EN–DE.v2.ipynb

Section 1.3: Contact details

This section records the name, affiliation, and email address of person completing this sheet, and of the contact author if different.

Section 1.3.1: Details of the person completing this sheet.

Question 1.3.1.1: Name of the person completing this sheet.

Enter the name of the person completing this sheet.

Filip Klubička

Question 1.3.1.2: Affiliation of the person completing this sheet.

Enter the affiliation of the person completing this sheet.

ADAPT Centre, Technological University Dublin

Question 1.3.1.3: Email address of the person completing this sheet.

Enter the email address of the person completing this sheet.

filip.klubicka@tudublin.ie

Section 1.3.2: Details of the contact author

Question 1.3.2.1: Name of the contact author.
Enter the name of the contact author, enter N/A if it is the same person as in Question 1.3.1.1

N/A

Question 1.3.2.2: Affiliation of the contact author.
Enter the affiliation of the contact author, enter N/A if it is the same person as in Question 1.3.1.2

N/A

Question 1.3.2.3: Email address of the contact author.
Enter the email address of the contact author, enter N/A if it is the same person as in Question 1.3.1.3

N/A

Section 2: System Questions

Questions 2.1–2.5 record information about the system(s) (or human-authored stand-ins) whose outputs are evaluated in the Evaluation experiment that this sheet is being completed for. The input, output, and task questions in this section are closely interrelated: the value for one partially determines the others,as indicated for some combinations in Question 2.3.

Question 2.1: What type of input do the evaluated system(s) take?

This question is about the type(s) of input, where input refers to the representations and/or data structures shared by all evaluated systems. This question is about input type, regardless of number. E.g. if the input is a set of documents, you would still select text: document below.

Select all that apply. If none match, select 'other' and describe.

- [ ] 1. raw/structured data ⓘ
- [ ] 2. deep linguistic representation (DLR) ⓘ
- [ ] 3. shallow linguistic representation (SLR) ⓘ
- [x] 4. text: subsentential unit of text ⓘ
- [ ] 5. text: sentence ⓘ
- [ ] 6. text: multiple sentences ⓘ
- [ ] 7. text: document ⓘ
- [ ] 8. text: dialogue ⓘ
- [ ] 9. text: other (please describe) ⓘ
- [ ] 10. speech ⓘ
- [ ] 11. visual ⓘ
- [ ] 12. multi-modal ⓘ
- [ ] 13. control feature ⓘ
- [ ] 14. no input (human generation) ⓘ
- [ ] 15. other (please describe) ⓘ

Question 2.2: What type of output do the evaluated system(s) generate?

This question is about the type(s) of output, where output refers to the and/or data structures shared by all evaluated systems. This question is about output type, regardless of number. E.g. if the output is a set of documents, you would still select *text: document* below. Note that the options for outputs are the same as for inputs except that the *no input (human generation) option* is replaced with *human-generated 'outputs'*, and the *control feature* option is removed.

Select all that apply. If none match, select 'other' and describe.

- [x] 1. raw/structured data ⓘ
- [ ] 2. deep linguistic representation (DLR) ⓘ
- [ ] 3. Shallow linguistic representation (SLR) ⓘ
- [ ] 4. text: subsentential unit of text ⓘ
- [ ] 5. text: sentence ⓘ

- 6. text: multiple sentences
- 7. text: document
- 8. text: dialogue
- 9. text: other (please describe)
- 10. speech
- 11. visual
- 12. multi-modal
- 13. human generated 'outputs'
- 14. other (please describe)

Question 2.3: How would you describe the task that the evaluated system(s) perform in mapping the inputs in Q2.1 to the outputs in Q2.2?

This question is about the task(s) performed by the system(s) being evaluated. This is independent of the application domain (financial reporting, weather forecasting, etc.), or the specific method (rule-based, neural, etc.) implemented in the system. We indicate mutual constraints between inputs, outputs and task for some of the options below.

Occasionally, more than one of the options below may apply. Select all that apply. If none match, select 'other' and describe.

- 1. content selection/determination
- 2. content ordering/structuring
- 3. aggregation
- 4. referring expression generation
- 5. lexicalisation
- 6. deep generation
- 7. surface realisation (SLR to text)
- 8. feature-controlled text generation
- 9. data-to-text generation
- 10. dialogue turn generation
- 11. question generation
- 12. question answering
- 13. paraphrasing/lossless simplification
- 14. compression/lossy simplification
- 15. machine translation
- 16. summarisation (text-to-text)
- 17. end-to-end text generation

- [ ] 18. image/video description
- [ ] 19. post-editing/correction
- [x] 20. other (please describe)

Please describe:

It's binary classification in a sense, predicting 0 or 1, mapped to 'Undertranslation' or 'Overtranslation' labels

Please provide further details for your above selection(s)

Question 2.4: What are the input languages that are used by the system?

This question is about the language(s) of the inputs accepted by the system(s) being evaluated. Select any language name(s) that apply, mapped to standardised full language names in ISO 639-1 (2019). E.g. English, Herero, Hindi. If no language is accepted as (part of) the input, select 'N/A'.

Select all that apply. If any languages you are using are not covered by this list, select 'other' and describe.

- [ ] 1. Abkhazian
- [ ] 2. Afar
- [ ] 3. Afrikaans
- [ ] 4. Akan
- [ ] 5. Albanian
- [ ] 6. Amharic
- [ ] 7. Arabic
- [ ] 8. Aragonese
- [ ] 9. Armenian
- [ ] 10. Assamese
- [ ] 11. Avaric
- [ ] 12. Avestan
- [ ] 13. Aymara
- [ ] 14. Azerbaijani
- [ ] 15. Bambara
- [ ] 16. Bashkir

- [ ] 17. Basque
- [ ] 18. Belarusian
- [ ] 19. Bengali ⓘ
- [ ] 20. Bislama ⓘ
- [ ] 21. Bosnian
- [ ] 22. Breton
- [ ] 23. Bulgarian
- [ ] 24. Burmese ⓘ
- [ ] 25. Catalan, Valencian
- [ ] 26. Chamorro
- [ ] 27. Chechen
- [ ] 28. Chichewa, Chewa, Nyanja
- [ ] 29. Chinese
- [ ] 30. Church Slavic, Old Slavonic, Church Slavonic, Old Bulgarian, Old Church Slavonic ⓘ
- [ ] 31. Chuvash
- [ ] 32. Cornish
- [ ] 33. Corsican
- [ ] 34. Cree
- [ ] 35. Croatian
- [ ] 36. Czech
- [ ] 37. Danish
- [ ] 38. Divehi, Dhivehi, Maldivian
- [ ] 39. Dutch, Flemish ⓘ
- [ ] 40. Dzongkha
- [x] 41. English
- [ ] 42. Esperanto ⓘ
- [ ] 43. Estonian
- [ ] 44. Ewe
- [ ] 45. Faroese
- [ ] 46. Fijian
- [ ] 47. Finnish
- [ ] 48. French
- [ ] 49. Western Frisian ⓘ
- [ ] 50. Fulah ⓘ
- [ ] 51. Gaelic, Scottish Gaelic

- [ ] 52. Galician
- [ ] 53. Ganda
- [ ] 54. Georgian
- [x] 55. German
- [ ] 56. Greek, Modern (1453–)
- [ ] 57. Kalaallisut, Greenlandic
- [ ] 58. Guarani
- [ ] 59. Gujarati
- [ ] 60. Haitian, Haitian Creole
- [ ] 61. Hausa
- [ ] 62. Hebrew ⓘ
- [ ] 63. Herero
- [ ] 64. Hindi
- [ ] 65. Hiri Motu
- [ ] 66. Hungarian
- [ ] 67. Icelandic
- [ ] 68. Ido ⓘ
- [ ] 69. Igbo
- [ ] 70. Indonesian
- [ ] 71. Interlingua (International Auxiliary Language Association) ⓘ
- [ ] 72. Interlingue, Occidental ⓘ
- [ ] 73. Inuktitut
- [ ] 74. Inupiaq
- [ ] 75. Irish
- [ ] 76. Italian
- [ ] 77. Japanese
- [ ] 78. Javanese
- [ ] 79. Kannada
- [ ] 80. Kanuri
- [ ] 81. Kashmiri
- [ ] 82. Kazakh
- [ ] 83. Central Khmer ⓘ
- [ ] 84. Kikuyu, Gikuyu
- [ ] 85. Kinyarwanda
- [ ] 86. Kirghiz, Kyrgyz
- [ ] 87. Komi

- 88. Kongo
- 89. Korean
- 90. Kuanyama, Kwanyama
- 91. Kurdish
- 92. Lao
- 93. Latin
- 94. Latvian
- 95. Limburgan, Limburger, Limburgish
- 96. Lingala
- 97. Lithuanian
- 98. Luba-Katanga
- 99. Luxembourgish, Letzeburgesch
- 100. Macedonian
- 101. Malagasy
- 102. Malay
- 103. Malayalam
- 104. Maltese
- 105. Manx
- 106. Maori
- 107. Marathi
- 108. Marshallese
- 109. Mongolian
- 110. Nauru
- 111. Navajo, Navaho
- 112. North Ndebele
- 113. South Ndebele
- 114. Ndonga
- 115. Nepali
- 116. Norwegian
- 117. Norwegian Bokmål
- 118. Norwegian Nynorsk
- 119. Sichuan Yi, Nuosu
- 120. Occitan
- 121. Ojibwa
- 122. Oriya

- 123. Oromo
- 124. Ossetian, Ossetic
- 125. Pali ⓘ
- 126. Pashto, Pushto
- 127. Persian ⓘ
- 128. Polish
- 129. Portuguese
- 130. Punjabi, Panjabi
- 131. Quechua
- 132. Romanian, Moldavian, Moldovan
- 133. Romansh
- 134. Rundi ⓘ
- 135. Russian
- 136. Northern Sami
- 137. Samoan
- 138. Sango
- 139. Sanskrit ⓘ
- 140. Sardinian
- 141. Serbian
- 142. Shona
- 143. Sindhi
- 144. Sinhala, Sinhalese
- 145. Slovak
- 146. Slovenian ⓘ
- 147. Somali
- 148. Southern Sotho
- 149. Spanish, Castilian
- 150. Sundanese
- 151. Swahili
- 152. Swati ⓘ
- 153. Swedish
- 154. Tagalog
- 155. Tahitian ⓘ
- 156. Tajik
- 157. Tamil
- 158. Tatar

- 159. Telugu
- 160. Thai
- 161. Tibetan ⓘ
- 162. Tigrinya
- 163. Tonga (Tonga Islands) ⓘ
- 164. Tsonga
- 165. Tswana
- 166. Turkish
- 167. Turkmen
- 168. Twi
- 169. Uighur, Uyghur
- 170. Ukrainian
- 171. Urdu
- 172. Uzbek
- 173. Venda
- 174. Vietnamese
- 175. Volapük ⓘ
- 176. Walloon
- 177. Welsh
- 178. Wolof
- 179. Xhosa
- 180. Yiddish
- 181. Yoruba
- 182. Zhuang, Chuang
- 183. Zulu
- 184. Other (please describe) ⓘ
- 185. N/A (please describe) ⓘ

Question 2.5: What are the output languages that are used by the system?

This field question the language(s) of the outputs generated by the system(s) being evaluated. Select any language name(s) that apply, mapped to standardised full language names in ISO 639-1 (2019). E.g. English, Herero, Hindi. If no language is generated, select 'N/A'.

Select all that apply. If any languages you are using are not covered by this list, select 'other' and describe.

- 1. Abkhazian ⓘ

- 2. Afar
- 3. Afrikaans
- 4. Akan
- 5. Albanian
- 6. Amharic
- 7. Arabic
- 8. Aragonese
- 9. Armenian
- 10. Assamese
- 11. Avaric ⓘ
- 12. Avestan ⓘ
- 13. Aymara
- 14. Azerbaijani ⓘ
- 15. Bambara
- 16. Bashkir
- 17. Basque
- 18. Belarusian
- 19. Bengali ⓘ
- 20. Bislama ⓘ
- 21. Bosnian
- 22. Breton
- 23. Bulgarian
- 24. Burmese ⓘ
- 25. Catalan, Valencian
- 26. Chamorro
- 27. Chechen
- 28. Chichewa, Chewa, Nyanja
- 29. Chinese
- 30. Church Slavic, Old Slavonic, Church Slavonic, Old Bulgarian, Old Church Slavonic ⓘ
- 31. Chuvash
- 32. Cornish
- 33. Corsican
- 34. Cree
- 35. Croatian
- 36. Czech

- [ ] 37. Danish
- [ ] 38. Divehi, Dhivehi, Maldivian
- [ ] 39. Dutch, Flemish ⓘ
- [ ] 40. Dzongkha
- [x] 41. English
- [ ] 42. Esperanto ⓘ
- [ ] 43. Estonian
- [ ] 44. Ewe
- [ ] 45. Faroese
- [ ] 46. Fijian
- [ ] 47. Finnish
- [ ] 48. French
- [ ] 49. Western Frisian ⓘ
- [ ] 50. Fulah ⓘ
- [ ] 51. Gaelic, Scottish Gaelic
- [ ] 52. Galician
- [ ] 53. Ganda
- [ ] 54. Georgian
- [x] 55. German
- [ ] 56. Greek, Modern (1453–)
- [ ] 57. Kalaallisut, Greenlandic
- [ ] 58. Guarani
- [ ] 59. Gujarati
- [ ] 60. Haitian, Haitian Creole
- [ ] 61. Hausa
- [ ] 62. Hebrew ⓘ
- [ ] 63. Herero
- [ ] 64. Hindi
- [ ] 65. Hiri Motu
- [ ] 66. Hungarian
- [ ] 67. Icelandic
- [ ] 68. Ido ⓘ
- [ ] 69. Igbo
- [ ] 70. Indonesian
- [ ] 71. Interlingua (International Auxiliary Language Association) ⓘ

- ☐ 72. Interlingue, Occidental ⓘ
- ☐ 73. Inuktitut
- ☐ 74. Inupiaq
- ☐ 75. Irish
- ☐ 76. Italian
- ☐ 77. Japanese
- ☐ 78. Javanese
- ☐ 79. Kannada
- ☐ 80. Kanuri
- ☐ 81. Kashmiri
- ☐ 82. Kazakh
- ☐ 83. Central Khmer ⓘ
- ☐ 84. Kikuyu, Gikuyu
- ☐ 85. Kinyarwanda
- ☐ 86. Kirghiz, Kyrgyz
- ☐ 87. Komi
- ☐ 88. Kongo
- ☐ 89. Korean
- ☐ 90. Kuanyama, Kwanyama
- ☐ 91. Kurdish
- ☐ 92. Lao
- ☐ 93. Latin ⓘ
- ☐ 94. Latvian
- ☐ 95. Limburgan, Limburger, Limburgish
- ☐ 96. Lingala
- ☐ 97. Lithuanian
- ☐ 98. Luba-Katanga ⓘ
- ☐ 99. Luxembourgish, Letzeburgesch
- ☐ 100. Macedonian
- ☐ 101. Malagasy
- ☐ 102. Malay
- ☐ 103. Malayalam
- ☐ 104. Maltese
- ☐ 105. Manx
- ☐ 106. Maori ⓘ
- ☐ 107. Marathi ⓘ

- [ ] 108. Marshallese
- [ ] 109. Mongolian
- [ ] 110. Nauru ⓘ
- [ ] 111. Navajo, Navaho
- [ ] 112. North Ndebele ⓘ
- [ ] 113. South Ndebele ⓘ
- [ ] 114. Ndonga
- [ ] 115. Nepali
- [ ] 116. Norwegian
- [ ] 117. Norwegian Bokmål
- [ ] 118. Norwegian Nynorsk
- [ ] 119. Sichuan Yi, Nuosu ⓘ
- [ ] 120. Occitan
- [ ] 121. Ojibwa ⓘ
- [ ] 122. Oriya ⓘ
- [ ] 123. Oromo
- [ ] 124. Ossetian, Ossetic
- [ ] 125. Pali ⓘ
- [ ] 126. Pashto, Pushto
- [ ] 127. Persian ⓘ
- [ ] 128. Polish
- [ ] 129. Portuguese
- [ ] 130. Punjabi, Panjabi
- [ ] 131. Quechua
- [ ] 132. Romanian, Moldavian, Moldovan
- [ ] 133. Romansh
- [ ] 134. Rundi ⓘ
- [ ] 135. Russian
- [ ] 136. Northern Sami
- [ ] 137. Samoan
- [ ] 138. Sango
- [ ] 139. Sanskrit ⓘ
- [ ] 140. Sardinian
- [ ] 141. Serbian
- [ ] 142. Shona

- 143. Sindhi
- 144. Sinhala, Sinhalese
- 145. Slovak
- 146. Slovenian
- 147. Somali
- 148. Southern Sotho
- 149. Spanish, Castilian
- 150. Sundanese
- 151. Swahili
- 152. Swati
- 153. Swedish
- 154. Tagalog
- 155. Tahitian
- 156. Tajik
- 157. Tamil
- 158. Tatar
- 159. Telugu
- 160. Thai
- 161. Tibetan
- 162. Tigrinya
- 163. Tonga (Tonga Islands)
- 164. Tsonga
- 165. Tswana
- 166. Turkish
- 167. Turkmen
- 168. Twi
- 169. Uighur, Uyghur
- 170. Ukrainian
- 171. Urdu
- 172. Uzbek
- 173. Venda
- 174. Vietnamese
- 175. Volapük
- 176. Walloon
- 177. Welsh
- 178. Wolof

- 179. Xhosa
- 180. Yiddish
- 181. Yoruba
- 182. Zhuang, Chuang
- 183. Zulu
- 184. Other (please describe)
- 185. N/A (please describe)

Section 3: Sample of system outputs, evaluators, and experimental design

Section 3.1: Sample of system outputs

Questions 3.1.1–3.1.3 record information about the size of the sample of outputs (or human-authored stand-ins) evaluated per system, how the sample was selected, and what its statistical power is.

Question 3.1.1: How many system outputs (or other evaluation items) are evaluated per system in the evaluation experiment?

Enter the number of system outputs (or other evaluation items) that are evaluated per system by at least one evaluator in the experiment. For most experiments this should be an integer, although if the number of outputs varies please provide further details here.

1505

Question 3.1.2: How are system outputs (or other evaluation items) selected for inclusion in the evaluation experiment?

Select one option. If none match, select 'other' and describe:

- ○ 1. by an automatic random process ⓘ
- ○ 2. by an automatic random process but using stratified sampling over given properties ⓘ
- ◉ 3. by manual, arbitrary selection ⓘ
- ○ 4. by manual selection aimed at achieving balance or variety relative to given properties ⓘ
- ○ 5. other (please describe) ⓘ

Section 3.1.3: Statistical power of the sample size.

Section 3.2: Evaluators

Questions 3.2.1–3.2.5 record information about the evaluators participating in the experiment.

Question 3.2.1: How many evaluators are there in this experiment?
Enter the total number of evaluators participating in the experiment, as an integer.

2

Section 3.2.2: Evaluator Type

Question 3.2.3: How are evaluators recruited?
Please explain how your evaluators are recruited. Do you send emails to a given list? Do you post invitations on social media? Posters on university walls? Were there any gatekeepers involved? What are the exclusion/inclusion criteria?

The evaluators came highly recommended by a colleague who teaches the translation studies course.

Question 3.2.4: What training and/or practice are evaluators given before starting on the evaluation itself?

Use this space to describe any training evaluators were given as part of the experiment to prepare them for the evaluation task, including any practice evaluations they did. This includes any introductory explanations they're given, e.g. on the start page of an online evaluation tool.

Shared official annotation guidelines and had a brief virtual meeting with the evaluator (<1 hour) to introduce the experiment and talk through any questions or concerns. Had them evaluate a smaller sample (10%) of the data first to get a feel for the task, before sending them the full dataset for evaluation.

Question 3.2.5: What other characteristics do the evaluators have? Known either because these were qualifying criteria, or from information gathered as part of the evaluation.

Use this space to list any characteristics not covered in previous questions that the evaluators are known to have, either because evaluators were selected on the basis of a characteristic, or because information about a characteristic was collected as part of the evaluation. This might include geographic location of IP address, educational level, or demographic information such as gender, age, etc. Where characteristics differ among evaluators (e.g. gender, age, location etc.), also give numbers for each subgroup.

Key characteristic was their proficiency in both German and English, as well as a linguistics and translation background, crucial for evaluating a MT-based task on the two languages.

Section 3.3: Experimental Design

Sections 3.3.1–3.3.8 record information about the experimental design of the evaluation experiment.

Question 3.3.1: Has the experimental design been preregistered? If yes, on which registry?

Select 'Yes' or 'No'; if 'Yes' also give the name of the registry and a link to the registration page for the experiment.

- ○ 1. yes
- ● 2. no

Question 3.3.2: How are responses collected?
Describe here the method used to collect responses, e.g. paper forms, Google forms, SurveyMonkey, Mechanical Turk, CrowdFlower, audio/video recording, etc.

Google Sheets spreadsheet exported into CSV and processed.

Section 3.3.3: Quality assurance

Section 3.3.3: Form/Interface

Question 3.3.5: How free are evaluators regarding when and how quickly to carry out evaluations?

Select all that apply:

- ☐ 1. evaluators have to complete each individual assessment within a set time ⓘ
- ☐ 2. evaluators have to complete the whole evaluation in one sitting ⓘ
- ☑ 3. neither of the above (please describe) ⓘ

Please describe:

It was assessed that the annotation would take about 10 hours of work and there was a significant amount of flexibility regarding when it is carried out, with a tentative 4-week deadline. Both evaluators copleted the annotations before the deadline was passed.

Please provide further details for your above selection(s)

Question 3.3.6: Are evaluators told they can ask questions about the evaluation and/or provide feedback?

Select all that apply.

- [x] 1. evaluators are told they can ask any questions during/after receiving initial training/instructions, and before the start of the evaluation ⓘ
- [x] 2. evaluators are told they can ask any questions during the evaluation ⓘ
- [ ] 3. evaluators are asked for feedback and/or comments after the evaluation, e.g. via an exit questionnaire or a comment box ⓘ
- [ ] 4. other (please describe) ⓘ
- [ ] 5. None of the above ⓘ

Question 3.3.7: What are the experimental conditions in which evaluators carry out the evaluations?

Multiple-choice options (select one). If none match, select 'other' and describe.

- (•) 1. evaluation carried out by evaluators at a place of their own choosing, e.g. online, using a paper form, etc. ⓘ
- ( ) 2. evaluation carried out in a lab, and conditions are the same for each evaluator ⓘ
- ( ) 3. evaluation carried out in a lab, and conditions vary for different evaluators ⓘ
- ( ) 4. evaluation carried out in a real-life situation, and conditions are the same for each evaluator ⓘ
- ( ) 5. evaluation carried out in a real-life situation, and conditions vary for different evaluators ⓘ

6. evaluation carried out outside of the lab, in a situation designed to resemble a real-life situation, and conditions are the same for each evaluator

7. evaluation carried out outside of the lab, in a situation designed to resemble a real-life situation, and conditions vary for different evaluators

8. other (please describe)

Question 3.3.8: Briefly describe the (range of different) conditions in which evaluators carry out the evaluations.

Use this space to describe the variations in the conditions in which evaluators carry out the evaluation, for both situations where those variations are controlled,and situations where they are not controlled. If the evaluation is carried out at a place of the evaluators' own choosing, enter 'N/A'

On a laptop or computer, either at home or at university.

Section 4: Quality Criteria – Definition and Operationalisation

Questions in this section collect information about each quality criterion assessed in the single human evaluation experiment that this sheet is being completed for.

Many Criteria : Quality Criterion - Definition and Operationalisation

In this section you can create named subsections for each criterion that is being evaluated. The form is then duplicated for each criterion. To create a criterion type its name in the field and press the *New* button, it will then appear on tab that will allow you to toggle the active criterion. To delete the current criterion press the *Delete current* button.

...

New | Delete Current

Section 5: Ethics

The questions in this section relate to ethical aspects of the evaluation. Information can be entered in the text box provided, and/or by linking to a source where complete information can be found.

Question 5.1: Has the evaluation experiment this sheet is being completed for, or the larger study it is part of, been approved by a research ethics committee? If yes, which research ethics committee?

Typically, research organisations, universities and other higher-education institutions require some form ethical approval before experiments involving human participants, however innocuous, are permitted to proceed. Please provide here the name of the body that approved the experiment, or state 'No' if approval has not (yet) been obtained.

Yes, it is covered under general approval of the TU Dublin research ethics committee.

Question 5.2: Do any of the system outputs (or human-authored stand-ins) evaluated, or do any of the responses collected, in the experiment contain personal data (as defined in GDPR Art. 4, §1: https://gdpr.eu/article-4-definitions)? If yes, describe data and state how addressed.

State 'No' if no personal data as defined by GDPR was recorded or collected, otherwise explain how conformity with GDPR requirements such as privacy and security was ensured, e.g. by linking to the (successful) application for ethics approval from Question 5.1.

No.

Question 5.3: Do any of the system outputs (or human-authored stand-ins) evaluated, or do any of the responses collected, in the experiment contain special category information (as defined in GDPR Art. 9, §1: https://gdpr.eu/article-9-processing-special-categories-of-personal-data-prohibited)? If yes, describe data and state how addressed.

State 'No' if no special-category data as defined by GDPR was recorded or collected, otherwise explain how conformity with GDPR requirements relating to special-category data was ensured, e.g. by linking to the (successful) application for ethics approval from Question 5.1.

No.

Question 5.4: Have any impact assessments been carried out for the evaluation experiment, and/or any data collected/evaluated in connection with it? If yes, summarise approach(es) and outcomes.

Use this box to describe any *ex ante* or *ex post* impact assessments that have been carried out in relation to the evaluation experiment, such that the assessment plan and process, well as the outcomes, were captured in written form. Link to documents if possible. Types of impact assessment include data protection impact assessments, e.g. under GDPR. Environmental and social impact assessment frameworks are also available.

No.

B Copy of the HEDS sheet

All Form Errors

Same Trends, Different Answers: Insights from a Replication Study of Human Plausibility Judgments on Narrative Continuations

Yiru Li, Huiyuan Lai, Antonio Toral, Malvina Nissim
CLCG, University of Groningen / The Netherlands
y.li.170@student.rug.nl
{h.lai, a.toral.ruiz, m.nissim}@rug.nl

Abstract

We reproduced the human-based evaluation of the *continuation of narratives* task presented by Chakrabarty et al. (2022). This experiment is performed as part of the ReproNLP Shared Task on Reproducibility of Evaluations in NLP. Our main goal is to reproduce the original study under conditions as similar as possible. Specifically, we follow the original experimental design and perform human evaluations of the data from the original study, while describing the differences between the two studies. We then present the results of these two studies together with an analysis of similarities between them. Inter-annotator agreement (Krippendorff's alpha) in the reproduction study is lower than in the original study, while the human evaluation results of both studies have the same trends, that is, our results support the findings in the original study.

1 Introduction

Reproduction studies of human evaluations in the field of Natural Language Processing (NLP) are attracting increasing attention (Belz et al., 2021b, 2022b). Due to the inherent limitations of automatic evaluation, especially in Natural Language Generation tasks which often imply high variability in the output, human evaluation is often considered to provide more reliable assessments (van der Lee et al., 2019). However, initial results observed in the context of ReproHum[1], a coordinated, multi-lab reproducibility project which the present work is also part of, suggest that the majority of human evaluations in NLP face the challenge of being unreproducible due to various reasons (Belz et al., 2023). This clashes with the importance of ensuring high levels of experimental reproducibility, which has been gaining increasing recognition in the NLP community (Fokkens et al., 2013; Belz et al., 2021a, 2022a).

In the context of our participation in the ReproNLP Shared Task on Reproducibility of Evaluations in NLP (Track C – ReproHum Project)[2], this paper reports on our experience when trying to reproduce as closely as possible a previously run human evaluation. Specifically, we aimed to reproduce human evaluations conducted by Chakrabarty et al. (2022) on the continuations of narratives generated with various systems or written by humans. In order to harmonise and coordinate all replication efforts within ReproHum, the project leaders have created a spreadsheet that each lab in charge of a reporduction experiment was asked to fill in and submit, acting as pre-registration for the replication. This Human Evaluation Datasheet (HEDS) is included in Appendix B. Following the shared reproduction approach provided by the ReproHum's coordinators, we first summarize the original study explaining the task addressed, and the human evaluation setting (Section 2), followed by our replicated experiment (Section 3). Although we did try to perform our new experiments under conditions as similar as possible to those of the original study, we still ended up with some differences between our setup and the original paper (e.g. we raise the payment to give the annotator a fairer reward); we discuss these in detail. Finally, we report and analyze the results obtained in our reproduction study by comparing them to the original experiments (Section 4), and draw some conclusions on the feasibility of a full experimental reproduction (Section 5).

2 Original Study

We aim to repeat the experiment conducted in "*It's not Rocket Science: Interpreting Figurative Language in Narratives*" by Chakrabarty et al. (2022).

[1] https://reprohum.github.io/

[2] https://repronlp.github.io/

Proceedings of the Third Workshop on Human Evaluation of NLP Systems, pages 190–203, Varna, Bulgaria, Sep 7, 2023.
https://doi.org/10.26615/978-954-452-088-5_015

Given Narrative	Continuations	Produced by	Plausible
Dreams of being taken prisoner in iraq began to haunt his dreams. Then the dream of being shot in the chest by cramer; pushing lindsey aside and taking the bullet himself. As the projectile impacted his chest like the kick of a mule, he started and woke up suddenly, eyes wide and looking around as if expecting enemies from any and all directions. He sweated profusely. Between him and the shed, heat waves shimmered and danced once again in erratic patterns. The camp was **like a cemetery**.	The smell of death was in the air	Model (baseline)	yes
	Was in a panic as he looked around	Model (+Context)	yes
	The usual welcomed silence is not welcomed here...it makes for crazy dreams.	Human	no
	You could hear a pin drop with the lack of sounds.	Human	yes

Table 1: An example of narrative ending in simile with corresponding continuations either generated by NLP systems or written by humans.

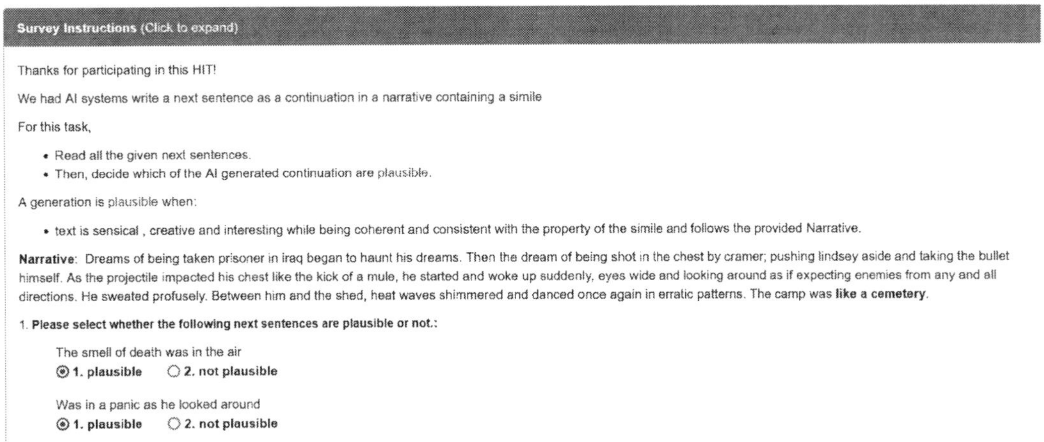
Survey Instructions (Click to expand)

Thanks for participating in this HIT!

We had AI systems write a next sentence as a continuation in a narrative containing a simile

For this task,

- Read all the given next sentences.
- Then, decide which of the AI generated continuation are plausible.

A generation is plausible when:

- text is sensical , creative and interesting while being coherent and consistent with the property of the simile and follows the provided Narrative.

Narrative: Dreams of being taken prisoner in iraq began to haunt his dreams. Then the dream of being shot in the chest by cramer; pushing lindsey aside and taking the bullet himself. As the projectile impacted his chest like the kick of a mule, he started and woke up suddenly, eyes wide and looking around as if expecting enemies from any and all directions. He sweated profusely. Between him and the shed, heat waves shimmered and danced once again in erratic patterns. The camp was **like a cemetery**.

1. **Please select whether the following next sentences are plausible or not.:**

The smell of death was in the air
◉ **1. plausible** ○ **2. not plausible**

Was in a panic as he looked around
◉ **1. plausible** ○ **2. not plausible**

Figure 1: A screenshot of the annotation interface.

This paper studies the interpretation of two figures of speech in narratives, namely *idioms* and *similes*, by means of a generation task.

2.1 Task and Models

The task consists in producing a plausible continuation of a given paragraph ending with a figure of speech, ensuring such continuation is coherent with the narrative and complies with the meaning of the figurative expression. A plausible continuation would serve as an indication that the given figure of speech is interpreted correctly. Table 1 shows an example of a provided narrative with human- or machine-generated continuations, some of which are deemed plausible, and some implausible.

To perform the task, the large pre-trained model GPT-2 XL (Radford et al., 2019) is fine-tuned on narrative-continuation pairs. Also, the authors propose two knowledge-enhanced models ("context-enhanced model" and "literal-enhanced model") that add, respectively, some context or a literal explanation of the figurative expression at the beginning of the narrative.

The continuations generated by different systems are assessed by means of human evaluation and also used for comparison with human-written ones.

2.2 Human Evaluation Settings

The original paper includes two types of human evaluations for both the simile task and the idiom task: absolute evaluation and comparative evaluation. The absolute evaluation asks the worker to evaluate whether the single continuation is plausible, independent of other continuations. The comparative evaluation asks the workers to compare multiple continuations and then choose the most plausible (neither or all are plausible are also possible options). We reproduce only the absolute evaluation as described in the original paper.

For the absolute evaluation, the authors of the original paper randomly sampled 25 narratives for each task, with each narrative containing 5 corresponding human-written continuations for the simile task or 3 for the idiom task. Three

Parameter	Original Setting	Replicated Setting
Reward	0.50 (U.S. Dollar)	**2.21** (U.S. Dollar)
Max Assignments	3	3
Assignment Duration	2 (hour)	2 (hour)
Auto Approval Delay	3 (day)	3 (day)
Expires in	7 (day)	7 (day)
Annotators	7 (simile) + 4 (idiom)	**75** (simile) + **75** (idiom)

Table 2: Parameters of the HIT publication settings, and the changed setting is marked bold.

continuations generated by the baseline GPT2-XL model, context-enhanced model, and literal-enhanced model are assessed by means of human evaluation along with human references.

The evaluation was conducted on *Amazon Mechanical Turk* (MTurk), a crowdsourcing platform, on which requesters may publish so-called Human Intelligence Tasks (HITs) for workers to complete. Each HIT (survey) was designed to have two major parts with instructions: the first part is an example, and the second part is the evaluation questions unique for each HIT. Figure 1 shows a screenshot of the annotation interface.

The example in the HIT is the same for all HITs of the same tasks, and the continuations of one of the selected similes/ idioms are evaluated in the second part. The example has the same layout as the questions: it includes one narrative which uses a given simile/idiom, the meaning of the presented simile/idiom, three model-generated continuations, and several human-written continuations. For the simile task, five human-written continuations are presented; for the idiom task, three are presented.

In all HITs, the positions of continuations were not randomly shuffled, i.e., the first continuation to be evaluated is always generated by the baseline model. Also, the workers are instructed to answer all questions, but it is technically possible for them to submit a HIT with questions unanswered (the script does not include a force-answering mechanism). For each continuation, the workers are instructed to answer a binary question, specifying whether any given continuation is judged as plausible or not.

Each HIT was completed by three unique workers, and each worker was rewarded $0.5 for completing one HIT. Seven and four unique workers were recruited for the simile task and the idiom task, respectively, as we could infer from the provided result file (this information was not included in the original paper, and it is unclear how this was enforced or allowed on the crowdsourcing platform). In the end, 25 HITs were put up for evaluation for each of the two tasks, and 3 responses for each HIT were collected, resulting in 75 responses for each task, and 150 responses in total. We did not observe any rejected or republished HIT in the collected responses, and since no approval time was included, we infer that all HITs were automatically approved.

3 Reproduction study

As mentioned, we only replicated the absolute evaluation from the original paper. Three differences between the reproduced experiment setting and the original one exist.

First of all, we recruited a total of 75 workers for each task with no additional requirements. This was done after thorough consideration: the total number and requirements of workers employed for absolute evaluation are not mentioned in the original paper. Still from the file containing the result data, we could infer, via anonymised ids, that the total number of annotators is much smaller than the number of HITs. However, since all HITs were published in one row, the selecting criteria for workers were unclear and we received no further clarification from the original authors; hence, we chose to also publish the HITs with no additional restrictions on workers in one row for each task, which ultimately led to recruiting one worker for each HIT. No control on whether one worker can work on both the idiom and simile tasks was put in place: in other words, one worker can potentially work on at most two HITs in total, one HIT of each task. Due to invalid results received, we re-published some of the HITs to obtain new assessments so that evaluations from a total of 127 workers were collected. In the original study, no rejecting or re-publishing of HITs was observed, but one invalid result is included in the original outputs for the simile task.

	Idiom		Simile	
	original	**reproduced**	**original**	**reproduced**
GPT2-XL	56	76	60	68
+Context	68	**92**	68	72
+Literal	48	68	76 (60)	**80**
Human	**80**	68	**88**	68
Difference Rate (%)	38.7		34	

Table 3: Summarized results of original and replicated experiments. The result we fail to reproduce is marked in red, with our calculated result in parentheses. The best result of each task is marked in bold. We also calculated the difference rate between each evaluated result from the replicated study and the original study to find how well our replicated results agree with the original result. See Table 4 and 5 for more details.

Secondly, we raised the monetary compensation from \$0.5 per HIT to \$2.21 per HIT, following the general recommendation of the ReproHum project to meet the minimum hourly salary in the UK, assuming it takes 10 minutes to finish one HIT properly. Besides setting differences, we received some invalid responses due to the original survey layout and thus had to re-publish some HITs. Table 2 presents key HIT parameters in the original and the present study.

Thirdly, we changed the examples given in the idiom tasks. Only the specific simile examples were made available by the authors, therefore we chose a narrative including an idiom and its corresponding continuations from the development set and then used them as examples for the crowdworkers.

4 Results

In this section, we report our results compared to the original experiment, and the reproducibility assessment. For each narrative-continuations pair we collect three responses, and whether a continuation is plausible is determined by majority voting, following what was described in the original paper.

As a first check, we assess inter-annotator agreement (IAA) using Krippendorff's α, which is appropriate for categorical labels attached to text spans, and which was used in the original experiment. The original experiment reports Krippendorff's $\alpha = 0.68$, while our replicated experiment shows Krippendorff's $\alpha = 0.11$ and the Krippendorff's α of the original experiment is 0.33 using our calculation method. This discrepancy might have to do with the fact that in our replication there are many more annotators, and with the way the score was calculated (accounting or not for the same annotator possibly doing more HITs in the original study).

The original paper reports quantitative results of each model for each task, and describes the reported data as the "percent of times that the generation from each of the models and human-written references was chosen as plausible by the majority of workers."

Since in each task we only collect assessments from each worker for one single continuation per model, there is no confusion on how to calculate the quantitative results. However, responses of multiple human-written continuations from each worker are collected, and the original paper did not detail how they came to the reported results for the human-produced continuations. After several attempts, 7 out of 8 the original results of the plausibility of human-written continuations were successfully reproduced using the following procedure:

1. determine whether a human-written continuation is plausible using majority voting;
2. count the total number of plausible continuations for each task;
3. divide the total by the number of human-written continuations in each HIT (3 and 5 for HITs in the idiom and simile task, respectively);
4. round up the calculated mean to an integer;
5. divide the rounded mean by the number of HITs (25 for both tasks) to calculate the percentage.

The calculated results are shown in Table 3.[3] The best result in each column is marked in bold, while the only result that our recalculation procedure described above could not reproduce as reported in the original study is marked in red (we include our recalculated result in brackets).

Surprisingly, our replicated experiments show that knowledge-enhanced models outperform humans, which was not the case in the original study. One plausible assumption is that the workers recruited in the original study have all been given additional training on evaluating continuations. Another possible reason is that the workers in the original study might unconsciously think that the second half of continuations is more plausible. Each of them works on multiple HITs, and in each HIT the first three continuations are always model-generated continuations and the rest are human-written continuations. The second problem is avoided in our replicated study as we avoided letting one worker evaluate several HITs. Nevertheless, both the performance difference and low IAA suggest that normal workers cannot fully understand, or reach an agreement on determining whether a continuation is plausible, with only the example and instructions given on the HIT page.

Overall, the original paper concludes from the results that "a knowledge-enhanced model outperformed the baseline GPT-2 model...the context model was favored for idioms while the literal model was favored for similes," and the general trend of our results, albeit at times largely different in scores, also supports this conclusion.

5 Conclusions

Although the results of our replicated experiment support the general findings of the original paper, the human evaluation process of the original paper could not be fully reproduced properly.

Two aspects need particular attention. First, the reproducing process is intrinsically difficult. Even though we tried our best, and we gained substantial help from the original authors, several questions still emerged during the replication stage which could not be answered. The detail of the worker recruitment process for example was not available and might be not fully known to the original authors either, due to platform specifications that can be not in full control of the researcher. We did stick to the original crowdsourcing platform used although it would not have been our primary choice, also due to logistic issues related to payment and, as said, full control over workers' recruitment.

Secondly, as shown in Table 3, the two rounds of experiments disagree with each other on more than one-third of continuations. Comparing the replicated results to the original results, we see that the high difference rates indicate disagreement between the reproduction results on the original output. We draw the conclusion from these mentioned problems that human evaluation of the plausibility of continuations, no matter the generated ones or the human written ones, is precarious.

[3] Table 4 and Table 5 in Appendix A show the detailed results collected from the original and the replicated experiments.

Acknowledgments

We are very grateful to the anonymous reviewers for their useful comments, which contributed to strengthening this paper. We would also like to thank the annotators for helping us evaluate the data. Finally, we thank the reproHum project leaders for all their help including bridging contacts with the authors of the original study and project coordination.

References

Anya Belz, Shubham Agarwal, Anastasia Shimorina, and Ehud Reiter. 2021a. A systematic review of reproducibility research in natural language processing. In *Proceedings of the 16th Conference of the European Chapter of the Association for Computational Linguistics: Main Volume*, pages 381–393, Online. Association for Computational Linguistics.

Anya Belz, Simon Mille, and David M. Howcroft. 2020. Disentangling the properties of human evaluation methods: A classification system to support comparability, meta-evaluation and reproducibility testing. In *Proceedings of the 13th International Conference on Natural Language Generation*, pages 183–194, Dublin, Ireland. Association for Computational Linguistics.

Anya Belz, Maja Popovic, and Simon Mille. 2022a. Quantified reproducibility assessment of NLP results. In *Proceedings of the 60th Annual Meeting of the Association for Computational Linguistics (Volume 1: Long Papers)*, pages 16–28, Dublin, Ireland. Association for Computational Linguistics.

Anya Belz, Anastasia Shimorina, Shubham Agarwal, and Ehud Reiter. 2021b. The ReproGen shared task on reproducibility of human evaluations in NLG: Overview and results. In *Proceedings of the 14th*

International Conference on Natural Language Generation, pages 249–258, Aberdeen, Scotland, UK. Association for Computational Linguistics.

Anya Belz, Anastasia Shimorina, Maja Popović, and Ehud Reiter. 2022b. The 2022 ReproGen shared task on reproducibility of evaluations in NLG: Overview and results. In *Proceedings of the 15th International Conference on Natural Language Generation: Generation Challenges*, pages 43–51, Waterville, Maine, USA and virtual meeting. Association for Computational Linguistics.

Anya Belz, Craig Thomson, and Ehud Reiter. 2023. Missing information, unresponsive authors, experimental flaws: The impossibility of assessing the reproducibility of previous human evaluations in NLP. In *The Fourth Workshop on Insights from Negative Results in NLP*, pages 1–10, Dubrovnik, Croatia. Association for Computational Linguistics.

Tuhin Chakrabarty, Yejin Choi, and Vered Shwartz. 2022. It's not rocket science: Interpreting figurative language in narratives. *Transactions of the Association for Computational Linguistics*, 10:589–606.

Antske Fokkens, Marieke van Erp, Marten Postma, Ted Pedersen, Piek Vossen, and Nuno Freire. 2013. Offspring from reproduction problems: What replication failure teaches us. In *Proceedings of the 51st Annual Meeting of the Association for Computational Linguistics (Volume 1: Long Papers)*, pages 1691–1701, Sofia, Bulgaria. Association for Computational Linguistics.

David M. Howcroft, Anya Belz, Miruna-Adriana Clinciu, Dimitra Gkatzia, Sadid A. Hasan, Saad Mahamood, Simon Mille, Emiel van Miltenburg, Sashank Santhanam, and Verena Rieser. 2020. Twenty years of confusion in human evaluation: NLG needs evaluation sheets and standardised definitions. In *Proceedings of the 13th International Conference on Natural Language Generation*, pages 169–182, Dublin, Ireland. Association for Computational Linguistics.

Chris van der Lee, Albert Gatt, Emiel van Miltenburg, Sander Wubben, and Emiel Krahmer. 2019. Best practices for the human evaluation of automatically generated text. In *Proceedings of the 12th International Conference on Natural Language Generation*, pages 355–368, Tokyo, Japan. Association for Computational Linguistics.

Alec Radford, Jeffrey Wu, Rewon Child, David Luan, Dario Amodei, Ilya Sutskever, et al. 2019. Language models are unsupervised multitask learners. *OpenAI blog*, 1(8):9.

A Examples and Result Tables

	GPT2-XL	+Context	+Literal	H. 1	H. 2	H. 3
Idiom Results	1	1	0	1	1	1
	0	1	1	1	1	1
	0	0	1	1	0	1
	1	1	0	1	1	1
	0	1	0	1	1	1
	0	1	0	0	1	1
	1	1	0	1	1	0
	1	1	1	1	0	1
	1	0	1	1	0	0
	1	0	0	1	1	1
	0	1	1	0	1	1
	1	1	1	1	1	0
	0	1	0	1	1	1
	0	0	1	1	1	1
	0	0	1	1	0	1
	0	1	1	1	1	0
	1	0	0	0	1	1
	1	1	0	1	1	0
	1	1	0	1	1	1
	0	1	0	1	1	1
	1	0	0	1	1	1
	1	1	1	1	1	1
	0	0	1	1	0	1
	1	1	0	0	0	1
	1	1	1	1	0	1
Difference Rate (%) Overall: 38.7	36	40	52	32	44	28

Table 4: Results of the original voted plausibility of continuations generated/ collected for idioms. "H." is the abbreviation of Human Reference. 1 represents plausible continuation, and 0 represents non-plausible continuation. If the determined plausibility of the continuation is different in replicated study, the value is marked red.

	GPT2-XL	+Context	+Literal	H. 1	H. 2	H. 3	H. 4	H. 5
	0	1	1	1	1	1	0	1
	1	1	1	1	1	0	1	1
	1	0	0	1	1	1	1	1
	0	1	1	0	1	1	1	1
	1	0	1	1	1	1	1	1
	0	0	1	1	1	1	1	1
	0	1	1	1	1	1	1	1
	1	1	0	1	1	1	1	1
	1	1	1	1	1	1	1	1
	0	1	0	1	1	1	1	0
	1	1	0	1	1	1	1	0
Simile	1	1	1	1	1	1	0	1
Results	1	1	1	1	1	1	1	1
	1	0	1	1	1	1	1	1
	1	0	1	0	1	1	1	1
	0	0	0	1	1	1	1	0
	1	1	0	1	1	1	1	1
	1	1	1	1	0	1	1	1
	0	1	1	1	1	0	1	0
	1	1	0	1	1	1	1	1
	1	1	1	1	1	1	0	0
	0	1	1	1	1	1	1	1
	0	0	0	1	1	1	1	0
	0	0	0	1	1	1	1	1
	1	1	0	1	0	1	0	0
Difference Rate (%) Overall: 34	40	28	36	40	48	20	12	48

Table 5: Results of the original voted plausibility of continuations generated/ collected for similes. "H." is the abbreviation of Human Reference. 1 represents plausible continuation, and 0 represents non-plausible continuation. If the determined plausibility of the continuation is different in the replicated study, the value is marked red.

Survey Instructions (Click to expand)

Thanks for participating in this HIT!

We had AI systems write a next sentence as a continuation in a narrative containing a simile

For this task,

- Read all the given next sentences.
- Then, decide which of the AI generated continuation are plausible.

A generation is plausible when:

- text is sensical , creative and interesting while being coherent and consistent with the property of the simile and follows the provided Narrative.

Narrative: Dreams of being taken prisoner in iraq began to haunt his dreams. Then the dream of being shot in the chest by cramer; pushing lindsey aside and taking the bullet himself. As the projectile impacted his chest like the kick of a mule, he started and woke up suddenly, eyes wide and looking around as if expecting enemies from any and all directions. He sweated profusely. Between him and the shed, heat waves shimmered and danced once again in erratic patterns. The camp was **like a cemetery**.

1. **Please select whether the following next sentences are plausible or not.:**

The smell of death was in the air
◉ **1. plausible** ○ **2. not plausible**

Was in a panic as he looked around
◉ **1. plausible** ○ **2. not plausible**

The quiet was eerie, it inspired a creeping fear
◉ **1. plausible** ○ **2. not plausible**

It was eerily quiet and nobody moved within the space.
◉ **1. plausible** ○ **2. not plausible**

The usual welcomed silence is not welcomed here...it makes for crazy dreams.
○ **1. plausible** ◉ **2. not plausible**

The silence made it harder to get back to sleep.
○ **1. plausible** ◉ **2. not plausible**

The quiet helped soothe his frazzled nerves.
◉ **1. plausible** ○ **2. not plausible**

You could hear a pin drop with the lack of sounds.
◉ **1. plausible** ○ **2. not plausible**

1. **Please select whether the following next sentences are plausible or not.:**

Narrative: So tell me, were you sleeping with william before you married tony or just when you figured out you might get some money out of it?\" She made a cry of outrage and re-aimed the gun. I saw the decision in her eyes the split second she decided to kill me. In a final attempt to save myself, I leapt to the side as the gun went off, grabbing william around the waist and using him as a shield. I felt his body jerk as we both landed hard on the floor with him on top of me. He was **like a huge block of cement.**
Meaning: heavy

a) I was unable to move at all
○ **1. plausible** ○ **2. not plausible**

a) I felt I could not move him an inch and I was afraid he would roll away from me
○ **1. plausible** ○ **2. not plausible**

a) His strength was undeniable and I struggled to breathe
○ **1. plausible** ○ **2. not plausible**

a) He was so heavy, I couldn't get him off of me.
○ **1. plausible** ○ **2. not plausible**

a) His dead weight knocked the wind out of me and I laid there forever trying to breath.
○ **1. plausible** ○ **2. not plausible**

a) I struggled to breath.
○ **1. plausible** ○ **2. not plausible**

a) As we laid there, I suddenly felt wetness and saw blood coming from him.
○ **1. plausible** ○ **2. not plausible**

b) He knocked the breath out of me and I struggled to push him off.
○ **1. plausible** ○ **2. not plausible**

ATTENTION We have taken measures to prevent cheating and if you do not complete the task honestly we will know and the HIT will be rejected.

(Optional) Please provide any comments that you have about this HIT. Thanks for doing our HIT! We appreciate your input!

Figure 2: Example HIT question page.

B HEDS Sheet

B.1 Paper and supplementary resources

Sections 1.1–1.3 record bibliographic and related information. These are straightforward and don't warrant much in-depth explanation.

1.1 Details of paper reporting the evaluation experiment

1.1.1 Link to paper reporting the evaluation experiment.
ReproHum: pre-experiment record

1.1.2 Which experiment within the paper is this form being completed for?
Absolute evaluation of plausibility (idiom and simile) in Section 5.

1.2 Link to resources

1.2.1 Link(s) to website(s) providing resources used in the evaluation experiment.
https://drive.google.com/drive/folders/
1ruTV4tnkfzTkGuF8VnmxgQr2ToQ3R
gDO?usp=sharing

1.3 Contact details

This section records the name, affiliation, and email address of person completing this sheet, and of the contact author if different.

1.3.1 Details of the person completing this sheet

1.3.1.1 Name of the person completing this sheet.
Huiyuan Lai

1.3.1.2 Affiliation of the person completing this sheet.
University of Groningen

1.3.1.3 Email address of the person completing this sheet.
h.lai@rug.nl

1.3.2 Details of the contact author

1.3.2.1 Name of the contact author.
Malvina Nissim

1.3.2.2 Affiliation of the contact author.
University of Groningen

1.3.2.3 Email address of the contact author.
m.nissim@rug.nl

B.2 System Questions

Questions 2.1–2.5 record information about the system(s) (or human-authored stand-ins) whose outputs are evaluated in the Evaluation experiment that this sheet is being completed for. The input, output, and task questions in this section are closely interrelated: the value for one partially determines the others,as indicated for some combinations in Question 2.3.

2.1 What type of input do the evaluated system(s) take?
6. text: multiple sentences

2.2 What type of output do the evaluated system(s) generate?
5. text: sentence

2.3 How would you describe the task that the evaluated system(s) perform in mapping the inputs in Q2.1 to the outputs in Q2.2?
17. end-to-end text generation

2.4 What are the input languages that are used by the system?
41. English

2.5 What are the output languages that are used by the system?
41. English

B.3 Sample of system outputs, evaluators, and experimental design

3.1 Sample of system outputs

Questions 3.1.1–3.1.3 record information about the size of the sample of outputs (or human-authored stand-ins) evaluated per system, how the sample was selected, and what its statistical power is.

3.1.1 How many system outputs (or other evaluation items) are evaluated per system in the evaluation experiment?
25 outputs per system

3.1.2 How are system outputs (or other evaluation items) selected for inclusion in the evaluation experiment?
1. by an automatic random process

3.1.3 Statistical power of the sample size.

3.1.3.1 What method was used to determine the statistical power of the sample size?
N/A. Follow the original experiment.

3.1.3.2 What is the statistical power of the sample size?
N/A

3.1.3.3 Where can other researchers find details of the script used?
N/A

3.2 Evaluators

Questions 3.2.1–3.2.5 record information about the evaluators participating in the experiment.

3.2.1 How many evaluators are there in this experiment?
N/A

3.2.2 Evaluator Type

Questions 3.2.2.1–3.2.2.5 record information about the type of evaluators participating in the experiment.

3.2.2.1 What kind of evaluators are in this experiment?
2. non-experts

3.2.2.2 Were the participants paid or unpaid?
1. paid (monetary compensation)

3.2.2.3 Were the participants previously known to the authors?
2. not previously known to authors

3.2.2.4 Were one or more of the authors among the participants?
2. evaluators do not include any of the authors

3.2.2.5 Further details for participant type.
N/A

3.2.3 How are evaluators recruited?
Post tasks in the crowdsourcing platform (MTurk).

3.2.4 What training and/or practice are evaluators given before starting on the evaluation itself?
We can provide evaluators with detailed guidelines and examples of generated sentences along with plausible assessments. However, it is not known if guidelines and examples were provided in the original paper.

3.2.5 What other characteristics do the evaluators have?
To ensure the quality of annotations, we will require that workers have an acceptance rate of at least 99%. No other demographic constraints are considered, only English as mother tongue (see below). Nothing is known regarding this from the original paper.

3.3 Experimental Design

Sections 3.3.1–3.3.8 record information about the experimental design of the evaluation experiment.

3.3.1 Has the experimental design been preregistered? If yes, on which registry?

2. no

3.3.2 How are responses collected?

Mechanical Turk

3.3.3 Quality assurance

Questions 3.3.3.1 and 3.3.3.2 record information about quality assurance.

3.3.3.1 What quality assurance methods are used to ensure evaluators and/or their responses are suitable?

1. evaluators are required to be native speakers of the language they evaluate.
2. automatic quality checking methods are used during/post evaluation
4. evaluators are excluded if they fail quality checks (often or badly enough)

3.3.3.2 Please describe in detail the quality assurance methods that were used.

2. = pre-selection based on master qualification on MTurk + post-selection based on minimum completion time required

4. = if non masters then excluded; if completion time too short, evaluators excluded.

Unclear, but unlikely, if quality control was done in original experiment and in case what (in paper 100% retention of evaluators)

3.3.4 Form/Interface

Questions 3.3.4.1 and 3.4.3.2 record information about the form or user interface that was shown to participants.

3.3.4.1 Please include a link to online copies of the form/interface that was shown to participants.

N/A

3.3.4.2 What do evaluators see when carrying out evaluations?

A task instruction, a short narrative and its meaning, and six outputs

3.3.5 How free are evaluators regarding when and how quickly to carry out evaluations?

2. evaluators have to complete the whole evaluation in one sitting

3.3.6 Are evaluators told they can ask questions about the evaluation and/or provide feedback?

5. None of the above

3.3.7 What are the experimental conditions in which evaluators carry out the evaluations?

1. evaluation carried out by evaluators at a place of their own choosing, e.g. online, using a paper form, etc.

3.3.8 Briefly describe the (range of different) conditions in which evaluators carry out the evaluations.

N/A

B.4 Quality Criteria - Definition and Operationalisation

Questions in this section collect information about each quality criterion assessed in the single human evaluation experiment that this sheet is being completed for.

4.1 Quality Criteria

Questions 4.1.1–4.1.3 capture the aspect of quality that is assessed by a given quality criterion in terms of three orthogonal properties. They help determine whether or not the same aspect of quality is being evaluated in different evaluation experiments. The three properties characterise quality criteria in terms of (i) what type of quality is being assessed; (ii) what aspect of the system output is being assessed; and (iii) whether system outputs are assessed in their own right or with reference to some system-internal or system-external frame of reference. For full explanations see Belz et al. (2020).

4.1.1 What type of quality is assessed by the quality criterion?
1. Correctness

4.1.2 Which aspect of system outputs is assessed by the quality criterion?
2. Content of output

4.1.3 Is each output assessed for quality in its own right, or with reference to a system-internal or external frame of reference?
2. Quality of output relative to the input

4.2 Evaluation mode properties

Questions 4.2.1–4.2.3 record properties that are orthogonal to quality criteria (covered by questions in the preceding section), i.e. any given quality criterion can in principle be combined with any of the modes (although some combinations are more common than others).

4.2.1 Does an individual assessment involve an objective or a subjective judgment
2. Subjective

4.2.2 Are outputs assessed in absolute or relative terms?
1. Absolute

4.2.3 Is the evaluation intrinsic or extrinsic?
1. Intrinsic

4.3 Response elicitation

The questions in this section concern response elicitation, by which we mean how the ratings or other measurements that represent assessments for the quality criterion in question are obtained, covering what is presented to evaluators, how they select response and via what type of tool, etc. The eleven questions (4.3.1–4.3.11) are based on the information annotated in the large scale survey of human evaluation methods in NLG by Howcroft et al. (2020).

4.3.1 What do you call the quality criterion in explanations/interfaces to evaluators? Enter 'N/A' if no definition given.
Coherence

4.3.2 Question 4.3.2: What definition do you give for the quality criterion in explanations/interfaces to evaluators? Enter 'N/A' if no definition given.
Coherence: Given a short narrative containing an idiomatic expression, the generated next sentence in the story is plausible.

4.3.3 Are the rating instrument response values discrete or continuous? If so, please also indicate the size.
1. Discrete
Size of the instrument: 0 or 1

4.3.4 List or range of possible values of the scale or other rating instrument. Enter 'N/A', if there is no rating instrument.
0 or 1

4.3.5 How is the scale or other rating instrument presented to evaluators? If none match, select 'Other' and describe.
1. Multiple-choice options

4.3.6 If there is no rating instrument, describe briefly what task the evaluators perform (e.g. ranking multiple outputs, finding information, playing a game, etc.), and what information is recorded. Enter 'N/A' if there is a rating instrument.
N/A

4.3.7 What is the verbatim question, prompt or instruction given to evaluators (visible to them during each individual assessment)?
Title: Choose if generated next sentence in a story containing an idiom is plausible.
Description: Given a short narrative containing an idiomatic expression, annotators need to choose if generated next sentence in the story is plausible.

4.3.8 Form of response elicitation. If none match, select 'Other' and describe.

1. (dis)agreement with quality statement

4.3.9 How are raw responses from participants aggregated or otherwise processed to obtain reported scores for this quality criterion?

For ground truth we will use majority label. Aggregation strategies are not mentioned in the original paper. We will also keep all assessments for more qualitative and in-depth analysis of single instances.

4.3.10 Method(s) used for determining effect size and significance of findings for this quality criterion.

None

4.3.11 Inter-annotator agreement

Questions 4.3.11.1 and 4.3.11.2 record information about inter-annotator agreement.

4.3.11.1 Has the inter-annotator agreement between evaluators for this quality criterion been measured? If yes, what method was used?

1. yes, Krippendorff's alpha

4.3.11.2 What was the inter-annotator agreement score?

N/A

4.3.12 Intra-annotator agreement

Questions 4.3.12.1 and 4.3.12.2 record information about intra-annotator agreement.

4.3.11.1 Has the intra-annotator agreement between evaluators for this quality criterion been measured? If yes, what method was used?

2. no

4.3.11.2 What was the intra-annotator agreement score?

N/A

B.5 Ethics

The questions in this section relate to ethical aspects of the evaluation. Information can be entered in the text box provided, and/or by linking to a source where complete information can be found.

5.1 Has the evaluation experiment this sheet is being completed for, or the larger study it is part of, been approved by a research ethics committee? If yes, which research ethics committee?

Yes! The Research Ethics Committee (CETO) of the Faculty of Arts, University of Groningen.

5.2 Do any of the system outputs (or human-authored stand-ins) evaluated, or do any of the responses collected, in the experiment contain personal data (as defined in GDPR Art. 4, §1: https://gdpr.eu/article-4-definitions)? If yes, describe data and state how addressed.

No

5.3 Do any of the system outputs (or human-authored stand-ins) evaluated, or do any of the responses collected, in the experiment contain special category information (as defined in GDPR Art. 9, §1: https://gdpr.eu/article-9-processing-special-categories-of-personal-data-prohibited)? If yes, describe data and state how addressed.

No

5.4 Have any impact assessments been carried out for the evaluation experiment, and/or any data collected/evaluated in connection with it? If yes, summarise approach(es) and outcomes.

No

Reproduction of Human Evaluations in: "It's not Rocket Science: Interpreting Figurative Language in Narratives"

Saad Mahamood
trivago N.V.
Düsseldorf, Germany
saad.mahamood@trivago.com

Abstract

We describe in this paper an attempt to reproduce some of the human of evaluation results from the paper "It's not Rocket Science: Interpreting Figurative Language in Narratives". In particular, we describe the methodology used to reproduce the chosen human evaluation, the challenges faced, and the results that were gathered. We will also make some recommendations on the learnings obtained from this reproduction attempt and what improvements are needed to enable more robust reproductions of future NLP human evaluations.

1 Introduction

Reproducible and repeatable evaluations lay at the heart of good science. However, there has been increasing concern with Natural Language Processing (NLP) on whether human evaluations are in fact reproducible and repeatable. This is particularly important within the field of NLP as human evaluations are seen as the "gold standard" as compared to automatic metric based evaluations. This has lead to an interest in trying to understand and quantify the degree to which evaluations are reproducible.

One such effort is the ReproHum project[1], which attempts to investigate human evaluations within NLP by systematically uncovering the extent of problems of reproducibility. As part of this project multiple partner labs, consisting of both academic and industry institutions, were invited to participate in a multi-lab study reproducing human evaluations from a chosen set of research papers. These papers were vetted by the organising committee of the ReproHum project to ensure that sufficient details in terms of materials (code, data, etc.) and evaluation procedures were present for a successful attempt at reproduction by a given partner lab. In addition to the original paper author(s) consent and co-operation was sought to enable the reproduction of human evaluations in their paper.

In this paper, we describe the current challenges facing human evaluations in NLP and reproducibility (section 2). Afterwards we give details on the attempt to reproduce a specific human evaluation within the paper "It's not Rocket Science: Interpreting Figurative Language in Narratives" by Chakrabarty et al. (2022) (section 3) and how the reproduction of the paper was conducted with details on the challenges involved (section 4). Finally, we detail the results obtained from the reproduction (section 5) and the recommendations (section 6) we would make based on the experiences of this experiment that would enable more robust reproductions of future NLP human evaluations.

2 Background

Within recent years there has been a great interest in understanding and quantifying the reproducibility of experiments across several areas of scientific research. This also includes experiments in the field of Natural Language Understanding (NLU), where researchers have questioned the degree to which experiments and results can reliably be reproduced. Recent work exploring the reproducibility of past NLU work has found significant issues such as only a minority of systems reproducing previously reported scores and systems not working due to non-functional code or resource limits (Belz et al., 2021b). In fact some estimates place the percentage of papers being repeatable without any significant barriers as low as 5% and at 20% if the original author(s) help is sought (Belz et al., 2023). Additionally, there has been growing awareness of systematic issues with regard to how human evaluations are being conducted. In particular, the lack of standardisation and significant underreporting of key human evaluation details (Howcroft et al.,

[1] ReproHum - https://reprohum.github.io

Proceedings of the Third Workshop on Human Evaluation of NLP Systems, pages 204–209, Varna, Bulgaria, Sep 7, 2023.
https://doi.org/10.26615/978-954-452-088-5_016

2020). There has been an attempt to make human evaluation reporting more standardised and comparable between different papers through an introduction of a classification system that defines quality criterion properties (Belz et al., 2020b). However, as noted by Gehrmann et al. (2023), whilst the problems of evaluations are known and proposals have been made to improve the situation, the adoption of best practices remains lacking.

The ReproHum project is a subsequent follow-up of the ReproGen shared tasks[2] (Belz et al., 2020a) in 2021 and 2022. In these shared tasks participants either selected a paper proposed by the organisers or self-selected a paper for human evaluation reproduction. The results from these shared tasks showed some indications that human evaluations that have different evaluation cohorts can disadvantage the reproducibility of a given experiment (Belz et al., 2021a). However, lowering the cognitive loads on individual evaluators could potentially lead to be better reproducibility of results (Belz et al., 2022).

3 Reproduction Experiment

For this reproduction experiment we were tasked with reproducing a specific human evaluation in the paper "It's not Rocket Science: Interpreting Figurative Language in Narratives" by Chakrabarty et al. (2022). The paper explores the interpretation of figurative languages (idioms and similes) in English by exploring plausible and implausible continuations from a given fictional narrative. The authors of the paper used models to generate plausible idioms and similes from a given narrative. These generated texts were compared to human written ones in both automatic and human evaluations.

The focus for this experiment is to reproduce the human evaluation conducted by authors. In particular, reproducing the absolute human evaluation, which asked human Amazon Mechanical Turk workers on whether the computer generated and/or the human references are plausible or not for the given narrative. This task is illustrated in figure 1, which is taken from Chakrabarty et al. (2022). In the original experiment crowd workers were shown a narrative, the meaning of the idiom or the property of the simile and a list of three automatically generated continuations. One from a baseline supervised GPT-2 model, one from a context model, and the third from the literal model. In addition to the automatic continuations, participants were shown three human alternatives for idioms or five for similes. For each continuation (automatic or human) participants were asked to rate whether the text is plausible or not. Each example was rated by three workers and the result aggregated using majority voting.

[2]ReproGen - https://reprogen.github.io/

Both evaluations were done on 25 randomly sampled narrative texts for both the absolute idiom and simile scenarios. This equates to 50 narrative texts in total. The original paper incorrectly states "50 narratives for each task", however prior to the reproduction experiment this was clarified by the authors to be a mistake.

In the original evaluation the authors of the paper reported the following results for the absolute evaluation:

- Moderate inter-annotator agreement using Krippendorf's $\alpha = 0.68$.
- 80% of human-written continuations for the idiom and 88% for simile tasks were judged as plausible.
- 56% of the baseline GPT-2 model continuations for the idiom and 60% for the simile tasks were judged as plausible.
- 68% of the context model continuations for both idiom and simile tasks were judged as plausible.
- 48% of the literal model continuations for the idiom and 76% for the simile tasks were judged as plausible.

In addition to the above reported results the authors also make a mention of the fact that "the context model was favoured for idioms, the literal model was favoured for similes". This result will also be checked in this reproduction attempt.

4 Methodology & Challenges

The original evaluation collected human evaluations using Amazon Mechanical Turk (MTurk) crowd workers. Like the original, the reproduction also used Amazon Mechanical Turk as well. However, the paper by Chakrabarty et al. (2022) does not detail whether any controls were applied or not for the selection of crowd workers. Nor were any details provided about the cohort of participants in terms of demographic data and the total number of participants recruited.

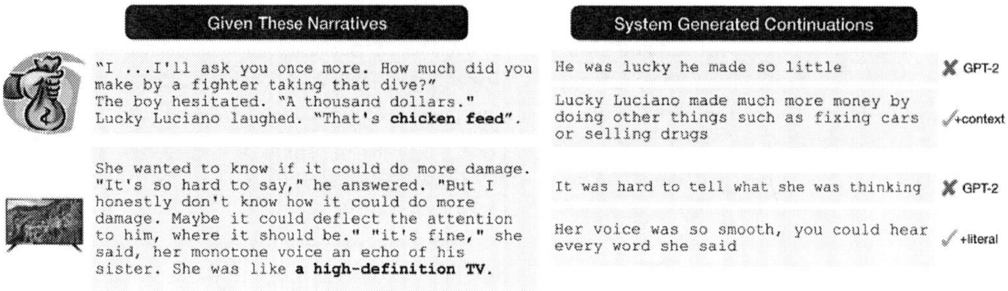

Figure 1: Diagram illustrating the judging of whether a given continuation is plausible or not with the top being an idiom and the bottom a simile. Taken from Chakrabarty et al. (2022).

For the reproduction experiment a total of 80 workers were recruited across both tasks (35 for idiom and 45 for simile). In agreement with the ReproHum organisers each worker was paid the UK living wage[3] of £10.90, in a US dollar equivalent amount, to give fair compensation for the workers time and effort across both tasks.

The experimental data and user interface was taken from the original published source code repository[4]. However several challenges were encountered in attempting to reuse the original experimental data and user interface:

- The CSV data used to prepare the idiom and simile tasks (HITs) on the MTurk platform were not present in the authors code repository.
- The interface for the idiom plausibility task was missing and not present in the code repository.
- The interface for the simile plausibility task, whilst present, was incomplete due to CSS code being commented out in the file. This left a visually inadequate interface as show in figure 2.

To re-create the CSV files needed for the plausibility idiom and simile tasks on MTurk the output JSON files from the original experiment were used. In particular, the narrative, the automatic and human continuation texts for each of the scenarios were extracted from these JSON files using a Python script.

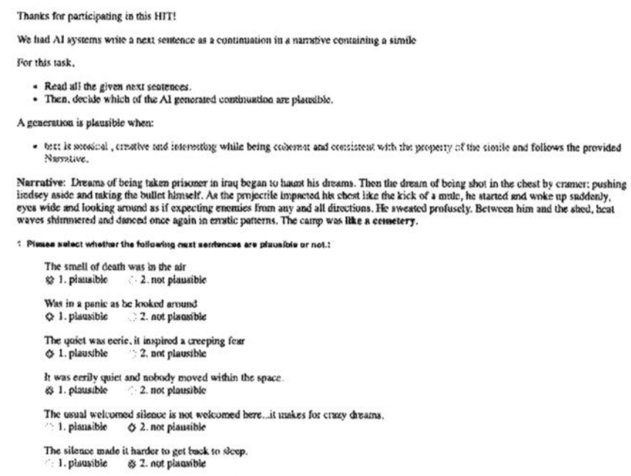

Figure 2: The simile plausibility interface with the missing CSS styling.

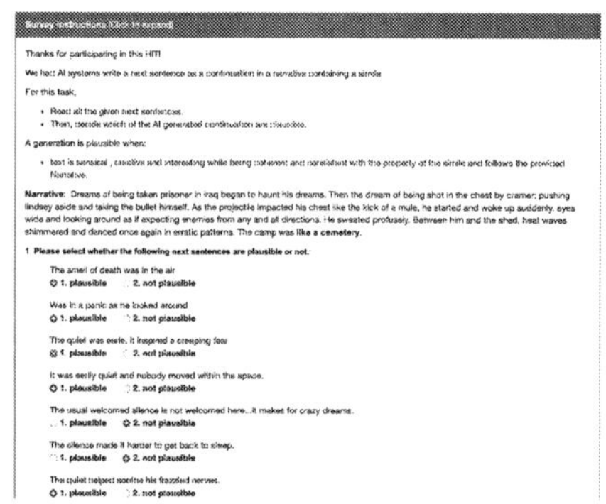

Figure 3: The simile plausibility interface with the restored CSS styling.

The missing CSS for the simile plausibility task was simply dealt with by re-instating the CSS by uncommenting the code in the interface HTML file resulting the interface as shown in figure 3. As for the missing interface file, after consultation with an organiser from the ReproHum project, a decision was made to copy the interface used from the simile task and make the relevant adaptions for the idiom task. In particular, this involved reducing the number of human text options from five to three

[3]UK Living Wage - `https://www.livingwage.org.uk`

[4]Figurative Narrative Benchmark - `https://github.com/tuhinjubcse/FigurativeNarrativeBenchmark`

and using a randomly picked narrative text from the development set, and amending any mention of similes in the interface code to that of idioms.

Due to the limitations mentioned above, this reproduction experiment cannot be an exact replication of the experiment as conducted by Chakrabarty et al. (2022). Therefore the results presented later in this paper must take these limitations into account when considering any potential differences in the results obtained.

5 Results

Model	Original		Reproduction	
	Idiom	Simile	Idiom	Simile
GPT2-XL	56	60	58	64
+Context	68	68	83.33	48
+Literal	48	76	66.66	64
Human	80	88	80.55	84

Table 1: Percentage of model and human generated texts were majority rated as plausible by human evaluators. Original results are from (Chakrabarty et al., 2022).

Out of the 45 workers who participated on the simile plausibility evaluation only 5 workers had answered all 25 texts. In the idiom plausibility evaluation out of the 35 workers that had participated only 2 had completed all 25 texts, with the next highest participant completing 17 in total. Whilst this is lower than the original experiment, we believe this should not affect the results reported significantly as the analyses for idioms were constrained to 17 instead of 25 texts. Additionally, as shown later, a similar percentage of the idiom human texts were rated as plausible as the original study. For the analysis, the code was written independently from scratch as no analysis code is present within the authors code repository.

Table 1 shows the results from this analysis and results obtained from the reproduction study for each of the different text types that were rated plausible by a majority of human evaluators. We were able to get near exact or very close replication results for human and the baseline (GPT2-XL) generated texts. However, majority preference for the context and literal model texts are substantially different from the results reported by Chakrabarty et al. (2022).

When analysing inter-annotator agreement, the difference between the original study and the reproduction is a drop in the absolute Krippendorf's α score from 0.68 to 0.39. More granular analysis showed that the Krippendorf's α inter-annotator agreement was 0.3761 for the idiom task and 0.3971 for the simile task between the three respective annotators. It is possible that a difference in the type of annotators used in reproduction as compared the original study resulted in a difference in the inter-annotator results seen between two the studies.

When evaluating majority worker preference between the context model and the literal model for idioms and similes, we observed that for idioms preference was greater with the context model (83.33%) than the literal model (66.66%). For similes we were able to see a larger preference for the literal model (64%) over the context model (48%). This confirms the preferences that Chakrabarty et al. (2022) observed with human annotators in their original experiment.

Whilst we could not replicate the moderate inter-annotator agreement found in the original study nor the preference for the context model for idioms, we were able to successfully replicate the results for the percentage of idioms and similes considered plausible through majority worker voting for human and the baseline model generated texts. Additionally, we were able to replicate the preference for the context model for idioms and the literal model for similes. The fact that the results were either the same or very close to the original study shows in some aspects shows that some results were successfully replicated in this reproduction study.

6 Conclusion & Recommendations

In this paper we have conducted a partially successful reproduction of the results obtained in the absolute idiom and simile human evaluations. Whilst we were able to reconfirm the results for the judgement on whether human and baseline model generated texts idioms and similes are plausible, the same could not be said for the literal and context model texts. Additionally, inter-annotator agreement scores show that there is a significant difference between the results obtained as compared to the original study. One possible reason for this could be due to the difference in the cohorts of annotators recruited between the two studies. A similar challenge was found in the reproduction experiment by Mahamood (2021) where the difference in recruited participant cohorts was speculated as a possible probable cause for the inability to reproduce results from the original study. Nevertheless, it has been noted that recruiting MTurk crowd workers that have high inter-annotator agreement with each other can be challenging even with a structured process in place to filter out unsuitable workers (Zhang et al., 2023) and therefore in itself may not guarantee reproduction success.

Based on the experiences of this reproduction study there are several key recommendations to reduce uncertainty for reproduction attempts:

1. Give information on the type of participants in a given evaluation such as including demographic data.
2. State the inclusion and exclusion criteria for participants in an evaluation.
3. Provide the datasets, including any data preparation code, used to create crowd worker tasks and the respective task interfaces.
4. The analysis code used to compute the results from an evaluation should be included in the experiment's source code repository.

The first recommendation is very straightforward. Without the information on the type of participants that were used for the evaluation it is very likely that any reproduction attempt may not succeed as the differences between the two recruited groups might be too far significant to enable a comparable evaluation. Therefore, data, such as participant demographics, would enable any reproduction attempt to focus on recruiting the right participants for a given study. When combined with the second recommendation, this would help to give confidence to ensure that participants who do not qualify for the experiment are rightfully excluded. Once having recruited the right participants, it is important the exact same datasets and user interfaces are provided to ensure comparability with the original experiment and armed with the same analysis code to reduce any possibilities of discrepancies occurring. With these recommendations and the learnings from others in this area, it is hoped that future attempts at performing reproduction experiments will be more successful than at present.

Acknowledgments

Many thanks to *Evgeniya Pushenko* and *Srinivas Ramesh Kamath* of trivago for their time in reviewing this paper and for the improvements suggested.

References

Anja Belz, Anastasia Shimorina, Shubham Agarwal, and Ehud Reiter. 2021a. The ReproGen shared task on reproducibility of human evaluations in NLG: Overview and results. In *Proceedings of the 14th International Conference on Natural Language Generation*, pages 249–258.

Anya Belz, Shubham Agarwal, Anastasia Shimorina, and Ehud Reiter. 2020a. ReproGen: Proposal for a shared task on reproducibility of human evaluations in NLG. In *Proceedings of the 13th International Conference on Natural Language Generation*, pages 232–236, Dublin, Ireland. Association for Computational Linguistics.

Anya Belz, Shubham Agarwal, Anastasia Shimorina, and Ehud Reiter. 2021b. A systematic review of reproducibility research in natural language processing. In *Proceedings of the 16th Conference of the European Chapter of the Association for Computational Linguistics: Main Volume*, pages 381–393, Online. Association for Computational Linguistics.

Anya Belz, Simon Mille, and David M. Howcroft. 2020b. Disentangling the properties of human evaluation methods: A classification system to support comparability, meta-evaluation and reproducibility testing. In *Proceedings of the 13th International Conference on Natural Language Generation*, pages 183–194, Dublin, Ireland. Association for Computational Linguistics.

Anya Belz, Anastasia Shimorina, Maja Popović, and Ehud Reiter. 2022. The 2022 ReproGen shared task on reproducibility of evaluations in NLG: overview and results. Association for Computational Linguistics (ACL).

Anya Belz, Craig Thomson, Ehud Reiter, and Simon Mille. 2023. Non-repeatable experiments and non-reproducible results: The reproducibility crisis in human evaluation in NLP. In *Findings of the Association for Computational Linguistics: ACL 2023*, pages 3676–3687, Toronto, Canada. Association for Computational Linguistics.

Tuhin Chakrabarty, Yejin Choi, and Vered Shwartz. 2022. It's not rocket science: Interpreting figurative language in narratives. *Transactions of the Association for Computational Linguistics*, 10:589–606.

Sebastian Gehrmann, Elizabeth Clark, and Thibault Sellam. 2023. Repairing the cracked foundation: A survey of obstacles in evaluation practices for generated text. *Journal of Artificial Intelligence Research*, 77:103–166.

David M. Howcroft, Anya Belz, Miruna-Adriana Clinciu, Dimitra Gkatzia, Sadid A. Hasan, Saad Mahamood, Simon Mille, Emiel van Miltenburg, Sashank Santhanam, and Verena Rieser. 2020. Twenty years of confusion in human evaluation: NLG needs evaluation sheets and standardised definitions. In *Proceedings of the 13th International Conference on Natural Language Generation*, pages 169–182, Dublin, Ireland. Association for Computational Linguistics.

Saad Mahamood. 2021. Reproducing a comparison of hedged and non-hedged NLG texts. In *Proceedings of the 14th International Conference on Natural Language Generation*, pages 282–285, Aberdeen, Scotland, UK. Association for Computational Linguistics.

Lining Zhang, Simon Mille, Yufang Hou, Daniel Deutsch, Elizabeth Clark, Yixin Liu, Saad Mahamood, Sebastian Gehrmann, Miruna Clinciu, Khyathi Raghavi Chandu, and João Sedoc. 2023. A needle in a haystack: An analysis of high-agreement workers on MTurk for summarization. In *Proceedings of the 61st Annual Meeting of the Association for Computational Linguistics (Volume 1: Long Papers)*, pages 14944–14982, Toronto, Canada. Association for Computational Linguistics.

Author Index

Association for Computational Linguistics
209 N. Eighth Street
Stroudsburg, Pennsylvania 18360

ISBN 978-1-7138-9052-2

CURRAN ASSOCIATES INC.
proceedings.com